ORDERING VI

ORDERING VIOLENCE

Explaining Armed Group-State
Relations from Conflict to Cooperation

Paul Staniland

CORNELL UNIVERSITY PRESS   **ITHACA AND LONDON**

First published 2021 by Cornell University Press

Library of Congress Cataloging-in-Publication Data

Names: Staniland, Paul, 1982– author.
Title: Ordering violence : explaining armed group-state relations from conflict to cooperation / Paul Staniland.
Description: Ithaca [New York] : Cornell University Press, 2021. | Includes bibliographical references and index.
Identifiers: LCCN 2021009243 (print) | LCCN 2021009244 (ebook) | ISBN 9781501761102 (hardcover) | ISBN 9781501761119 (paperback) | ISBN 9781501761126 (ebook) | ISBN 9781501761133 (pdf)
Subjects: LCSH: Political violence. | Conflict management. | Political violence—South Asia—Case studies. | Conflict management—South Asia—Case studies. | Non-state actors (International relations) | Insurgency—Government policy.
Classification: LCC JC328.6 .S696 2021 (print) | LCC JC328.6 (ebook) | DDC 303.60954—dc23
LC record available at https://lccn.loc.gov/2021009243

For Rebecca

Contents

Figures and Tables

Figures

Tables

Acknowledgments

This book has taken rather longer than I optimistically had expected, and during research and writing I have incurred innumerable debts. Colleagues, friends, and interlocutors made time for me in India, Sri Lanka, Thailand, Burma/Myanmar, and Singapore over the last dozen years as I tried to understand complicated, often confusing patterns of cooperation and conflict between governments and armed groups. I owe particular thanks to Mirza Zulfiqur Rahman, David Mathieson, Pratap Bhanu Mehta, and Terence Lee for providing exceptional help in facilitating this research, and the Centre for Policy Research in New Delhi and ISEAS–Yusof Ishak Institute in Singapore for institutional bases.

Two recurring workshop series have been valuable in helping me develop the ideas in this manuscript. First, the Program on International Security Policy and its successor, the Workshop on International Politics, at the University of Chicago has long been a place to hear incredibly smart people play with ideas; it has also helped me hone my own thinking. John Mearsheimer, Bob Pape, Bobby Gulotty, Rochelle Terman, Austin Carson, and Paul Poast have built an exceptional workshop culture. All of them have also provided incisive feedback on this project. Second, the annual India Security Studies workshop, hosted first by the Center for the Advanced Study of India at the University of Pennsylvania, and now by the Johns Hopkins University School of Advanced International Studies and the Carnegie Endowment for International Peace, has been a unique home for rigorous but policy-engaged work on India. I thank Devesh Kapur for his years of leadership.

I was lucky enough to receive detailed feedback on the project at two events. First, I organized a small conference at the University of Chicago on ideas and political violence in 2016 that featured research by and feedback from Elisabeth Wood, Ron Hassner, Scott Straus, the late and much-missed Lee Ann Fujii, Rich Nielsen, and Jonathan Maynard Leader. I am in their debt. Second, the Harry Frank Guggenheim Foundation, spearheaded by the incomparable Joel Wallman, hosted a book workshop for me in 2019. I am deeply grateful to Lisa Blaydes, Sameer Lalwani, Jake Shapiro, Erica Chenoweth, Laia Balcells, Carter Malkasian, and Eugene Finkel for taking the time to give exceptional feedback on the project. The book is dramatically better as a result of their comments.

I am extremely grateful to participants at seminars and conferences at Princeton, Northwestern, Brown, George Washington, Emory, Ohio State, the

University of Pennsylvania, Boston College, MIT, Yale, Uppsala University, Wisconsin, Texas A&M, Michigan, the National University of Singapore, the University of California at Berkeley, the University of Connecticut, and Northern Illinois University. I also hope this book carries forward the spirit of Yale's Program on Order, Conflict, and Violence.

Numerous other individuals have been gracious with their time and insights. Ben Lessing and I have had many conversations on the themes covered in the following pages. I owe a great deal to his incredibly creative mind. I cotaught a course on civil wars in 2018 with Lisa Wedeen that sharpened my thinking on key issues. Roger Petersen's early reaction to this project, centered around an anecdote from The Wire, is an example of how he has spurred new ideas for generations of students. Dann Naseemullah and I have worked collaboratively and individually on topics related to this book, and I have greatly benefited from his incredible range and expertise; his own book will be a major contribution. I am especially indebted to Asfandyar Mir and Sameer Lalwani for their coauthorship of an article that forms part of chapter 6, as well as teaching me so much about South Asia's conflict landscape. As always, I am deeply grateful to Vipin Narang and Caitlin Talmadge for being dear friends and wise professional sounding boards. The University of Chicago Center for International Social Science Research, led by the indefatigable Jenny Trinitapoli, was the home to a wonderful Thursday afternoon writing group that kept this project afloat even in the busiest of times.

For valuable feedback and insightful conversations, I thank Dan Slater, Stathis Kalyvas, Abbey Steele, Kristine Eck, Jason Lyall, Severine Autesserre, Yuhki Tajima, Anit Mukherjee, Charles Glaser, Michael Weintraub, Ana Arjona, Amit Ahuja, Christian Davenport, Josh Shifrinson, Rahul Sagar, Will Norris, Jeremy Pressman, Betty Hanson, Monika Nalepa, Stephen Biddle, Ashutosh Varshney, Janet Lewis, Aila Matanock, Lee Seymour, Rajesh Rajagopalan, Keren Yarhi-Milo, Taylor Fravel, Tanisha Fazal, Stein Tønnesson, Steven Wilkinson, Austin Long, Michael Horowitz, Elizabeth Saunders, Joakim Kreutz, Will Reno, James Mahoney, Milan Vaishnav, Maya Tudor, Wendy Pearlman, Dan Krcmaric, Karen Alter, Dan Reiter, Peter Krause, Austin Long, Ches Thurber, Barbara Walter, Mike Albertus, Ian Chong, Bethany Lacina, Joshua White, Srinath Raghavan, Manjari Chatterjee Miller, Jessica Weeks, Peter Andreas, Rikhil Bhavnani, Sarah Daly, Forrest Stuart, Matthias Staisch, Erica Simmons, Michael Reese, Nadav Shalef, and Alberto Simpser. Apologies to those whom I have inadvertently omitted.

A group of excellent University of Chicago PhD and MA students have offered their thoughts on this project, both in early and advanced forms, over the years. I sincerely thank Asfandyar Mir, Ahsan Butt, Sana Jaffrey, Morgan Kaplan, Drew Stommes, Lindsey O'Rourke, Aidan Milliff, Mashail Malik, Alexandra

Chinchilla, Sarah Parkinson, Chris Price, Jon DePoyster, Jonathan Obert, Kevin Weng, Genevieve Bates, Noah Schouela, Katy Lindquist, Madeleine Stevens, and Andres Uribe for their insights.

A stellar group of research assistants worked on the Armed Orders in South Asia (AOSA) data project over the last half-decade. Their work has been invaluable. Winston Berg, Wenyan Deng, Bryan Popoola, Erik Mueller, Nasir Almasri, and Basil Bastaki provided exceptional leadership of these teams. I am grateful to Drew Stommes, Norm Kemble, Reja Younis, Christian Godwin, Matthew Koo, Elayne Stecher, Nandhana Sajeev, Gamarnik, Rida Ashfaq, Mengting Luo, Xunchao Zhang, Robin Morris, Joseph Greenbaum, Maddie Stevens, Rhea Mahanta, Chris Dictus, Purnia Siddiqui, Rashmi Muraleedhar, Noa Levin, Raghuveer Nidumolu, and Patrick Burke.

I am extremely grateful to a number of institutions for their financial support. The Harry Frank Guggenheim Foundation funded essential field research in 2013 and a book workshop in 2019. The East Asian Peace program at Uppsala University, led by Stein Tønnesson, provided exceptional assistance during a crucial early period for the project. The Smith Richardson Foundation took a chance on the project and funded extensive data collection. Award W911-NF- 1710044 from the Department of Defense and US Army Research Office/Army Research Laboratory under the Minerva Research Initiative, with Ben Lessing, was essential for funding the dataset and qualitative narratives, and for buying out courses that provided time for research. The views expressed are those of the author and should not be attributed to the Department of Defense or the Army Research Office/Army Research Laboratory. I am deeply appreciative of the University of Chicago's Social Sciences Division and its deans during this project—Mario Small, David Nirenberg, and Amanda Woodward—for funding and research support.

Roger Haydon showed early interest in this project, even when it was years away from completion, and provided astute and candid advice through to the offer of a contract. I very much hope he is enjoying his retirement. Mahinder Kingra, Ellen Labbate, and Karen Laun skillfully moved the manuscript forward. I am grateful to Jack Rummel for his excellent copyediting and to Judy Kip for her indexing skills. Two exceptional anonymous reviewers provided remarkably insightful, rigorous, and detailed feedback.

Earlier versions of some of the material in this book were previously published in "Politics and Threat Perception: Explaining Pakistani Military Strategy on the North West Frontier," with Asfandyar Mir and Sameer Lalwani, Security Studies 27, no. 4 (2018): 535–74; "Armed Politics and the Study of Intrastate Conflict," Journal of Peace Research 54, no. 4 (July 2017): 459–67; and "Militias, Ideology, and the State," Journal of Conflict Resolution 59, no. 5 (August 2015): 770–93. I thank the publishers of these journals for their permission.

Finally, I owe my greatest debts to my family. My parents, Alberta Sbragia and Martin Staniland, and sister Laura Trybus have been unwaveringly supportive over the years. I thank them from the bottom of my heart. My father passed away just as I was completing this book. I miss him dearly, but I remember him with great love and enduring gratitude. My wonderful sons, Ethan and Leo, were both born while I was working on this project; I have since had a lot less sleep but a lot more fun. My wife Rebecca Incledon has been an amazing life partner, and I dedicate this book to her.

ORDERING VIOLENCE

ARMED POLITICS AND STATE POWER

On the side of the muddy road to the village of Khonoma in the Indian state of Nagaland, two monuments stand perched over a deep valley. Each memorializes Naga political and military separatist leaders, honoring them for defending the rights of the Naga people and for advancing the cause of a Naga nation. This is no surprise: Khonoma has been a historical center of armed resistance; first, to British colonial, and then Indian government, authority, including a protracted insurgency in the area since the mid-1950s. The fact that the Indian state allows these monuments to exist suggests that government authority must be weak; such a display would be unacceptable in war-torn Kashmir.

This roadside vignette seems to mark a classical anti-state rebellion. But this is not quite right. There is almost no violence in the area because cease-fires have dramatically reduced conflict, despite neither ending ongoing political disagreements nor demobilizing the most powerful Naga armed groups. Indian military convoys rumble along key arteries and police garrison important towns, but rarely fight armed groups. In turn, these groups sometimes fight one another, but more regularly engage in extortion, social control, and recruitment. The Indian government and Naga groups have had numerous rounds of negotiations over the decades, mixed in with long stretches of both cease-fires and fighting.[1]

The Naga conflict hovers somewhere between war and peace—it does not look like an archetypal civil war, but there is also not a government monopoly over legitimate violence. Nor is it unique. In Iraq and Syria, powerful Kurdish armed groups have worked with central governments and the United States: they

are neither pro-state militias controlled by a central regime, nor insurgents wag-
ing a pitched war against governments. In Burma, decades-long cease-fires have
bought relative peace without delivering deeper political stability. Even within
the same countries or conflicts we can see a remarkable spectrum of conflict and
cooperation among states and armed groups: ISIS has been locked in total war
against both Baghdad and a set of proregime Shiite militias, while some insurgents spent the 2010s fighting against the Myanmar military even as others cut
cease-fire deals or joined the side of the state.

I conceptualize these state–armed group relationships as "armed orders."[2]
Studying them lets us systematically compare state-group interactions during
periods of both high and low or nonexistent violence, across types of groups
(including armed political parties, militias, private armies, and insurgents), and
over time. We can see shifting trajectories of armed politics, as groups move
between different forms of conflict and cooperation, and also examine how these
orders come to an end. There is enormous variation, within countries, across
them, and over time, in patterns of these armed politics.

What drives this variation? The core claim of this book is that the ideological threats that governments perceive from armed groups drive state responses.
Rather than straightforwardly worrying about the size, power, or organizational
characteristics of armed groups, regimes assess how groups' politics align with
the government's own goals. Governments' ideological projects lead them to
perceive groups as occupying an ideologically aligned, opposed, or interme-
diate "gray zone" position. These projects are rooted in the deep history of a
regime and are difficult, though not impossible, to change. This helps explain
why we often see governments using extreme repression against tiny and irrelevant armed groups, while working with or tolerating much larger and more
powerful armed groups. Seemingly puzzling or disproportionate behavior often
makes much more sense when understood through an ideological lens: government have widely varying threat perceptions that drive different patterns of
armed politics.

Governments' ideological projects play a central role in generating armed
orders. But this is more useful for understanding broad patterns than the nuances
of specific interactions. Groups and governments can also share tactical incentives to work together—even across ideological divides. Sometimes ideologically
aligned groups offer little tactical value to the state, while, in admittedly rare
cases, even a government and ideologically opposed group may have instrumental reasons to cooperate against a shared enemy. Transnational civil wars, counterinsurgency, electoral violence, and periphery management are all domains in
which tactical overlap can emerge and help us understand armed orders at a
more fine-grained level.

This argument politicizes political violence. Rather than taking goals and fears of governments for granted or assuming that they are similar across states, I seek to explain how and why they vary. I then offer a theory of how government ideological projects can lead to patterns of conflict and cooperation with armed actors. Empirically, the book systematically measures and compares armed orders in large swathes of South Asia, from Nagaland's distant hill marches to Karachi's blend of urban violence and voting to Shan State's myriad armed actors, to show the importance of the armed politics approach, to develop a theory of armed orders, and to provide comparative evidence for evaluating the theory. Using qualitative and quantitative data drawn from fieldwork, primary sources, and a new dataset of armed orders, the empirical sections of the book leverage different cross-national, subnational, and chronological comparisons of ideological projects, tactical incentives, and state-group political relationships to explore when and how the argument succeeds and fails. South Asia is my empirical focus, but the themes and claims of the book travel beyond the region.

What Are Armed Orders?

Exploring these questions requires introducing and defining a set of new concepts. An armed order is the political relationship between a central government and a nonstate armed group at any point in time.[3] I identify four armed orders: total war, containment, limited cooperation, and alliance. They begin when an armed group emerges as a coherent actor and is perceived by the government. For a group to be included in an armed order, we need clear evidence of cadres being training and equipped with lethal weaponry under the control of a leadership group within a formal organization. The state's awareness of the group and choice of strategy toward it creates an initial order. Armed politics, by definition, do not include a total state monopoly over all coercive capacity in a society, but also may not involve any actual violence or conflict. Table I.1 summarizes these orders.

Crucially, orders can be dynamic, shifting fluidly as political relationships change. Local Sunni groups in Iraq's Anbar province, for instance, moved from total war to limited cooperation to alliance and, in some cases, back to total war or containment between 2003 and 2015. The limited cooperation between the Pakistani military and the Mullah Nazir group in South Waziristan during the height of Pakistan's brutal civil war in the Northwest from 2007 to 2014 was different than either total war between the military and Maulana Fazlullah's Tehrik-i-Taliban Pakistan (TTP) or the military's alliance with the Lashkar-e-Taiba.[4]

TABLE I.1   Armed orders

ORDER	OBSERVABLE FEATURES
Alliance	Close, visible coordination of state and nonstate policy; substantial sharing of resources and information
Limited cooperation	Managed boundaries of influence along functional and/or territorial lines; restricted sharing of information or resources; occasional clashes and continual bargaining; Formal: ceasefires, signed deals; Informal: communicated, mutually acknowledged arrangements without document
Containment	Mutual combat but with relatively low intensity and substantial restraint shown in the application of military force
Total war	A high level of military effort by each side aimed at the other, with few discernible restraints—large deployments, leadership decapitation (or efforts thereof), and broad targeting

Some orders continue indefinitely, but when they end, it is through one of several pathways: the collapse of the group or (less likely) the state, the incorporation of a group via its demobilization, absorption into another armed organization, or disarmament without demobilization. Understanding patterns of termination can help us explain variation in both state strategy and armed groups' positioning toward the government.

Armed Orders

Conflictual armed orders are characterized by some degree of mutual combat, clashes, sweeps, and attacks between a state and an armed group. However, this is a very broad category, so I offer a more fine-grained distinction between containment and total war. In both, forces systematically and consistently pursue one another, but with important variation in the intensity and nature of this conflict.

Containment orders often involve relatively little violence and frequently accompany sustained campaigns of peripheral insurgency, with sporadic offensives and comparatively limited combat. This is an order in which the regime has lower levels of resolve to destroy the group and can tolerate its existence as long as it is kept below a particular threshold. Leadership decapitation is avoided, violence is relatively restrained and limited, and "normal" political processes often continue to operate, sometimes in complex fusions with violence or coercion. The Armed Forces of the Philippines have pursued containment against the New People's Army (NPA) for extended periods, aiming to slowly wear the group out rather than seeking a decisive military victory.

By contrast, total war orders involve large amounts of violence and huge state resource investments in repression. The resolve to destroy the group is high: aggressive military strategies of leadership decapitation, sustained and indiscriminate attacks on civilian populations, and large-scale investments in militarized state building are much less common in containment orders than in total war orders. The Sri Lankan government and the Liberation Tigers of Tamil Eelam (LTTE) engaged in total war between 2006 and 2009 (and much of the previous three decades) prior to the LTTE's collapse.

Dyads can move between these orders: the Indonesian military and Gerakan Aceh Merdeka (GAM) in Aceh oscillated between containment and total war until a period of limited cooperation during peace negotiations eventually led to incorporation in 2003.[5] As we will see in the empirics, sometimes it is impossible to measure an order at this level of detail. When unable to distinguish between containment and total war empirically, a dyad-year is coded as "military hostilities," which is an untheorized general coding identifying some kind of conflict.

Armed groups can also cooperate with the state. A *limited cooperation* order is constituted by formal cease-fires or informal live-and-let-live bargains between a state and armed group. This is the result of a strategy that seeks a degree of collusion, without political resolve to destroy the group. Some form of arrangement limits mutual violence without formal demobilization, a full peace settlement, or military victory. Both sides continue to exist as distinct actors engaged in bargaining and compromise, though tension and fragility often accompany this bargaining. Unlike in conflictual orders, we do not see significant attacks by either side, and military forces are kept apart. Unlike in alliance orders, however, there is not tight policy coordination toward shared purposes, but instead a delimitation of territorial and functional authority and the maintenance of appropriate "rules" of interaction.[6] This order often resembles what Richards refers to as contexts of "no war, no peace."[7]

Limited cooperation can occur through formal agreements, such as cease-fires or peace deals, that specify the rules of political-military interaction without requiring either side to disarm. In Northeast India, Suspension of Operations (SoO) agreements that act as renewable cease-fires are common.[8] In northwestern Pakistan, numerous deals have been signed between the military and local armed actors that do not actually involve demobilization; instead, they establish mutual expectations and the "red lines" at which the state will shift to hostilities.[9] Limited cooperation can occur through informal, but still stable and even prolonged, mutual understandings between governments and armed actors. In northern Iraq since 2003, tension between Baghdad and Kurdish armed groups has certainly existed, but an uneasy equilibrium has mostly held in which security forces and the Peshmerga avoided large-scale, sustained clashes.[10] In the Philippines, security forces often simply avoid targeting local private armies of politically powerful families and patrons, and in turn these private armies refrain from targeting the state security apparatus.[11] These understandings are not codified in formal, written deals; nevertheless, there is ongoing communication between armed actors to try to avoid misunderstandings and unnecessary conflict.

Alliance involves tight, institutionalized cooperation between a state and armed group, generally involving targeting of a shared enemy, observable coordination of policies, and sharing of organizational resources.[12] States and nonstate actors are active partners.[13] Pro-state militias and paramilitaries, electoral armed groups, and former insurgents cooperating with the government are most commonly involved in alliance orders. These are not tacit arrangements or live-and-let-live deals, as in limited cooperation. Instead, the security apparatus closely and consistently operates alongside and in dialogue with armed groups; coordination is much more ambitious and intensive than with limited cooperation.

Coding a dyad-year as one of alliance requires substantial evidence of government support for the activities of armed actors and regular communication between them. The linkages between Shiite militias and the Iraqi government in battling the Islamic State in 2014 are a clear example of an alliance order.[14] In Indian-administered Jammu and Kashmir, the Indian security forces closely cooperated with former insurgent groups to attack mutual enemies during the mid-1990s.[15] In Kenya in 2007, local armed actors were supported by the incumbent government as an electoral strategy.[16] In post-1998 Indonesia, some state actors and politicians have become aligned with local armed gangs and militias.[17] Interwar Europe saw several cases of intertwined relationships between regimes and nonstate paramilitaries.[18] Alliances yoke state and nonstate violence together.

How Armed Orders End

The armed politics approach is especially useful for exploring how armed groups end. Many groups stop existing years after they stop fighting at a level sufficient for entering into civil war datasets. Some decline militarily and end up collapsing after years of low activity, while others enter into cease-fires and negotiations prior to a peace deal or demobilization. Some groups never fight the state at all, so we need to study them independent of the use of violence. I identify and then measure several ways that armed orders can come to an end.

TABLE I.2   Measuring armed orders

FORM OF TERMINATION	OBSERVABLE FEATURES
Collapse	Group unable to deploy organization in a sustained or coordinated way; state/regime unable to hold capital and to deploy state security forces in a sustained or coordinated way
Incorporation	Actor ends as independent organization through some mutual agreement with the state about demobilizing (whether formal or informal)
Disarmament	Groups lay down arms and order ends, without group itself terminating as an autonomous organization
Absorption	Group becomes part of another group and no longer exists as a distinctive organization

Collapse occurs when the group cannot consistently mobilize followers or engage in basic organizational activities. It disintegrates or becomes an empty shell unable to sustain core functions related to revenue extraction, military mobilization, recruitment, or political claim making. This can be the result of military destruction or internal dissension that undermine the organization. Examples of collapse include the annihilation of the Tamil Tigers in 2009, internal splintering of the Communist Party of Burma in 1989, and defeat of Sikh separatist militants in India's Punjab.[19] These groups did not switch to a limited cooperation or alliance order, or become incorporated into "mainstream" politics; instead, they were wiped out by counterinsurgents or broken apart by internal strife.

In rare circumstances, the central state collapses, either in the face of a full-scale military victory by the armed actor or when it can no longer maintain a presence on a contested periphery, allowing secession. Rebel victories in Cambodia, Ethiopia, and Cuba are cases in which the overthrow of central authority led to the transformation of state structures at the hands of armed groups. The destruction of Pakistani military power in 1971 East Pakistan led to the emergence of Bangladesh and the end of its total war with the Mukti Bahini, though not the collapse of the central state. I code a state collapse outcome as an armed group victory.

Incorporation, by contrast, generally occurs when a group demobilizes as part of a deal with the government and enters the unarmed political sphere. This may occur through be a formal deal, such as the 1993 Bodo Accord in Northeast India, 1998 Good Friday Agreement in Northern Ireland, 2005 peace agreement in Aceh, creation of Border Guard Forces (BGFs) from insurgents and militias in Myanmar, and demobilization of AUC paramilitaries in Colombia. This can also be a much less formal process, without signed agreements. In Karachi and

West Bengal, we have seen armed actors being absorbed into the structures of ruling parties, and in the Philippines local private armies have sometimes simply been granted imprimatur as part of the state apparatus.[20] State centralization of control over violence is very often built around the incorporation of a wide range of armed groups, turning "bandits into bureaucrats" or militias into police.[21]

Two more niche forms of termination can also occur. Absorption involves a group becoming part of another group or when forming a new group: for instance, the People's War Group and Maoist Communist Centre merged in 2004 to form the Communist Party of India-Maoist (CPI-M). This is largely irrelevant to my argument, since the group continues on in a new form. Disarmament involves a group giving up violence without demobilizing as an organization. A number of Tamil pro-state paramilitary parties in Sri Lanka disarmed after the end of the war against the LTTE in 2009, for instance, laying down arms without dissolving themselves as actors.

This framework encompasses diverse forms of state–armed group interactions, from classical civil wars to murky militarized elections to the culmination of peace processes. Even if the theory I offer is wrong or limited, the armed orders framework can still be used by others to build and evaluate their own theories. As I discuss below and in detail in chapter 3 in this book, I present unique new data from the Armed Orders in South Asia (AOSA) project that quantifies orders on a dyad-year basis, providing qualitative narratives to justify the codings.

Armed Politics in the Study of Political Violence

There has been an extraordinary, and hugely valuable, outpouring of research on political violence in the last twenty-five years. What does studying armed politics contribute to this rich literature? First, exploring armed politics helps us overcome the problem of intellectual "siloes" that can limit our understanding of how politics and violence can be connected. Civil war research starts with some degree of violence as its scope condition. Scholars study insurgent groups, counterinsurgency, patterns of violence, or civilian agency, among many other topics, only in situations where enough conflict has emerged to count as a civil war.[22] This is a reasonable area of focus if the question under study is explicitly about either the onset of a particular level of violence, or if the topic to be studied only occurs during periods of open violence above a certain threshold of deaths.

However, this is not the right approach for this book: state-group relations occur outside of contexts and periods of traditional civil conflicts (as well as within them), and so restricting our observations exclusively to civil wars would artificially truncate the scope of the study. For instance, many groups start out as minor irritants, escalate into direct challengers to the state, then shift into either combatants in long-term but low-level conflicts or transform into militias, armed political parties, or partners in live-and-let-live deals with government power. Some groups never fight the state at all, but still carry arms and deploy coercion to win elections, attack nonstate rivals, or benefit from war economies, all while cooperating at some level with state power. And yet others move from positions of relative quiescence to open rebellion. Studying all of these relationships under a shared framework of armed orders can help us better understand when civil wars break out, when they end or turn into something new, and what armed groups, in their full diversity, are doing before, during, and after open civil wars.

Second, this move then helps us identify the numerous roles that armed actors can carve out for themselves in politics. We can move beyond thinking of armed groups primarily as anti-state insurgents or pro-state militias to see them instead as semiautonomous local governors, collusive partners with regimes, electoral strategists, criminal enterprises, cross-border proxy fighters, local armies of powerful strongmen—or some combination of these different roles.[23] The Kurdish Peshmerga of northern Iraq have been insurgents, political parties, partners with American conventional and special forces, counterinsurgents, agents of corruption and repression, and bargaining counterparts with Baghdad. Some of these roles have been sequential; others have been simultaneous. Widening the aperture beyond straightforward civil war allows us to see all of the ways that armed groups can operate in both intra- and antisystemic politics. In doing so, it can bring together under one framework existing work on electoral violence, civil war, state building, policing, and other areas in which violence and politics are related.

Third, armed politics provides a useful bridge between the study of violent and nonviolent political mobilization and between the study of macro- and microlevel analyses of conflict.[24] There is a growing literature on nonviolent resistance, but we know that the boundary between violence and nonviolence can be quite porous, as organizations move back and forth between—or even combine—strategies of resistance.[25] Studying armed politics may help us understand more precisely when and how armed groups cross between and mix strategies of violence and nonviolence.[26] The basic approach may even be portable to purely unarmed groups. It may be that governments categorize and respond to dissidents, unions, protest campaigns, regionalist movements, and other actors through similar ideological lenses as armed groups.[27]

Similarly, we have excellent research on the microdynamics of violence in civil war, exploring why some places experience violence at some times, why people decide to join rebellions (and to avoid them), and how to understand patterns of civilian victimization, among other topics.[28] This book does not challenge that line of inquiry, which is hugely important. Instead, it aims to illuminate the broader politics of the conflicts within which microdynamics play out. This may help us understand why the on-the-ground nature of violence, civilian agency, and order-building can differ so much across conflict settings and explain outcomes that are currently difficult to tackle without a higher level of aggregation. Armed group and state strategies are both hugely important for shaping fine-grained interactions, for instance, and they are descended at least in part from the "high politics" of internal conflicts that my approach examines.

Finally, this framework pursues answers to a set of deeply political questions that have not been fully answered in existing research: Why would a government ever tolerate an armed group? Why might it work with a very powerful armed actor—or a very weak one? Which kinds of groups are seen as the biggest threats, and why do governments seem to differ so much in their answers to that question? What does it mean to be a strong state? These are fundamental questions about the nature of political violence.

The best research in this vein has focused on the threat side of the equation: Straus emphasizes the agency of postcolonial leaders to include or exclude ethnic categories, Boudreau points to the initial threats facing new authoritarian regimes, Walter examines how reputational concerns drive responses to separatist groups, Kaufman highlights how symbolic politics can undermine rationalist bargaining, Roessler explores the trade-offs between coup threats and insurgent threats that determine regime responses, and Reno examines how groups' position in patronage networks shapes their threat to the government.[29] I draw directly on these arguments in this book, especially Straus's important study of how regime narratives can drive mass violence against civilians.

This book, however, advances on this work in a variety of ways: it systematically theorizes the full range of threat perceptions (from highly threatening to politically unproblematic); identifies and measures variation across both countries and within them; examines a wider variety, and combinations, of ideological dimensions beyond ethnic inclusion/exclusion; and explores a spectrum from total war to alliances. While a key part of any story of armed politics is about which groups the state finds highly threatening—the focus of the excellent existing literature—an equally important question is which groups it finds tolerable, if unsavory, and which are seen as actually friendly and helpful.

Government Ideology and Armed Orders

Government ideology is at the core of my argument.[30] In the medium- and high-capacity states that this book studies, states have some degree of choice in deciding how to deal with armed groups. Sometimes, of course, there are unavoidably severe military threats that demand a specific response. But much, probably most, of the time there is far more ambiguity and room for maneuver. How much of a threat do right-wing militias in the United States pose? What exactly is the problem posed by Hindu nationalist organizations linked to riots and lynching? Do tiny Rohingya insurgent groups in Myanmar need to be brutally wiped out— or instead lightly managed as a law enforcement issue, or accommodated via negotiations? Can the FARC in Colombia be trusted to implement a peace deal, or is it ultimately a corrupt and irreconcilable group that needs to be destroyed? Are armed settlers in the West Bank an existential threat to the idea of Israel, a serious nuisance but ultimately not a major threat, or instead do they advance a desirable vision of what Israel should aspire to be?

The answers to these questions vary dramatically depending on which leader, political party, or regime is answering them. There is often not an obvious, consensus view of internal security threats, or even which groups and issues count as being politically relevant to internal security at all. Governments' ideological projects can vary along (at least) three key dimensions: the nature and extent of ethnonationalist inclusion, the place of religion versus secularism in politics, and the desirability of redistribution along a classic left-right axis. These are radical simplifications, and their specifics vary by context, but systematically placing regimes, governments, and leaders at different points along these dimensions allows us to compare their projects. These projects, I show empirically, are frequently rooted in long-term processes of movement formation, state building, and political competition that make them sticky and resilient, though not static.

Regime projects categorize armed groups into different ideological positions. Their threat or alignment depends on the demands they make, the political cleavages they mobilize, and the rhetoric and symbols they deploy. Since there is often deep ambiguity about the "objective" military threat—if any—that groups pose, ideational factors play a central role in how governments manage violence. Though we associate armed groups with failed states in the developing world, this basic insight can travel even into highly capable states: for a Likud government in Israel, armed settlers are seen differently than under a Labor government, and would be seen yet differently by a more radically religious-right government; the Trump administration made clear early on that it did not view rightist armed groups as a major problem in American politics despite their ability to summon large numbers of men with guns.

Crackdowns and quiescence are not straightforward. Groups that are seen as ideologically opposed will be likely to find themselves locked in total warfare; those that are ideologically aligned will either be allies or fully incorporated into mainstream politics. The orders that emerge may be unrelated to groups' objective military power or the structural characteristics of a government such as its regime type or level of economic wealth. The ideological extremes drive toward broad patterns of either conflict or cooperation. But armed orders within the "gray zone" between these extremes are more complicated. The specific order that emerges in the gray zone depends heavily on whether there are shared tactical interests between the government and group in question. If there are, limited cooperation can emerge, with live-and-let-live deals and collusive bargains; if not, a grinding, low-intensity containment conflict is likely to result.

Ideological projects frequently precede the emergence of armed groups by years or decades. They are formed when "carrier movements"—ranging from anticolonial movements to political parties to praetorian militaries—politically mobilize prior to taking power as a government or regime.[31] Their goals and beliefs are inevitably mapped onto these questions of internal security and armed politics. The broader politics that a government seeks to build shape the ways that it assesses and reacts to armed groups.

Armed orders can change over time. The most dramatic pathway is a major regime change that replaces one project with a very different one, reshuffling threat perception and patterns of order. More incremental changes can emerge from political party or leadership turnover within a political system, from armed groups radicalizing or moderating their ideological positions relative to the government, and from shifts in the tactical incentives that both states and groups have to work with one another.

Scope Conditions

Armed orders are incredibly complicated. My argument offers a radical simplification that cannot accommodate all of this complexity. There are important scope conditions within which the argument should perform best, and outside of which it will have less to contribute.

State and Regime Coherence. Deeply divided regimes without any central control over security policy need to be disaggregated into distinct actors with differing, often competing, strategies toward armed actors. In failed or very weak states, military force may not exist that can be used to contain, cooperate with, or suppress armed actors. While my basic framework may still be applicable to the feuding parts of a regime, it is impossible to identify overall "state" strategies. In these contexts, studies of failed states will likely be more helpful. There is not much to theorize about state behavior when the state barely exists. An explanation of armed orders in failed and fractured regimes will need to focus on the bargaining and battles among warlords, militias, security forces, and factions. In 2014–15 Iraq, for instance, the collapse of large parts of the security apparatus and the rise of Shiite militias as key security providers made the central state a less important actor, and one beset by numerous basic organizational challenges in generating military power, compared to a more coherent regime-state like Ho Chi Minh's North Vietnam in the 1950s or Nehru's India.

The key puzzle is therefore policy variation by regimes that have faced armed groups *and* possess substantial coercive power. These medium- and high-capacity states are quite common; some still lack a monopoly of violence, while others have become hegemonic wielders of political violence only after long periods of interactions with armed groups.[32] They have options but still face scarcity that imposes hard, theoretically important, choices: why do they prioritize some strategies, and armed groups, over others?

I therefore focus the theory on contexts in which there is a basic degree of state capacity, including a coherent national military, extensive internal security forces, and a central decision-making authority that at least broadly guides policy formulation (this locus of authority over internal security can be either civilian or military). The case selection of this study follows that logic, examining regimes that can deploy large-scale military force under the control of a central civilian or military authority but that, at least at the beginning of the study, do not possess total control of political violence. The empirics comparatively explore how these regimes have allocated coercion and compromise across space and time.

Armed Actors. This book seeks to understand the specific dynamics of armed orders, which by definition must include armed nonstate groups at some point. This focuses our attention on groups typically understood as insurgents, militias, private armies, and armed political parties.[33] I do not study unarmed groups in this book, except when identifying the termination of armed orders in the incorporation or disarmament of formerly armed groups. It is possible that my broader argument about threat perception and ideological projects can be fruitfully applied to state responses to unarmed political actors, such as trade unions, opposition parties, or religious organizations. The specific nature of these interactions is likely to be somewhat different because unarmed groups have very different capacities to inflict harm on or advance the interests of a government, but future work can explore whether relevant aspects of my approach can travel to this important set of questions.[34]

Research Design

The inferential approach is multifaceted: I rely on a mix of comparisons, change over time, and quantitative data with primary, secondary, and interview sources. I offer a transparent combination of different sorts of data and comparisons to make the theory more credible and plausible while openly acknowledging limitations.[35] This approach to social science stresses a substantial degree of humility, but it is best suited to the kinds of long-run, endogenous, and frankly messy processes that characterize armed politics.[36] The steady accumulation of different kinds of evidence is intended to persuade the reader that there is an important process of ideological categorization at work that consistently—though far from universally—helps us understand why states interact with armed groups in such varied ways. The armed orders framework and my theory are simplifications, and throughout this book I call attention to their limits. But their value lies in systematically organizing an incredibly complex empirical landscape in new ways while providing clear theory on how to make sense of variation within it.

Case Selection: Why South Asia?

I study South Asia—specifically India, Pakistan, Sri Lanka, and Burma/ Myanmar—for two reasons. First, the countries I focus on were all enmeshed within the British colonial Raj. While this certainly has not induced absolute uniformity across the territories and eventual nation-states in the region, it provides a broad shared political context within which to study the emergence and evolution of carrier movements' ideological projects.[37] This includes both movements that took power immediately after independence and the "roads not taken" that articulated alternative visions of the nation. I do not include Nepal because it operated outside of this colonial context. I also do not study Bangladesh in detail because its emergence was actually a consequence of the processes of threat perception and state response I study in the Pakistan case. However, I engage with the Bangladeshi case throughout the book. It is actually very supportive of the theory: contestation about the role of ethnicity/language versus religion has deeply structured how political parties and the military frame Bangladeshi nationalism and their approach toward dissidents, insurgents, and opponents.

Second, the content of postcolonial regimes' ideological projects differed dramatically along key dimensions of politics (language, religion, redistribution), while these regimes all were forced to deal with various kinds of armed groups over time. For the most part, armed politics emerged after the formation of ideological projects in the colonial and immediate postcolonial period, allowing us to examine state-group interactions after the formation of broad categories of ideological fit. There is also fine-grained variation in the tactical incentives of states and armed groups, which are contextual and vary with time. The region thus provides extensive variation in the key independent variables, while operating within a context of broad historical similarities. As I note throughout, there are also serious limits to confident inference, but the case selection strategy allows at least an assessment with caveats of whether we should be more or less confident in the argument after examining the empirical evidence.

Data and Comparison

Within this context, chapter 3 first provides an overview of unique new quantitative data from the AOSA project on patterns of armed order within South Asia. It shows important variation in state-group relations and suggests some interesting aggregate patterns. The armed order conceptualization can be systematically measured and compared, and even this simple exercise reveals clear evidence that there are important puzzles to be explained. The second half of chapter 3 then shifts to an overview of the key ideological projects at play in colonial and postcolonial South Asia, providing a comparative guide to the country-specific cases to come. I map out the broad position of major carrier movements along the dimensions of language, religion, and redistribution.

The remaining chapters tackle individual countries, but each draws on the comparisons in chapter 3 to situate both ideological projects and patterns of armed politics in a comparative perspective. Chapter 4 assesses the most complex case of India, in which armed groups have mobilized in a huge variety of ways and along multiple political cleavages, and multiple nationalist projects have vied for control of the political system. Chapter 5 provides the closest comparison to India in Pakistan, which shares some degree of political inheritance but whose security managers have perceived internal threats quite differently. Chapter 6 tackles the grim and bloody history of armed politics in Burma/Myanmar, and chapter 7 examines Sri Lanka. Each chapter mixes broad patterns of quantitative data, macrohistorical claims, and more fine-grained case studies of specific armed orders, seeking to accumulate different forms of evidence in a compelling way. The conclusion explores how both the theory and evidence can guide future research and what implications for policy and analysis we can draw from the book.

The next two chapters lay the theoretical basis of these empirics. Chapter 1 defines an ideological project, discusses the origins of projects, and then links these threat perceptions with tactical incentives to generate predictions about the creation of different patterns of armed order. Chapter 2 explores mechanisms of change over time, highlighting both government and armed group processes that can set armed politics into motion.

1

THE POLITICS OF THREAT PERCEPTION

Governments need to decide how to deal with armed groups: which to tolerate, which to destroy, with which to cooperate. This is a simple statement, but a complex problem. In the United States, private firearms are widely available and armed militias of various sorts exist, as, at various points, have leftist radicals, white supremacists, Islamist cells, and organized criminal organizations. In some of these cases, the response by US policymaking and security elites has been unified and highly resolved. Yet in others, the very definitions of what is political versus criminal violence, acceptable versus unacceptable repertoires of action, and palatable versus intolerable types of actors are deeply, often bitterly, contested.[1] Both consensus and contestation represent fundamentally *political* views of how the American polity should be structured.

The United States is, in turn, different in how it manages violence than other industrialized democracies. The responses of postwar Europe's "militant democracies" to perceived threats from within have in turn been profoundly influenced by their own distinctive histories: they have used sweeping emergency powers and limits on free speech and association to try to hold the radical Left and Right at bay.[2] Despite their larger size and spread, right-wing militants in Japan have been viewed as a less serious political threat than left-wing militants: this has contributed to a pattern of containment or limited cooperation with armed groups linked to the right wing, as opposed to total war against those on the Left.[3]

These examples are especially illuminating because they do not occur in the weak or failed states that dominate studies of political violence. Government approaches to armed order are not simple functions of capacity. All governments try to police politics, seeking to lay down *cordons sanitaire* against ideas, actions, and groups they see as beyond as pale, while tolerating or supporting armed actors they see as more or less politically palatable. Some actors are militarily unambiguous threats, and armed orders then simply reflect straightforward battlefield calculations of necessity. But in most states, most of the time, which groups count as "political," which are threatening or unproblematic, and which are existentially worrisome, as opposed to a nuisance, is far from obvious or given.

This chapter provides a new way of understanding these politics by making two arguments. First, ideology plays a central role in how governments perceive threats from armed groups, which in turn drive the armed orders they pursue toward these groups. A government's *ideological project* identifies its desired structure of politics. I especially focus on the extent and content of nationalist inclusion, the government's position on the religious-secular dimension, and the left-right redistributive ideology that the government pursues. Ideological projects are rooted in contingent history: past coalition building and political innovation by "carrier movements" produce and institutionalize a set of political preferences that inform government policy once these movements take power.[4] State policy toward an armed group depends on how it fits with the government's ideological project.

Second, under some conditions, tactical incentives explain more fine-grained patterns of armed politics. Messy exigencies of governing coercion, whether winning violent elections or seeking partners against shared insurgent enemies, can make armed groups operationally valuable to governments. In turn, despite some degree of ideological disagreement, armed groups may find working with the government useful. The combination of ideological position and tactical overlap generates distinct "political roles" that an armed group can occupy in the eyes of the state. Tactical dynamics are particularly important for understanding the orders that emerge with "gray zone" groups, since this is where there is the greatest indeterminacy in threat perception.

The chapter first makes the case for my conceptualization of ideological projects and identifies historical roots of ideological projects. It then turns to how these projects inform threat perception. Finally, it considers how tactical dynamics interact with these ideological assessments to categorize groups into political roles, determine state strategies, and create particular patterns of armed order.

Ideological Projects and Internal Security

Ideology is an incredibly contested concept.[5] In this book, I focus on three key dimensions along which a government's ideological goals can vary, represented in table 1.1. These are complex and context-dependent dimensions that may need to be expanded or restricted in particular situations, but the typology makes them more concrete as a launching point for analysis. The dimensions do not necessarily align with one another; theocratic regimes may not identify a single ethno-linguistic community as their political constituency, while aggressively atheistic regimes could be either on the ideological Left or Right. We can map regime projects onto a variety of combinations of positions on these dimensions; in some cases, we can also combine them—for instance, sometimes language and religion reinforce one another. This allows a richer and much more flexible conceptualization than existing applications of ideology to violence, which usually focus on either Left versus Right or ethnic inclusion/exclusion.[6]

Governments vary in the inclusiveness of the primary ethnic community that they perceive as linked to the state.[7] At one end are highly exclusionary minoritarian governments that privilege a minority as the dominant "owner" of the state, and majoritarian regimes that either exclude or make second-class citizens out of minority categories. Toward the other end of the spectrum, we can see state-nations that accommodate multiple ethno-linguistic categories and civic nationalist projects that at least formally avoid any identity-based distinctions among citizens.[8] Rwanda in the run-up to the 1994 genocide was a majoritarian regime; Canadian federalism represents a state-nation, while the United States is technically an example of civic nationalism (though powerful strands within it prefer a majoritarian view).[9]

In specific cases, I further measure the *content* of these ideologies—which groups are in the nation, out of it, or that occupy a second-class status while still being seen as a lower-status part of the nation.[10] This can be hugely important for variation; some minority groups may be excluded in some contexts, but included in others where different minorities are excluded or marginalized. This allows us to comparatively distinguish between varieties of inclusion and exclusion.

I then examine the government's views of the role of religion in political and social life. At one extreme, theocratic regimes explicitly place religion at the

TABLE 1.1 Dimensions of government ideological project

ETHNO-LINGUISTIC	MINORITARIAN	MAJORITARIAN	STATE-NATION	CIVIC
Religious-secular	Theocratic	State involved in religion, with varying degrees of favor/equidistance	State distinct from religion	Anticlerical/militantly atheist
Left-right	Communist	Democratic socialist	Democratic capitalist	Authoritarian anticommunist

center of governance. Others are not theocratic but do engage directly with supporting religion in the public sphere, ranging from favoring one religion over others to equidistantly engaging with all of them. Some governments seek separation of church and state, while the furthest extreme seeks to wipe out religion in both political and social life.

This helps to capture variation ranging from postrevolutionary Iran to the brutal anticlericalism of the Jacobins. India's founding ruling party formally embraced equidistance between religions, while the United States technically is a separation of church and state political system, though with continual political pressures on that separation. We can certainly see religion and ethnicity overlapping and these dimensions starting to merge: the "sons of the soil" of Malaysia are simultaneously Malay and Muslim. But we can also see crucial distance between the two: the radical transnational vision of ISIS seeks to delink ethnicity from religion. In other cases, this fusion is the object of politics: in contemporary Israel, the political meaning of the religious practice of Judaism is intensely contested even within the broad right wing; the French political sphere has experienced tensions between formal practices of *laïcité* and implicit assumptions about the place of Catholicism in French nationalism.

I finally identify variation in ideological projects along the classic left-right redistributive spectrum. Governments can range from hard Left to hard Right, while occupying a variety of positions in between. Drawn from the European experience, this spectrum has run into serious trouble as a catchall conceptualization of politics elsewhere. Instead of trying to fit everything into such an approach, I scale it back to focus specifically on the question of how democracy and markets do or do not fit. Broadly, I array communist regimes to the left, anticommunist authoritarian regimes to the right, and varieties of democratic capitalism and socialism in the center-right/center-left space.

This helps to capture one of the core competitions of the twentieth century, including communist and anticommunist regimes and the battle over the nature and extent of the welfare state. There are other dimensions that can cross cut these distinctions—above all, pulling apart views of democracy from capitalism in a far more nuanced way—but they provide a starting point for comparative analysis. Suharto's New Order viewed even unarmed communists as a subversive, alien threat that needed to be bloodily scoured from the body politic, while India adopted a comparatively relaxed approach to the hard Left. Communist regimes emphasized class categories as likely sources of threats; though they frequently became enmeshed in labyrinthine factional struggles, there was a general template for thinking about the structure of society that shaped internal threat perceptions.

These are of course radical simplifications: the specific relevance, meaning, and nature of these dimensions differ enormously across countries, and other cleavages and divisions can be highly salient instead or as well.[11] Sometimes they also overlap or fold into another. In the empirical chapters, I address in detail these challenges of applying sparse concepts to rich contexts. But this analytical scaffolding gives us a starting point for comparing government ideological projects, whether across countries, across carrier movements that aspire to be governments, or over time within governments and regimes. Each government/regime/leader can be roughly placed somewhere along these core dimensions to represent key aspects of their ideological project.

For instance, we can use the template to see how the Khmer Rouge combined ultra-Left ideology with radical ethno-nationalist Khmer chauvinism and a virulent opposition to religious sentiment, and how the Indian National Congress mixed a mostly inclusive ethnic vision with center-left political economy and an approach to religion that stood in between both the "pure" secularism of church-state separation and an explicitly religious language of politics. In Israel we can see how the commanding heights of Israeli politics have shifted along all three dimensions (though to different extents) as the once-dominant Labor/Mapai Left has been marginalized by an ascendant religious right.[12] The framework can be productively taken out into the world and used for comparison. It also moves past a dichotomy between "ethnic" and "ideological" conflicts; multiple cleavages can be contested at once.[13]

Threat Perceptions

These ideological projects generate internal "maps" of alignment and opposition: governments categorize groups according to how they mobilize cleavages, make demands, and deploy symbols. Ideology helps to determine which political claims on the state by citizens are perceived by ruling elites as legitimate, tolerable, or unacceptable. Claims advanced on the basis of ideas, symbols, and social groupings that are seen by leaders as compatible with their ideological project will be treated as more "legitimate" than those that pursue agendas seen as beyond the pale. This is a clear act of political power: "Every such project tends to exclude certain propositions, political interests, and social groups from influence, while furthering the political interests, social vision, and the position of the social groups that the 'state project' seeks to represent and consolidate."[14]

As a result, small and militarily unthreatening armed groups can be seen as a much bigger threat than far more objectively powerful groups when the former make demands and mobilize political ideas that are seen as existentially threatening to the government's project. By contrast, if a large, militarily powerful group stays within the lanes of "mainstream" politics it may be seen as politically unproblematic. I focus on armed actors, but we could easily imagine how the same processes of threat perception could apply to a whole variety of unarmed political groups, from labor unions to dissident networks to political parties.[15]

This approach establishes a political basis for regime threat perception. In contemporary Rwanda, the mobilization of ethnic identities is seen as dangerous by the leadership, which instead seeks to publicly enforce a particular vision of universal citizenship.[16] In the Soviet Union, by contrast, the polity was understood through, and organized around, the lens of class and a particular view of (essentialized) nationality and ethnicity.[17] Many European rulers in the wake of World War I were driven by visceral fears of the Left, despite the fact that "there was no close correlation between the actual size of the revolutionary threat and the fear of Bolshevism";[18] indeed, in Germany, "even if the actual threat of a Bolshevik revolution was minimal, the perception was very different indeed."[19] In some of these countries, right-wing regimes would ally with or tolerate counterrevolutionary paramilitaries of far greater military potency than the leftists they sought to annihilate.

This emphasis does not mean that armed groups are simply what governments make of them, or that ideology is the sole source of government threat perceptions. There are direct, unambiguous military threats that leave little room for interpretation: the Spanish Republicans in 1939 and the Lon Nol regime in March 1975 Cambodia, for instance, faced clear, objectively alarming challenges that left little discretion in how to allocate coercive resources. Once armed groups have the size and effectiveness to conventionally threaten core regime centers of power, we should expect a purely military-strategic dynamic to kick in. Other factors, from class interests to international geopolitics, undoubtedly influence state policies as well, exacerbating or diminishing the ideological basis of evaluations. The argument here is instead simply that a government's ideological projects should consistently orient its security apparatus toward certain kind of groups, activities, and symbols over others, determining the broad space for conflict and cooperation: "Ideas about who is fighting whom, and for what purpose, shape how perpetrating authorities frame threat and develop responses."[20]

Where Do Ideological Projects Come From?

The obvious next question is where these ideological commitments come from. We have reason to worry that they are rationalizations of other interests (such as class), or are so fluid and malleable that we cannot use them as explanatory factors. There is no doubt that sometimes there is no discernible ideological project. In failed or deeply fragmented states, for instance, factional infighting and warlord maneuvering make politics simply about desperate survival. Personalist regimes may revolve exclusively around access to a central leader, with only a patina of ideology.[21] This is one reason why I focus my theory on medium- and high-capacity states, where I suspect the daily exigencies of survival are less pressing and the politics more complex.

Yet many governments do have measurable, relatively coherent ideological projects. Moreover, these are frequently historically rooted, often highly contingent, results of coalition building, innovation, and political entrepreneurship by "carrier" movements prior to taking power.[22] Carrier movements spend their time out of power crafting a set of political commitments that inform what they try to do as new regimes.[23] This "political and ideological entrepreneurship is the transmission belt which carries ideas with hegemonic potential forward into the political arena. It is practiced by bold leaders, intellectuals, and the organizations they build or control."[24]

Carrier movements lay the basis for future government ideology, creating stickiness and continuity in the core principles of governing movements. Methodologically, they provide a valuable starting point for studying later ideological perceptions, reducing concerns about backward causation or radical fluidity. We can measure movements' ideological projects ahead of time, including movements that never become governments. To be a carrier movement, we look for an organization or clearly identifiable and related set of networks with some sort of leadership that articulates ideas about the polity they aspire to enact.

This is a broad definition, but four types of carrier movements are especially common in the historical record. Nonviolent, anticolonial, and democratizing mass movements can overthrow state power or take over in the wake of decolonization. We should see a major shift in evaluations of armed groups if (as is common) the new movement has a different ideological project than its authoritarian/colonial predecessors and is able to control the security apparatus following regime change. The Indian National Congress advanced an explicitly different set of beliefs about politics than did the British imperialists who ruled India. Victorious insurgent and revolutionary groups also, unsurprisingly, tend to view politics very differently than the regime they have overthrown. Their projects develop during underground mobilization and (often protracted) armed struggles.[25] The Viet Minh, Khmer Rouge, and Rwandan Patriotic Front are examples of these kinds of carrier movements. Rebel seizures of power are rare but often hugely consequential, as in, for instance, 1917 Russia and 1949 China.

Praetorian militaries have also been important carrier movements in the postcolonial world. They usually develop political worldviews during a period of growing skepticism of and hostility to civilian rule, as internal doctrines, training, and education craft a particular vision of state and nation. These ideological goals should be most apparent in the aftermath of coups undertaken against civilian rivals with a very different political vision.[26] The "new professional" Brazilian military is a classic example, seeking to restructure the state and society to hold a perceived threat from the Left at bay.[27] The Indonesian Army spent much of the 1950s and early 1960s developing positions about which ideas and social categories it saw as acceptable, as opposed to antinational and subversive.[28] Policzer argues that in part as a result of Prussian-inspired military reforms in 1885, "anticommunism has been at the center of the modern Chilean military's ideology," a preference given more specific Cold War content and linked to a "systematic strategy" through the spread of Western (particularly French) counterinsurgency doctrines during the 1950s and 1960s.[29]

Finally, opposition parties in democratic systems usually have a somewhat different ideological profile than the ruling party/coalition. Turnover in a democratic system often does *not*, however, lead to fundamental changes in government ideology. In many democracies, regular turnover in leaders occurs within the boundaries of mainstream politics. Debates in contemporary Germany or the Netherlands in recent decades have rarely been over the foundational rules of politics: questions that were at stake in 1776, 1865, or 1949 are no longer as pressing, in part as a result of prior governments' efforts to exclude, control, and shape the political arena. While party turnover can, under some circumstances, drive major shifts in ideological evaluation, it is less likely to do so than coups, revolutionary seizures of power, or the toppling of authoritarian or colonial rule. That said, serious political stresses within the United States and Western Europe in recent years urgently show that clashing conceptions of nation and citizenship remain very important; ideological projects continue to be a fruitful, and politically important, area of study across the world.[30]

Ideological projects thus emerge from complex historical processes of political development, interaction, and accident: everything from anticolonial mobilization to electoral politics can shape and bring to power new visions of the political arena. There is no single root cause of variation in ideological projects; material, ideational, and contingent circumstances combine in unpredictable and frequently unintended ways that can merge power politics, tactical bargaining, factional rivalries, intellectual entrepreneurship, and deep political commitment.

Elites, Institutions, and Carrier Movements

Ideological projects are not necessarily—and often are emphatically not—embraced by the "masses" or everyday citizens writ large. I focus on elites and the organizations they build and control. Even though leaders of carrier movements may, and frequently do, understand politics differently from those they ostensibly lead,[31] they will control the coercive apparatus and internal security policy of the state once in power, so we need to pay careful attention to their politics prior to becoming the government.[32]

Institutionalized carrier movements are best equipped to manage inevitable internal debates and disagreements. The Viet Minh and Indian National Congress, for instance, were better organized than their competitors for power. Such movements fuse political meaning with organizational function: the normative unacceptability of British colonialism; the need for a centralized party-state run by a vanguard party acting on behalf of proletariat; the desirability of a national language and religion can be bound up in formal and informal processes of training, socialization, and education within a party, military, or rebel carrier movement. Institutions with clear hierarchies and processes of socialization and reproduction become repositories of particular commitment, goals, and fears. A project of crafting common sense is most powerfully advanced through institutions of political mobilization. Perceptions of affinity, belonging, and threat may become taken for granted as obvious and straightforward within highly institutionalized movements: as Straus argues in explaining how "foundational narratives" can lead to genocide, they "are deeply resonant among elites, and as such they can become focal points for generating elite consensus."[33]

By contrast, in some movements divisive disagreements over foundational principles are rife, undermining any coherent ideological project. These fractured movements are common when there is not major antiregime mobilization prior to a regime change; such "challengers" do not have the time or the incentive to develop and promulgate a clear ideological line.[34] This can breed regimes with weak ideological moorings, dominated by patronage, factional rivalry, and limited incentives to build state power. This is, for instance, Herbst's account of much of postcolonial Africa's politics, in sharp contrast to the mass anticolonial and revolutionary movements that swept to power after serious struggle in much of Asia.[35]

Many cases lie between these extremes, with a mix of consensual and contested strands within a broad project. Rather than ignoring these disagreements, I use them to help explain later outcomes. Internal tensions within carrier movements are inevitable and provide an opportunity to explain which ideological orientations should be most durable or tenuous. Areas of reasonably broad agreement should lead to continuity once a movement takes power. The Indochinese Communist Party was always a Marxist-Leninist party, even when there were internal disagreements about tactics or mid-range strategy, and it is little surprise

it acted as a Marxist-Leninist party upon taking power. Areas of enduring disagreement or contestation within a movement, by contrast, are open to future
change and variability: in India, for instance, we will see in chapter 4 recurring,
intense debates about what can be defined as Hindu communalism, when Hindu
majoritarianism is acceptable, and how to view Hindu nationalist organizations
like the Rashtriya Swayamsevak Sangh (RSS), reflecting disagreements and competition within Indian politics well prior to 1947.[36]

Governments and Internal Security

Once carrier movements become governments, they try to implement their projects. Prepower commitments do not straightforwardly become implemented
policies. New challenges arise: raising revenue, managing corruption, reforming
bureaucracies, controlling the security forces, competing with rivals, and creating and sustaining the basic institutional functions of the state can all bedevil
carrier movements as they transition into governments.[37]

Nevertheless, new regimes should pursue sustained, costly efforts toward
implementing their ideological goals once in power. These will vary across governments because "states" do not have universal internal security perceptions or
goals.[38] Ideological projects make sense of what the regime exists to do. Ideological projects powerfully bind institutions and elites around an overarching "political grammar of the state,"[39] informing how they evaluate groups. As Jayal argues,
"The particular elements that make up a citizenship regime in a given society at a
given point in time will differ from those in other societies and even in the same
society over time."[40]

When there are competing strands within a movement, space exists for other
political dynamics to decide in which direction a new government will tilt among
the open options carried over from the prepower period. Factional feuds, leadership rivalries, internal purges, and contingent events shape which strands emerge
victorious or which compromises emerge. Exactly how these debates play out,
mixing contingency and strategy, is beyond my ability to explain. These contested issues will be the locus of open, visible politics within the political system,
and consequently the most fluid and easy-to-change domains of internal security
policy. For instance, in Bangladesh, deep divisions within the military and ruling
elite after independence about the role of religion laid the basis for radical shifts
in government evaluation following both coups and electoral turnover.[41] The
Awami League, heir to the independence movement that birthed Bangladesh,
has highlighted the Bengali language and regional identity, while 1970s/1980s
military dictators and the Bangladesh National Party (BNP) have pushed for a

THE POLITICS OF THREAT PERCEPTION

definition of the nation that is more explicitly Muslim, distinct from a dominant focus on language and region.

In areas of relative consensus, by contrast, new regime leaders seek to build security and political institutions in which certain threats take priority in the allocation of scarce coercive and cooperative resources, political activities incompatible with the ideological project trigger red flags, and particular modes of response are prescribed as appropriate or unacceptable. Political leaders and bureaucracies advance a "language of politics" that defines mainstream discourse, aiming to forestall or sideline others.[42] Thai military and military-linked rulers have sought to radically limit public discourse about the monarchy; Burmese elites, both military and civilian, have largely marginalized the Rohingya in the political sphere, while military has also sought to excise federalism as a thinkable political end goal.[43]

These projects are already embedded in carrier movements, but this process of "value infusion" often occurs within broader state institutions after the carrier movement takes power.[44] Police and military forces are not simple, technical institutions; they are also deeply political. They can adopt a particular set of—often taken for granted—threat perceptions in training, doctrine, internal socialization, and political intervention by ruling elites. America's security apparatus, for instance, regularly uses racial cues in its patterns of targeting protesters and citizens, reflecting broader racial orders.[45]

These formal and informal processes reproduce rules of the political game, in part as focal points around which state political and military elites understand how to act. Corruption, venality, rivalries, and disagreements can easily exist within an ideological project as long as they do not directly challenge or threaten the core principles the government seeks to police.[46] Indonesia's military was notoriously corrupt and rife with rivalries during Suharto's New Order, yet it pursued a consistent internal security doctrine that sought to eliminate communists, repress ethnic separatists, and cooperate with politically palatable local power holders.

Unsavory or unacceptable ideas (in the eyes of the state) of course do not disappear even if elite security managers do not like them. As Krebs notes, "A dominant narrative, which excludes others from the zone of the respectable and legitimate, is compatible with diversity and dissent at the margins."[47] Citizens hold opinions about politics and discuss them among themselves, whether in open public debates, behind closed doors, through "hidden transcripts," or via the underground circulation of dissident literature.[48] Organizations ranging from mainstream political parties to hard-line insurgents may make public demands that fly in the face of government desires. Governments often fail to achieve their projects or meet unexpected resistance.[49] These are the contests at the heart of politics. Understanding how *opposition* emerges and what form it takes, however, requires first establishing the visions of politics held by elites and the security institutions they control.[50]

Armed Group Ideological Positions

Armed groups can be categorized by governments as ideologically opposed, aligned, or in the "gray zone." Ideological fit is a continuous spectrum, but this is a useful simplification for analysis. These assessments flow from the government's project. Opposed groups are those that fundamentally challenge regime ideology on at least one of its dimensions, and usually at least two. They are seen as making unacceptable political demands that cannot be easily managed within mainstream politics. Aligned groups are those that are in substantial agreement across the three dimensions, even if there are some areas of minor difference. Gray zone groups are those with substantial disagreement on at least one of the three core dimensions of ideology, but that are not mobilizing demands or cleavages that are seen as unacceptably out of bounds or impossible to resolve within standard political processes. Coding in specific cases requires careful contextual justification, but this gives a sense of how threat perception relates to ideology.

Opposed groups have political goals and deploy symbols that are seen by security managers as deeply incompatible with the government's ideological projects. These groups make demands and advance ideas that are perceived as illegitimate. Doing business with them is not on the table under most circumstances. Bargaining and compromise are seen as fruitless: acknowledging the legitimacy of such groups' goals will undermine key principles of the regime and nation while encouraging other similar challenges. They cannot be trusted to uphold any deal, and therefore they—and the subversive ideas they carry—must be scoured from the body polity.

Opposed groups are portrayed by regimes as alien, "other," and subversive; they exist beyond the acceptable bounds of the polity. Governments have high levels of political resolve for crackdowns and purges against these actors.[51] Suharto's New Order framed ethnic separatist armed groups as deeply inimical to the imagined nation, American presidents and security managers viewed the armed Far Left with undisguised contempt and suspicion in the 1960s, and Stalin perceived an extraordinary plethora of enemies of the state (armed and unarmed).[52]

By sharp contrast, *aligned* groups pursue goals, deploy symbols, and articulate discourses that are compatible with the government's project across the board. Militarily powerful, but ideologically aligned, groups may not be intrinsic threats to the government's vision of the political arena. Aligned groups do not challenge the right of the regime to rule and they reproduce the basic ideological themes of the government. Many pro-state militias, armed wings of ruling parties, and local private armies fall into this political role, as do even some groups that originated as anti-state insurgents but change sides.[53] They serve as shock troops of rulers, pursuing goals and deploying symbols that reinforce, rather than undermine, security managers' desired political system.

The Suharto regime deployed militias in East Timor and state-backed armed actors in the political heartland that amplified the political message of the government.[54] In 2007 Kenya, armed groups closely aligned with the ruling party were key players in large-scale electoral and ethnic violence. In the United States, a variety of armed individuals and groupings are not seen as intrinsically politically problematic by powerful forces within American politics: their right to bear arms is constitutionally protected and, in the case of the Republican Party and conservative activists, actively celebrated. The Trump administration repeatedly downplayed the threat posed by radical right militias and lone-wolf terrorists, preferring to focus instead on immigration and Islamist extremism as vastly higher internal security priorities. In Bangladesh, the often-violent student wings of ruling political parties are protected from repression, and instead operate as allies of the regime.

Gray zone groups are the most interesting, and least-studied, ideological category. Inspired by Auyero's study of "gray zone" contexts that blend mainstream politics with illegality, I conceptualize these as groups that pursue goals and advance ideas that are in tension with the government's desired political arena on one or more dimensions, but not seen as beyond the pale.[55] Gray zone groups tend to mobilize on political dimensions that are tolerable subjects of politics for the government, but they stake out positions and deploy goals and symbols that mark out extreme political positions on those dimensions relative to the desired "mainstream."

Gray zone groups are not actors a government wants to encourage: in an ideal world they and their ideas would not exist. Yet rulers believe they can do business with such groups because they do not pose an existential threat to its broader project. Their demands and activities are regrettable, not intolerable. Political space exists for bargaining, negotiation, and cooperation, even in the face of anti-state attacks, disruptive activities, or armed group social control and resource extraction. Israeli governments have often seen armed settler movements as gray zone actors (though their most extreme fringes bleed into ideological opposition).[56] Linguistic insurgents in India tend to be perceived as gray zone groups who can at least be talked to, and the armed parties of Iraqi Kurdistan have been gray zone actors in Baghdad's eyes since 2003, with deep underlying political disagreements over the distribution of resources and political decentralization, but not representing an existential challenge to the center.[57]

From Ideology to Armed Order

Ideological projects play the foundational role in determining how governments perceive groups. We should see general tendencies in armed orders emerge according to ideological fit: aligned groups are likely to receive much more cooperation than coercion, while opposed groups see the exact opposite. But this still leaves some indeterminacy, above all for gray zone groups.

A secondary variable enters my argument at this point: whether the government and armed group have shared tactical interests that can create a basis for cooperation even in the face of ideological disagreement. This is a tactical question about political exigencies. Given a set of ideological alignments, can an armed group help the state win elections, target shared enemies, or project power in regional rivalries and internationalized civil wars, and is it willing to do so?

Tactical overlap is generally not very important at the extremes of the ideological spectrum. Aligned groups that are able to help the government achieve its political goals will form alliances. Those that do not offer much to the government will still be treated well—they are likely to be incorporated or made into allies. There can be situations in which even opposed groups and governments have shared tactical interests, forming "strange bedfellow" limited cooperation orders, but this is rare. These extremes are also where my argument is mostly easily shown to be wrong in a case. We may, for instance, see personal or factional rivalries leading to conflict even with aligned groups: the purging of the SA brownshirts in early Nazi Germany is not an outcome my theory expects.[58] Similarly, a state may tolerate a group I code as ideologically opposed despite no discernible tactical/instrumental reason for doing so: it may simply be neglectful, or misperceive the situation.

More interesting are gray zone groups. These challenge the government's preferred polity on at least one ideological dimension, but are not making unacceptable demands. Here we see a complex set of calculations and interactions that determine whether containment or limited cooperation emerge; tactical overlap becomes essential since ideology sets only loose limits on the specific order that emerges.

Table 1.2 maps out how ideological fit combines with tactical overlap. We see six distinct armed group political roles emerge in the eyes of a regime. Armed allies and superfluous supporters are quite similar; both involve friendly relations with the government. Opposed groups can be broken into two types: mortal enemies and strange bedfellows. Realistically, strange bedfellows roles only rarely emerge because of the primacy of ideological difference, so the tendency is toward conflict with opposed groups. In the gray zone tactical overlap plays a key role. Business partners have shared instrumental interests with the government and thus mutually build limited cooperation, while undesirables do not, leading to containment orders. This section unpacks tactical overlap in more detail, then works through the different political roles that table 1.2 identifies.

Governments and armed groups have broad strategic goals that are deeply shaped by ideological visions. But they also have immediate tactical goals. When governments and armed groups have clear tactical reasons to cooperate, I code high tactical overlap; when there are few or no strong incentives for this tactical alignment, I code low overlap.[59] Armed groups have the greatest tactical value to the governments when they are capable of sustained campaigns of action that advance government interests. What counts as instrumentally valuable obviously is conditioned by ideological goals, which is why tactical incentives are secondary in my argument.

However, group characteristics vary in ways that can create analytical distance between the two. Groups have radically different strengths and weaknesses: some are simply ill-equipped to accomplish a particular goal, no matter their ideological sympathies. In turn, armed groups can find government assistance useful for advancing local interests—holding off rivals, controlling resource flows, and gaining some degree of autonomy. This also depends on what specific capabilities and resources the government is able to offer; even friendly governments may not be able to help armed groups deal with the political exigencies they face.

Tactical dynamics can create interesting tensions between government goals and group capabilities. First, sometimes relatively weak or small groups nevertheless are very useful because of their particular skills or support base: linking up with a niche local group in a particularly pivotal electoral constituency may be

TABLE 1.2   Group political roles, government strategies, and armed orders

	TACTICAL OVERLAP	
IDEOLOGICAL FIT	**HIGH**	**LOW**
Aligned	Armed ally	Superfluous supporter
	Order: Alliance	Order: Alliance or incorporation
Gray zone	Business partner	Undesirable
	Order: Limited cooperation	Order: Containment
Opposed	Strange bedfellow	Mortal enemy
	Order: Limited cooperation	Order: Total war

far more useful for winning an election than supporting a more powerful group that operates in an area of existing government dominance. Second, armed group power has no straightforward effect on government decision making. Relatively powerful groups can be hugely helpful or politically unproblematic. But they can also be a major problem when they are ideologically opposed or in the gray zone. These are more powerful enemies, not more helpful allies. Group strength is a double-edged sword, and its ultimate value or threat hinges crucially on politics.

Three contexts are most likely to create tactical overlap (though other mechanisms certainly exist): militarized elections, cross-border proxy conflicts, and multiparty civil wars.[60] For each, I identify conditions under which we are most likely to see mutual interests. These mechanisms can operate individually or in combination with others. They may change rapidly, helping to explain shifts in armed orders over time even when ideological variables remain constant. In chapter 2 I explore in more detail how these contexts can drive fine-grained changes over time.

First, multiparty civil wars make tactical overlap more likely than in a straightforward, two-actor insurgent-counterinsurgent conflict. Fotini Christia has shown that in extreme cases of total state breakdown, incredibly fluid alliance and conflict patterns can emerge.[61] Tactical cooperation can occur despite ideological disagreements in less dramatic cases as well. Gray zone groups engage in rivalries and feuds that lead them to approach the government for either protection or a lessening of repression that would let them deal with more pressing challenges from other armed groups. Actors facing serious threats from other groups or that see an opportunity to carve out de facto governance through a deal with the state are most likely to pursue limited cooperation.

In turn, governments may benefit from working with armed groups in this context: at the maximum, they can provide local information and even "deniable" violence, while at minimum, avoiding conflict with some armed groups can make fighting other groups easier. This is a context in which looking beyond dyads to more sophisticated interactions among three or more actors is very helpful.

Second, armed groups and governments can see each other as valuable partners for winning "militarized elections."[62] Armed groups are most useful when they can repress opposition politicians and supporters or deliver important blocs of votes. Groups in these contexts are often linked to the ruling party or state apparatus. But they can also be autonomous actors that work with the ruling party to pursue their own interests. Groups that cannot deliver votes or support government campaigns against opposition parties within this context provide little value to rulers. In turn, governments can also be valuable to groups by providing them with protection, patronage, and access to resources and power through proximity to mainstream politics.[63]

Third, the international system can provide powerful incentives for governments to collude with armed actors against rivals. Cross-border militancy is frequently used by states who perceive a pressing threat from neighbors or who are pursuing irredentist goals in nearby civil conflicts.[64] Armed groups that have ambitions in these neighboring conflict environments can benefit in a variety of ways from sanctuary, training, or military aid.[65] This value hinges on the ability to successfully impose costs on rival states. Many armed groups are singularly unsuited to this highly challenging task, however, and have little to offer the government in navigating geopolitical tides, even if they are ideologically aligned. Motivated, disciplined insurgent groups are likely to be most useful when facing a powerful rival state, while shambolic organizations only become useful in less militarily difficult contexts.

Political Roles

Having established how ideological fit and tactical overlap work, we can now work through the full typology of armed group political roles in table 1.2 to explore when and how different armed orders emerge.

Aligned: Armed Allies and Superfluous Supporters

Ideologically aligned groups receive the most cooperative treatment from governments, leading to alliances or incorporation. When there are overlapping tactical incentives, we see tight alliance between the government and group. State security forces and an armed ally coordinate policies and consistently share information and resources. This combination of ideological sympathy and mutual tactical utility is a powerful one. There is no incentive to radically change these rules of the game, even if some degree of disagreement and bargaining is inevitable.[66] An enduringly fragmented distribution of control over violence emerges from this political configuration, with government complicity in the intertwining of state and nonstate violence.

Some allies are linked to government patronage and support networks: this is the classic vision of "outsourced" violence.[67] But other armed allies are more autonomous. They coordinate with the state but are not reliant on or bound to it. This occurs because the most useful armed groups are often those with strong organizational structures and access to information, capabilities, and social constituencies that the government lacks.[68] They are the only ones that can deliver what the political leadership needs. Rather than being pawns, such groups have leverage in their dealings with the state.

Aligned groups that lack tactical overlap with the government can be categorized as superfluous supporters: not particularly helpful but also not especially problematic. I assume that there is little intrinsic benefit to rulers from allowing low-value groups to continue to exist, and expect that they will be targeted for incorporation.[69] Incorporation efforts are most common either after a government has surmounted a major political challenge and has the opportunity to centralize its control over violence, or when its dalliance with nonstate violence has led to unexpected and unwanted costs. That said, this is a weak prediction: a group could want to maintain itself as an autonomous organization, and since it poses little political threat, the government may simply let it continue to exist.

Incorporation sometimes involves a formal demobilization deal and a signed agreement that specifies a process for the termination of the group and its incorporation into the state, ruling party, or "mainstream" politics. In other situations, incorporation is an informal process of placing group members on the state payroll, or conveying the message that their activities are no longer needed and that their dissolution will be rewarded.[70] These rewards are diverse, ranging from direct cash payments to influence in the halls of power. Aligned groups are relatively easily absorbed into patronage networks, ruling parties, or the security apparatus. In contrast to gray zone or opposed groups, major political concessions or disruptions are not necessary to bring superfluous supporters into "mainstream politics."

Opposed: Mortal Enemies and Strange Bedfellows

Being an opposed group does not just mean disagreeing with the government, but instead levying demands and deploying symbols perceived as fundamentally incompatible with security managers' ideology on at least one core dimension. These are not actors, or ideas, that the government wants to countenance or feels it can do business with. Some ideological projects identify many opposed groups, while for most others the number of truly subversive, existentially threatening groups is much lower.

The dominant political role for opposed groups is being seen as a *mortal enemy*. Rather than having to make unacceptable concessions, governments try to break such groups. These are total internal wars, rather than containment efforts. Without understanding the roots of political resolve for crackdowns, variation in government's willingness to repress or make deals is hard to explain. The available "bargaining range" is very narrow when a state interacts with a group seen as a mortal enemy, while deep (generally mutual) mistrust heightens commitment problems, making it difficult to avoid violent conflict.[71] Such perceptions help explain policies that seem gratuitously indiscriminate or disproportionately intense: the state's security forces perceive a major threat that needs to be eliminated, even at a high price. This can be true of both militarily strong and weak groups because the threat is often understood in "dispositional" terms.[72]

When a mortal enemy is relatively weak or fragmented, total war is likely to quickly destroy it. The armed order comes to an end with the group's collapse. Such dyads often disappear before reaching the point of civil war because their interactions never escalate into protracted mutual combat. Conflict datasets often do not capture these kinds of short-lived, preemptive total war purges but they are essential if we are to understand patterns of challenge, repression, and order.[73]

When a mortal enemy instead has enough capacity to stand and fight, and refuses to shift its political positioning, we see protracted, intense hostilities with little concession or conciliation. Governments are often surprised by a group's resilience, leading to unintended conflict escalation as both sides up the ante in hopes of achieving major breakthroughs; this can end in the collapse of one side, intense long-running wars, or eventual shifts in political positioning.[74]

There are rare circumstances when an opposed group and the state can have shared tactical interests, putting the group in a *strange bedfellows* political role. These are likely to be situations of government desperation, attempting to collude and forge a limited cooperation order around mutual, but temporary, tactical interests. If the perceived strange bedfellow reciprocates, collusion can occur even among bitter enemies. This is most likely when they are both deeply threatened by a common enemy. Intense, existential, multiparty civil wars, cut-throat electoral competition, and pitched international rivalries can create enough mutual desperation to allow some degree of cooperation between ideological foes.[75] Limited cooperation with strange bedfellows will be rare. The overlap of interests giving rise to it is so narrow that even when cooperation occurs, it is fragile and can break down quickly in the face of minor changes. Once the shared interest disappears, we should see a rapid return to total war.

Gray Zone: Business Partners and Undesirables

The "gray zone" is the murkiest space on the ideological spectrum.[76] Gray zone groups seriously challenge the government on at least one important ideological dimension, but the symbols and demands they deploy can be potentially accommodated within the government's vision of the mainstream political sphere. This means that ideology does not generate very clear predictions on its own, beyond there being less cooperation than with aligned groups and less conflict than with opposed groups. Tactical dynamics play a central role in understanding variation in this political context.

Gray zone groups that share tactical interests with the government are business partners. They are likely to end up in a limited cooperation order. Like armed allies, these are frequently powerful, cohesive organizations that can achieve tasks the government itself cannot. Limited cooperation with business partners takes on the form of formal or informal live-and-let-live deals, cease-fires, and modern variants of indirect rule.[77] These actors do not see eye-to-eye on key ideological questions and, alongside powerful incentives to cooperate, their relationships are fraught with tension and ambiguity. The business partner group is generally granted a substantial degree of space to operate, influence in its area of operation, and freedom from repression by the state. The government in turn is better equipped to achieve its instrumental goals.

Power and authority are negotiated and divided within the shell of the ostensibly sovereign state.[78] This outcome straddles the boundaries between war and peace, representing a political bargain that reduces violence without either settling core political conflicts or forging a state monopoly of violence. These orders can be highly enduring, but are always vulnerable to a shift in tactical interests. Even if the group remains in the gray zone, limited cooperation is fragile and can crack as a result of unexpected shocks, misunderstandings, and escalating local feuds or clashes. Because of its political origins, this order is more like cooperation between states under anarchy than the tightly collusive embrace of alliances.[79]

Undesirables are not ideologically aligned nor do they have overlapping tactical interests with the state. Crucially, however, they are also not seen by security managers as existentially dangerous. Their moderate level of political threat is not worth the military, financial, and political costs of total war. Governments instead prefer to keep a lid on disruption linked to these groups. This leads to wars of violence management rather than violence monopolization. The government hopes that containment will grind the undesirable group down until it collapses or shifts its ideological positioning into alignment with the state (a common prelude to incorporation). A long period of containment is seen as an acceptable price, either to hold the line until the group eventually falls apart, or to simply stop it from causing undue trouble.

Undesirable groups make the opposite bet, that the state will eventually grow weary of containment and make concessions, or that some outside shock will open new space for the armed group to operate.[80] Such groups may also benefit from continuing access to illicit resources, or gain de facto political and social influence below the threshold of activity that would trigger crackdowns and suppression. The actual level of violence in these armed orders can vary dramatically, sometimes well below the standard threshold of "civil war," but the underlying political conflict endures.

Understanding Armed Politics

This chapter has outlined a new approach to studying politics and violence. Armed orders emerge from the ideological projects of governments, which identify the kinds of political demands that make a group more or less threatening. Ideological fit largely determines armed orders with aligned and opposed groups. Within the gray zone category, tactical incentives play an important role in explaining whether containment or limited cooperation emerge. I have not argued that this argument is the only one able to account for variation: this is an extremely complex phenomenon.

The key insight driving my theory is the central importance of ideology as a historically rooted source of threat perceptions that varies across countries, across carrier movements and governments within countries, and over time. I conceptualize ideological projects along three dimensions—ethno-linguistic cleavages, the role of the state in religion, and left-right redistribution—as a starting point for measuring and comparing governments' ideological projects. Ideology can be combined with tactical overlap to generate predictions about the orders that should emerge between a government with a given ideological project and different kinds of armed groups within it. This argument helps make sense of important puzzles: why some tiny, marginal armed groups face seemingly disproportionate repression, why some powerful groups are left alone or worked with, and why we see long-running cease-fires emerge with some groups but not others that have similar organizational or military characteristics.

This chapter has focused on historical origins and a broadly static set of conceptualizations of armed group political roles. The next chapter builds on these arguments to identify pathways of change over time in armed orders. Even if government ideologies are contingent and sticky, they are not locked in stone; the same applies to armed groups' ideological positions. Tactical incentives can also be highly fluid, creating the potential for extremely dynamic shifts in armed orders over time. This chapter laid the foundations of armed politics—the next moves to armed politics in motion.

HOW ARMED ORDERS CHANGE

Armed orders may have deep political roots, but they are not locked in place. The two Kurdish armed parties of northern Iraq, the PUK and KDP, are a classic example: they have oscillated between various forms of conflict and cooperation with Baghdad over the decades. At different times they have both fought against the central Iraqi government, fought each other and as a result looked for support even from Saddam Hussein's government, built a live-and-let-live relationship with the central government, and in response to the surge of ISIS in northern Iraq in 2014–15, even worked closely with Baghdad—before then clashing with government forces over control of Kirkuk.

The Kurds face a conundrum of nationalism in Iraq. Both Sunni-minority Baathist rule and Shiite-majority post-2003 governance left the Kurds potentially on the outside of the ruling coalition, without a clear claim to dominance over the state. Yet within this broad structure, armed orders have shifted around dramatically. Some of these changes have been driven by tactical considerations, with infighting and the rise of ISIS creating incentives at various points for Kurdish groups to try to establish a modus vivendi with Baghdad against their rivals. Some changes have been influenced by ideological dynamics among armed groups themselves: accusations of selling out and the rise and fall of different tribal, ethno-nationalist, and leftist strands within Kurdish politics have created more and less radical factions. And finally, regime politics in Baghdad played a central role in determining how rulers saw the Kurdish question in general and what political exigencies they faced that shaped their approaches to specific groups.[1]

How can we understand these complex processes of change? This chapter explores how the core variables introduced in the previous chapter—ideological alignment and tactical overlap—can make sense of mechanisms of change. Both armed groups and governments can shift their ideological positions, altering their political relationship. These are the most consequential changes, affecting the core contours of the political system and the group's place within it. Yet they are also not common: for both groups and governments, major shifts in ideological position are slow, difficult, and usually contested processes. More common, though less dramatic, are changes in tactical overlap. These can be quite fluid, as governments and groups deal with highly dynamic on-the-ground challenges. This suggests that most of the change in groups' political roles we see will be *within* ideological categories, especially shifts between business partner and undesirable roles within the "gray zone." But the most important changes in group roles will be *across* ideological categories.

There are a staggering number of factors that can explain why tactical incentives and ideological positions change. This chapter focuses on a small number of pathways that seem likely to recur across contexts and that are built on the argument of the previous chapter. The argument remains ultimately state-centric, but this chapter opens the space for more dynamic interactions and armed group agency. The pathways I identify provide an analytical starting point that can be built on in future research. I first examine fluid shifts in alignment choices, holding constant ideological factors. The chapter then moves to the bigger question of why governments and armed groups shift their ideological projects.

Changes in Tactical Overlap

Political challenges and tactical needs can be very fluid: elections come and go, international rivalries wax and wane, rebel fragmentation emerges and disappears, and insurgencies rise and collapse. These are the kinds of changes that have attracted the most attention in research on political violence, focusing on instrumental, tactical incentives for shifting alignments. This chapter builds on this literature in three ways. First, it pulls together different mechanisms under a shared framework. Second, it specifies more clearly when particular contexts will turn into actual incentives for cooperation. Third, it agrees with existing work that tactical dynamics are very important, but argues that they are ultimately secondary to the larger political struggles at play within political systems and regime politics. Tactics valuably fill out fine-grained variation, while larger patterns emerge from the clash of political projects at the national level. We need to take both of them seriously, in dialogue with one another.

The challenge is identifying and predicting tactical overlap without tautology: rather than seeing cooperation and assuming it had some functional source, we need to explicitly theorize conditions under which tactical overlap is most likely. I focus on three contexts in which armed groups and governments are most likely to find reasons to cooperate. Violent elections, international politics, and intense civil wars can all create strong reasons for states and armed groups to work together. Within each, I identify specific conditions under which tactical overlap might emerge or disappear and discuss what characteristics of groups will be more useful than others. I devote particular attention to ideological gray zone groups, since they are the most indeterminate category. This is of course only a limited set of instrumental mechanisms, but the dynamics I theorize seem likely to occur with some degree of frequency across a wide range of contexts and can provide a basis for future research.

Militarized Elections

The rise and aftermath of "militarized elections" can drive shifts in how much groups and states need each other.[2] Sometimes violence and coercion around elections is purely a government affair: police and military forces repress the opposition or manipulate the electoral process. But election-linked violence often involves nonstate armed groups: in Bangladesh and Kenya, organizations linked to political parties have been actors in electoral violence; in Northern Ireland and Northeast India, insurgents have weighed in on the electoral process; in Nigeria, local armed groups are linked to political patrons as part of a grim fusing of "mainstream" politics with political violence.[3] This is an area in which normal, mainstream politics can be partially armed politics: the exigencies of elections can create armed allies, business partners, and even strange bedfellows. But shifts in electoral coalitions and pressures can just as quickly eliminate tactical overlap, driving rapid realignments. This leads to incredibly dynamic and complicated politics, with groups and governments jockeying for power and influence under very short time horizons.

What are the roots of tactical overlap around elections? Armed groups can actively and directly support the ruling party, using their influence to encourage voters to back the party. They can target opposition candidates and supporters with violence or threats. This may also involve electoral irregularities like ballot stuffing. Groups that are political parties or that represent an important constituency may be seen as valuable current or future coalition partners who the ruling leadership wants to work with. Crucially, violence by nonstate groups can let ruling parties deny responsibility to international and domestic critics, allowing an "outsourcing" of election violence.[4] Some groups, whether ideologically aligned or not, will be useless for these tasks, but others may have reach and capabilities that give them particular political value to the regime. This is why we cannot use objective group characteristics, like size or military power, as indicators of electoral overlap; there can be contextual reasons why different kinds of groups are more or less useful.

In turn, governments can provide protection, resources, and political access that may be very valuable to armed groups as they pursue their own agendas, expanding the scope of an armed group's influence and range of action. At an extreme, armed groups can become part of or protected by the ruling regime, providing extraordinary access to political power. This is most relevant for aligned and gray zone groups, since opposed groups are least likely to either want or be granted direct access to mainstream politics. Many of the armed electoral groups that operate in contexts like Nigeria, the Philippines, and Bangladesh do so in open or tacit collusion with state agencies and ruling parties.[5]

How does this help us understand change over time? These government motivations to tolerate or work with armed groups should be strongest under the shadow of tight, competitive, and uncertain elections in weakly institutionalized environments.[6] The run-up to elections should see increasingly overlap between ruling parties and electorally valuable armed groups, resulting in campaigns of state-sponsored or tolerated coercion, direct violence, and armed mobilization. Kenya in 2007 and Bangladesh in numerous elections are classic examples of how ruling parties can facilitate violence by nominally nonstate armed groups as a strategy to try to maintain power.

Tactical overlap in this context should usually decrease after an election. Either the incumbents win and can now move to contain or, more often, incorporate armed groups, or a new government comes to power opposed to the groups it had been targeted by in the previous election. Electoral victory provides both motive and opportunity to at least rein such actors in. When incumbents win, they often reward their nonstate allies with incorporation that gives them access to power and patronage within the party or government. When the opposition wins, groups backed by the previous government are likely to be recategorized as threats, leading to conflict or at least much more limited and tenuous cooperation.

There may be contexts, however, in which electoral armed groups have no interest in being demobilized and have the organizational autonomy to resist incorporation, while governments do not view them as major threats.[7] They can persist within an electoral system, often as "intrasystem" free agents willing to cut deals with ruling parties while maintaining some degree of independence.[8] These tend to be gray zone and aligned groups, generally taking the form of armed parties and local private armies. Business partners and armed allies can therefore endure in a context in which militarization of domestic politics is a characteristic of the system, rather than emerging and then disappearing around elections themselves.

International Politics

International politics can create radical shifts in tactical overlap between governments and armed groups. As a rich literature has pointed out, the rise and decline of conflicts and rivalries can make groups more or less useful as tools of cross-border power projection.[9] A state locked in rivalry with another state often has very strong reasons to want to work with armed groups that target the rival or its allies. Armed groups can benefit from this relationship when they receive sanctuary, material, training, or diplomatic support. Many cases of alliance and limited cooperation emerge from these tactical alignments: Thailand backed ethnic separatist groups fighting the Burmese military, Syria has hosted anti-Israel groups, and Iran supported anti-Saddam Shiite militants, among many other cases.

This overlap should be most durable when international rivalry is most intense. Armed groups can be key players in proxy conflicts. Pakistan, with extensive US support, provided sanctuary and arms to Afghan mujahideen fighting the Soviets in the 1970s and 1980s, for instance.[10] The height of Arab-Israeli wars and tension saw extensive support among a number of states for Palestinian armed groups.

Yet shifts at the international level also can decrease tactical overlap, leaving armed groups out in the cold. When Thailand and Myanmar improved their ties during the 1990s, ethnic armed groups began to feel increasing pressure from the Thai government to end their wars.[11] As Israel has grown closer to a number of Arab states against Iran, meaningful support for Palestinian armed struggle has clearly decreased. When the Soviets left Afghanistan, the Americans largely lost interest.[12] Iran-Iraq rapprochement in the mid-1970s badly undermined Kurdish armed actors who had relied on Iranian support.[13]

Therefore, while most research focuses on how international conflict can spur state-group collusion, it is equally important to study how international rapprochements can *decrease* the overlap of tactical goals between governments and armed groups. Sometimes international interventions are driven by deep ideological compatibility between sponsors and armed groups, and in these contexts changes at the international level are less likely. But when support for transnational armed groups is a largely tactical, instrumental tool, it is very likely to shift when these interests change. Armed groups left in the lurch may end up marginalized and irrelevant, but sometimes they turn against their former sponsor or find a new state willing to support the cause. Armed groups may also decide to stop working with governments that they believe are simply using them as cannon fodder or that they perceive as meddling, sometimes leading them to abandon cooperation.

This all means that there is a complicated, dynamic relationship between international relations and armed politics. Not only do we see waves of transnational ideological diffusion helping to shape the basic contours of political life, but interstate rivalries, "internationalized civil wars," and proxy wars create variation across time in tactical overlap between governments and armed groups.[14] This is an area in which boundaries between international relations and comparative politics are entirely porous, and the fusion of the two creates important and fine-grained variation in tactical overlap. Conflicts in Syria, Afghanistan, and Iraq are examples in which domestic and international forces have shaped the tactical incentives of actors in important ways.

Civil Wars

Civil wars, especially multiparty civil wars, generate incredibly complex incentives that can create tactical overlap between even ideological enemies.[15] For instance, the intertwined Syrian civil war and broader counter-ISIS conflict of the last decade has seen as an extraordinary array of relationships. The Assad regime temporarily ignored ISIS while fighting other rebels before returning to anti-ISIS operations, and carved out a tenuous live-and-let-live arrangement with the Kurdish YPG for a substantial period of the war. The United States has worked with Kurdish, Arab, government, and nongovernment actors, ranging from tight alliances with the Peshmerga to grudging tacit cooperation with Iran-linked Iraqi Shiite paramilitaries, as it attempted to roll back ISIS.[16] The Iraqi government has similarly tried to manage a remarkably complex array of armed groups, from Kurdish and Shiite paramilitary parties to local Sunni Arab militias. A dizzying set of alignment choices have emerged as tactical needs, local rivalries, and battlefield dynamics have shifted around. Ideological projects have obviously not been irrelevant: ISIS has fought everyone, and the Assad regime has pursued most of its enemies with unmitigated violence. Nevertheless, at least in some cases, there has been substantial fluidity.

I outline two logics that can create tactical overlap in civil wars. The first occurs in the simple setting of a two-party conflict.[17] Ideological fit does most of the work in shaping conflict and cooperation in such wars. However, for gray zone and even opposed insurgents, tactical reasons to do business with the state, and vice versa, may emerge over time. War weariness is discussed more below as a cause of insurgent ideological change, but it can also cause limited tactical overlap when both sides can gain from a cessation of open fighting.[18] If grinding conflicts are making it difficult to maintain local power and control for insurgents, and if the state is tired of bearing the costs of endless war, the two sides may agree to at least attempt a cease-fire or other form of limited cooperation to provide mutual breathing space, an opportunity to explore political changes, or a chance to rearm before the next round of clashes.

The Tamil Tigers and government of Sri Lanka, for instance, found themselves at such an impasse in late 2001 and early 2002, leading to a cease-fire of several years despite severe ideological incompatibilities and providing an opportunity for the Tigers to consolidate their governance.[19] These arrangements may be long lasting, but regardless of their duration they are fragile unless there is a deeper political shift in alignment. This is especially true for opposed groups: if either side decides that it is not gaining from a tactical cessation of conflict, we will see a return to intense warfare. This mechanism can help explain waxing and waning conflicts, with periods of relative quiet when neither side sees a short-term benefit to continuing fighting, and shifts in power, expectations, or internal political pressures potentially undermining these periods and leading to reescalation.[20]

The second, and more complex, cause of tactical overlap occurs in multisided civil wars as states and armed groups jockey for survival and influence.[21] As I discussed in chapter 1, this is a particularly common context for the rise of tactical overlap. Governments look for armed actors who can provide local intelligence and deniable violence, as well as those whose cooperation can fracture or divide an insurgent movement. Armed groups in turn look for protection against other armed groups and local power and influence from government sponsorship. In a conflict with multiple actors, this creates space for cooperation across the full ideological spectrum. As these incentives diminish, however, so too does tactical overlap, which helps to explain variation over time.

Groups become attractive potential partners to governments if they have information, social support, or fighting power that could undermine a shared enemy.[22] Superfluous supporters may suddenly acquire new value as deniable proxies or arms'-length enforcers of state power and become armed allies in the eyes of the state. Undesirables previously seen as tolerable but unsavory can become business partners if they are willing to work with the state. This context is also where we are most likely to see the strange bedfellow political role emerge, if only temporarily: grim, existential battles for survival can bring together bitter foes.

Armed groups also have reasons to avoid cooperating with the state: cooperation can be seen as selling out by anti-state civilians, open the group up to attack from rivals, and reduce organizational autonomy if the government begins to interfere in group operations.[23] But weighed against these are very real and pressing fears of destruction by other armed groups or, less dramatically, loss of influence and power to such groups. When the government can offer protection and resources that give a group a chance of surviving and maintaining some degree of power, the group will have powerful instrumental reasons to consider at least temporary cooperation to deal with more pressing threats from other groups.

The process of internal conflict can also generate new splinters emerging out of feuds between factions who look to the state for protection and support.[24] This can be the result of intentional government strategies of divide and rule, but cooperating groups often do so for reasons of their own, driven by rivalries and feuds with other armed groups.[25] This means that the "supply" of cooperators is not a straightforward function of regime demand; there is huge variation in when willing armed groups appear.[26]

In general, we should expect gray zone and aligned groups to be the most likely groups that states will seek to work with. But, intriguingly, under some very complex multiparty scenarios, ideologically opposed groups can become strange bedfellows who combat shared enemies with the government. The Assad regime and ISIS maintained limited cooperation for parts of the Syrian civil war, not out of ideological sympathy, but because both had more urgent and pressing mortal enemies to deal with. Similarly, the Liberation Tigers of Tamil Eelam and the Sri Lankan government had a brief rapprochement in 1989–90 as a way to get rid of the Indian Peacekeeping Force and Eelam People's Revolutionary Liberation Front.[27]

These enemy-of-my-enemy dynamics are not, however, likely to be very long lasting if the combat situation or political context shifts.[28] Limited cooperation with strange bedfellows is extremely tenuous and largely driven by the balance of military forces within a war, which is likely to change in response to battlefield shifts and international interventions. Ideologically opposed groups generally find themselves at war with the government, sooner or later, though periods of limited cooperation may be very important for a war's course. The defeat, degradation, or realignment of the shared enemy should be the trigger for a shift in state incentives to work with such a group.

For gray zone and aligned groups, victory, or at least the dramatic degradation of a mutually targeted armed group, is likely to be the end of their usefulness to the government. The decline or end of insurgent conflicts, as with elections, should see efforts to absorb or marginalize groups in these tolerable ideological categories. The distinctive value of deniable counterinsurgent forces comes to an end, and efforts at postconflict state building may begin with strategies for consolidating the counterinsurgent side.[29] As with elections, such groups can sometimes resist absorption and stake out an enduring role as a free agent, but the general tendency should be a shift in the armed order between that group and the government. If ongoing instability endures, by contrast, they may remain perpetually useful as a backstop against conflict recurrence. Comprehensive military victories or fully implemented peace deals should therefore be the clearest signal of the end of counterinsurgent groups' value to the state and precede a shifting armed order away from alliance or limited cooperation. Groups may also abandon the state if they feel that it is becoming a liability to their interests or in anticipation of a future shift in tactical alignment.

We can therefore identify two important mechanisms through which civil wars can create—and possibly undermine—tactical overlap. The first, in a strictly dyadic relationship, sees mutual incentives for conflict reduction lead to limited cooperation, though such arrangements can be highly unstable. The second involves complex multisided wars in which dyadic relationships are deeply influenced by third actors, especially shared enemies, that can create tactical overlap even among ideologically distant states and groups. These mechanisms can help make sense of a phenomenon we see in many civil wars: even as the structural "master cleavage" of a war remains fairly stable over time, more fine-grained armed orders can see substantial change and fluidity.[30] Bringing in tactical incentives adds insights into why and when we see this this disjuncture between levels of analysis.

Ideological Change: Governments

The mechanisms given above are fluid and common, but often quite temporary and narrow. The fundamental political structures in place do not change, only the specific calculations within them. The most substantial and enduring shifts in armed politics are instead driven by changes in ideological position, either by states or armed groups. These are quite rare, but their effects are far more fundamental than the tactical dynamics discussed above. The structure of politics itself can shift. This claim is consistent with the overall theme of this book: politics matters to political violence.

Major ideological shifts in the government's position are not common or easy because leaders and ruling institutions rarely have dramatic epiphanies about basic questions of politics. Even when elites begin to reconsider previously dominant ideological positions, change can be slow and incremental.[31] History constrains leaders' ability to easily shift the ideological orientation of their regimes or governments. Once in place, the "political grammar of the state" and its associated "language of politics" limit not only how dissent can be voiced, but also the boundaries of what leaders themselves can say and do.[32]

This stickiness is a result of several factors. Individuals and groups tend to be resistant to radically rethinking the foundational terms of politics, mass publics can hold preferences that militate against major shifts by regime elites, leaders may lose credibility if they radically revise their past statements, and powerful state institutions (such as the military) may resist changes that threaten or undermine their core organizational mission and worldview. It is striking how many ruling projects collapse or are forced to retreat from power rather than being able to nimbly adapt to new challenges or fluidly reorient their ideological framing in response to changing circumstances.[33] We should not expect unyielding inertia, but instead substantial continuity even in the face of new incentives: the public and private legitimation of a regime project, the way in which bureaucracies have been trained to conceive of the world, and the complex interactions between public and elite preferences all can create barriers to rapid change.[34]

Nevertheless, changes can happen; I focus on two pathways that are likely to recur across contexts. As with the discussion of tactical overlap, this is not intended to be comprehensive. The most dramatic and far-reaching pathway is a fundamental shift in project resulting from regime change that is accompanied by a very different ideological vision than its predecessor. The new government stakes out major changes in its position along the core dimensions of an ideological project. This is the stuff of new regimes with new projects, often aiming at ambitious and ruthless transformations of the political arena: the collapse of the old regime and rise of a fundamentally new set of political agendas in 1789 France is a classic example. Incremental shifts are less dramatic: rather than a new regime with a new project, we see leadership or party turnover within mainstream politics or a regime change that simply reshuffles the elite decks. Here we may see change on one major dimension of politics, but not a thoroughgoing revision of the basic structure of politics. The evolution of the Soviet Union after Stalin is an example of selective rethinking of previously firm commitments. Leaders do have agency, even if it is broadly constrained by past history. This is important because it reminds us that leaders and institutions remain morally culpable for their behavior: it is rare that history totally and determinatively locks in a particular course of action.

Fundamental changes are the most important and easiest to measure; incremental changes are harder to observe and often less clear cut, but unsurprisingly more common.[35] Regime changes have the greatest potential to radically reshuffle threat perception across the entire ideological spectrum, while incremental changes are more likely to move groups only partially across the spectrum. Both are essential for making sense of major changes over time in how a state seeks to govern coercion. I focus, however, on the more dramatic and far-reaching shifts, since they are easy to empirically identify and will have the largest effect on patterns of armed politics.

Fundamental Changes

Fundamental shifts occur when regimes change and the new leaders and ruling institutions that come to power hold substantially different positions across multiple ideological dimensions than their predecessors. This must be further-reaching than a simple cabinet reshuffle or revised secret police doctrine; it also cannot be a regime change in which ideological projects nevertheless remain constant or control over security policy does not shift. If control over security policy does not change or if the new regime has a similar ideology of the polity as the old regime, we should not expect substantial effects on state strategy or armed orders. In Pakistan and Thailand, even democratic transitions and coups have not changed control over security policy, as powerful militaries retain influence over violence management strategies.[36] In the Philippines, shifts among regimes and rulers have occurred, but a broad vision of the nation is shared among many elites. Internecine factional competition is entirely compatible with identifying Muslim (especially) and leftist armed groups as foes to be combated.[37] Fundamental shifts are therefore far less common than regime changes, leadership turnover, or alternations of ruling parties.

Instead, fundamental change requires a new ruling elite taking power with very different understandings of what they want the political system to look like what and what kinds of political threats are most dangerous. In these types of transition, regimes seek to refound the political arena according to their ideological goals. Decolonization, coups, revolutions, and democratization are common moments of radical change. Examples include the 1917 Bolshevik, 1975 Cambodian, and 1979 Iranian revolutions, military coups in 1952 Egypt, 1962 Burma, and 1965 Indonesia, 1868 beginning of the Meiji era in Japan, creation of Bangladesh, Nazi seizure of power, transition from Sunni to Shiite dominance of the Iraqi state after 2003, and bloody collapses of colonial rule in French Indochina and British India.[38]

These were obviously not total breaks: some remnants of the past carried over, and new political goals were not seamlessly implemented. But carrier movements became governments that consciously and determinedly tried to alter the basic symbolic orientation of and distribution of power within the political system. Whether along the religious, ethnic, or redistributive dimensions, there was a new set of goals and fears. The French Revolution is a classic example: new ideas entered the political arena, driven by a shifting variety of carrier movements jockeying for power and identifying very different threats than those perceived by the ancien régime. The new regimes from 1789 battled clerical influence, aristocratic power, and rural counterrevolutionary tendencies, alongside a byzantine array of intrarevolutionary factional and personal rivalries. Though the revolutionary forces never consolidated themselves into a single, lasting regime, the transformation of French politics proved impossible to fully reverse.

After a fundamental change in ideological project occurs, political evaluations of armed groups are reshuffled. When a leftist revolution sweeps to power, groups that were previously ideologically aligned with a right-wing oligarchy are likely to recategorized as opposed by the new regime; gray zone private armies may become allies after a more politically sympathetic regime takes over; separatist rebels are newly portrayed as unacceptable enemies or brought in from the cold as business partners.[39] Threat perception is driven by politics: as the government pursues its goals and ambitions, it assesses the armed landscape to decide who stands in its way, who aims to advance shared goals, and who can be tolerated.

These fundamental regime changes are fairly easy to measure: they are moments of major political rupture as a new project comes to power.[40] Regime changes (both internally and externally driven) and decolonization/independence are the most visible signals of a new project rising and can form the pool of most likely cases for examining fundamental ideological shifts. Crucially, there is often reliable historical evidence on the nature of regime shifts that can provide insights into when an ideological change has occurred (distinct from simply a change in rulers); this can help us distinguish between transformational shifts and those that simply reshuffle the deck chairs without meaningful ideological change.

Prior research has noted how violent and unstable the periods following revolutions, democratization, coups, and decolonization can be, pointing to weak institutions and pressing problems of bad information and mistrust as the culprits.[41] There is no doubt that these are incredibly important, but work on political instability tends to ignore the ideological ambitions of new regimes. They have goals, momentums, and a deep set of fears and suspicion that interact with institutional weakness to trigger often-bloody wars, crackdowns, and purges: the blood-stained campaigns in the Vendée, the extraordinarily violent pursuit of communists in 1965–66 Indonesia, and bloody rise of the Ba'ath in Iraq accompanied the birth of a new ruling project.

Incremental Shifts

Incremental shifts are more common, but less dramatic. They occur when new governments or leaders modify, but do not fundamentally alter, prior assessments about the political sphere along more than one core ideological dimension. This often comes as a response to government/leadership transitions without a major

change in the regime: the mainstream stays broadly the same, but different parties or factions rise and fall within this system. Regime changes can also lead
to incremental shifts if the new regime has a similar ideological profile to its
predecessor. Turnover is extremely common, but change in ideological projects
is dramatically rarer.

Coalitions may be modified, leaders drop in and out of power, and political
entrepreneurs shift the framing of issues, but not in the ways we see when a fundamental change occurs. Examples include the 1977 Zia al-Huq coup in Pakistan
and the post-2008 political liberalization in Myanmar. In Israel, the rise of the
Likud has put shifted the religious-ethnic dimension most dramatically, with left-
right economic shifts substantially less dramatic. In Bangladesh, the post-1990
alternation between the Awami League and the Bangladesh National Party has
been very meaningful, especially on the religion-state dimension of politics, but
not as dramatic as the 1975 military seizure of power that killed the state's founding leader, Sheikh Mujibur Rahman, or the 1990 democratization that limited
direct military influence in politics.[42] For instance, Rahman was "intent to create
a secular and democratic nation" while his military successor Ziaur Rehman in
Bangladesh "removed the constitutional commitment to secularism" and under
Ershad, the next military dictator, "the Islamization of Bangladesh continued to
expand."[43]

These are all important changes that are the responsibility, for good or ill,
of political entrepreneurs who created substantial shifts in how states govern
coercion. They can eventually lead to full-scale transformations over time. The
rise of the Bharatiya Janata Party (BJP) in India, as I discuss in chapter 4, has
had a major effect on the place of the Hindu majority in the government's
articulation of the nation, even as some other approaches have remained the
same.[44] Such changes are nevertheless less total and fully encompassing than
fundamental shifts.

In the research to come, I examine cases of leadership turnover, whether
regime or government changes, and study what projects new leaders bring to
governance. Most of the political action caused by incremental changes should
lead to groups moving between gray zone and either aligned or opposed positions, not a full realignment across the entire spectrum. This approach gives
weight to historical path-dependence: rapid reversals and dramatic changes
in political direction should be rare. However, it leaves open space within
that broad trajectory. Leaders are never locked in, and we will see cases in the
empirics in which leaders and institutions shifted the course of their nation's
politics. The choices plausibly available to leaders are in part constrained
by historical context, but this does not eliminate their responsibility for the
choices they make.

Ideological Change: Armed Groups

Armed groups can change their ideological positioning, growing closer to or farther from government on one or more dimensions. This is a very noisy and contingent process, and this chapter only begins to unpack some of the dynamics that can drive shifts. In part, this is because governments need to perceive, interpret, and accept changes in group politics, so change is not always as simple as a group announcing a change of goal. Moreover, major shifts may require abandoning or modifying the core goals groups have mobilized around and fought over for years or decades.[45] Such changes can leave a group open to charges of selling out or abandoning the cause from supporters or rivals, even as they are attempting to signal new aims to an often-skeptical government.[46] This combination helps explain why most of the groups I discuss in the empirical chapters do not fluidly or frequent change their stated political aims. Generally, there might be one or two major shifts; sometimes there is no change, despite long, intense conflicts that impose high costs.

Yet we do see changes, even if they are far from straightforward. Groups can move closer to the regime's political preferences, but also against them—both moderation and radicalization are real possibilities. The rest of this section unpacks key mechanisms that can drive these shifts. As with the other pathways I outline in this chapter, they are far from comprehensive, but offering a coherent "toolkit" helps us systematically understand when and how shifts tend to occur. I examine the effects of internal fragmentation, international pressures, and state policies.

Each can lead to either moderation or radicalization, so I identify the conditions under which each outcome occurs. Selective, sustained state repression over time can induce moderation, while indiscriminate violence—if it does not cause group collapse—is likely to stiffen the backs of hardliners and encourage maximalist war aims. Internal splintering and fragmentation tend to drive simultaneous moderation and radicalization, as movements separate into competing blocs that often stake out different ideological positions. Finally, international politics can force groups to shift their politics in order to satisfy powerful external states on whom they are highly dependent; this mechanism will matter much less when groups do not rely heavily on sponsors, and its direction depends on the political preferences of sponsors.

Government Targeting

A crucial source of change is government strategy that endogenously shifts a group's ideological position.[47] As with the other mechanisms below, this variable can cut in both directions, so I specify which types of state strategy are most likely to lead to "moderation" as compared to "radicalization" relative to state preferences. The most likely pathway toward moderation is protracted but reasonably selective government repression that simultaneously raises the costs of continued conflict while offering a way out if the group shifts its political demands.[48] Such a combination can provide strong incentives for a group to shift itself from opposed to gray zone or gray zone to aligned.[49]

This is essentially a war-weariness mechanism: selective violence (at least at the group, if not the individual, level) provides confidence that a shift into a more favorable ideological position is likely to be reciprocated by the government while making clear that continued conflict will incur serious costs. As the odds of achieving the group's maximal aims drop, we should see a growing likelihood of shifting toward the state's position.

This is an extremely common pattern in protracted, low-level conflicts: groups learn over time that they cannot win and that they have options for incorporation or limited cooperation if they are willing to make substantial shifts in political positioning.[50] Many insurgent groups end up negotiating with the government after a process of internal debate that leads to an acceptance of key elements of the status quo.[51] Becoming aligned is often a precondition for rulers to agree to incorporation, while entering the gray zone is frequently necessary for peace talks to begin or cease-fires to occur.

Convergence toward the state over extended conflicts, however, is not guaranteed. There are certainly holdouts who continue to fight even against extremely long odds, a reminder that processes of change are very complex and contingent. Paresh Baruah of the United Liberation Front of Asom is an example; even as large parts of his organization have split and made a separate peace with Delhi, he and his remaining faction continue a long-odds fight. Such groups often act as attempted "spoilers" in negotiation processes.[52]

However, state strategy can also have precisely the opposite effect, driving spiraling radicalization. *Indiscriminate* crackdowns that fail to destroy a group create powerful incentives to abandon efforts at moderation or dialogue, especially if groups are treated as opposed groups unless they unconditionally surrender.[53] Radicalization can ensue as groups realize that there is simply no reason to try to do business with the government—they will suffer from state repression regardless. In many cases, civilians are also supportive of hard-line stances because of their experiences with government violence.[54] Armed groups may decide that there is nothing to gain by trying to move into the gray zone or from the gray zone into ideological alignment.

The only path forward in these cases is staking out an opposed position while mobilizing manpower and resources to survive a long, bitter conflict with an unaccommodating regime. This helps us understand why seemingly costly, inefficient conflicts persist: groups may fundamentally distrust the government to honor any commitments, as the government conversely views these groups as malignant and subversive forces that cannot be given any ground.[55] Enduring total war or containment orders can persist over years, even decades, if the groups are able to successfully hold themselves together under sustained, but not highly discriminating, military pressure. These are the contexts most likely to end in total military collapse for armed groups, with brute force destruction resulting from the deep incompatibility of unyielding political claims coupled with deep mutual distrust.

Internal Tensions and Splintering

A second important trigger of group ideological change is intramovement/organization competition. This can cut in both directions and often interacts with government strategy. Internal fragmentation—or its threat—has several sources. Government strategy can help drive wedges between factions or organizations, and may therefore be a result of the mechanism above. However, many fissures and tensions are derived from clashing political interests, disparate social bases, and leadership rivalries within movements/groups.[56] Internal competition can emerge without intentional regime manipulation, making it analytically distinguishable from state strategy. Fragmentation often leads to separation and sorting, driving simultaneous moderation and radicalization as groups stake out a political position in the face of competition and rivalry. In some cases, however, there is movement only in one direction, such as toward shared radicalization. Given this complexity, I can only provide a broad overview of mechanisms that may drive variation in groups' ideological stance.[57]

Splintering can drive moderation (relative to the state) when groups/factions break away from a hard-line leadership that has been unable to show substantial gains for the group over long periods of time. This may be a variant of the war-weariness mechanism mentioned above: when there is a plausible route to deal making, dissatisfied factions may decide to get closer to the state and abandon former compatriots who they see as leading a hopeless war. This requires some degree of civilian and militant factional support for changing sides or at least adopting a neutral ideological position. Kathleen Cunningham's important work shows that governments may be able to strategically peel off moderates, and this seems most likely to occur when there are distinct factions available to collectively shift position.[58]

Splintering can also lead to simultaneous moderation and radicalization when military defeats, offers of peace processes, elections, or other major shifts in political context create "hard"- and "soft"-line factions. These positions can be hard to measure ex ante, as individual and factional preferences are quite malleable.[59] Nevertheless, as shocks put pressure on groups to adjust to new realities, we frequently see infighting and disagreement between emerging factional blocs over the political path forward.[60] When there are significant numbers of civilians and fighters lined up on each side of this divide, groups/movements will often polarize, with some shifting into a gray zone or aligned position, and others moving toward or doubling-down on an opposed political role. The full spectrum of ideological positions becomes populated with the fragments of a previously unified movement or organization.

Finally, internal tensions can drive *all* groups toward radicalization in spirals of "out bidding" that force leaders to adopt ever more hard-line ideological postures in order to retain support from a civilian population increasingly supportive of escalated fighting.[61] In this mechanism, leaders seek to forestall charges of selling out or being traitors to the cause.[62] Competition can shift an entire bloc along the spectrum toward opposition. This may be particularly likely after major regime changes at the center bring deeply feared governments to power, leading to the rise of a successful insurgent entrepreneur able to attract support for a harder-line stance, or result from intensifying military conflicts that favor more radical fighters.[63]

Depending on what individuals and groups think, we can therefore see wildly different consequences emerge from internal dissension and conflict. This makes it difficult to offer simple predictions. Instead, we need to understand the alignment of political forces across armed groups, their interaction with states and potentially external sponsors, and the preferences of civilian social bases. This lends itself to contextual explanation rather than cross-case generalizations.

International Politics

Finally, armed groups' ideological positions can shift, in both directions, as a result of international politics. Groups reliant on external support may adopt demands and symbols favored by foreign patrons. This can lead to radicalization when external backers are profoundly opposed to the government and looking to support hard-line opposed groups, bolstering them against more "moderate" (i.e., closer to gray zone) actors. Yet it can also induce shifts toward the regime when external backers decide that their proxies need to cut a deal, and push proxies into positions closer to the governments. A mix of persuasion and threats from foreign powers can move armed groups in different ways along the ideological spectrum.[64]

This will be the least common pathway of change in strategic positioning. Intragroup/movement politics and state strategy are pervasive across armed politics. External involvement, though common, is not. Moreover, many armed groups that receive external support are not reliant on this backing, and thus can ignore their backers' wishes.[65] This mechanism will be irrelevant in the absence of external support (or its prospect) and when it comes to the choices of autonomous, well-organized groups with diversified resource streams.[66]

By contrast, for groups that are dependent on external support for resources and political cover, shifts in sponsors' demands can be a powerful cause of ideological change. In this situation, whether among many of the rebel groups in Syria or the eastern DRC, the international context can be a prime mover of ideological sorting, with groups echoing their outside backers' political lines in hoping of maintaining favor and thus survival.[67] Complex multiparty wars with weak armed groups highly dependent on external support are where we should expect this mechanism to be most important.

This chapter has provided a set of mechanisms for systematically analyzing when and how changes are most likely to occur. This is a domain of messy, endogenous interaction and contingency. Nevertheless, laying out key pathways of change provides a place to start when analyzing shifts over time, making it possible to develop and refine future theory and empirics that blend together historically sensitive, path-dependent processes with strategic interactions and calculations.

The rest of the book turns to empirical research, exploring the foundations of ideological projects, their changes over time, and the armed politics that result as governments pursue their goals in interaction with armed actors. The next chapter provides a description of and broad findings from the Armed Orders in South Asia (AOSA) dataset and a comparative overview of the ideological projects of carrier movements and governments during and after colonialism in India, Pakistan, Sri Lanka, and Burma/Myanmar. I then devote a chapter to each country, mixing historical narratives, quantitative data, and specific case studies on regions and dyads to assess what my theory helps us understand about each country, as well as areas in which it fails. The conclusion chapter identifies open questions for future research and implications for how to think about important policy questions.

3

ARMED ORDERS AND IDEOLOGICAL PROJECTS IN SOUTH ASIA

In this chapter, I move from theory to evidence and explain how I measured armed orders and ideological projects. First, I introduce unique new data on armed politics in South Asia and use them to illustrate the extraordinary range of armed orders in the subcontinent. Violence and its threat are part of a far broader, and more ambiguous, range of political interactions than just conventional insurgent-counterinsurgent conflict. Every armed order has substantial representation in the dataset, from pitched total wars to tight alliances to various gradations in between. The data reveal interesting general patterns that inform the more detailed country-specific case studies to come.

Second, I provide a comparative overview of ideological projects across countries and over time within them, allowing us to see differences in governments' positions on core political questions. I discuss how I qualitatively measure projects and preview the more detailed arguments I make in each chapter. This systematic comparison provides a framework for the cases. We see that India is an outlier across the region in its approach to ethno-linguistic minorities, and that Pakistan is unusual in its ambiguities about the relationship between religion and nationalism. In Sri Lanka and Myanmar by contrast, majoritarian religious-linguistic projects emerged that fused language/ethnicity with religion. I also identify changes over time in ruling projects, both as a result of military coups and shifts in electoral power.

This empirical groundwork lays the basis for country-specific research in chapters 4 through 7. I leave discussions of tactical overlap for these chapters.

These can be systematically measured, but doing so requires a substantial level of detail and background that is best provided in the specific cases and contexts in the chapters to come.

Measuring Armed Orders

A central empirical challenge of this project is measuring armed orders in a systematic and transparent manner. There are excellent datasets on civil conflict, but they tend to focus on comparatively straightforward internal wars, using a total or annual death toll threshold to determine which conflicts and years enter the data.[1] This approach is essential for studying protracted cases of substantial civil conflict but is not a good methodological fit for the armed politics approach. There are other datasets that separately tackle violence between nonstate actors and the existence of progovernment militias, but each of these research agendas risks operating within silos, and often have different dependent variables of interest.[2] Limited cooperation and alliance orders rarely include high levels of direct state versus group violence, while many containment orders can sputter along below standard death thresholds.[3]

To more closely tie the concepts at the heart of this book with empirical data, I constructed a new dataset of state-group orders in six post-1947 South Asian countries. The Armed Orders in South Asia (AOSA) project aims to provide systematic and transparent coding of how states and armed groups have interacted across countries, levels of violence, and types of armed groups, from the rough-and-tumble of West Bengal's electoral politics to the killing fields of northeastern Sri Lanka to the state-backed militias of Pakistan. The project has generated data from Bangladesh, India, Pakistan, Burma/Myanmar, Nepal, and Sri Lanka.

The research continues beyond this book, which uses a subset of the data thus far. This book excludes systematic discussion of Nepal, which did not emerge from the British colonial context, and Bangladesh, which does not fit into the post-1947 comparative framework of the book. Both involve ideological projects and armed politics. For instance, Bangladesh sees important contestation over the meaning of nationalism and the place of Islam within it. The regime oscillations among different understandings of Bangladesh's nationalist project are important for understanding state policies, and at least broadly the case seems supportive of my theory.[4] But neither fits straightforwardly into the comparative case selection, so I leave detailed discussion of the armed politics of these two countries to future research.

Within the four countries the book focuses on, there are 211 groups and 3,684 dyad-years. The groups average 17.5 years of existence. Each dyad is backed by a qualitative case study that will be made publicly available alongside the quantitative dataset. The goal of the case narratives is to explain key codings and outline the sources used to arrive at this decision. Part of this process is to be extremely transparent about gaps and limits to our understanding of these cases: there are surely many mistakes, omissions, and arguable coding choices, so it is essential to give researchers the opportunity to examine how decisions were made and, if desired, to change them. This book is one step of a broader iterative process.

One striking takeaway from the process of building the data and narratives is how little we know about much of the world; whether in Manipur, Shan State, or the final days of Sri Lanka's Tamil rebellion, secrecy and ambiguity shroud even recent history. Nevertheless, it was encouraging how much the research team could still find by being entrepreneurial about the range and types of sources we consulted, including local newspapers, specialized history books, and online material. The coding scheme also evolved over time, as we encountered outcomes that were not part of the original plan. For instance, I had not been aware of disarmament (demobilization without a formal or public deal) as a conceptual category, but it became clear that some groups transitioned out of being armed groups either unilaterally or via a tacit understanding with the government. The data collection was iterative over time, with excellent research assistants playing an essential role in pointing out the problems with existing coding rules and often suggesting solutions.

The data are structured to be dyad-year, with each state-group pairing starting from its beginning of interaction with the state (whether that involved violence or not) through its termination or the last year in which coding was completed. This allows us to capture some degree of over-time change in both potential explanatory variables and in the outcome of interest. In many of the analyses below, I stop at 2016 or 2017 (depending on the context) since that is often when coding ended, though some continue into 2019 in the fuller data. For each year, the team determined whether the dyad continued through the year or whether it terminated in that year. The orders could be total war, containment, limited cooperation, or alliance, as well as a loose coding of "military hostilities" used when total war could not be distinguished from containment. This hostilities coding became increasingly rare as the project moved on and we improved our process, but does appear in some cases. For each dyad in each year, we measured an armed order, and also whether the year in question marked a change. The approach obviously remains crude, since changes could happen at a monthly or weekly level, but such granularity was often not available across cases, and it at least broadly captures trajectories of change.

Figure 3.1 shows an illustration of the data, mapping the annual distribution of order-dyad-years in Burma/Myanmar over time. Despite admittedly severe limits of sourcing and data quality, the general pattern aligns with an intuitive understanding of the country's trajectory: we see diverse orders in the early

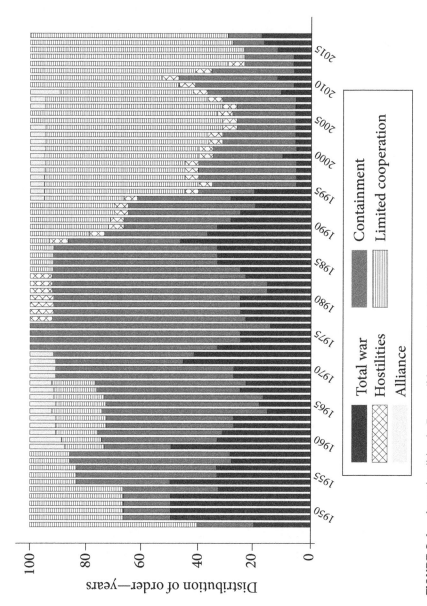

FIGURE 3.1. Armed politics in Burma/Myanmar, 1948–2017

democratic period under U Nu, a consequent intense conflict under military dictator Ne Win from 1962 to 1988, and then a dramatic growth in limited cooperation as a series of post-1989 cease-fires took hold, as well as a small but noticeable increase in conflict as we approach 2017. There is no doubt that specialists of particular groups and contexts could plausibly contest coding decisions, but the overall trend aligns well with qualitative accounts, which is reassuring, while also providing a new way to systematically measure and track conflict dynamics.

Armed orders were usually measured at the level of the national government's interaction with an armed group. However, we took advantage of the remarkable variation within India and its federal system to measure a number of dyads between a subnational state government and an armed group. They give new insights into the ways that militarized electoral politics (i.e., in West Bengal, Kerala, Bihar) and local counterinsurgency (COIN) operations (subnational state-led operations in Jharkhand, Chhattisgarh, and others versus Naxalites) can work in a sprawling federal system, and they also expand the number of observations into domains in which the central government has had little interest. In analyses, these state-level dyads are sometimes dropped to avoid duplication of dyads and noncomparability with other countries; they are most useful for understanding militarized politics in a selection of Indian states, but future research can hopefully expand this approach.

The armed order coding is accompanied by a confidence variable that aims to make transparent the quality of the coding. The lowest confidence was assigned when scant or contradictory evidence was the best available in making the judgment; the highest was when there was consensus across multiple quality sources; medium confidence occurred when there were consistent accounts across multiple sources but those sources are limited in either quantity or quality. Unsurprisingly, there is a clear trend in confidence—opaque, complex wars in peripheral areas had the lowest confidence.

The research team also examined whether a given dyad ended in a year. If so, they searched for evidence of how the dyad terminated: the armed group could collapse, win a victory, disarm without a deal, be absorbed into another group, or be incorporated in some form into "mainstream" politics. This takes us beyond the traditional approach to conflict termination in civil wars by looking at a broader range of groups and more diverse set of pathways through which something like a state monopoly of violence can occur. Many dyads endure through the end of the dataset, some violent and some not.

The annual dyadic armed order data is the most unique empirical contribution of the project. But to explore the relationship between armed orders and other variables, the AOSA project also coded a set of other attributes of armed groups, governments, and their interactions. A full accounting is not necessary for the purposes of this book—more detailed assessments are better suited to specialized articles—but several clusters of variables are important in moving from description of armed orders toward a richer understanding of why they vary.

First, there are variables that include the self-description of armed groups (as anti-state, a mainstream party, pro-state, or something else), their goals (such as autonomy, independence, control of the central government, or reform/policy change), and the political cleavages they mobilize around (e.g., redistributive, leftist, or religious). These are essential for assessing my argument—we need to be able to distinguish ideologically opposed, gray zone, and aligned groups from one another, so we need to know what they are demanding, how they position themselves in the political system, and which issues they are contesting.

For instance, the Kashmiri insurgent organization Hizbul Mujahideen is an anti-state rebel group demanding independence that mobilizes along a Muslim religious cleavage; by contrast, the Shiv Sena in Mumbai is an electoral political party that has mobilized both a Hindu religious cleavage and a nativist ethnolinguistic cleavage, and operates as a group seeking to reform government policy. Indian governments should treat the two radically differently—the Hizbul should be opposed while the Shiv Sena should be either aligned or gray zone (depending on the party in power in Delhi). We need to able to measure these differences within and across countries, which will be the focus of chapters 4 through 7, since political factors are only meaningful in a specific national and comparative context.

Second, there are a cluster of variables that seek to identify outcomes that overlap with, but are distinct from, the armed order variable. We measure ceasefires, amnesties, and peace deals, including both their onset and their duration. This provides greater specificity about the precise form of state-group interaction, allowing a comparison with research that examines formal manifestations of state-group bargaining and cooperation.[5]

Finally, there are a set of contextual variables, such as the provision of external support, the existence of an armed group's political wing, rebel governance, and whether the dyad is primarily located at the level of the national or subnational state government. All of these covariates can be used to disaggregate the data and explore the impact of variables on armed orders.

Creating the Data: Sources, Limitations, and Caveats

These data need to be used with great care, and to be complemented with other kinds of evidence. The quality of the underlying sourcing varies dramatically; we have extensive information on the LTTE relative to the numerous tiny splinters in hard-to-study Manipur. We similarly know much more about formal, institutionalized party-linked violence in West Bengal and Kerala than highly localized lynchings and vigilantism in Madhya Pradesh or Uttar Pradesh, leading to an overrepresentation of some contexts compared to others. Each dyad-year armed order coding was given a confidence coding from 1 (lowest) to 3 (the highest), and there is definitely substantial variation across dyads in the average confidence level. India (2.61) and Sri Lanka (2.58) on average generated the highest confidence, followed by Pakistan (2.28) and Myanmar (2.21), where the average confidence was lowest. Confidence was highest for mainstream political parties (2.8), and similar for the other three categories of self-identification (2.35–2.44). We replicated a number of case narratives and codings to try to limit this variation, and performed a series of quality control checks to look for errors, but some dyads are much better sourced than others. The case narratives thus differ dramatically in their length and quality.[6] These limitations are openly acknowledged in the qualitative materials: in the future, researchers can correct and improve on this initial effort. Data collection will continue into the future and will surely revise and improve on the work in this book.

Second, the AOSA quantitative data do not tell us everything we need to know. For instance, the brutal 1971 Pakistani crackdown in East Pakistan appears as only 1 dyad-year of armed order (total war): compared to the dozens or hundreds of observations in Manipur, Kerala, or Balochistan, it may appear minor and irrelevant. But this extraordinary explosion of violence killed hundreds of thousands of people and birthed a new state. We need to keep in mind that many observations in the data are from low-level, but very long-running, conflicts, while hugely important events may be far shorter and thus seem to carry less weight in the data. The accumulation of dyad-years may simply reflect a single dyad over long periods of time.

In order to avoid overvaluing these aggregated dyad-years, I use numerous case studies and disaggregate the quantitative data in various ways. Nowhere do I rely exclusively on quantitative data to make strong inferences. Nevertheless, the data are valuable in moving us closer to a systematic understanding of armed politics: they show that orders can be systematically and transparently measured, provide evidence of trends across time and across numerous comparative variables, and let us "see" state-group interactions even when they are not highly violent.

Armed Orders in South Asia

We can now turn to a simple description of empirical patterns in armed orders. Across the entire sample of 3,684 dyad-order-years, roughly half of the orders are some form of cooperation, and the other half is some form of conflict.[7]

Limited cooperation and containment orders are by far the two most common orders (figure 3.2). Ironically enough, the two most ambiguous outcomes that have received the least attention in existing literature are in fact, by far, the most *common* result of state-group interaction in the sample. This is strong empirical support for the core conceptual basis of the book: states and armed groups engage in remarkably variable relationships, conflicts are often not brute force contests of mutual destruction but instead are driven by political calculations, and violence and politics can be interweaved in a variety of ways.

A key motivation for the quantitative portion of this book, despite the very substantial time and resources it required, was to help answer the simple descriptive question of how common state–armed group cooperation actually is. Indeed, the extent of limited cooperation across the sample is striking: rather than being idiosyncratic and quirky exceptions, such orders are quite common. In much of independent South Asia, much of the time, armed groups have operated in manageably comfortable relationships with states. They are not intrinsic threats to state power, can be tolerated even by political and military leaders who ruthlessly attack other armed groups, and have been deeply involved in "mainstream" politics. Just as individuals in conflict zones occupy different positions on a range, from committed supporters of one side or another to fence sitters to

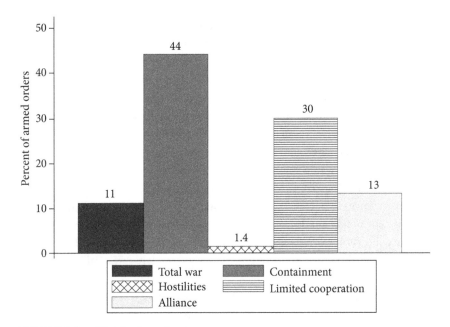

FIGURE 3.2. Distribution of order-years

lightly committed supporters, armed groups occupy different relationships with the state.[8] It is possible that these dynamics are unique to South Asia, but scholars have identified similar examples from all over the world, which suggests that these findings are tapping into a broader reality.

We can see substantial variation in orders when we examine the proportion of the years in a group's existence that were some form of conflict (i.e., total war, containment, hostilities). About half of groups are entirely cooperative (18 percent) or entirely conflictual (44 percent), but a substantial minority have some blend of conflict with cooperation over their lifetime. The mean proportion of conflict-years across all group is 0.66. There is a huge spread in state-group relations.

Figure 3.3 moves back to order-years to explore how orders relate to groups' self-identification, which can change over time (thirty order-years see a change in self-identification, involving twenty-five groups, about 10 percent of the groups in the dataset). We distinguish between groups during years in which they self-identify as mainstream political parties rhetorically focused on electoral competition (20 percent of order-years), as pro-state combatants like militias (6 percent), and anti-state rebels (53 percent), as well as a category of "other" (21 percent). These are admittedly very challenging categorizations, since some groups combine multiple goals and attributes, and since professed goals and rhetoric may or may not relate to actual behavior—some Tamil armed political parties in Sri Lanka, for instance, were both formally registered political parties that ran in elections and pro-state paramilitaries working closely with Sri Lanka's government. As I have emphasized throughout, the data need to be taken with major caveats. Nevertheless, there is a clear, and thankfully unsurprising, relationship between professed self-identification and the distribution of order-years across these categories. Even here there are some interesting disjunctures between identification and armed politics—some anti-state rebels cooperate, and some parties and even pro-state groups clash with the state.

In the anti-state rebel contexts that most closely align with the classic conceptualization of civil war, we still see a range of armed orders, with containment years predominating (64 percent of dyad-order-years), and limited cooperation order-years (14 percent) not far behind total war (20 percent) in frequency. States do not simply hurl their coercive capacity at any given rebel group: there is extensive discrimination in targeting strategies, including a substantial number of cases in which limited cooperation or even (extremely rarely) alliance occur. Most rebels are engaged in conflict with state forces, but that conflict is often relatively low level, and there are possibilities for actual cooperation.

Armed political parties are far more likely to cluster in limited cooperation and alliance orders than self-described insurgent groups.[9] They often do business

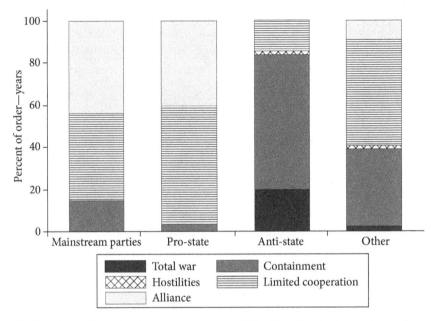

FIGURE 3.3. Armed order dyad-years by self-identification (Indian state-level dyads are included here; dropping them makes little difference to the overall distribution of orders)

with the government around elections, coalitions, and patronage, while occupying ideological positions compatible with mainstream electoral competition. The "Other" category examines groups in years during which we had trouble clearly categorizing in terms of self-description: they often are not explicitly pro- or anti-state, while also not engaging in electoral politics. An example of this "other" category is the National Socialist Council of Nagaland (Isak-Muivah) (NSCN-IM) after 1997—it explicitly moderated its ideological stance, but remained in the gray zone. Private armies and criminally oriented, but formally political, groups also frequently exist in this category. Figure 3.3 reveals a huge realm of armed politics that would—for, to be clear, good reason—never show up in standard civil war datasets, but that demands attention.

There is also evidence of change over time. We measured the incidence of a changed armed order from the previous year and in the middle of a year. Though a very crude measure, roughly 11 percent of years in a dyad are different than the year before, including cases in which the prior year saw a change midway through the year or in which a new group emerges. This shows meaningful dynamism. There are good reasons to adopt the time-varying approach, since it captures important shifts in political alignments. However, it also shows substantial continuity over time: groups do not radically change their relations with state power very often, or in huge swings across the spectrum of political roles. Indeed, we count twenty-eight groups that had at least one stretch of ten consecutive years of limited cooperation, and there are numerous cases of enduring containment orders.

Groups range from the United Wa State Army (UWSA) in Burma/Myanmar, which had limited cooperation from 1989 to present, to the Naga National Council, which had six years of change over two decades from 1955 to 1975. The Liberation Tigers of Tamil Eelam swung from low-level conflict to intense warfare with the Sri Lankan state, then a brief period of alignment while it and Colombo tried to expel an Indian peacekeeping force, before a return to total war, marked by several periods of cease-fire, ending in the group's collapse in 2009. This approach is still overly aggregated, since there were changes within years, but it shows a basic trajectory that both aligns with the historical literature and offers interesting possibilities for exploring variation.

There are obviously limits to the AOSA quantitative date. But they show that violent and nonviolent, and cooperative and conflictual, state-group interactions can be integrated into a shared conceptual and empirical framework that lets us "see" the world in a valuable way. This reveals the extent of state–armed group cooperation, the variation in state repression even against explicit rebels, and the importance of armed parties, militias, and private armies.

Cross-Country Variation

To provide a general sense of how these patterns vary, I explored cross-national variation. There are no clear predictions from my theory for countries' overall levels of repression. The key variation is across different kinds of political cleavages within each context, rather than general repression or accommodation. Figure 3.4 therefore is simply aimed at introducing descriptive patterns, showing cross-country variation in the proportion of armed orders. It includes all types of armed groups, so it is a very noisy picture. Nevertheless, we see Myanmar standing out for its high incidence of total war; Pakistan for extensive alliances and limited cooperation; India for a high reliance on containment orders, which we will see reflect its long-running counterinsurgency strategy in the Northeast and Naxalite areas. Limited cooperation is common in general, though its incidence varies a bit, and we will see in the case chapters that the conditions under which it occurs are very different across countries.

Pakistan and Sri Lanka have a high percentages of alliance orders, and Myanmar very few. These largely reflect Sri Lanka's close embrace of Tamil pro-state militias during a long civil war and Pakistan's heavy support for cross-border armed groups

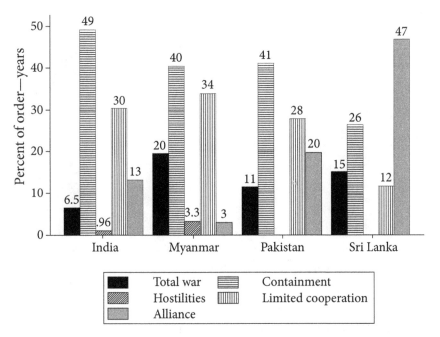

FIGURE 3.4. Cross-national patterns of armed order

aimed at India and Afghanistan across decades. As we will see below, Myanmar's governments have avoided tight alliances with major armed groups, preferring instead limited cooperation or some form of repression. The greatest raw number of alliance orders, however, are found in India: both national and state governments have aligned tightly with armed political parties and party-linked private armies, particularly communist and Hindu nationalist groups.

We see more striking variation in figure 3.5, which provides subsets of the sample for groups during periods that we identify as clearly anti-state insurgents. It restricts our focus to very explicitly anti-state armed group-periods; these are largely counterinsurgency campaigns and traditional civil wars. The coding that is used to identify groups in this category excludes a number of observations of insurgents that have moderated their war aims, so this is capturing the most intense and unambiguous conflict-years in the subcontinent. We might expect convergence toward similar strategies in civil wars, but striking variation instead emerges: there does not seem to be any straightforward "functional" approach to managing rebels.

Pakistan, Myanmar, and Sri Lanka all stand out for very heavy reliance on total war armed orders. These are highly repressive counterinsurgency states, while India seems to default more readily to containment. India, Sri Lanka, and Myanmar have a substantial amount of limited cooperation, which largely capture cease-fires: India in the Northeast, several periods of cease-fire in Sri Lanka, and a long

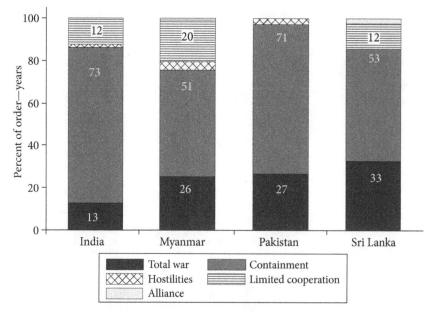

FIGURE 3.5. Armed orders by country, insurgents

stretch of post-1989 cease-fires in Myanmar. Pakistan's responses, by contrast, cluster almost entirely toward repressive options: its cooperation with armed groups instead is heavily focused on a variety of transnational militant groups and, in some periods, armed political parties in Karachi. As I discuss in much more detail in the Myanmar chapter, the Myanmar finding is highly period-dependent: the 1962–88 period has far less limited cooperation than the periods before or after it. India stands out for its relatively limited use of total war even toward explicit insurgent groups, though where it does pursue total war, as in Kashmir, it is very highly motivated for repression. Sri Lanka has the highest (by a tiny amount) incidence of total war, reflecting its brutally intense conflicts with the LTTE and the Janatha Vimukthi Peramuna (JVP), but also some limited cooperation, often involving short cease-fire/negotiation periods. There is meaningful heterogeneity in counterinsurgency across countries, despite COIN being an area with seemingly the most straightforward and unambiguous challenge to state power.

General Influences on Order: Group Goals and External State Support

My argument is contextual—the political meaning of groups' activities and rhetoric depend on the historical construction of a government's threat perception.

But we also want to know whether there are "thinner" generalizations we can make across contexts that provide valuable insights. Here I briefly probe now how two general variables—the ambition of war aims and the presence of external support—can shape broad patterns of armed politics. They are not necessarily alternatives, but can act as complements to my richer but more complex theory and need to be acknowledged as important.

An obvious starting point is to determine whether armed group goals are related to patterns of order. We would expect so, as a general matter. For figure 3.6, I created a simple dichotomous variable of "radical goals"—I coded these as a Yes if the group either sought full secession or central control, and No for groups seeking reform of central policy, autonomy short of secession, or some other goal. This variable is difficult to array on a spectrum (is secession more or less radical than revolution?), so I disaggregate it into distinct broad categories.

The correspondence is clear: groups with "radical" goals are four times more likely to be in total war and almost twice as likely to be in containment, but only 25 percent as likely to be in limited cooperation and exceptionally unlikely to end up in an alliance order. This suggests a political basis to the construction of armed orders. Governments respond differently to different kinds of demands. They do not appear to simply be reading off relative capabilities or group size. Moving beyond this simple, though very important, claim requires country-level

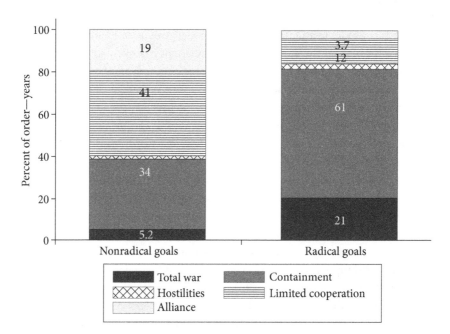

FIGURE 3.6. Goals and armed orders

research, since the meaning of radicalism varies across countries: an Islamist center-seeking group may be treated more lightly than a linguistic secessionist in Pakistan, for instance, while an Islamist secessionist is likely to be treated much more harshly than a linguistic secessionist in India. Nevertheless, this gives a rough sense that the nature of armed group political demands is a key factor in creating political orders. Moreover, we still see 40 percent of nonradical order-years engaged in conflict of some sort, and 16 percent of radical order-years engaged in some sort of cooperation with the state despite what we would expect to be highly conflictual relations.

I disaggregate these goals to see if more fine-grained patterns emerge. Table 3.1 examines the armed group goals that we coded, plus "unclear," and their relationship to armed orders. Even secessionist and center-seeking groups still end up in limited cooperation with some frequency—9 percent and 20 percent, respectively. Alliances, however, are rarer. Containment instead remains the main form of order for these groups. Autonomy-seekers cluster heavily in the middle of the distribution—almost exclusively limited cooperation and containment. Central "reform" groups tend to be the most mainstream of political actors in the dataset—primarily political parties—and they exist heavily on the cooperative end of the spectrum, with more than 80 percent in limited cooperation or alliance orders. However, the line between reformist and center-seeking groups can be very ambiguous, so distinguishing between the two in a highly aggregated analysis should only be taken as suggestive. There is a clear correspondence between the nature of armed group demands and their relationship with the state. Yet this remains a very blunt relationship, and not one that gives us an enormous amount to work with beyond the simple claim that relations are likely to be worse the more ambitious a group is. This leaves a lot of variation to explore, such as why both revolutionary and autonomy-seeking groups experience such a broad range of orders, and why secessionists are sometimes intensely targeted and sometimes contained. The case chapters pursue these questions in specific contexts.

The most straightforward alternative arguments to my own are found in excellent work by Ahsan Butt and Barbara Walter, though both are exclusively about secessionists, so only capture part of my theoretical domain. Butt's important book argues that external support drives higher levels of threat perception and thus more hard-line state responses against groups with such support.[10] I examine this relationship in figure 3.7. We see a clear correspondence between intensive counterinsurgency and external support—insurgent groups with confirmed external support are more likely to be locked in total war orders (33 percent of order-years versus 16 percent), though not dramatically more likely to be in overall conflictual relationships with the state. This difference does not exist when we only have *allegations* of external support; for these, the proportion

TABLE 3.1 Order-years by group goals

	UNCLEAR	SECESSION	AUTONOMY	CENTRAL CONTROL	CENTRAL REFORM	CRIMINAL	
Total war	22 (5%)	224 (21%)	89 (9%)	69 (18%)	4 (1%)	2 (3%)	410 (11%)
Containment	178 (37%)	715 (68%)	394 (40%)	156 (41%)	140 (20%)	52 (68%)	1,635 (44%)
Military hostilities	0	12 (1%)	0	25 (7%)	8 (1%)	6 (8%)	51 (1%)
Limited cooperation	108 (22%)	96 (9%)	459 (47%)	75 (20%)	355 (50%)	7 (9%)	1,100 (30%)
Alliance	178 (36%)	2 (0.2%)	38 (4%)	51 (14%)	209 (29%)	10 (13%)	488 (13%)
Total	486	1,049	980	376	716	77	3,684

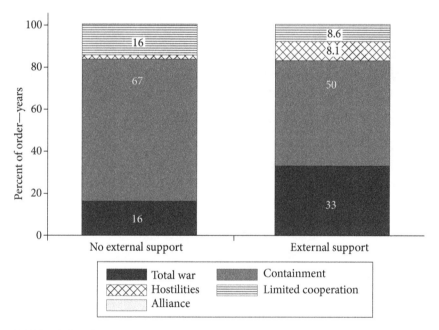

FIGURE 3.7. External support and armed orders

of total war and containment order-years is almost identical. This suggests that the relationship is most robust in clearer cases, and once we move into a more ambiguous category of unconfirmed allegations it disappears.

There is clearly evidence for Butt's theory, and it has important explanatory power. My best assessment is that external support can interact in complex ways with domestic political ideologies. I view such support as a potent "threat multiplier" that can trigger heightened concerns over conflict cleavages that are already seen as sensitive.[11] The following chapters will provide evidence that perceptions of particular political cleavages are often formed decades *prior* to actual armed mobilization, much less the onset of external support. For instance, Bengali regionalism was seen as a dangerous political movement by Pakistani elites decades before India began backing the Mukti Bahini. Kashmir was always treated as a worrisome region by Delhi, even in long periods without any armed movement or Pakistani backing. If external backers are strategic, they may support groups that are the ones most likely to draw a costly, bloody response from the rival counterinsurgent state, so external support may sometimes be an endogenous outcome of a deeper process.

There are also cases of clear insurgents with external support that are met with containment or even limited cooperation. The Nagas of Northeast India are a classic case—even when receiving Chinese aid (and attacking civilians, such as in train bombings in Assam) in the mid/late-1960s, they continued to be part of limited cooperation and cease-fires for years. This is true of many of the armed groups in India's Northeast more broadly; external support can be seen as a tactical expedient rather than signaling unacceptable war aims.[12] Thus, Butt's argument seems most powerful when applied to already-sensitive political cleavages, especially when the external support is from a state linked in some ways to the stakes of that conflict. In the case chapters, I will pay particular attention to external support.

Walter's argument is that early secessionist groups will attract more intense repression than later aspirational secessionists because governments are interested in establishing a reputation for resolve.[13] With only four countries, we have limited ability to make inferences. That said, there is clearly something to her argument. The earliest responses to secessionism in all four countries was repressive—the Karen National Union in 1948–49 Burma, Naga National Council in 1955–56 India, Baloch rebels in 1950s Pakistan, and Tamil proto-insurgency in 1970s Sri Lanka all met with crackdowns. Yet following this, we see huge variation over time. India has quickly moved into a negotiating posture with its separatists, Pakistan does not accommodate secessionists (indeed, it cracked down much harder in 1971 East Pakistan), Sri Lankan repression escalated over time even while it was interspersed with periods of cease-fire, while Burma's most hard-line repression occurred not in the late 1940s but instead during the military-personalist regime of Ne Win from 1962–88. There is important variation across countries and over time within them that needs to be grappled with to offer a more comprehensive explanation of how governments respond to separatism, as well as other group goals.

How Orders End

How do these orders come to an end? There are 137 dyad-years that involve a group termination, summarized in figure 3.8. In a few cases, a group reemerges years later with the same name after an extended period of disappearance; these can be tricky to code and these decisions are discussed in individual case narratives. However, in the vast majority of cases, a termination means the group comes to an end and it does not later reemerge as an armed actor.

Of groups that terminate, the overwhelmingly most common form is through their organizational collapse (59 percent). This is a broad category, ranging from groups that are militarily defeated to those that fritter away into nothing to those that split and have different factions carrying on under different names. The stresses on armed groups are extraordinarily severe, and there are many pathways to ultimate collapse. South Asia's governments tend to be reasonably militarily strong and highly motivated when faced with what they perceive as direct political challenges, while civilian discontent, ideological and personal factionalization, rival armed groups, and the difficulties of extracting resources create other serious barriers to survival.[14] In this grim and demanding environment, many groups simply cannot hold together.

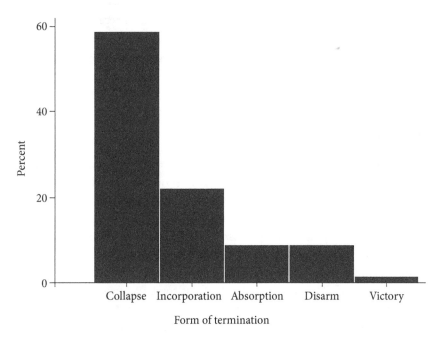

FIGURE 3.8. Forms of termination

The next most common outcome is incorporation (22 percent). This is a very heterogeneous category, but largely involves groups demobilizing through formal deals with the state. As I discuss in the conclusion, a number of groups demobilize without the international involvement so prominent in the existing literature on civil war termination. This does not disprove the existing literature, but it does suggest possibilities for conflict management that do not center on international support for a peace process.[15] Combined with the extensive limited cooperation we see in the data, there are intriguing dynamics of conflict stabilization and even termination that seem different from traditional arguments about civil war termination: there may be organic, heterodox approaches to building something like stability in environments where international involvement and peacebuilding is implausible.[16]

There are other forms of terminations. A number of groups ended by being absorbed in another group (9 percent). Others terminated through the somewhat odd category of disarmament; they demobilize without a formal deal (9 percent). A large proportion of these occur in Sri Lanka, where Tamil armed party paramilitaries mostly disarmed in the wake of the end of the war against the LTTE, and where the JVP moved in and out of violence before ultimately turning into a mainstream political party. Only one group won a clear and absolutely decisive victory—the Mukti Bahini, who fought for the independence of East Pakistan and won (with Indian help) the creation of Bangladesh.[17] There is also one case in which the form of termination is unclear, with the waning of the first wave of Baloch revolt in the late 1950s; it is simply not very clear exactly what happened in this period.

Moving Forward

The reason for gathering these data was to better "see" state-group interactions across time, space, and levels of violence. They show that armed orders can be systematically measured and that there is substantial variation in state-group relations in this large and important context. Moreover, they begin to reveal some patterns: different types of groups seem to receive different types of treatment, and countries seem to vary, at least in some ways, in how they manage armed groups. Yet we quickly run into limits in what we can draw from the quantitative data alone. Instead, it is most meaningful in close combination with comparative-historical qualitative data, and chapters 4 through 7 fuse the two. The rest of this chapter shifts to an overview of that evidence, previewing and comparing major ideological projects, both during and after colonialism, that sought to capture the commanding heights of state power in South Asia.

Comparing Ideological Projects

Measuring ideological projects is challenging—there are many possible dimensions of ideology, huge contextual differences across cases, divisions within governments and movements that make simple codings difficult, and ambiguity about what leaders and institutions really "believe."[18] This means that I make claims about ideological projects with caveats and caution. But the goal of comparison is to gain valuable new leverage on an analytical question, even at risk of missing important nuance. The claims below receive dramatically more detail in the country chapters, but placing them together here provides a comparative framework to guide the empirics to come.

The carrier movements I focus on were key players under colonialism, including those that emerged dominant at independence and those who were sidelined. One important reason to include the paths not (initially, at least) taken is to show how many *potential* answers existed to the pressing political questions of the day; there were few policies that were accepted as obviously straightforward. It is striking how much the politics of the colonial period tell us about politics after independence, as many key organizations and ideological projects that only became politically influential decades after independence can still be traced back to before 1947. Obviously, there has been enormous churn in South Asia's politics, but many of the most foundational questions and goals have endured.

Colonial Politics: An Overview

Colonial South Asia was a site of intense political mobilization and contestation. British colonial rule was established across what would become India, Pakistan (and then Bangladesh), Burma/Myanmar, and Ceylon/Sri Lanka by the late 1880s. Blending war, coercion, patronage, and co-optation, British rule was intended to last indefinitely. But it would end in the partition of India in 1947 and independence of Burma and Ceylon in 1948. During the decades leading up to the British withdrawal, several distinct carrier movements emerged to articulate some form of nationalist politics, aiming at greater autonomy for self-rule, independence, or a shifting blend of the two: independence eventually became the goal even for groups that started with more limited aims. Table 3.2 summarizes the broad positions of the carrier movements along the three main ideological dimensions I introduced in chapter 1.

The best-known struggle over the future of politics in the region occurred within British India. The core contest was a complex three-sided competition among the British, Gandhi and Nehru's Indian National Congress (INC), and Jinnah's Muslim League. In addition, powerful regional political groupings

TABLE 3.2 Colonial carrier movements

MOVEMENT	ETHNO-LINGUISTIC	RELIGION	REDISTRIBUTIVE
Indian National Congress	Multilingual state-nation	Equidistant/divisions over Hinduism; skeptical of religious minority political claims	Democratic socialist/center-left
Muslim League	Urdu as central to Muslim nationalism	Preference to Muslims	Right/center-right
Ceylon National Congress	"Ceylonese" nationalism	Ambiguous; de facto preference to Buddhism	Center-right
AFPFL	Bamar nationalism	Preference to Buddhism	Left/center-left
Sinhala Maha Sabha/ Sinhala-Buddhist nationalist movement	Sinhala-Buddhist nationalism	Preference to Buddhism	Unclear
Awami League	Bengali nationalism	Secular/equidistant	Left/center-left
Hindu nationalist movement	Priority on Hindi	Preference to Hindus	Ambiguous

existed in Bengal and Punjab, communists tried to mobilize within the chaos of late colonial politics, and Hindu nationalist forces sought to build up an alternative vision to the Congress. At the moment of partition and independence, the League and Congress would stand triumphant. But even after this "moment of departure,"[19] the legacies of colonial politics and threats that the new governments perceived in the political arena persisted. In Pakistan, questions of how to manage region and religion plagued the League after independence. The rise of the Awami League as a carrier movement for what eventually became Bangladesh in postindependence Pakistan was directly caused by the inability of the League's "Muslim nationalism," combining Urdu with the identity category of Muslim (distinct from actual Islamic practice), to accommodate Bengali regionalism. In independent India, Congress hegemony would last far longer, but eventually Hindu nationalism rose to the fore as India's new dominant political force.

The Congress was formed in 1885 and the League in 1906. The Congress originally began as a reformist program aimed at gaining a greater role for Indians in the governance of British India. It drew on a relatively elite, educated social base that initially pursued a relatively cooperative approach to the British. During World War I, it supported the war effort, and initially made an agreement for a kind of consociationalism with the League in the Lucknow Pact of 1916. Yet this accommodation with the League would not last, and from the 1920s the two organizations were bitter rivals. It became an increasingly institutionalized, though never fully cohesive, organization from 1920 onward, combining mass mobilization with a steady central leadership.

The Congress' approach to the question of religion requires some care, which chapter 4 delves into in far greater detail.[20] Overall, it sought to advance a secular nationalism that did not formally define Indian nationalism by religious identity or practice. The Congress made secularism—defined as state equidistance between religions, not separation from religion—an explicit part of its ideology, especially as Jawaharlal Nehru became more prominent. The top leadership of the INC feared the implications of an avowedly "communal" turn in the organization's policy: building an autonomous, much less independent, India would require avoiding enervating religious conflict.[21] However, some key individuals and factions, especially but not exclusively at the local level, tended to favor Hindus in growing communal rivalries and tensions. Over time a broader cleavage emerged within Congress between what Jaffrelot terms "Hindu traditionalists" and secularists.[22] Hindu traditionalists continued to have an expansive definition of the Indian nation, but thought it only natural that Hindu symbols and practices would receive greater de facto prominence because of the Hindu majority. Secularists feared that this represented the thin end of a wedge that would undo secularism: under Nehru's leadership, the secularist faction ultimately, but not indefinitely, won out. Thus we can plausibly code the INC as a primarily secular carrier movement—but need to also be attentive to the endurance of other currents within the party and their implications for postindependence politics.

Language, a cleavage that haunted postcolonial polities in Asia and Africa, was approached in a novel and innovative way by the INC's ideological project: rather than trying to align the nation with a single language (the classic European model), by the late 1920s the Congress formally endorsed multilingual politics. From the early 1920s (including the 1928 Nehru Committee Report), the Congress accepted provincial languages as a basis for administrative reorganization. English would continue to be useful, and there was an expectation that Hindustani would become the language of central government, but extensive political space was carved out for multiple official languages. Stepan et al. refer to this approach as a "state-nation" conceptualization of nationalism, in which multiple linguistic communities could nestle within a national category, rather than language defining the national community.[23] This is a sharp contrast to the other carrier movements mobilizing around the region: for the Muslim League, Urdu was a central component of nation building; for the Burmese nationalist movement, Burmese; for the Sinhalese Buddhist movement, Sinhala.

Finally, the Congress occupied a loosely center-left position on the redistributive dimension. It had several distinct factions—some were socialist, others tended toward probusiness policies, and some lay in between. All, however, expected a major state role in the economy; the question was what exactly the state would do and who its policies would favor.[24] By the late 1940s, the more radically left factions of the Congress had been expelled, split, or been marginalized. There was nevertheless an openness to both land reform and a mainstream communist Left that were lacking in many peer regimes in postcolonial Asia.

This combination crafted an unusual ideological project for the Congress: center-left, multilingual, and notably more secular than either the League or Hindu nationalist competitors. It created substantial space for ethno-linguistic (and tribal) politics and mainstream leftist mobilization. However, built into the Congress project was a lesson from its battles with the League and the chaos of Partition: the unacceptability of explicitly religious appeals as the basis for redrawing state boundaries or making political accommodations on a communal basis.[25] The specter of religious conflict haunted the Congress. Its factions disagreed, however, on precisely who was most worrisome: for Hindu traditionalists, it was Muslims above all; for secularists like Nehru, Hindu nationalists were just as problematic as Muslim separatism. But they agreed on the threat posed by Muslim, and to a lesser extent, Sikh political mobilization: the key to a secular policy was to avoid making concessions along overtly religious lines. This did not mean the state could not be involved in religion as a cultural matter, whether in sponsoring holidays or pilgrimages, but it did mean that line had to be held against a repeat of the experience of religious Partition.

The Hindu nationalist movement, in retrospect the most important alternative (though at the time, the Left seemed urgently important), was driven by the Rashtriya Swayamsevak Sangh (RSS), as well as various other organizations (like the Hindu Mahasabha) and leaders. Under colonialism they were unable to capture a central political place, but articulated an important project that made Hinduism and Hindus central to the nation.[26] This included deep skepticism of Muslims and Urdu, and a general aversion to the Left. Though Hindu nationalists were largely held at bay by the Congress, they survived into independence as an alternative conceptualization of the nation that would eventually capture the commanding heights of Indian politics.[27]

The Muslim League was an often-divided organization that waxed and waned in importance and cohesion.[28] This makes it even more complicated to assess—it was heavily personalized around Jinnah, its rise to power occurred quite late in the game, and it articulated different goals at different times in different provinces. Moreover, Jinnah's personal political beliefs appear to have sometimes been in direct tension with the political claims and mobilizational strategies he and the League embraced.

Nevertheless, we can construct a looser approximation of the League project, which established broad contours of politics in the Pakistan to come. The League is regarded by many scholars to have adopted "Muslim nationalism."[29] The point at which Jinnah and the League actually wanted an independent Pakistan, as opposed to a highly decentralized power-sharing deal within a unified India, is a matter of debate, but the political community that the League identified with were the Muslims of South Asia. The idea of Pakistan was that of a Muslim homeland, free from domination by the subcontinent's Hindu majority. This made Muslims central to the League's ideological project, and to the definition of Pakistani nationalism.[30]

Defining the nation along religious grounds created a deep legitimacy vulnerability for consequent regimes—future governments could be condemned and criticized for not supporting proper religious practices. These tensions were apparent before independence: in the 1946 elections, for instance, the League's explicit claim that Islam was in danger, the role of clerics on the campaign trail, and the explicit use of religious imagery all made clear that Muslim as a category could not be easily separated from Islam as an admittedly vague set of practices and beliefs.[31] Establishing what precisely this relationship should be challenged both the League before 1947 and rulers of Pakistan after 1947.[32] A language of politics emerged that built religion into the political system and that predisposed non-Muslims to a second-class status within politics, both formally and informally. Maintaining inclusion in a political project built around one religious category would prove enormously difficult.

Combined with the focus on Muslims (and, in some ambiguous and contested way, Islam) was the primacy of Urdu as the intended language of the nation. It was the language of the north Indian elite that played such a central role in building the League, but not the language of most of the majority-Muslim regions of what would become Pakistan, nor did this elite have firm roots in these areas.[33] Punjab and Bengal were particularly resistant to coming under Jinnah's control, and they eluded him until near the endgame of the British empire. Bengal was a particular problem for the League: it was deeply attached to the Bengali language, had a substantial Hindu minority, and included more left-wing movements and tendencies than in the other areas the League sought to mobilize. As partition loomed, Jinnah was finally able to wrangle the Muslim communities of Punjab and Bengal under the League's banner. But this did not solve the basic problem of the role of ethnic/linguistic regions within the nation. Making matters even more complicated, the League was dominated by right-leaning elites, many of them landowners, who saw little to like about the Left.[34] The League did not offer particularly detailed thoughts on future redistributive and economic questions, but its general leanings were to the right.

In Burma and Ceylon, colonial-era carrier movements rose that would immediately or soon shift the center of political gravity in each country. In both, emerging nationalist carrier movements centered on language and religion as key components of the authentic, indigenous nation. In Ceylon, this Sinhala Buddhist nationalism remained marginalized under colonialism, but it would soon spring forth after independence to reshape the terms of political debate. In Burma, Bamar nationalism combined with leftism to forge a fractured but hugely influential anticolonial movement that would take power in 1948. In sharp contrast to the elite-led nationalist movements of the Congress and League, in Ceylon and Burma nationalist projects emerged largely from below—these were "sons of the soil"[35] movements that took aim at indigenous elites as well as British rule. A fusion of ethnicity, language, and religion took place: while the Muslim League looked to religion and a minority, elite language to cross-cut ethnicities and Congress sought a kind of civic nationalism, in Ceylon and Burma, a majority ethnic "core" was made central to the nation by movements that radically restructured politics after independence.

Ceylon had the calmest colonial politics in the region: there was not the sustained anti-British mobilization we see elsewhere. Instead, a comparatively somnolent elite of ethnically Sinhalese planters and merchants cooperated with British rule. They eventually formed the Ceylon National Congress (CNC), which would turn into the United National Party (UNP) that became one of the two major parties after independence.[36] The CNC's lack of sustained mass mobilization or conflict with the British meant that it never articulated a clear ideology of the polity: its leadership referred to "Ceylonese" nationalism but did little to explain what precisely that meant. This was a crucial question in Ceylon because the Sinhalese majority was joined by substantial Tamil and Muslim minorities. The CNC sought to include them all, but without much detail or conviction.

Moreover, the CNC was a fractious and poorly institutionalized organization, without socialization of cadres or a coherent party line. Rather than laying out and sticking to a clear Ceylonese nationalist vision, important leaders and factions had already flirted with Sinhalese Buddhist primacy in the 1930s and 1940s. This combination of organizational fragmentation with a thin and underdeveloped ideological project would make the CNC/UNP highly vulnerable after independence. The CNC took power in 1948 as the UNP, but its nationalist project had not been forged in contentious politics like that of the League, Congress, or Burma's Anti-Fascist People's Freedom League (AFPFL).

Instead, the key ideological-political innovation of the late colonial era was Sinhala Buddhist nationalism.[37] It found its clearest organizational manifestation in the Sinhala Maha Sabha (SMS), but was a more inchoate movement that also infiltrated parts of the CNC. S. W. R. D. Bandaranaike, for instance, was both part of the CNC and a key political figure in cultivating Sinhalese Buddhist nationalism. The SMS was not a highly institutionalized political party, but it captured an upsurge of resentment by largely rural Sinhalese Buddhists against the British, the Tamil minority, and elite Sinhalese collaborators with British rule. This carrier movement combined a small group of elites like Bandaranaike with local notables, clerics, and citizens, mostly in the densely populated rural areas.

The Sinhalese language and Buddhist religion were to be given pride of place for two reasons: first, their majority status on the island, and second, their tiny and minority status within South Asia and the broader world. This combination would contribute to the common framing of the Sinhalese as being a majority that nevertheless viewed itself as a minority: dominant within Ceylon, but constantly worried about being swamped by massive non–Sinhala Buddhist populations in the broader region.[38] The movement was religiously and linguistically majoritarian, fusing together religious and language categories into a more "traditional" version of ethnicity than that advanced by the League or INC. This movement was also broadly toward the redistributive Left, given the relatively modest economic status of many of its members; in contrast, the CNC/UNP occupied a center-right space. But while left-right competition was meaningful in Ceylon—there was a vibrant though deeply divided hard Left as well—the key axis of contention would be the place of ethnic minorities (especially Tamils) relative to the Sinhalese majority. Here the Sinhala Maha Sabha and its sympathizers sought Sinhala as the language of state, explicit primacy for Buddhism, and a substantial downgrading of the status of Tamils, who had become heavily overrepresented in the colonial bureaucracy due to their English education.[39]

Burma was the most violent context under colonialism, both due to the British wars of conquest and the extraordinary devastation accompanying the Japanese invasion and Allied counterinvasion. Even prior to World War II, politics had become highly militarized, with loosely organized parties having armed wings. The most important anticolonial nationalists were—unlike in India—not involved in the colonial governance system. Instead, a set of radical Bamar nationalist leftists mobilized in the 1920s and 1930s against British rule. Like the Sinhalese Buddhist movement, these nationalists focused their grievance on the "downgrading"[40] of the Bamar majority and the Buddhist religion as a result of colonial divide-and-rule tactics that favored Burma's ethnic minorities, as well as foreigners. More than in Ceylon, radical leftist thought was embraced by the emerging nationalists, who often self-identified as socialists or communists.[41]

A substantial number of these nationalists collaborated with the Japanese after the invasion, seeing a rare opportunity to acquire meaningful power with the British driven out. During the war, these forces clashed viciously with ethnic minorities armed and supported by the Allies, especially the Karen. Extremely intense ethnic violence occurred that further hardened ethnic divisions and distrust. As the tide of war turned, some Bamar nationalists, especially the Burma National Army led by Aung San, switched sides. It combined with the Communist Party of Burma (CPB) and others to form the AFPFL, which aligned with the Allies against the Japanese in the final days of the war.[42]

The AFPFL, with Aung San's Socialist Party at its core, would become the key carrier movement that took over Burma at independence. The CPB was marginalized in 1946–47, and the Socialists stood ascendant heading into independence (despite Aung San's assassination).[43] The AFPFL combined leftism with a version of Bamar nationalism. It was not as radically exclusionary as the later Ne Win regime, but was largely built around ethnic Bamar Buddhists in Burma's "heartland" and viewed the ethnic minorities—Karen, Kachin, Mon, and others—with suspicion for their past collaboration with the British and their desires for enduring autonomy. These minority communities in turn worried about the implications of a rising Bamar nationalist project taking power in Rangoon. The seeds for decades of conflict were sown in the 1930s and 1940s.[44]

This is obviously just a rough sketch, but even this overview gives a clear sense of the varying ideological projects at work under British colonialism. The Muslim League and Indian National Congress were locked in bitter conflict over how religion should relate to nationality and state formation; these movements also faced intense internal debates about which language(s) to privilege and how to manage regionalism. The SMS and CNC in Ceylon did not see this same kind of direct competition; instead, the CNC's weaknesses allowed Sinhalese Buddhist nationalism to rise from below. In Burma, Bamar nationalism squared off with autonomy-seeking ethnic minorities. Across the region, the question of redistribution and leftism were also important: communists (some armed, some not) sought to mobilize incredibly poor and unequal societies.

Postindependence Politics

After independence, these carrier movements either came to power immediately or survived as contenders that in some cases eventually triumphed. As with the colonial period, here I outline in only broad but useful sketches the contending projects at work in South Asia's politics. Despite the region's extraordinary political complexity, it is striking how much continuity there was from the colonial period in the basic political cleavages and questions central to each country's politics. Independence did not magically transform these countries' political foundations. Instead, it forced to the surface tensions and decisions that had at times been submerged or elided under colonialism. In some cases, we see substantial continuity in the "rules" governing state coercion; in others, regime changes induced substantial shifts in ideological project. Even in these latter cases, however, new governments often drew on strands of politics that had existed previously. There is no way to study South Asia's politics without taking historical legacies seriously—the range of plausible options available to political leaders was heavily constrained. Table 3.3 provides a summary.

TABLE 3.3 Key postindependence governments and carrier movements

COUNTRY	GOVERNMENT/REGIME	ETHNO-LINGUISTIC	RELIGION	REDISTRIBUTIVE
India	Congress	Multilingual state-nation	Secular/equidistant	Democratic socialist/ center-left
	BJP	State-nation, but with priority on Hindi	Preference to Hindus	Center-right
Pakistan	Civilian parties	Urdu as priority	Variation	Center-left/right
	Military/Ayub	Urdu as priority	Preference to Islam	Right
	Military/Zia	Urdu as priority	Strong theocratic preference toward Islam	Right
	Military/Musharraf	Urdu as priority	Preference to Islam	Right
	Military (general)	Urdu as priority	Preference to Islam	Right
Sri Lanka	SLFP	Sinhala-Buddhist nationalism	Preference to Buddhism	Center-left
	UNP/pre-1956	"Ceylonese" nationalism	Ambiguous	Center-right
	UNP/post-1956	Sinhala-Buddhist nationalism	Preference to Buddhism	Center-right
Myanmar	U Nu	Preference to Bamar nationalism	Preference to Buddhism	Center-left
	Ne Win/Army/BSPP	Preference to Bamar nationalism	Preference to Buddhism	Left
	SPDC/SLORC	Preference to Bamar nationalism	Preference to Buddhism	Ambiguous
	NLD	Preference to Bamar nationalism	Preference to Buddhism	Center-left

The Congress in India is the easiest case. It took over as India's ruling party in 1947 and continued in power almost continuously until 1989.[45] There were important shifts and oscillations within the party over this time, but some basic viewpoints endured: there was substantial space for linguistic and tribal demands to be accommodated within the Indian Constitution, the nonviolent Left could enter the mainstream, and religious minority groups could mobilize in the cultural sphere, but were viewed with deep suspicion when making explicit political demands on religious grounds. Though there was ambivalence and hypocrisy over time in its commitment to secularism, the Congress was, in general, skeptical of Hindu nationalist groups like the RSS. Even after the "Congress system" ended, the coalition era of 1989–2014 kept many of these basic precepts in place.[46]

The key change has been the rise of the Hindu nationalist movement.[47] From a marginal position in the early 1980s, the Bharatiya Janata Party (BJP) rose to lead a coalition government from 1998–2004. This period began to see efforts to reshape the "common sense" understanding of Indian nationalism. But the major breakthrough came with Narendra Modi's decisive victory in 2014, followed by an even more dramatic win in 2019. This is a case of a change in ideological project occurring through partisan turnover. The BJP continued to adhere to the broad parameters of linguistic, tribal, and left/redistributive claim making within mainstream politics. This has often been the grudging result of having to come to terms with enduring realities of Indian society (like the need for multilingualism rather than Hindi dominance).

The main, and hugely important, shift has instead been along the religious dimension—the BJP and its associated network of organizations place priority on Hindus as central to the nation, with Muslims (above all) and Christians occupying the position of foreign guests that ultimately lack loyalty to the land.[48] The suspicion toward explicitly Hindu nationalist organizations that characterized some past Congress governments is gone; those organizations have instead captured the state. The threat perceptions aimed at Muslims as a social category in BJP ideology are clear, and so we should expect shifts in how the state views and coerces Muslims.[49] This is a major change, even if not a reversal or transformation in its approach to India's other politicized cleavages.

The Sri Lankan case saw a much earlier change driven by electoral politics. "Ceylonese" nationalism was never clearly defined or institutionalized by the UNP, and the rising tide of Sinhalese Buddhist nationalism destroyed this hazy nationalist imagining by 1956. In 1951, S. W. R. D. Bandaranaike founded the Sri Lanka Freedom Party (SLFP) as the political vessel of Sinhalese nationalism. Complemented by (sometimes violent) contentious politics and mobilization by monks and Sinhalese civil society, it immediately put pressure on the ruling UNP. Arguing that the UNP was selling out the Sinhalese masses and unduly favoring

Tamils, the SLFP triggered a process of "outbidding" that culminated in its victory in the 1956 elections.[50] The UNP then pursued a similar strategy to come back to power in 1960. By the mid-1960s, the two Sinhalese-majority parties had destroyed each other's attempts to cut a sustainable deal with Tamil political parties, including through the deployment of riots toward Tamils.

In the early 1970s, Mrs. Bandaranaike's SLFP took the final plunge toward open Sinhalese majoritarianism, advancing both Buddhism and Sinhala as dominant within the Constitution. This was the culmination of a process of "lock-in," as the key parties embraced a policy of discrimination against the Tamil minority along the language and religion dimensions.[51] This was a striking case of pressure from below incentivizing politicians to adopt a particular ideological position, making this project a highly resilient political stance rather than an attempted imposition by elites. Deep suspicion of the Tamil minority and an assertion of Sinhalese "ownership" of the island would characterize politics in the run-up and during most of the long war with Tamil insurgents. There were important differences between the UNP and SLFP on redistribution, with the former leaning right and the latter leaning left, but these held few implications for armed politics.

More complex are the cases in which militaries alternated power with civilian political parties or seriously constrained their power over internal security, namely in Burma/Myanmar and Pakistan. I focus my theory on the actors that control internal security, which leads to a strong emphasis on the Pakistani and Burmese militaries as the central players since the late 1950s, even during periods of formal civilian rule. This is not to say that civilians did not sometimes play an important role or that there was no politics outside of the military. But it is the case that even after formal democratization (2015 in Myanmar, and 1971–72, 1988, and 2008 in Pakistan), militaries were the key security managers that could act with substantial autonomy from civilian oversight and control.[52]

Pakistan has seen the most ambiguous and complex patterns of ideological articulation, in part because of the unanswered questions that accompanied the Muslim League's mobilization before independence. "Muslim nationalism" privileged Muslims, Urdu, and the redistributive right/center right. But the boundary between Muslim and "Islamic" nationalism was potentially quite porous: What was the use of Muslim nationalism if Muslims did not adhere to the proper practice of Islam? How should Christians, Sikhs, and Hindus be treated in a "Muslim homeland"? What relation could there be between Islam and nation after the creation of Bangladesh forged another Muslim-majority state in South Asia? What was the role of Shia and Ahmadis in a Sunni-majority Pakistan? And how much should Pakistan look to the broader Muslim, especially Arab, world for cues about how to be appropriate Muslim nationalists? Jinnah made some statements that tilted more toward, ironically, a Congress style of secularism, but the

League's language of politics had very explicitly linked religion with Pakistan, a language that carried over into independence. Jinnah's death soon after independence made his personal beliefs largely irrelevant to the new political arena.

The Muslim League fractured badly in the 1950s amid enduring disagreements about the constitution. These disagreements, flowing directly from tensions within the League during late colonial politics, occurred over religion, redistribution, and region (combining language with geography). They combined conflict among elites, street politics (like anti-Ahmadi riots in Lahore), and growing suspicion in East Pakistan of the Muhajir and Punjabi dominance of the bureaucracy and military. By the time a constitution was finally created, this bureaucratic-military combine had begun to shunt aside civilian parties—especially those with a leftist or Bengali regionalist hue.

By the time of the 1958 military takeover, the military and many of its civilian supporters had come to view regionalism as an unacceptable threat, Islam as necessary to hold the country together even if Islamic practice was not, and the Left as alien and subversive. Pakistani nationalism could still contain a variety of groups, but it would give priority to Muslims, to Punjabis, Muhajirs, and Pashtuns over Sindhis, Baloch, and (majority) Bengalis, and would tilt to the ideological Right under the guardianship of the military and its bureaucratic junior partners. These politics emerged from the British colonial approach to the military in Punjab, international linkages, and the ethnic composition of the army, as well as the chaotic politics of Pakistan in the 1950s. Together they forged a political project that took key aspects of the League—Islam as a crucial category even if not practice (Ayub Khan, for instance, loathed clerics but deployed Islam as a unifying narrative), Urdu as language of nation, West Pakistan dominance, and opposition to the Left—and fastened onto them an authoritarian "military guardian" exoskeleton.

The army emerged with an organizational threat perception that saw regionalism as deeply fissiparous and antithetical to a stable and loyal population, that opposed the Left, and that was at least open to demands made on the grounds of Islam. My focus on the military means that the complex civilian politics of Pakistan get less attention. It is worth noting that some of these threat perceptions are shared among civilian parties, especially skepticism of regionalism. Zulfikar Bhutto was, for instance, a disastrously hard-line foe of Bengali and Baloch regionalism, while both the Nawaz Sharif and Benazir Bhutto governments were not implacably opposed to state linkages with Islamist armed groups like the Taliban and Lashkar-e-Taiba.

This military ideological project was not locked in stone. The main change I identify is the Zia military regime's embrace of a more openly Islamist approach to politics. Zia pushed religious practice into a more central symbolic place in

Pakistani politics, cultivated sectarian tensions against Shiites, and accelerated close state links with Islamist armed and unarmed political actors. After Zia's death in 1988, the military shifted somewhat back toward Muslim nationalism when it came to the symbolic focus on practice and theology. Crucially, however, the legacies of Zia's embrace of political Islam endured, and the basic friendliness toward Islamist armed groups continued. In table 3.3, I offer a general military coding, as well as somewhat more specific codings for individual military dictators, and I summarize the "civilian" project, while acknowledging that this is a radical simplification.

Burma also saw the rise of a powerful military. But first it had roughly a decade of civilian rule under the AFPFL government of U Nu. U Nu carried over key components of the AFPFL project: a general sympathy for the Bamar majority and Buddhism relative to minority ethnicities and religions combined with a center-left redistributive tilt, but without a hard-line exclusionary project like that of his (military) successor Ne Win. His government immediately faced near-collapse, and the first several years were basically a desperate bid for survival. As the state consolidated, U Nu had more space to maneuver.

Unlike in Pakistan, this was not a direct carryover from the British colonial military.[53] It was one of the successors of the anticolonial nationalist movement. Key military elites had been in anti-British militant networks that collaborated with the Japanese and participated in the interethnic clashes of World War II. After the war, the Burmese Army combined this faction with minority Karen who had worked with the British, but in 1948–50, the Karen rebellion led to a predominantly Bamar military driven by a fusion of nationalism and leftism. Over the course of the 1950s, the military waged intense counterinsurgency against both an array of minority ethnic armed groups and the Communist Party of Burma. This experience combined with the historical ideological goals of the Bamar nationalist movement and fears of entrapment in the Cold War to create a siege mentality under army chief Ne Win.[54] The army—even before taking power—came to view itself as surrounded by irreconcilable enemies that needed to either surrender or be destroyed. These threats were alleged to come from the hard Left, a distrusted civilian party system and civil society, and the ever-growing set of ethnic minority insurgent groups. We also see the early glimmerings of the full-throated rejection of the Rohingya for being not part of the nation, which accelerated in the following decades.

Ne Win's sidelining in 1988 led to a partial softening under the junta that took over. As I discuss in chapter 6, the end of the Cold War and shift in the nature of insurgent mobilization on the periphery also contributed to some rethinking of the military project. But key continuities have endured: an unwillingness to accept federalism that would empower ethnic minorities, enduring suspicion of dissent, opposition to civilians having power over security issues, and exclusion of the Rohingya.[55] The latter sentiment is broadly shared among the civilian government that came into power in 2015, though without control over internal security. The centrality of Burmese and Buddhism to the dominant nationalist vision of regime elites, military and civilian, has endured even alongside substantial formal democratization and enduring military power and prerogatives.

History, Politics, and Violence

This chapter laid the basis of the more detailed, specialized chapters to come. Measuring armed orders and ideological projects requires substantial contextual research and knowledge, as well as serious humility. Nevertheless, I show that both can be systematically operationalized, opening new directions for comparative research on the dynamics of political violence.

Three themes emerge from this chapter that guide the rest of the book. The first is understanding state-group relations as a spectrum rather than a dichotomy. The data above show huge variation across orders, and provide suggestive evidence of political dynamics driving some of this variation. This reorientation in how we think about the relationship of politics and violence allows a broad conversation, ranging from militia politics to insurgency to elections, that pulls together disparate political phenomena. We can explore how regimes try to navigate across different types of groups, social and political cleavages, and political goals. We can see which differences matter, and which disappear once subjected to systematic comparison.

Second, the book takes seriously governments' understanding of politics, specifically which linguistic, religious, and redistributive positions they staked out and which they most feared.[56] This is a challenging task, and many caveats are necessary. Nevertheless, a combination of comparison, triangulation of sources, and appropriate caveats can move us toward credible and usable assessments of the general projects and threat perceptions of rulers. Part of the goal is to denaturalize what is now taken for granted as the obvious course of politics in these countries: What alternatives existed? What processes led to one project triumphing over another? What other paths could have been taken in responding to a particular armed group, and how might we understand why they were not?

A third theme that runs through the book is the weight of history. We see continuity in the armed orders data: there are certainly changes, but also a fairly substantial inertia. In the ideological projects coding, we do not see major changes happening with enormous regularity. Though there are important shifts, they are the exception rather than the rule, and are difficult to easily roll back. Without making sense of events decades prior, we cannot understand many critical contemporary dynamics of armed politics. This does not take responsibility away from leaders and institutions for the choices they make, but does show the relationship between those choices and broader historical trends.

With these three themes in mind, the rest of the book explores the origins and evolution of government ideological projects and patterns of armed order in India, Pakistan, Burma/Myanmar, and Sri Lanka. While each is a self-contained chapter, they all draw on the comparative framework of this chapter.

INDIA

4

India is one of the world's most complicated countries, and the same is true of its armed politics. There has been, and remains, a staggering variety of state–armed group relations across space and time, including private armies, anti-state insurgents, pro-state militias, armed political parties, and in-name-only rebels that do business with Delhi. This landscape stretches from bitter total wars to tight alliances, with extensive containment and limited cooperation in between. India sees a large number of groups ending in military collapse, but also a substantial number that have been incorporated into mainstream politics.

This chapter sets out to explain India's distinctive patterns of armed politics.[1] It offers a comparative historical account of the nationalist projects that survived into independence, showing how the slow but steady collapse of the Congress' nationalist project opened space for Hindu nationalism to seize the commanding heights of national power. The nationalist projects are also contrasted to India's neighbors, revealing a very different orientation toward language in particular and, under Congress, religion. A clear set of predictions emerge across ideological projects about how the state should generally deal with armed groups mobilizing on language, tribe, and the Left. By contrast, it suggests that fundamental questions of religion depend, at least in part, on whether the BJP or Congress rule in Delhi: how the Hindu majority relates to the Indian nation is a fundamental contested cleavage in Indian politics, and the ruling government's answer to this question has shifted dramatically in recent years.

The chapter then compares these expectations to reality, using the AOSA data to explore whether these ideological projects match patterns of actual state internal security policies. I systematically study Delhi's relations with insurgents, militias, and armed political parties, examining variation across and within each of these categories. Across them, I argue that a key factor in explaining state policy is the political acceptability of the demands made by armed groups. I also more tentatively examine state-level dynamics in several Indian states. There are clearly other variables at play, and there are also differences between national- and state-level dynamics that I engage with, but the general tendencies linking politics to conflict hold. The chapter builds on a rich existing line of research that highlights how important political cleavages—especially religion—are to state patterns of response to mobilization in India.[2] The discussion covers everything from the Kashmir insurgency to communal riots to West Bengal's militarized elections. The chapter's final empirical section delves more deeply into the Naga conflict to explore in greater detail how tactical overlap emerges and vanishes, and how armed groups can change their ideological positioning. The chapter concludes with what the argument tells us about contemporary Indian politics, as a majoritarian political project has captured the commanding heights of state power.

Making India: Political Projects before and after 1947

Battles over the meaning of Indian nationalism occurred under both colonial and postcolonial politics.[3] First, under colonialism, the Congress fashioned a distinctive, though not hegemonic, project in competition with the Muslim League. Second, after independence, this project dominated for decades. In the 1980s, it began facing an increasingly potent, ultimately victorious, challenge from a rising Hindu nationalism politically represented by the BJP.

This part of the chapter takes each period in turn. It outlines how the Congress project emerged and consolidated in a complex three-way competition with the British and the League. It then shows the solidification of internal threat perception after independence. However, the question of how the Indian nation related to the Hindu majority remained open. The BJP dramatically rose to power with a very different answer than the Congress' and now dominates the national political stage. This approach is in line with Chhibber and Verma's broader characterization of "Indian politics as deeply ideological," though I focus on state and political elites: without understanding rulers' conceptions of state and nation,

TABLE 4.1 Carrier movements and ruling governments

MOVEMENT	ETHNO-LINGUISTIC	RELIGION	REDISTRIBUTIVE
Indian National Congress	Multilingual state-nation	Secular-equidistant/ internal divisions	Center-left
Hindu nationalist movement/BJP	Priority on Hindi (colonialism)/ Grudging acceptance of multilingualism (independence)	Preference to Hindus	Center-right

we have limited insight into how the state apparatus they control tries to govern coercion.[4] Table 4.1 broadly summarizes the two projects I focus on, acknowledging that there are of course many subtleties within each.

Colonial Politics and the Rise of the Indian National Congress

The INC was formed in 1885 as a forum for a rising class of educated Indians to voice demands for greater inclusion in British colonial rule. Dominated by English-educated lawyers and run for a time by a retired British bureaucrat, the INC attempted to appeal to British liberal values in order to gain a greater role for educated elites.[5] Indeed, Congress would not explicitly demand full independence from British rule until 1930.[6] The Congress staked out an aspirationally national position that avoided the embrace of explicit religious appeals or symbols.[7] It represented a "bourgeois, step-in-your-shoes sort of nationalism until the time of Tilak and the 'extremist' tendency in the INC in the 1890s and 1900s."[8]

Yet many Congress-linked leaders became involved in movements with religious overtones.[9] Accordingly, "the nature of Indian National Congress secularism was therefore, from the very beginning, compromised by this dual political register," especially where local and provincial mobilization drew on Hindu symbols, rituals, and the Hindi language.[10] Enduring tensions over the place of Hindus in the Indian nation can be found even in the early days of India's most prominent secular political party.

This is not to say that Congress was a "communal" party: it explicitly and repeatedly invoked national principles of a particular form of secularism. But when its supporters sought to build support, life grew far more complicated. Hindu symbols and appeals became fused to the INC in certain places and periods even as early as the 1890s, an early precursor of similar local dynamics in the 1920s and 1930s.[11] However, this tendency must be distinguished from the Hindu nationalist position that would emerge: "None of these [traditionalist] leaders advocated an exclusively Hindu nation, they envisioned an Indian nation as a balanced alliance between distinct and self-conscious cultural communities."[12]

The INC sought to stake out the position that "the Indian nation was to be defined according to the territorial criterion, not on the basis of cultural features: it encompassed all those who happened to live within the borders of British India."[13] In the face of these tensions, by the 1910s INC elites sought "to steer a course between an open commitment to a Hindu community/nation that could generate considerable popular support but also endless violence, and continued cooperation with a Muslim leadership that remained skeptical toward the intentions of Congress."[14] Yet after efforts to work with both the British and League during World War I, "by the second decade of the twentieth century, the idea of a nation became a dominant force in Indian politics" and after the turn of the century "a new political language was clearly coming into being."[15]

The Congress under Colonialism

Mahatma Gandhi offered a new strategic approach in 1919–20. He introduced both a new idiom of politics and array of organizational strategies for mass mobilization. Gandhi pushed for large-scale protests that could move challenges to the British out of the realm of elite bargaining. Ideological projects were explicitly being built, compared, and attacked in this period: "The two decades before independence are a cornucopia of rival and competing conceptions of citizenship,"[16] and "the 1920s was a period in which the divergent visions of the Indian nation, which since the turn of the century had cohabited under the slogan of 'swaraj' (self-rule), now developed into competing nationalist discourses. These competing visions all tried to address the most pertinent question of the day, namely, the relation between cultural communities and the question of which community the Indian nation was going to belong to."[17]

Language was a daunting question in a country with numerous regional languages, the presence of English an administrative link language, and battles in north India over Hindi, Urdu, and Hindustani. Given the primacy of language in many understandings of nationalism, it would seem odd to have a nation without a national language. Indeed, Hindu nationalists and Hindi supporters (not the same thing) explicitly argued that without Hindi to bind India together, national integrity could not be assured.[18] In a crucial innovation, the Congress decided that linguistic diversity could be preserved without undermining the imagined community: it was "forced to look for unity of India in terms other than religious or linguistic unity."[19] After 1920 Congress worked on the basic of linguistic province units.[20] Strategically, this also allowed the INC to reach across India, including into non-Hindi speaking regions that might otherwise be averse to signing onto the movement. The INC's multilingual posture was a mix of deeply considered principled commitment and instrumental coalition building.

Nehru recognized that "the cultural form of Indian nationalism must be different from the European norm" while "Gandhi was also receptive to claims of linguistic diversity, which he considered fully compatible with civic nationalism."[21] This "historical debate around language was therefore critical to the ideological formation of Indianness and the Indian nation," delinking a single dominant national language from the idea of India.[22] Powerful proponents of Hindi remained, both in and out of the Congress, but the 1928 Nehru Report— "the first major Indian effort to draft a constitutional framework for the country"[23]—explicitly outlined a multilingual polity in which provinces would be reorganized along linguistic lines. This move "foreshadowed many provisions of the Indian constitution."[24] As Ayres argues, English proved a valuable link language that could sidestep key questions about the overlap between language and nation for the Congress, pushing it in a radically different direction than either the ethno-linguistic nationalisms from below that we see in Ceylon and Burma or the unusual religious-linguistic emphasis on Urdu from above that the Muslim League advanced.[25] The territorial, universalizing nature of the Congress project did not evoke a "true" nation surrounded by guests or interlopers.

It is important not to read history too far backward: powerful pro-Hindi sentiments existed in north India, and even those INC leaders who were comfortable with English and linguistic diversity assumed that Hindi would eventually, naturally assume a de facto pride of place. But the explicit decisions in the 1920s to accept linguistic heterogeneity and to organize political mobilization at least in part along language lines were enshrined both in doctrine and in practice: it committed Congress to granting legitimacy to demands made along linguistic lines.

A far more challenging, and never fully resolved, question arose in this period around the political implications of religious mobilization: "Unlike the settlement of the relation between the regional and national identities, that between the national and religious identities remained deeply contentious."[26] Most vexing was how to deal with the fact of the Hindu majority. Here we see a difference within the Congress between elites who feared Hindu majoritarianism, on the one hand, and those who were far more comfortable with a dominant place for claims advanced on the basis of Hindus, on the other. I borrow Jaffrelot's distinction between the Nehruvian modernizers who expected religious cleavages in general to soon fade after independence, and the Congress "traditionalists" who saw themselves as noncommunal but who believed that it was appropriate for a Hindu majority country to be influenced by Hindu interests and symbols.[27] Gandhi, for instance, mobilized religious imagery to assist with mass outreach and mobilization.

There was substantial consensus, by contrast, around the "Muslim question" by the late 1920s. Pandey argues that "in the eyes of advocates of a composite Indian nationalism, led by the Indian National Congress, communalism (which here refers to a condition of suspicion, fear, and conflict between people belonging to different religious denominations) had in the years after the First World War become the most important political problem to be overcome in the struggle against British colonialism."[28] This cleavage was seen to undermine the prospects for a powerful, unified future nation-state: "The question of 'communalism' touched on fundamental issues of nationalist construction."[29]

Communalism became the "other" against which the Congress arrayed itself, a disreputable and disintegrative tendency that the INC linked to the British, the Muslim League, and some princely state leaders. Nehru was a central figure in the Congress' articulation of the polity: he "attempted to position the party in a way that was completely at odds with what he described as 'communal' organisations. His view of organisations like the Hindu Mahasabha and Muslim League was based on the principle that they were politically reactionary as a result of their limited social bases."[30] He viewed Jinnah's demands for a Muslim homeland "with horror and shock."[31] This resistance to communalism was central to a broader project of nationalist imagining: "Nehru and many leftists in the 1930s developed the idea of the Indian nation as an abstract, modern (synthetic) ideal that could transcend older identifications with community and caste by relegating them to the realm of the irrational and premodern, and eventually render them irrelevant."[32] In Chatterjee's influential formulation, Nehru engaged in an "entirely novel ideological reconstruction of the elements of nationalist thought."[33]

On the question of the relationship between Hinduism and Indian nationalism, however, the politics within Congress were much more divided. The Nehruvian faction was influential: "For Congressmen like Nehru this ideology [Hindu nationalism]—like that of the Muslim League or of Sikh separatists—had nothing to do with nationalism,"[34] while "from the 1930s onward, Hindu nationalism was declared by the leaders of Congress to be out of keeping with an Indian definition of nationality . . . the Congress party promoted a definition of Indian nationality that was based on a composite notion of culture."[35] Nehru in 1938, for instance, argued that "what is called the religious or communal problem is really a dispute among upper-class people for a divisions of the spoils of office or of representation in a legislature."[36]

This was not the only powerful view, however. Congressmen who disagreed with Nehru did *not* seek the *Hindu rashtra* of the Hindu nationalist movement, but they did view Hinduism as naturally part of an Indian nationalism.[37] As Jaffrelot argues, "The Congress contained several variants of nationalism and that proposed by the party's Hindu traditionalists, who also considered that Hindu values and customs should be fostered, resembled Hindu nationalism in certain respects."[38] Many Congressmen deployed Hindu symbols as they attempted to mobilize the masses: "Congress propaganda, especially at lower levels, had also been far from consistently secular—Ram-Rajya, after all, was not a concept with much meaning or attraction for Muslims" and "the meaning of secularism, even in relation to the Indian National Congress, became ambivalent at these [district and town/city] levels."[39]

A powerful cadre of INC saw the biggest challenge to the INC project arising from Muslim separatists, with Hindu nationalists a secondary concern. As a result, "if top Congress leaders in the late-1930s now insisted more than ever before on the need for secularism, their attitudes were by no means universally shared or sincerely implemented, lower down in the party hierarchy or even by all Congress ministers."[40] This disjuncture found expression when the Congress took power at the provinces in 1937: "Despite its national and multi-class ideals, Congress as a ruling party found it almost impossible to go on pleasing Hindus and Muslims, landlords and peasants, or businessmen and workers at the same time."[41] Traditionalists were key provincial players, and their heated competition with the Muslim League fueled growing communal divisions that the Congress was unable to overcome. This situation left space even within Congress for future challenges along this dimension—Nehru, as we will see, emerged triumphant after independence, but his victory did not eliminate either Hindu traditionalism or nationalism in the broader political system and society.

Redistribution was the final key dimension that would become relevant to armed politics after independence. Congress staked out a position that allowed much more space for the Left than many other eventual regimes in Asia, but it also identified clear "red lines" beyond which leftist redistributive and revolutionary demands would become unacceptable. This commitment did not derive from a specific class commitment: "If the new Indian proletariat was thus quite far from being an unequivocal bearer of any 'modern' ideology, the same comment seems to apply even more to the emerging Indian capitalist class" and "no unambiguous link can be drawn between class interests and party politics."[42]

The Indian Left was fractured by the 1930s. The Communist Party of India (CPI) emerged in the mid-1920s and began to stake out a distinct space from the Congress.[43] Within the Congress, left-wing factions evolved, including the Congress Socialist Party (CSP), a more radical leftism led by Subhas Chandra Bose, and Nehruvians who attempted to straddle different parts of the party. Even these factions were heterogeneous, making the consolidation of a clear Left line impossible: radicals on the Left "never came to wield the influence they could have exercised had they stayed together" while "Communists pulled along in isolation" (though they would mount a Popular Front in the late 1930s).[44]

Arrayed against the Left within the Congress were industrialists and merchants who "were strong opponents . . . of anything that smacked of social revolution. Gandhi, so Ambalal Sarabhai once remarked, was the best guarantee against communism which India possessed."[45] This was because Gandhi's particular economic viewpoint was not readily compatible with the historical materialism of the Left. This combination of Gandhian economics with the power of right-wing INC leaders, including people like Sardar Patel, explains the "basic conservatism" of the 1928 Nehru Report's framers on question of property and redistribution.[46]

This left the real battle within the INC between Nehru, the Congress Socialist Party, and the right wing. As on the religious question, the Congress ended up adopting a stance that blended Nehru's interests with those of the traditionalist right: this would account for what Chatterjee calls India's "passive revolution."[47] Despite a left tilt in 1935–36, "in the end the Right within the Congress was able to skillfully and effectively ride and indeed utilize the storm."[48] In turn, Nehru and his socialist bloc within the party (especially those on the Congress Working Committee) were able to articulate a socialist vision that would place the state at the center of an industrializing, modernizing project—but one that favored national elites, could be compatible with existing industrial interests, and at least nominally placed modernity, technocracy, and the factory ahead of revolution, the countryside, or the nonindustrial.

The intra-Congress bargain allowed a role for left-wing politics within the Congress and an acceptance of nonviolent communism outside the Congress, but with the substantial protection of private property and economic elite power.[49] Communism was not at all integral to any understanding of Indian nationalism—a key part of anticommunist mobilization in the 1930s and 1940s was painting the CPI as a tool of the Soviet Union rather than as an organization grounded in indigenous politics. The CPI would therefore enter independence viewed as tolerable but with goals in serious tension with the Congress project.

World War II saw Congress leaders imprisoned and the movement targeted for repression by the British, a result of both opposition to the Viceroy's unilateral involvement of India in the war in 1939 and the Quit India movement of 1942. Its key leaders spent much of the war in jail. Yet during this period it became increasingly clear that Britain's ability and will to maintain the status quo were slipping away. The Congress High Command by the elections of 1945–46 was ready to press its case for power. In doing so, it articulated a set of clear demands: it opposed separate electorates along religious lines, demanded the option of appointing Muslims as INC representatives, and favored a centralized state rather than some form of weak-center "grouping" scheme. It aggressively criticized League communalism; instead of religious cleavages, the INC Election Manifesto of 1946 explicitly proposed "such territorial areas or provinces should be constituted, as far as possible, on a linguistic and cultural basis."[50]

We can see in Jawaharlal Nehru's writing and speeches tenets of Congress nationalism.[51] The communal question that haunted Congress could be sidestepped in favor of secularism by Nehru because "once these premises of the national state were granted there could not exist a 'communal' problem any more."[52] Key aspects of the Congress ideological project had been agreed on: linguistic reorganization was in principle acceptable (if not necessarily desirable on administrative and economic grounds), the Left was to be accommodated but the far Left purged, and tribal peoples were seen as a distinct social category worthy of special treatment.

The key remaining tension, which would never be decisively settled, was the Hindu-Muslim question. The particular brand of secular nationalism that Nehru advanced was not hegemonic: "It was not clear in the mid-1940s that Nehru's sketches for a future India would survive either the 'leftist' politics of Bose and his allies (not to mention the communist insurgencies in Bengal and Telengana), or the conservative political instincts of Patel and his many supporters."[53]

The Hindu-Muslim violence that occurred in the run-up to independence brought to the fore tensions about the relationship between Hinduism and nationalism that divided Nehruvian and traditionalist Congressmen: "Confronted by [violence in] Calcutta, Noakhali, Bihar, and Punjab, the secular ideals of many within the Congress ranks and leadership tended to evaporate."[54] This was true even at the very highest summits of the INC: while Nehru "was not inclined to give the Sangh the benefit of the doubt,"[55] Sardar Patel had greater sympathy for the broad strands of Hindu traditionalism. These basic strands of both consensus and debate formed the Congress ideological project moving into independence.

A Path Not (Yet) Taken: The Hindu Nationalist Movement

The Congress was split over the relationship of Hinduism to nationalism, but its "traditionalists" were not members of the Hindu nationalist movement. The alternative nationalist approach was "constructed as an ideology between the 1870s and 1920s" on the basis of Hindu revivalist and reformist organizations.[56] Hindu nationalism was given particular further spur by the rise of the Muslim League, which was seen as a looming threat that needed to be met by a unified Hindu nation.[57] This was a new construction: indeed, the influential thinker Vinayak Damodar Savarkar "learnt what nationalism was from western experiments and then tried to apply this imported concept to his own country, a process that relied on a new construction of nationalism."[58]

While the Hindu nationalist movement was never the exclusive domain of a single organization, the Rashtriya Swayamsevak Sangh (RSS) took on increasing prominence from its founding in the 1920s. Hindu nationalists more explicitly and aggressively sought to define nationalism along religious lines: "In these ideological constructions, there was little space for notions of plurality, either social or religious, and so evidence of fissiparous tendencies along those lines could not be easily accommodated."[59] For V. D. Savarkar, "to be free, Hindus would have to do more than merely acquire geographical control over the territory of British India—they would need to construct a state that could protect and nourish their particular identity" and as a consequence they believed that Congress "had committed a fundamental error in disregarding the religious, racial, and cultural unity that was essential to the forming of a nation."[60] Savarkar's "defining analytic maneuver . . . was to frame the question of nationhood in terms of identity. He thereby forced the question of which identity, which group, would be recognized as belonging in the Indian context."[61] This led to the subordination of non-Hindus, not necessarily exclusion—this is where hierarchies need to join our analysis of boundaries.[62]

The basic vision of Hindutva thinkers was to be a "nation of Hindus," with Christians and Muslims being guests or second-class citizens.[63] For the 1940s RSS leader M. S. Golwalkar, "religious minorities were required . . . to owe allegiance to Hindu symbols of identity because these were the embodiment of the Hindu nation."[64] It "developed an alternative political culture to the dominant idiom in Indian politics" both in rejection of nonviolence and "because it rejected the Gandhian conception of the Indian nation."[65] Unlike the Hindu Mahasabha, the RSS avoided direct party politics, seeking a cultural transformation prior to a direct entry into competition against the Congress.

This stance resembles that of Sinhalese nationalists in Ceylon at a similar period, but the RSS was far better organized and politically sophisticated. It advanced "one of several contingent outcomes of a protracted struggle over the definition of Indian nationhood."[66] The fact that it did not build a hegemonic movement prior to independence was obviously of enormous importance, but did not mean that it would drop away in independent India. The Hindu Mahasabha faded as a major political force over the course of the 1930s and 1940s, but the RSS carefully cultivated an alternative political common sense, an ideology of the polity that sought to redefine what an Indian nation would be with very different boundaries and hierarchies than that of the Congress. This alternative ideological project haunted Nehru following 1947, and it carved out a resilient niche in India's politics. The RSS continued its work of social transformation, while the movement's party (the Bharatiya Jana Sangh, BJS; later the Bharatiya Janata Party, BJP) would eventually capture the commanding heights of the state.

Regimes and Ideological Projects after Independence

Congress became India's ruling party at independence. It immediately had to grapple with an extraordinary variety of challenges. The two key players in crafting the basic goals and structures of the state in this period were Sardar Patel and Jawaharlal Nehru. After Patel's death in late 1950, Nehru would become the preeminent policymaker. Though Nehru and Patel disagreed on some issues—including the question of Hindu mobilization—they also overlapped on foundational questions about how the new Indian nation should be constructed.[67]

Nehru's primacy was a contested and contingent outcome that signaled only temporary victory for his strand of Congress nationalism, rather than a decisive hegemony over Indian politics. Nevertheless, this victory set the course of Indian internal security policy for decades. Crucially for methodological purposes, the early years of Indian independence saw primarily unarmed mobilization along different cleavages that provide insights into threat perception *prior* to actual armed politics. There was a scattered communist insurgency in the late 1940s alongside independence. But even the onset of Naga revolt in 1955–56 was preceded by years of Naga demand making and policy formulation in Delhi. The waves of armed politics I discuss later in this chapter all lay almost a decade or more into the future after independence.

In line with Walter, I find that the Indian leadership cared about building a reputation—but the reputations they sought to build differed dramatically *across* issue areas, leading to a pattern of policy inconsistent with Walter's argument about how regimes crack down hard on early separatist movements.[68] Accommodation with explicit Muslim and Sikh religious separatism (armed or unarmed) was seen as unacceptable, falling into the ideologically opposed category. By sharp contrast, linguistic and tribal demands could be negotiated, within bounds, making groups mobilizing these demands fall in the gray zone. The Left was not seen as an existential threat but could not be allowed free rein. Yet even armed manifestations were seen as a gray zone that could plausibly be incorporated and bargained with: there was plenty of space for the hard Left to come in from the cold. Hindu nationalist organizations were generally seen as problematic by Delhi's Congress elite in this period of Nehruvian dominance.

A wide range of theoretically plausible options were radically narrowed by the ideological commitments of key leaders. What seems retrospectively obvious, natural, and unproblematic was in fact a radically new and innovative project. For all of Congress' rhetoric about decolonization marking the reemergence of a deep, historically rooted idea of India, its leaders were very well aware that they were engaged in the creation of their own conception of state and nation.[69] According to Khosla, in the eyes of India's founders, "A hallmark of modernity was the idea that one's political universe could be constructed: it was neither natural nor inherited," and "to have frozen interests was to be apolitical, for it was to presume that certain interests were fixed and outside the realm of politics."[70] They intentionally sought to construct a new political universe.

Patel and Nehru began their state-consolidating task with several key commitments in mind that reflected the Congress' explanation for and critique of colonialism and partition. In Patel's words, "It is the lesson of history that it was owing to the country's politically fragmented condition and our inability to take a united stand that India succumbed to successive waves of invaders . . . we cannot afford to fall into those errors or traps again."[71] As Nehru wrote in 1949, without a strong Congress "we shall then have separatisms in every form, provincialism, communalism, apart from all kinds of splinter groups sailing under the name of socialism and communism."[72]

The most fundamental, dangerous cleavage that new state elites perceived was the communal divide among Hindus, Muslims, and Sikhs—Varshney refers to the Hindu-Muslim cleavage as a core of modern Indian politics.[73] The politics of religion dominated regime leaders' fears of the future and perceptions of threat. There was strong consensus that Muslim and Sikh political mobilization could completely undo Congress' ideological project. To be clear, demands for cultural space were different—it was instead political demands on explicit religious grounds by these groups could not be accommodated. Patel argued that that "it is equally dangerous to form a party or to lay down a programme on a religious basis. It would not pay. Now that the country got its freedom for anybody to say that any religion is in danger is a very dangerous precedent to set up,"[74] while Nehru wrote to the state chief ministers that "I should like to repeat that the danger to us is not so much external as internal. Reactionary forces and communal organisations are trying to disrupt the structure of free India."[75]

One initial indication of how the regime was perceiving threat can be found in its views of Sikh agitation in the Punjab (by the Akali Dal, a Sikh party), which Congress leaders believed was intended to build a religious component into the Constitution and thus the basic structure of the new polity. Nehru and Patel clearly saw this as a fundamental challenge that needed to be dealt with aggressively. He wrote to Patel on February 8, 1949: "The Akalis are bent on trouble and are dragging the refugees and RSS people in their wake. Open challenges are being made. . . . it is clear that a major crisis is ahead," while Patel in response to Nehru made sure to note that "we will not allow such a religious gathering [Akali conference planned to be in Delhi] to be turned into a political gathering."[76] The state was laying down its cordon sanitaire.

History weighed heavily on these assessments. For instance, Patel, in a letter to Nehru in May 1949, explicitly linked contemporary postindependence politics to the disaster of Partition:

> We have seen, and indeed have had bitter experience of past policies which have divided and separated India in the name of helping a particular community. You are well aware of the terrible result that has flowed from this policy, and it would be extreme folly on our part if we did not profit from this experience . . . perpetuation of communal or separatist tendencies by means of constitutional provisions, in particular, has cost India a great deal in valuable human lives, in property and in national interests. We must, therefore, avoid at all costs encouraging any communal or separatist tendencies and try to eradicate them from people's hearts and minds.[77]

Nehru in turn, to the chief ministers, wrote in November 1947 of the "disastrous results of the evil policy followed by the Muslim League and the Pakistanis during the last few years. All of us are fully aware of it and we have seen the consequence of it. We have to continue to be vigilant, for the consequences of that evil policy have not exhausted themselves yet."[78] The Constituent Assembly "abolished the statutory basis of communalism," institutionalizing resistance to mobilization along religious cleavage—and especially to the kinds of minority electorates that had been so prominent in the colonial period.[79]

State elites cracked down preventively on nonviolent Sikh mobilization, trying to set a clear precedent for future interactions over Sikh religious politics. Threat perception here clearly, and by far, preceded the armed Sikh mobilization of the late 1970s. Patel wrote to Baldev Singh on the Sikh issue in 1948: "It is quite clear that the Constitution cannot be disfigured by provisions which we conceive are opposed to the very principles or which we feel would be inappropriate in a permanent measure of that kind. The demands are at best temporary; the Constitution is intended to exist for all time."[80] At a most fundamental level, Patel justified the March 1949 detention of Sikh leader Master Tara Singh because "he wanted to destroy what we wish to construct."[81]

On December 6, 1948, Nehru wrote of Sikh mobilization in east Punjab that "claims are made which go completely counter to our declared policy and which are based entirely on an acceptance of communalism."[82] He linked this set of religious-political demands to the broader question of the relationship between Indian nationalism and the state's relationship to society: "On this question of principle in regard to introducing communalism in our constitutional structure there is going to be no compromise and no giving in on our part. That is exactly what led to Pakistan and all the trouble that followed."[83]

Resistance to Sikh mobilization continued into the 1950s and 1960s. Nehru wrote of the Sikhs and SGPC elections in December 1954 that "it is a very great concern of all of us how far communal and separatist tendencies grow in this country . . . they represent a mentality which has no place today in India and which can only lead to evil results."[84] Nehru linked Sikh religious politics to the much-hated Muslim League: "With communalism, casteism and other separatist tendencies, we can make no compromise . . . the activities of the Akali Dal and its leaders are singularly like those of the Muslim League."[85] In the 1960s, Sikh political demands simply would not be countenanced on religious grounds; as Brass shows, only once they became at least nominally based on language, not religion, could a division of Punjab be conceded.[86]

These essential precepts, with more visceral fear, guided responses to the Muslim question. Patel represents a harder-line version, in which Muslim loyalties were to be doubted and needed to be proved.[87] In 1949, he publicly stated that "the Government does not expect from the Muslim anything more than what it demands from other communities, namely a complete and unquestioned loyalty to their State,"[88] while in correspondence with Nehru, Patel wrote, "As regards Muslims, I entirely agree with you as to the dangerous possibilities inherent in the presence in India of a section of disloyal elements. Here also, we are taking such measures as we can consistent with the needs of security and the secular nature of our State."[89] In a speech to students in Nagpur in 1948, Patel argued that "the real danger inside lies in our disunity. What poison has been spread in the past by communalism, you should not forget."[90]

For Nehru, the path to building the right kind of nation was to equally protect all religions, rather than focusing on Muslims. Yet he too feared the disintegrative potential of Muslim separatism, which he had battled so vociferously under the Raj. Nehru linked the Kashmir question to the broader Muslim question in India; Kashmir must be held as a proof that India could be a multireligious polity. Kashmir came to stand, in Nehru's mind, for the very idea of India: of other countries watching Kashmir issues, he wrote, "They follow them in order to judge of what India stands for and is going to be."[91] This forged the political basis for Delhi's broadly consistent Kashmir policy across governments: its fusion to the idea of the nation was complete by the end of the first India-Pakistan war of 1947–49.[92]

Nehru perceived a severe threat from the RSS as well, which is why communal cleavages writ large were so important to him. Of the group, he writes, "In fact their ideology strikes at the root of our constitution, present and future."[93] Of Hindu mobilization in Jammu in 1952–53, he writes in January 1953 that "even apart from the effect on Jammu or Kashmir, this agitation is so basically communal and opposed to our policy that to *surrender to it in any way would mean a complete reversal of the all-India policy that we have pursued*. So long as the present Government of India is functioning, this cannot happen."[94] Of such Hindu nationalist organizations he wrote in 1951 that "essentially their appeal is more dangerous for India's future, because it is insidious, than many other appeals, coming from obviously dangerous quarters."[95]

The "rules" that Brass identified thus have their roots in the colonial and immediately postcolonial period of state building; they are products of India's political history.[96] Nehru succinctly summed up this approach: "It is clear that we cannot tolerate communalism or accept any demand which is so totally opposed to our general policy."[97] These cleavages remained Nehru's greatest concern well into independence—"And yet in our thinking and action we are often influenced by the communal outlook. That way danger lies. I have been more troubled by this than any other matter in India."[98] In 1959, he wrote of communal incidents, "There is nothing more dangerous for the future of India than the communal approach."[99]

Ideological considerations were of course not the only factors weighing on the Indian policy-making elite. International politics, elections, functional needs to restore basic order, and economic incentives all influenced state policy. But the weight of the past carried through to perceptions of political acceptability and threat: "We in India have the ghost of Pakistan coming in the way of our normal activities. Behind that ghost, there lies the history not only of the past ten years of freedom, but also of the years that preceded it, with all the communal bitterness and hatred which resulted in the partition of India."[100]

By comparison, tribal issues had not remotely attracted major attention during the nationalist movement, whether in the Northeast or in areas of central India that are now the states of Jharkhand and Chhattisgarh. Yet a set of debates in the Constituent Assembly carved out a special place for tribals: these communities were portrayed (often in a deeply patronizing way) as oppressed, downtrodden communities. The Sixth Schedule of the Indian Constitution provided local autonomy and land rights, as well as concessions over mining revenue sharing.[101] In the cases of a number of groups in the Northeast, tribe and language became intertwined or overlapping, so some of these actors fell under the Sixth Schedule, while others were handled through other institutional mechanisms.

The earliest tribal challenge emerged in the Naga Hills on India's far Northeast, where the Naga National Council (NNC) and its army pursued independence from India starting in 1955–56. Yet we have evidence on Delhi's views of the question *prior* to armed politics emerging. The Naga question thus provides a crucial case of state policy toward ethno-tribal separatism prior to insurgency. The NNC emerged as a nonviolent political force in 1946, trying to determine the status of Nagas within the new state of India. In 1946, Nehru told a senior Naga leader that he would be happy for the Nagas to have autonomy, but that independence was out of the question. Though disputes remain about the nature of the interaction between governor of Assam Akbar Hydari and NNC leaders in 1947, the response they later received from national political leaders was that autonomy was the best they could hope for. This is not surprising: central governments rarely are open to secession.

But openness to autonomy and political concessions clearly differed from contemporary perceptions of religious minority mobilization. For instance, Nehru wrote in 1951 that "it is obvious that the Nagas or any tribes on our borders cannot have independence. But we are very anxious to give them a large measure of autonomy and to help them in every way, while respecting their traditions and ways of life. I am personally an admirer of the Nagas and I like many of their fine qualities."[102] Nehru wrote of the Sixth Schedule that it "was a very wise provision. It is quite essential that these tribal people should be given the largest possible measure of local autonomy."[103]

Leaders of the then-undivided state of Assam had little interest in granting any concessions, Delhi had other things to worry about, and no progress was made. The Northeast, especially its tribal hills, was extremely peripheral to Indian politics.[104] So the Naga conflict began to escalate, eventually turning into armed revolt in 1955–56. But the evidence from before 1956 shows that the Congress regime considered tribal mobilization an acceptable form of politics—insurgency was instead the result of central apathy and Assamese resistance rather than resulting from a hard-line anticoncession stance.[105] There were established mechanisms within the Constitution for managing this kind of demand making, even prior to the onset of the actual rebellion, and in sharp contrast to the communal question.

We see similar accommodation of language. Paul Brass famously identified how Delhi responds to demands for new subnational states: never on openly religious grounds, and on language grounds only when there is substantial support from the region in question.[106] India's leaders were very conscious that their initial policy decisions were setting enormous precedents and that ideological guideposts were necessary to guide these choices. For instance, Nehru wrote to Patel of linguistic politics that "I think the safest way to consider this question is on the basis of some principles which we wish to apply to all India."[107] This was not a series of ad hoc decisions but instead deeply considered strategy.

Congress' articulation of the nation explicitly included space for multiple languages from 1920 onward. These decisions about multilingualism would be repeatedly referred to and invoked in the late 1940s, as legitimating pillars of the INC project.[108] The precise linguistic structure of the future state was unclear at independence. Two issues presented themselves. First, what would be the national language/s? Second, how, if at all, would states be reorganized along linguistic lines? Over the course of their deliberations, the Constituent Assembly reached a temporary compromise on the issue of national language, letting Hindi and English coexist for the time being, though with an expectation of eventual Hindi dominance. In this compromise, it became clear that "the large majority of the Assembly believed that the use of many Indian languages and of English was compatible with national unity and with the evolution of a national spirit."[109]

The Congress high command was skeptical of rapid and far-reaching linguistic reorganization for fear of administrative bloat, inefficiency, and the weakening of the central power that was seen as necessary for spurring rapid industrialization and economic growth. Yet this was not a matter of unalterable principle; instead, it acknowledged that linguistic politics were acceptable, but that the timing was wrong to engage in substantial reorganization. Nehru wrote in 1948, for instance, that "the demand for provincial redistribution and rectification of provincial boundaries is a perfectly legitimate demand and must claim attention" but needs to wait for functional/logistical reasons.[110] The contrast with minority religious claim making is striking.

Ultimately, after intense debate, an opening was created for linguistic reorganization of states. In Austin's words: "The Constitution has been accepted as the charter of Indian unity. Within its limits are held the negotiations over the workings of the federal system. The realignment of state boundaries on linguistic lines was done within its definition of Indian nationalism."[111] Nehru explicitly articulated general "rules" to guide the application of this division: "(1) that decisions can only be largely by consent and cannot be imposed by a majority over a minority, (2) that every language should be given full scope and, in our Services, nothing should be done which puts a person from a non-Hindi area at a disadvantage."[112] The contrast with Pakistan and Urdu's supremacy or Ceylon/Sri Lanka and Sinhala linguistic dominance is very striking. Linguistic and tribal mobilization, therefore, were located in the ideological gray zone in Delhi's eyes.

It is more difficult to precisely locate leftist armed mobilization on the ideological spectrum, for two reasons. First, there were multiple views of the Left within the government and multiple forms of the Left outside of government. Second, a scattered leftist insurgency emerged concurrent with independence that limits the "distance" between measuring ideological perception and actual state responses. I suggest that armed leftist mobilization against the state was broadly, though not universally, seen as *primarily* a gray zone affair—the violent Left would need to be contained, but key elements of its demands could be negotiated short of regime overthrow. There was space in mainstream politics within which to incorporate leftist, even formally Communist, tides in ways that were distinctly absent in much of noncommunist Asia at the same time.[113]

Patel and Nehru differed in their views of the severity of the threat from the Left. Patel saw the Left as a more worrisome force than Nehru: he leaned to the right and found favor with India's capitalist class. Even Patel, however, saw a place for leftist movements in the mainstream: "We do not interfere in their open activities. We do not interfere so long as they are working for the uplift of labour or the peasant. But if they invite labour to violence, we have to deal with them firmly. Their object has been to create dislocation and disruption. We cannot allow the breakdown of Government or organized machinery by force or coercion . . . it is generally left to the Provinces to deal with them with the guidance of the Centre."[114] There was a pathway to the mainstream: "There are some people who say Communism should be banned. But we do not do it except in some provinces like Madras where we are forced to do it. We do not want to ban them all over India because we still want to allow them a free field if they want to take to constitutional methods. But if they do not adopt constitutional methods, then they have no place at the polls or in the field of liberty . . . do not start the hoax of Communism or communalism."[115]

Nehru's rhetoric about the hard Left was very different than on the communal groups he was so worried about: "If they wanted to spread the ideology of communism, they were welcome to do so, provided there was no violence about. It must be remembered that the Communist Party has not been declared illegal in India, except in Western Bengal. We have tried to avoid taking any steps restricting the functioning of organisations except when we were forced to, as in regard to some communal organisations."[116] He was careful to explain that banning was only the result of violence, not ideology: "We should try to keep apart the violence and sabotage part of the Communist Party's programme in India from their normal ideological approach. That is to say our action against the Communist Party members is because they indulge in violence and sabotage and openly say so in their circulars, etc., and not because they hold certain opinions."[117] Indeed, "I should like to repeat here that this banning is entirely due to the violent activities of the Communist Party. It has nothing to do with ideology or theory."[118] As the Communist Party of India abandoned the revolutionary road, Nehru largely welcomed its incorporation.[119] It is difficult to imagine him writing so positively of explicitly Hindu or Muslim communal groups.

Stability and Change over Time after Independence: The Rise of Hindu Nationalism

These basic foundations of the Congress project were laid by Nehru. There was not dramatic movement on *most* of these dimensions in the governments that came after the founding period of India as a nation-state. Following Nehru's death in 1964 and that of his successor, Lal Bahadur Shastri, in 1966, Nehru's daughter Indira Gandhi came to power. While Prime Minister Gandhi tilted more to the left along the redistributive dimension, internal threat perception did not radically change. Mrs. Gandhi continued to worry about communal cleavages, was willing to bargain over tribal/linguistic mobilization, and drew a clear distinction between the parliamentary and antiparliamentary Left. These basic foundations did not shift radically even after the Congress lost its dominance in 1989.

Yet one dimension did see substantial, and hugely consequential, change in the decades after Nehru's death. The Hindu nationalist movement, anchored by the RSS as a social movement and the BJS/BJP as a political party, had been sidelined at independence but endured as an ideological alternative, even in its moments of political irrelevance.[120] Despite electoral marginalization, the organization continued to train cadres and articulate a worldview in which Congress' secularism was in fact hypocritical appeasement of Muslims, Hindus were disadvantaged relative to religious minorities, and the historical wounds of the Muslim conquests, British colonization, and violent partition had not been addressed.

The communal cleavage that Nehru had worried about in the 1950s returned with a vengeance in the 1980s.[121] The BJP deployed a wide variety of strategies to peel off Hindus from the Congress, cultivating a sense among many Hindus that the Congress catered to Muslim vote banks while disparaging Hindus. The Congress's dalliances with various kinds of religious symbols and appeals made secularism seem like a cynical and opportunistic strategy, especially in the 1980s as the older bases of Congress success began to fray. A combination of riots, mass mobilizations, and new forms of media consumption helped to fuel the BJP's rise, from a near wipeout in the 1984 election to having the first BJP prime minister head a coalition government in 1998.

The BJP's rise has been episodic and at times reversed since the early 1980s. Nevertheless, the party led the government from 1998 to 2004 and then won a pair of landslide election victories in 2014 and 2019 under Narendra Modi, who was chief minister of Gujarat during brutal anti-Muslim pogroms in 2002. The "saffron wave" has swept to power in dramatic fashion.[122] The Modi government has marked the most dramatic reshaping of regime priorities, which existed in a much more attenuated form under Vajpayee's rule from 1998 to 2004.

Vaishnav summarizes the project as of 2019: "Proponents of Hindu nationalism believe that Hinduism—not the precarious balancing of all ethnic and religious communities residing in India—is the ultimate source of the country's identity" and "the BJP espouses a distinct worldview that intrinsically favors one religious community—Hindus—over all others."[123] For Varshney:

> The Hindu nationalist claim is not that Muslims ought to be excluded from the Indian nation. While that may be the position of Hindu extremists, the generic Hindu nationalist argument is that to become part of the Indian nation, Muslims must agree to the following: 1) accept the centrality of Hinduism to Indian civilization; 2) acknowledge key Hindu figures such as Ram as civilizational heroes, and not regard them as mere religious figures of Hinduism; 3) accept that Muslim rulers in various parts of India (between roughly 1000 to 1857) destroyed the pillars of Hindu civilization, especially Hindu Temples; and 4) make no claims to special privileges such as the maintenance of religious personal laws, nor demand special state grants for their educational institutions. They must assimilate, not maintain their distinctiveness. Through *Ekya* (assimilation), they will prove their loyalty to the nation.[124]

This is where my discussion of hierarchies within an ideological project in chapter 1 becomes important: Muslims can be part of the nation, but they will be an intrinsically suspect category who can win the tolerance of Hindus by acknowledging the cultural and political dominance of the Hindu majority.

Some dimensions of the Congress project have not dramatically changed in the BJP's project. The BJP's nationalist project grudgingly made its peace with multilingualism despite a marked preference for Hindi, as it has faced the need to expand from its Hindi belt redoubts into non-Hindi speaking areas. The movement has prioritized Hindu over Hindi mobilization. Similarly, the various provisions in the Constitution for tribal categories have not been major targets of the BJP—indeed, the party has moved aggressively into the Northeast and has cultivated tribal mobilization in central India.[125] While the BJP intensely dislikes the Left, it is no more or less sympathetic to Maoist insurgents than the Congress, or for that matter the CPM, which suffered far more under the guns of the insurgent Left. The BJP's nationalist project leaves some core pillars of the Congress threat perception untouched, while dramatically shifting others.

What should we expect from armed politics under BJP rule? We should expect continued repression of religious minority armed groups, as well as repression of unarmed actors the BJP identifies with that religious community, though with a more explicitly communal framing than the Congress' and more open fervor. There should be much less change on the linguistic, tribal, and redistributive dimensions.

Thus, the most important consequence is in how violence linked to Hinduism and Hindu claims for primacy are viewed by BJP governments in Delhi (and in the states). They should be viewed with, at minimum, more tolerance, and at maximum, active favoritism, compared to Congress governments. We should expect less central repression toward them, opening space for more vigilantism and private violence. Hindu-identifying armed actors are likely to be murkily linked to local BJP and RSS organizations, and this is where I expect to find the biggest difference between BJP and Congress governments. For the BJP, Hindu nationalist armed actors are ideologically aligned, even if their value in any given moment hinges on complex calculations about the balance of benefit and backlash from actual use of organized violence.

The ambiguity is that local Hindutva activists are cloaked in deniability that seeks to shield the formal party and organizations from their activities—these are uneasy fits with the armed politics framework, which relies on more clearly defined armed actors in order to measure orders. Nevertheless, a basic expectation is more limited cooperation and alliance with violence linked to Hindu nationalist actors, at whatever level of formal organization, and a harder-line stance toward Muslim political demands.

Armed Politics in India

Based on this historical discussion, I identify five empirical expectations for patterns of state–armed group relations in India. First, under any regime, linguistic and tribal armed groups should be seen as in the gray zone and least likely to face severe repression and the most likely to see incorporation or cooperation. Second, minority religious groups—that is, Muslim and Sikh—should be the most threatening and face the greatest conflict, with the BJP even more intensely repressive than the Congress. Third, leftist groups should lie in between—closer to the gray zone than, for instance, Islamists, but closer to opposed than tribal/linguistic insurgents. Fourth, explicitly intrasystemic armed groups, even if large and violent, should be broadly tolerated. Finally, Hindu nationalist armed groups should receive more repression under Congress than the BJP, and be more likely to see support and collusion under the BJP. There are other dynamics that my armed politics approach cannot accommodate, like the repression of unarmed activists or localized lynchings that have state support; I touch on them in the conclusion.

The quantitative and qualitative data broadly, but not universally, bear out these expectations: we see a more repressive counterinsurgency stance toward the minority-religion rebels of Kashmir and Punjab than the linguistic and tribal rebels of the Northeast, a general tendency toward cooperation with armed parties, and variation in how Hindu-linked armed groups are treated. However, there are also some surprises that defy my theoretical expectations. I first identify broad patterns in armed politics. I spend substantial time discussing civil wars (including both rebel and pro-state groups), which includes the most compelling data, and more briefly survey the murky and incompletely measured world of electoral/communal violence.

We can start with the overall distribution of armed orders in India, both total and then disaggregated between national and state-only. The state-level dyads are idiosyncratic to India—these are situations in which the state government has a major role in interacting with armed groups that is not de facto controlled by Delhi. Moreover, as I noted in chapter 3, the data on armed political parties are quite crude and prone to error or ambiguity, so I exclude state-level and armed party dyads in a number of the analyses below.

The AOSA dataset includes 122 armed groups in India, covering 1,986 dyad-years. The average confidence in the armed order coding is 2.6 on a 1–3 scale, indicating reasonable but not total confidence in the general validity of the data. There are 107 national-level dyads, in which groups are directly interacting with the central government, while an additional 17 are primarily located at the level of the subnational state. Across all years and groups, the average armed order was dead set in the middle of the distribution—2.61 (5 = alliance, 1 = total war). Because using annual data can exaggerate patterns—a thirty-year stretch with one armed group can tilt the distribution dramatically—it worth looking at group-level patterns.

We can now shift to the annual orders data, with the caveat that these are treating individual years as independent observations. Table 4.2 summarizes the overall order-dyad-years, while also disaggregating those that involve interactions with the central government from those between subnational state governments and armed groups. We can immediately see that most of the conflict involves interactions with Delhi, which makes sense given the structure of Indian federalism: the central government is more likely to get involved the more violence there is. There remains quite substantial variation, however, with a third of the dyad-years even in national interactions being some form of cooperation and a similar proportion being conflictual in the state dyads.

TABLE 4.2 Armed orders in India: National versus state

	ALL	NATIONAL ONLY	STATE ONLY
Total war	129 (7%)	115 (9%)	14 (2%)
Containment	975 (49%)	814 (61%)	161 (25%)
Military hostilities	19 (1%)	19 (1 %)	
Limited cooperation	601 (30 %)	347 (26 %)	254 (40%)
Alliance	262 (13 %)	48 (4%)	214 (33%)
Total	1,986	1,343	643

It is commonly accepted that religion is a central cleavage in Indian politics. Figure 4.1 provides an overview of armed orders by the religious identity of armed groups in India, based on the kinds of symbols and demands the groups mobilize. The Northeast is coded as its own category, since the primary demands of mobilizing armed groups fuse religion, language, and tribe in different ways: they tend not to map onto the master religious cleavage and instead are best understand as tribal or linguistic actors. Hindu groups in figure 4.1 primarily refer to Hindutva-oriented parties and private organizations that have been credibly linked to the mobilization of violence. No Religion groups tend to be leftist insurgents or armed political parties that do not explicitly mobilize a distinctive religious cleavage. Muslim and Sikh groups are those are seen by the state to link religion to political demands (the reality has often been far more complicated), and which have often explicitly made that connection. These are obviously crude categorizations that can be recombined in various ways—but they capture an important big picture view of Indian internal security policy. Figure 4.2 then disaggregates between national and state-level dyads to see how politics shift once the central government is less involved and state governments are the dominant state actor.

Most of the patterns in figures 4.1 and 4.2 are as we would expect. There are barely any Hindu-identified groups in total war, and relatively few in the Northeast and "no religion" categories. The "no religion" category bifurcates into two radically different types of actors—when solely dealing with Delhi, this is primarily anti-Naxalite counterinsurgency; when at the state level, there is a split between conflict with Naxalites and then a rich array of cooperation between armed political parties and state governments. The state versus national difference does important work here, and reveals the complexities of armed politics in a federal system like India's. The Northeast is a domain in which Delhi has dominated, and we already see the extensive variation that I will discuss in more detail later.

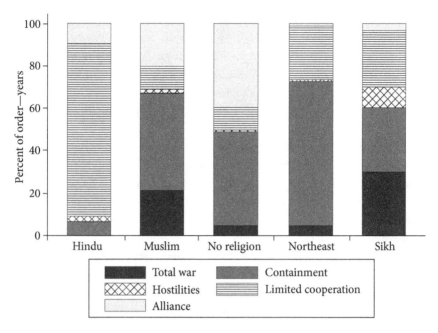

FIGURE 4.1. Armed orders by religion (all groups)

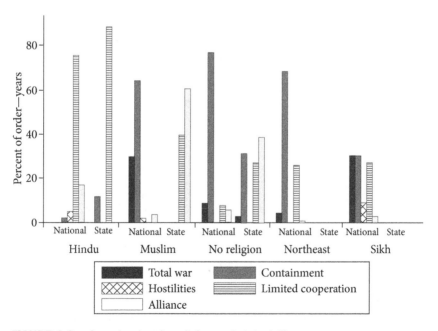

FIGURE 4.2. Armed orders by religion and state (all)

Muslim and Sikh groups are comparatively likely to end up in total war. The wars in Punjab and Kashmir saw religious-linguistic insurgencies for secession, and they involved a dramatically higher proportion of total war than India's other secessionist insurgencies in the Northeast. Delhi was centrally involved in managing these conflicts. A surprise in figure 4.1 is the proportion of Muslim armed actors in alliance orders (N=38). Once we pull apart the state versus national dyads, this becomes clearer. Muslim alliance orders are driven almost entirely (N=34) by the unusual Indian Union Muslim League in Kerala, a political party engaged in Kerala's violent and combative politics that has engaged in state-level alliances (we see this broken out at the state level in figure 4.2). The other Muslim alliance cases (N=4) are the "flipped" Ikhwan pro-state militias in 1990s Kashmir—they abandoned any political claims and worked closely with the state against Kashmiri rebel groups.[126]

The Sikh limited cooperation and alliance cases heavily cluster around a set of 1970s and 1980s Sikh militant groups that only became clear insurgents by the mid-1980s.[127] Indeed, the rise of the Sikh insurgency comes out of an ultimately disastrous strategy on the part of Congress elites to cooperate with the Sikh militant Jarnail Singh Bhindranwale as a way of dividing the Akali Dal, Punjab's main Sikh political party. In this case, limited cooperation eventually flipped over into containment and then total war. This is one of the conflicts that triggered my original interest in armed groups' relations with politics: there was a remarkable political alignment in the late 1970s between mainstream politicians and an ideologically opposed Sikh armed group, an alliance of convenience that bloodily fell apart once the thin instrumental basis of cooperation evaporated by 1984.

Figure 4.3 shows the distribution of armed order-years across categories of self-identification. Mainstream political parties and pro-state actors are unsurprisingly much more cooperative on average, though even here we see variation. Groups in periods in which they identify as anti-state insurgents are substantially more conflictual, but some cooperation still occurs. The final category of "Other" is quite murky and heterogenous, and sees a blend of limited conflict and limited cooperation for the most part: it includes quite a few groups that we might think of as insurgents but who have moderated their posture toward the state despite remaining armed (several Naga groups moved into this category, for instance). If we examine a difference between state- and national-level dyads, we see that many of the alliance orders occurs at the state level, with ruling governments either themselves being or working with armed parties, as in West Bengal or Kerala (other areas show substantial similarities, such as the dominance of containment at both state and national level when fighting groups identifying as insurgents).

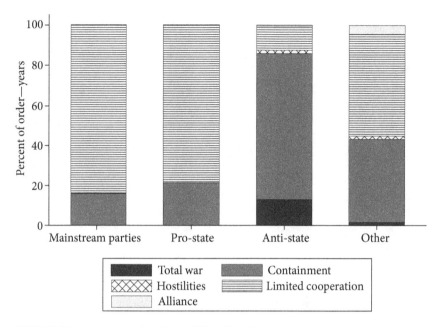

FIGURE 4.3. Armed orders by self-identification

Unsurprisingly, we see a broadly similar pattern when we examine armed group goals, as in figure 4.4 below. These are correlated with but not identical to armed group self-identification. To limit the complexities induced by state-level political parties, here I focus exclusively on national-level dyads. Politics are fundamentally shaping India's armed orders: groups that can find space for autonomy within the terms of the Indian constitution are primarily tribal/linguistic. For historical reasons, this not nearly as much of an option for Sikh and Muslim armed groups; the latter instead end up much more in the independence category and more conflictual relations. Reform-oriented tend to be armed political parties trying to shift policy and power within mainstream politics; they are disproportionately located at the state level and are most prone toward limited cooperation and alliance orders. Central control is primarily leftist insurgents, which meet repression, though there can be important coding ambiguities and overlap with reformist groups.

The results so far suggest important variation according to religion, state versus national dyads, goals, and self-identification. Political goals and perceptions profoundly shape state-group relations; there are radically different landscapes of violence across political contexts in India. Yet the analysis has been quite aggregated: there is a lot of "lumping" that needs to now be complemented by "splitting." The rest of the chapter shifts to a range of specific contexts in which we can

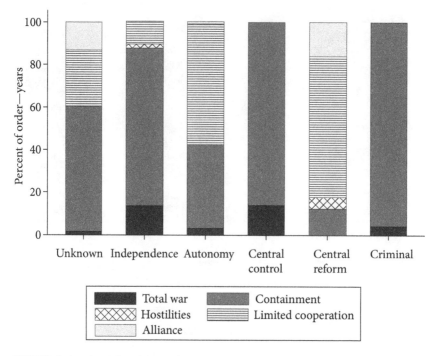

FIGURE 4.4. Armed orders and group goals

more clearly see how state-group relations unfold. I first examine clearly insurgent dyads across the Northeast, Punjab, Kashmir, and the Naxalite insurgencies and then look within these wars at patterns of pro-state paramilitarism and side switching. I consequently shift focus to militarized "mainstream" politics at both the state and national levels, exploring when and how violence is tolerated and even encouraged within the bounds of normal political life. Finally, delving into the Naga conflict in the Northeast provides an opportunity to explore how tactical overlap and armed group agency work over time, bringing groups themselves more squarely into the story.

The Three Worlds of Indian Counterinsurgency

Much of India's armed politics has occurred in the contexts of its numerous insurgent conflicts. Many of the groups in these conflicts do not end up acting like we might imagine insurgents do, but the broader contexts are nevertheless of rebellion, repression, and ongoing political conflict. What patterns emerge once we start comparing state responses to self-identified rebels?

If we restrict the analysis to periods in which groups self-identify as fighting against the state (with admitted caveats), as in figure 4.5, the pattern of repression and relative accommodation is very clear—Maoist and especially Northeast groups are substantially less likely to be in total war than Sikh and Muslim insurgents. The Northeast stands out for its extensive limited cooperation even with openly anti-state insurgents, while Naxalite left-wing insurgents are primarily targeted with containment. There is striking variation in patterns of counterinsurgency in India: having the same counterinsurgency doctrines, regime type, central political leaders, and security organizations at work has not led to convergence in approach to armed actors.

There are two, interrelated, political dynamics driving this pattern across counterinsurgency domains. The first is threat perception: for the reasons I introduced above, there is a very different historical meaning to mobilization around explicit religious cleavages (especially Muslim) in contrast with tribal or linguistic dimensions. The basic structure of how Delhi perceives the greatest danger is tilted toward some insurgents over others. A consequent selection effect then follows: given that autonomy on religious grounds is off the table constitutionally, armed groups that do emerge in minority religious contexts are likely to be more radical in their aims. Those that "select" into open revolt are those willing to take their chances in the face of a likely ferocious Indian state response. This combination reinforces itself, making compromise and even tacit deal making far more difficult than in the comparatively fluid world of the Northeast.

We see this difference more specifically when comparing Kashmiri, Mizo, Sikh, and Naga groups (including all groups linked to these conflicts, including pro-state militias) in table 4.3. Though Walter would expect India to fight the Nagas the hardest to establish a reputation for resolve because they were the first secessionist revolt after India's independence, this has actually been a substantially less intense conflict than in Kashmir.[128] A striking 53 percent of orders-years in this conflict were limited cooperation, including formal, extended cease-fires in the 1960s to early 1970s and since the late 1990s. The Mizo revolt, beginning in 1966, saw a vigorous early Indian counterinsurgency reaction of total war. However, after about five years of intense conflict, it then switched to a blend of limited cooperation and containment, before eventually ending in incorporation in 1986. This process involved open and far-reaching negotiations and cease-fires between the Mizo National Front (MNF) and Delhi.[129]

As I discuss below, limited cooperation and alliance in Kashmir has almost exclusively involved depoliticized militias that changed sides amid fratricidal fighting and did not make any political demands on the state. After the early period of limited cooperation with Sikh militants in Punjab, we see a shift over

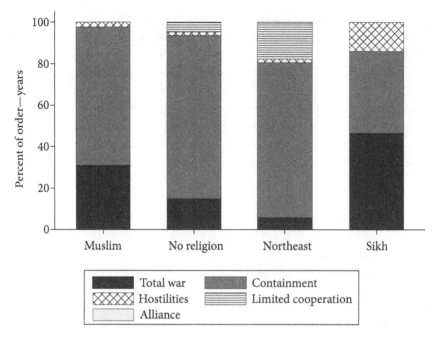

FIGURE 4.5. Armed orders by identity category, insurgent self-description

TABLE 4.3 Armed orders in Naga, Kashmir, Mizo, and Sikh/Khalistan conflicts

	NAGA	KASHMIR	MIZO	SIKH
Total war	10 (9%)	43 (29%)	6 (29%)	20 (30 %)
Containment	37 (33%)	96 (64%)	6 (29%)	20 (30 %)
Military hostilities		4 (3%)		6 (9%)
Limited cooperation	60 (53 %)	3 (2%)	9 (43%)	18 (27 %)
Alliance	5 (5%)	4 (3%)		2 (3 %)
Total	112	150	21	66

time—there is limited cooperation as late as 1987, but by 1990, every Sikh militant group was in some form of conflict, with total war predominating in 1990–93 and leading to the collapse of the insurgent movement.

It is apparent that the wars of Kashmir and Punjab have attracted a very different response than those of the Northeast, with the Naxalites in between. There are multiple reasons for this, but the pattern is consistent with what we would expect from the dominant understandings of Indian nationalism stretching back to the 1920s. This is even true of the BJP—the Modi and Vajpayee governments

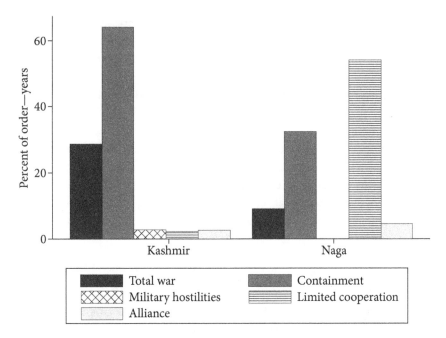

FIGURE 4.6.   Patterns of armed politics in Kashmir and Naga conflicts

have pursued extensive deal making in the Northeast, while in both cases there was substantial state repression in Kashmir.

The Northeast in Comparative Perspective

As I discuss more below, almost all of the cease-fires, peace deals, and incorporations in India have occurred with tribal and linguistic groups in the Northeast. Groups mobilizing these cleavages live in the gray zone and have largely been dealt with as either undesirables or business partners. There has been particularly extensive limited cooperation, especially outside of Manipur, largely in the form of long-running cease-fires. We have also seen some peace deals. This pattern applies to most of the major armed groups that have emerged in the region. Some groups in the Northeast have kept on fighting in low-level containment orders, above all the Paresh Barua core of ULFA and the stunningly numerous and highly opaque Meitei armed groups operating in the Imphal Valley.

There are very few alliance outcomes—armed groups that work with the state tend to cluster in limited cooperation until incorporation or a breakdown back into hostilities of some sort. This is an interesting contrast to Kashmir, where we see several clear counterinsurgent alliances. We know qualitatively in Punjab that the security forces cultivated flipped militants to work against the insurgency in a broadly similar way, although this is impossible to systematically code owing to the small size and opacity of these groups. Other than the Revolutionary Government of Nagaland (RGN) in Nagaland and, much more amorphously and murkily, surrendered militants in Assam, this has not been common in the Northeast.[130]

Unexpectedly for my argument, there have been some periods of total war in the Northeast. The initial state responses to the Naga, Mizo, and Assam (ULFA) insurgencies all involved total war—large force footprints, aggressive targeting, and maximalist war aims. These fairly quickly shifted to containment or limited cooperation, but the early years of each conflict does suggest a desire to limit or cap the amount of space given to insurgents before beginning a quite fluid process of bargaining.

Kashmir and Punjab: Higher Threat, Greater Conflict

The northwestern periphery—the insurgencies of Punjab and Kashmir—looks quite different. There is still a substantial amount of containment and some limited cooperation, but the overall distribution tends to the extremes much more than in the Northeast. Total war has been aimed at the major insurgent groups in Kashmir at different points, as well as some periods of the Khalistan militancy. These religious separatist groups tapped into the most existential pressure points of the Indian national project as it was constructed during and after colonialism. According to my theory, these challengers should be perceived as mortal enemies by state security managers. And we do indeed see much more total war here as a proportion of insurgent order-years than in the Northeast or Naxal wars. The Indian state has deployed huge forces to these war zones that have exerted enormous effort to try to break the militant movements. There has been leadership targeting, very limited public bargaining with armed groups, and a sustained push to monopolize violence.

Containment has also been common in these contexts, however. This seems to be aimed at two kinds of organizations. First, secondary armed groups (like Al-Badr in early 1990s Kashmir) that were not the dominant actor in their conflict environment at the time and, second, groups that had been beaten back and maintained a fairly limited posture following an earlier stretch of total war (Hizbul Mujahideen after 2003).[131] Even in these very intense and politically sensitive wars, the state can live with a certain amount of ongoing disorder if the final push toward violence monopolization is militarily or politically too daunting. The main failing of my argument in the northwestern conflict zones is that it underpredicts containment. Delhi is not interested in maximizing coercive pressure all the time even against groups I predict should be viewed as mortal enemies. The overall prediction of much greater repression compared to the Northeast clearly holds, however.

What have cooperative orders looked like in Kashmir and Punjab? First, there was limited cooperation in the early days of the Sikh militancy, as a blend of central and state politicians tried to manipulate Bhindranwale's group to try to split the Akali Dal in Punjab. Tactical overlap drove the deeply cynical strategy of manipulating militancy for electoral reasons: parts of the Congress party wanted a split Sikh vote, while Bhindranwale wanted political cover to mobilize. Tactical overlap emerged from this confluence of goals. This was a rare example of the strange bedfellows political role; by 1984, it had become clear that there were deep political incompatibilities that could no longer be papered over.[132]

Second, as discussed more below, there have been counterinsurgency-driven alliances between the state and former militants. These were deeply hierarchical arrangements with armed groups that abandoned any autonomous political demands—they did not bargain for concessions or deals, but instead sought shelter with the state as protection against their foes.[133] In both Kashmir and Punjab, we see a much firmer bifurcation between being pro- and anti-state than in the Northeast, where there is a far finer spectrum of variation that clusters more heavily around containment and limited cooperation.

In these war zones, there have been some efforts at cease-fires and limited cooperation, such as with the Hizbul Mujahideen in 2000, so these are not entirely negotiation-free contexts.[134] But they have failed quickly. I do not claim that these outcomes are purely the result of Indian state policy: the Lashkar-e-Taiba is not coming to the negotiating table regardless of anything. Reasons beyond state policy for the lack of meaningful negotiation outcomes also involve Pakistani meddling, interinsurgent fratricide, and the radicalism of key groups. However, it is striking how limited the political concessions on offer have been from Delhi, even toward more moderate and indigenous armed groups. The political sensitivity of these conflicts is far higher than in the distant, politically peripheral Northeast: a live-and-let-live bargain with Hizbul Mujahideen in Kashmir like that with the NSCN-IM in Nagaland is unthinkable, even if it could actually reduce violence.

The political structures of these situations are fundamentally different. While we take this as obvious and totally natural, this divergence is a result of historical contingencies and nationalist projects. In a different political context, the NSCN-IM could instead be like the Baloch or Bengali insurgents of Pakistan or the Kachin of Burma, relentlessly pursued by an unyielding state, while Kashmiri warlords are left mostly to their own devices, with Kashmir under de facto indirect rule as a peripheral mountainous hinterland. That this counterfactual sounds utterly bizarre is the result of contingent outcomes that established the dividing cleavages of the subcontinent, and were institutionalized in political parties, transmitted to the mass public, and used to establish boundaries of the polity after independence.

Naxalite Insurgency

The Kashmir/Punjab versus Northeast comparison is illuminating, and I return to the Naga conflict in the Northeast below. But what can we make of the communist insurgencies in India? The post-1967 Naxalite insurgency has been remarkably robust, at its peak spreading some degree of influence to more than 10 percent of India's territory (and allegedly higher) and controlling thousands of men under arms. There have even been substantial "liberated zones" in the interior where the CPI-Maoist and its predecessor factions held (and still hold) sway.[135] These have actually been identified by senior political leaders like Manmohan Singh as India's most serious internal security threat.[136] The Naxalites' raw military power and territorial influence dwarfs that of any other armed group in India's history. There are many other cases of intense state repression against powerful (and not so powerful) leftist movements, whether the pitched battles between the Burmese Tatmadaw and CPB or in the annihilation of the PKI in Indonesia.

Yet as table 4.4 shows, leftists are largely treated as undesirables in India. Above I noted the ambivalent place of the radical Left in Indian politics—while Maoist insurgents are undoubtedly seen as needing to be repressed, there has been vastly more communist involvement in mainstream electoral politics, the Congress had a powerful socialist bloc, and questions of redistribution are very much politically acceptable in Indian politics. The radical Left's political position is less sensitive and existentially worrisome in the political sphere. It also undoubtedly helps that the Naxalites' primary areas of operation have been the interior peripheries, far from major cities or borders; I certainly do not pretend that ideological fit is the only cause of the containment-focused posture of the state. In this case, it is likely that the two factors work together: an ideological challenge seen as manageable is combined with deeply peripheral locations that do not have either strategic or political importance to Delhi.

There have been important periods of total war, most notably the early 1970s in West Bengal and the late 2000s in interior India.[137] When leftist insurgents have grown too disruptive and powerful, the state has increased its repressive efforts. This is where functional imperatives kick in: Delhi does not want to allow utter chaos and widespread disorder. But once a trajectory of escalation has been broken, we see a quick shift back to a containment posture, aiming to wear the

Naxals out over time. This does not mean that these are pleasant operations—human rights abuses have been rife both under containment and total war. But the intensity of central crackdowns has varied over time. Interestingly, there have been some cease-fire talks with Naxal groups at the state level. There have been a few instances of limited cooperation with ultra-Left groups, including periods of ambiguity (1968 West Bengal), the very early years of groups mobilizing (like 1977 MCC), and occasional cease-fire efforts (like mid-1990s Andra Pradesh with the People's War Group). There have also been a set of anti-Naxal militias that the Indian government has worked with that I discuss below.

In general, though, the political salience of the Maoist Left is comparatively low—they are seen as deeply undesirable, but lack the serious threat perception, urgency, or political mobilization that surrounds a conflict like Kashmir. Counterinsurgency (COIN) efforts toward communist insurgents thus looks neither quite like the Northeast nor the Northwest—unlike Kashmir and Punjab, total war has not been so dominant, but unlike the Northeast, there has been much less limited cooperation, especially not protracted periods of cooperation, against a background of sustained repression. The undesirables political role seems to dominate in this domain, compared to a blend of business partners and undesirables in the Northeast and mortal enemies in Punjab and Kashmir.

There are three distinct worlds of counterinsurgency in India, despite the exact same national political leaders and many of the same security organizations being in charge of operations in each. COIN doctrine, regime type, and other structural variables are less useful than the political specificities of each conflict context. While no single variable can explain the incredibly complex variation we see, it is clear that politics matters enormously. The kinds of demands groups make and the cleavages they mobilize seem to drive systematically different government responses.

Yet there are misfires in my argument when applied to Indian counterinsurgency. The theory underpredicts total war in the Northeast, where it was very important in the early years of the Naga, Mizo, and Assam conflicts. At the same

TABLE 4.4 Leftist insurgency contexts

	FREQUENCY (%)
Total war	19 (15%)
Containment	100 (81%)
Limited cooperation	5 (4%)
Total	124

Note: This analysis includes Naxal groups and their successors and well as other leftist radicals (like the Dakshin Desh).

time, it overpredicts total war in Punjab and Kashmir; though repression dominated in both, there were periods and dyads of containment rather than universal high-intensity repression. Total war requires hugely costly military effort that may simply not be seen as sustainable or worth the costs. There is variation in orders even with groups I would code as mortal enemies. The general tendencies are what I expect across conflict categories, but there are nevertheless outliers that must be acknowledged. Straightforward military and functional imperatives show their importance here: on the one hand, the state wants to cap insurgents' mobilization in the early days of any revolt; on the other, even when fighting mortal enemies, resource constraints and other political calculations may induce greater restraint than ideological categorization would suggest.

The other limitation is that this analysis is best at distinguishing between ideologically aligned, gray zone, and opposed categories rather than being able to specify how tactical overlap emerges. This is most pressing in the gray zone, where highly contextual tactical dynamics and armed group agency play a central role in determining the difference between containment and limited coopera-tion. I explore these dynamics of tactical overlap and armed group agency below in the Naga conflict.

Pro-state Paramilitaries and the Sources of Alignment

I mentioned side switching and pro-state paramilitarism in some of the dis-cussion of counterinsurgency above. This section explores alliances or limited cooperation with groups that work alongside the government to actively target insurgents.[138] These are different than either live-and-let-live limited coopera-tion orders or collusion with armed political parties. Such alliances are also quite murky: the Indian government is loath to publicly discuss pro-state paramilita-rism, the groups often are implicated in severe human rights abuses, and the level and nature of cooperation can be very unclear and contested.[139] In Punjab, we know that there was widespread use of "cats"—turned militants used against their former colleagues.[140] But these groups did not have any real organizational exis-tence, being highly localized and ephemeral. This makes empirical measurement extremely challenging. The same is true of the so-called SULFA (Surrendered ULFA) in Assam; measuring armed orders does not seem appropriate, given the lack of a clear autonomous organization.

There are three primary sets of cases in which we do see unambiguous pro-state paramilitarism. They provide insight into how tactical overlap can emerge. In Kashmir, a set of insurgents "flipped" to work with the state after becoming

enmeshed in fratricidal conflict with the Hizbul Mujahideen.[141] The tactical cal-
culation was clear—they needed protection to survive, while the Indian state
was desperate for local intelligence and support. The side-switching factions
abandoned any political claim making, making cooperation with them politically palatable. These so-called Ikhwans were eventually absorbed into the formal security apparatus over time, having been effective in the mid-1990s but
losing value over time as their intelligence became dated, militants struck back
against them, and questions were increasingly raised about human rights abuses
by Ikhwan groups.

In Nagaland, we see a similar story in the rise of the Revolutionary Government of Nagaland (RGN) from 1968 from 1973. The RGN, as I discuss more
below, emerged from a tribally based split within the Naga National Council
(NNC). As this conflict escalated, including attempted assassinations, the RGN
looked to the state for protection. In turn, Delhi increasingly had its hands full
with an ever more adventurous NNC—even though technically the cease-fire
continued and limited cooperation endured, the NNC was testing its limits by
launching attacks and cultivating Chinese external support. In this tumultuous
context, the RGN-Government of India (GOI) alignment came to make good
tactical sense, since both sides had tactical reason to work with the other.[142]
The RGN increasingly gave up autonomy, culminating in its formal incorporation in 1973—parts of the group became integrated into the security apparatus against the backdrop of the renewed Indian offensive against the NNC of
1972–75.[143] As in Kashmir, intrainsurgent fratricide and rivalry triggered fears
of survival by armed groups that were able to offer valuable counterinsurgency
resources to the Indian government in return for protection. As in Kashmir,
the RGN lost value as an independent actor as time went on, as it became
increasingly reliant on Delhi and unable to provide new intelligence about the
insurgency. Like the Ikhwans, it slid toward being a superfluous supporter and
was demobilized.

The final major case of pro-state paramilitarism in India are a set of anti-
Naxalite militias in the interior combat zones. The pattern here is quite different than in either the murky, individual/small group collusion in Punjab or the
flipped militant dynamics in Nagaland and Kashmir. Instead, it appears that local
political figures and security force leaders helped establish or at least facilitated
the growth of local counter-Naxal groups.[144] These took different names—Jan
Jagran Abhiyan, Danteshwari Samanvay Samiti, and then, most importantly, the
Salwa Judum of 2005–11.

The Salwa Judum was the most dramatic and powerful of these forces. It was
supported by a variety of government forces, especially the state police (including its large array of murky Special Police Officers [SPO] enrolled to garrison

local areas). The Salwa Judum reflected an alignment of state interests—needing manpower, intelligence, and a public relations story of a spontaneous uprising—with the specific local rivalries and interests of both local elites and peasants. The Indian Supreme Court essentially broke the back of the Salwa Judum in 2011, but only after several years of very violent conflict in Chhattisgarh and the introduction of a much larger Ministry of Home Affairs (MHA) force footprint. This case does not align well with my armed politics approach, since it appears that elements of the state were essential to forming and building up the group in the first place.

We can see important sources of group ideological changes and tactical overlap in the Naga and Kashmiri paramilitary cases. Groups hard pressed by internal rivals looked to the state for support and survival. To be acceptable to the government, these groups needed to drop their political claims and slide into an aligned ideological position. This is how armed allies emerged despite having begun life as business partners or even mortal enemies; they were forced to adjust to unfavorable circumstances by changing their ideological positions, and luckily for them, they could offer valuable information and operations to the government. As that tactical value declined over time, the groups became incorporated into the security apparatus and ended as even nominally autonomous actors. By contrast, the case of anti-Naxalite militias is quite different and my argument does not help us understand it. This is a much more classical case of a government, or at least elements of it, helping to *set up* a paramilitary force, about which my approach has little to say. The armed politics framework is best suited to armed groups that have their origins at least somewhat distinct from the state, rather than pure creations of it.

"Mainstream" Political Violence in State and Nation

A consistent claim of this book is that a repressive government response to a group is not triggered just because its members are armed. Armed parties and private armies can be mainstream actors in Indian politics, and we see a remarkable cluster of limited cooperation and alliance with these groups.[145] They have been heavily located at the state level, enmeshed within complex political coalitions and competitions in West Bengal, Kerala, Bihar, and Maharashtra. However, because we have focused on a subset of particularly violent states, we do not have a full sample of the various ways that mainstream actors can use violence. Moreover, the book's focus on formal, recognizable organizations also makes it difficult to capture the highly localized, fluid nature of "institutionalized riot networks" and vigilante violence. This was also a domain in which coding errors and measurement ambiguities were far more common. Far more empirical research is needed in this area, but this tentative evidence does allow suggestive insights into the ways that armed actors can play within the rules of the game.

Table 4.5 summarizes armed orders for all groups in India that we code as describing themselves as either mainstream political parties (BJP, CPI, INC in some states; CPM, Shiv Sena in others) or as "other." This latter category brings in some noise, but also includes a number of organizations like the RSS and Bihar's 1990s caste militias that defy easy categorization. It also compares state- and national-level dyads with such groups. I found that consistent coding here was a real problem; while most of the time research assistants coded these groups as being "reform"-oriented, others were identified as center-seeking, and shifts over time were particularly challenging for consistent measurement. These major caveats must be kept in mind for assessing the findings below. This is an area that deserves much more future research.

We can see that much of the action in "mainstream" armed politics comes at the state-level—groups like the CPM and RSS are often operating with violence mainly within specific states, frequently as part of or aligned with state governments that politicize the use of law enforcement.[146] There is still much of this tendency at the national level, but the central government is more likely to engage in crackdowns than the state governments we examine. Alliance is, by contrast, dramatically more common in state-level dyads, with parties like the CPM, CPI, BJP, and Shiv Sena ruling or allying with ruling parties in major Indian states.

West Bengal and Kerala have the most clearly institutionalized systems of militarized elections, with violence linked to and controlled by mainstream electoral politics. Bihar saw an incredibly violent 1980s–1990s period of caste-based militia mobilization, sometimes linked to political parties, that has largely subsided. Maharashtra has been a site of armed party mobilization, largely led by the Shiv Sena.[147] Containment in these contexts is often the result of a new government coming to power in the state opposed to an armed party that then faces some degree of repression by the state police. There is no total war, and limited cooperation and alliance absolutely dominate the distribution of order-years. This is certainly an undercount of state-level armed politics, but the evidence shows how violence can be incorporated into mainstream political life.

Things are somewhat different when examining the central government's relationship with such groups. Total war and containment orders emanating from Delhi have been primarily oriented at groups like the RSS that are not formally political parties. But we do see some central crackdowns on even self-identified

TABLE 4.5 Mainstream parties and "other" actors in India

	ALL	NATIONAL	STATE
Total war	10 (1%)	8 (2%)	
Containment	303 (25%)	201 (42%)	84 (15 %)
Military hostilities	8 (1 %)	7 (1%)	
Limited cooperation	546 (45%)	232 (49%)	248 (45 %)
Alliance	341 (28%)	30 (6 %)	214 (39 %)
Total	1,208	478	546

mainstream parties. The cues for crackdowns in general largely seem to an escalation of violence that is seen by Delhi as getting out of control, such as atrocities in Bihar and the destruction of the Babri Masjid and related waves of riots by Hindu nationalist groups in the early 1990s.[148] This pattern of greater conflict at the national than at the state level makes sense given India's federal structure: only when the state government has lost control over law and order, or there are cross-state armed groups, does Delhi get deeply involved in bans and repression.[149] Nevertheless, limited cooperation is common even in interactions with the central government, which shows that noninsurgent armed groups can receive plenty of leeway from the central government.

India has been viewed for most of its history as a reasonably consolidated democracy: indeed, it is the outlier of outliers among poor developing countries when it comes to democratic survival.[150] But alongside that apparent consolidation is a fairly remarkable amount of quotidian violence and coercion linked to mainstream politics.[151] This book is certainly not the last word on these patterns; my approach struggles with highly localized and fluid forms of violence such as vigilante lynching and riot networks. Moreover, there is striking variation across states and time in the existence and nature of political violence that is beyond my ability to explain. Future research can build on this work to explore when and how "mainstream" politics are compatible with the threat and use of violence.[152]

Naga Armed Groups and Shifting Political Roles, 1955–2016

We now shift to a more fine-grained comparative study of one of Asia's longest-running armed conflicts. Armed politics in Naga areas of the Northeast have taken on a variety of forms, from intense warfare to close alliances to enduring limited cooperation arrangements.[153] I use this context to explore initial regime threat perception and shifts over time in armed orders. The variation across groups and time makes this a particularly valuable context to study. It also allows us to deal more directly with tactical overlap.

The current Indian state of Nagaland (created in 1963) contains most of the population of Nagas, but they are also in northern Manipur, parts of Assam, and in Burma/Myanmar, and the Naga armed groups have operated in all of these areas in addition to Nagaland state. The rebellion began in 1955–56 and armed groups continue to operate to the present day, now mostly in cease-fire arrangements with the Indian government. This was India's first separatist revolt, making it especially valuable for examining how policymakers considered this new challenge. We have good evidence on how policymakers thought about it and its implications for broader security policy through the mid-1970s. In recent decades the evidence is much weaker, but the pattern of policy responses established by the 1960s has been repeated since.

I examine five groups: the Naga National Council (NNC), Revolutionary Government of Nagaland (RGN), National Socialist Council of Nagaland (NSCN), NSCN-Isak-Muivah (NSCN-IM), and NSCN-Khaplang (NSCN-K). The NNC, NSCN-IM, and NSCN-K at different times fought and cooperated with India; the RGN was a splinter that allied with the Indian government; the NSCN, a splinter from the NNC, fought the state before it collapsed in a split between the factions that became the NSCN-IM and NSCN-K. This remarkable variation in armed orders occurred in a tiny slice of geographical space, and involved many of the same leaders and institutions over time. All of the groups have their origins in the NNC, allowing us to trace out how a single movement evolved, splintered, and interacted with the state.

Coding the Variables

Ideological fit is determined by the political goals these groups publicly advanced: in most cases, they demanded secession or autonomy along ethnic/tribal lines. The NNC, NSCN, NSCN-IM, and NSCN-K all started out demanding full independence; over time these goals largely moderated toward autonomy of some sort, and some groups abandoned major political demands by the end of their existence (RGN, NNC). The gray zone is where the NSCN-IM, NSCN-K, NNC before the mid-1970s, and pre-split NSCN are best coded. The late NNC and RGN started in the gray zone but ended up ideologically aligned.

How should we think about tactical overlap in this context? India had no interest in using Naga groups against Myanmar, so cross-border rivalry was irrelevant. But it did have strong functional reasons to try to stabilize the periphery at a low cost and to gain intelligence against other groups. But the political constraints to cooperation were fairly low because of ideological fit—this is in stark contrast to Kashmir and Punjab, where the government was unwilling to allow de facto indirect rule, and instead would only work with depoliticized hunter-killer militias able and willing to assist counterinsurgency operations. The lack of pressing conventional threats along the border combined with the political peripherality of the region loosened the government's motivation to pursue violence monopolization. Being in the gray zone opened more space for tactical collaboration.

However, there was some important variation in the intensity of groups' incentives to work with Delhi. Drawing on the discussion of tactical overlap in chapters 1 and 2, we see two broad conditions that seem to have driven greater group willingness to cooperate. First, periods of splintering or rivalry sometimes created incentives to work with Delhi.[154] This was most striking in the RGN's side switching, but also appears to have played a role in both the NSCN-IM and NSCN's calculations since 1997. Second, war weariness combined with a government offer to explore limited cooperation made Naga groups willing to at least consider cooperation. This is a less specific prediction, since it is hard to measure war weariness ex ante, but the first major wave of limited cooperation in 1963 came after years of hard fighting, the second wave in 1975 after a huge Indian crackdown, and third wave in 1997–2000 after two more decades of fighting that had not generated new political concessions.

Under what circumstances did tactical overlap disappear? First, there were periods in which armed groups tried to push the boundaries of limited cooperation and overshot the state's "red lines." This led to pushback when the government came to see the group as undermining stability rather than encouraging it.[155] Second, when groups lost their ability to provide valuable new local intelligence, they became less useful to the state, as we also saw in Kashmir. Third, when groups felt that cooperation was leading to them being frozen out or outflanked by rivals, they could abandon it: as scholars have argued in other contexts, rivalry and conflict within militant movements can shape willingness to cooperate with the state.[156] Table 4.6 outlines key claims.

The findings are generally supportive of the theory. When Naga groups were willing to control their territory without extensively attacking the state, limited cooperation emerged. Such deals often institutionalized a missing monopoly of state violence, but on broadly acceptable terms to Delhi that reduced its costs of governance. In turn, the groups received remarkable space to recruit, extract resources, and pursue their own political and social agendas on the ground. When groups pushed beyond acceptable limits or decided that cooperation was no longer working for them, containment orders emerged with ongoing low-level fighting. When a group was willing and able to be engaged in active

TABLE 4.6 Naga armed groups and armed politics

	IDEOLOGICAL FIT	TACTICAL OVERLAP	PREDICTED ARMED ORDERS	ACTUAL ARMED ORDERS
NNC	Gray zone (1955–74) aligned (1975)	High (1963–69) Low (1955–63) 1969–75)	Containment (1955–63; 1969–75) Limited cooperation (1963–69) Incorporation (1975)	Total war, 1955–57 Containment, 1957–64 Limited cooperation 1964–72 Total war, 1972–75 Incorporated, 1975
NSCN	Gray zone	Low (1980–88)	Containment (1980–88)	Containment, 1980–88 Collapse, 1988
NSCN-IM	Gray zone	Low (1988–95) High (1995–present)	Containment (1988–95) Limited cooperation (1995–present)	Containment, 1988–97 Limited cooperation, 1997–present
NSCN-K	Gray zone	Low (1988–2000) High (2000–2015) Low (2015–present)	Containment (1988–2000) Limited cooperation (2001–15) Containment (2015–present)	Containment, 1988–2001 Limited cooperation, 2001–15 Containment, 2015–present
RGN	Gray zone (1968) aligned (~1969–73)	High (1968–73)	Alliance (1968–73)	Alliance, 1968–73 Incorporated, 1973

counterinsurgency alongside the government, we see an alliance (the RGN from 1967 to 1973). When groups moved into ideological alignment and requested a deal, we see incorporation (NNC 1975, RGN 1973).

However, there are two areas in which my argument does not work. First, total war is not expected in my argument. Yet in the initial response to the uprising in 1955 and then again in 1972's crackdown, intensive combat that my argument does not predict did occur. Second, there is often a lag between when I predict an armed order will begin and when it actually does. For instance, the NSCN-IM signaled its openness to doing business with India in 1995, but limited cooperation did not occur until 1997. By the late 1960s, the NNC had made life difficult for Delhi in ways that my theory suggests should have decreased tactical overlap and caused a return to containment, but the shift away from limited cooperation did not occur until 1972 (and then, as noted above, this took the form of total war). These are not severe problems, but they do suggest much more friction than the theory can straightforwardly handle.

The First NNC Revolt and Delhi's Reaction: 1955–64

The Naga movement has its roots in late colonial politics. As the end of the British Empire began to loom, Naga civil society mobilized to try to establish its likely place in the new dispensation. The Naga National Council (NNC) emerged as a political body to represent Naga interests. In 1947, the NNC met with Sir Akbar Hydari, the governor of Assam, and a Nine-Point Understanding was reached that indicated that Naga areas would receive a degree of autonomy—and, possibly, that there would be an option to revisit the agreement in ten years. Delhi did not interpret the agreement as providing the NNC with the option to secede in a decade, but many Nagas did.

As the 1950s progressed, the NNC became increasingly convinced that secession was the right option, especially as the Assam government seemed uninterested in its hill peripheries. In the face of this growing discontent, and well *prior* to the onset of actual armed rebellion, Nehru outlined the approach that would come to govern India's internal security posture in the region:

> In Assam, the question of the Nagas has assumed prominence again and some leaders of the Nagas have been demanding independence. They are trying to hold a plebiscite for this purpose. It is obvious that the Nagas or any tribes on our borders cannot have independence. But we are very anxious to give them a large measure of autonomy and to help them in every way, while respecting their traditions and ways of life. I am personally an admirer of the Nagas and I like many of their fine qualities.[157]

He rejected any talk of independence, arguing that the assurances given by Hydari could be accommodated within the Sixth Schedule of the Constitution. Of autonomous district councils outlined in the Constitution, he writes:

> Five of these have been formed, but the sixth, in the Naga Hills district, has not been formed because of the non-cooperation of the Nagas there. They demand an independent State, which is rather absurd. But they have another grievance. According to them, the understanding arrived at on their behalf with Sir Akbar Hydari, then Governor of Assam, was not given effect to in the Sixth Schedule. In so far as this is so, we should be prepared to honour that understanding and even to vary the Sixth Schedule to some extent. That question, however, does not arise at present, though I should like to consider the grant of further powers to the district councils.[158]

These were the rules of the political game: secession would be redirected into autonomous administrative units, whether at the state- or substate level. The NNC increasingly dug in its heels, launching a growing campaign of noncooperation and defiance, including a boycott of the 1952 general election. This was observed from a distance by Delhi, but did not trigger a major military crackdown until Naga violence escalated in 1955–56. The NNC declared itself the Federal Government of Nagaland (FGN) in 1956, marking an unambiguous challenge to state sovereignty. Nehru sent the Indian Army into the Naga Hills to quell this uprising in 1956. Up to fifteen thousand fighters were in the FGN's Naga Army by the late 1950s.[159] In 1956, Nehru rather nonchalantly summarized the situation: "In the North-East of India, some of the Nagas have started an armed revolt. There is no need to get alarmed about this, although it is depressing that some of our countrymen should behave in this way. The real difficulty comes from the nature of the terrain and the lack of communications. We have put the Army in command of these operations, though the civil power will continue to perform its normal functions."[160]

Nehru's 1957 overview of this revolt and response, in a letter to his chief ministers, continues the basic theme of autonomy without secession. He writes of the Naga leader Phizo that "I told him then, and I have repeated it often, that the demand for independence was out of the question. But we were always prepared to consider anything else, even though this might involve some change in the Sixth Schedule of our Constitution. Our general policy was not to interfere with tribal people and to give them the largest measure of autonomy. . . . but gradually it [Naga movement] drifted toward violence."[161] In his telling, "It was decided to regroup the villages, so that we could give adequate protection to these new groups. This involved a good deal of inconvenience to the people, but it certainly gave them protection. This step led, to a large extent, to the isolation of the hostiles, and their morale began to suffer. Probably, it was mainly this step which induced most of the Nagas to decide to seek a settlement."[162]

Nehru's aside about "inconvenience" masked a major crackdown by Indian forces, accompanied by persistent accusations of human rights abuses. The 1955–57 period is reasonably coded as a period of total war, with large-scale surges of forces and the extensive use of force against militants, suspected militants, and civilians: "Armed confrontations at times resembled pitched battles."[163] Regroupment was a policy of population resettlement (repeated in Mizo areas from 1966) aimed at making the Naga population more easily controllable. Indeed, long-time Indian government adviser and policymaker on the Northeast Nari Rustomji writes that Indian policymakers thought that Nagas needed "the iron fist" in the mid-1950s and "the military applied themselves with full-blooded vigour to the business of 'softening up' the recalcitrant Naga."[164] As I noted above, the initial use of serious force is a common characteristic of Indian internal security posture, even in dyads that then shift to containment or limited cooperation (as in the Assam and Mizo conflicts).

Yet the basic tendency of the theory asserted itself very quickly in a shift toward containment by 1958 and then limited cooperation in 1964. As a concession to Naga demands (articulated by the Naga People's Convention, or NPC), the Naga Hills and Tuensang Frontier Division of the NEFA were to be "constituted into a single administrative unit under the Centre" with any claim for independence given up.[165] Nehru believed that, despite ongoing fighting and Phizo's refusal to accept this as sufficient, the basic problem had been resolved—Phizo would be isolated by a pro-peace majority.[166] In 1957, the Naga Hills-Tuensang Area (NHTA) was created and a general amnesty was offered that triggered a number of surrenders. In 1960, Nehru agreed to create a subnational state of Nagaland, providing the greatest degree of autonomy under the Constitution. He dealt with the NPC as the representative of the Nagas, whom the FGN derided as sellouts. In 1963, Nagaland was created. In less than a decade, the initial rebellion of the FGN/NNC had turned into a full-fledged subnational state, despite the tiny size and population of the new Nagaland.

Nehru's correspondence in 1960 continues to argue that, despite ongoing fighting, the basic path of concession and accommodation will bear fruit: "The hostile hard core are not likely to accept this agreement, even though the great majority of the Naga people might approve of it. And so we may still have to continue to deal with the activities of these hostile groups . . . the tide has turned in Nagaland and we move now towards more peaceful conditions and normality."[167] By 1962 he was arguing that Nagaland "has caused us many headaches, and I fear that our troubles are not over yet. But the step we have taken is a right step and I feel it will help us greatly in normalizing that area and in convincing the people who live in Nagaland that they can live in freedom and dignity in the larger family of India."[168]

This quick move to concession is not expected by Walter's influential theory, which expects the first separatists in a country to be fought very hard to avoid setting precedents.[169] In India, as I argued above, for historical and ideological reasons, the central government wanted to set the precedent that linguistic and tribal issues could be incorporated into mainstream politics through federalism and multilayered governance. The government aimed to build reputation as (boundedly) *open* to tribal and ethno-linguistic claims, since these could be handled within the Constitution. A hard-line reputation was instead aimed at the minority religious groups seen as more threatening to the future of India. The specific political context of India led to a radically different security posture toward such groups than in its neighbors; in Burma and Pakistan, by contrast, peripheral separatists would be exposed to brutal (and in the long run, often counterproductive, destructive) crackdowns. This was part of a broader strategy: Bhaumik writes that "the creation of Nagaland and the peace talks of the mid-1960s was intended to start a process of political reconciliation that would lead to the territorial reorganization in Assam."[170]

Limited Cooperation and Alliance: No War, No Peace, 1964–72

Creating the state of Nagaland did not lead to the collapse of the FGN or the end of armed politics in the region, however. The FGN core under Phizo kept on fighting, arguing that statehood within India was no substitute for independence outside of it. The armed order marched on, and Indian security forces maintained a heavy footprint even as the tempo and tenor of operations moved more toward a containment order rather than total war. In 1963, as part of a political effort to pair statehood with the demobilization of the FGN, Nehru created a Peace Mission to Nagaland. These representatives went to Nagaland to meet with the underground in direct negotiations. In September 1964, a ceasefire was signed that shifted this dyad into limited cooperation, which would last until 1972.

The basic contours of the possible remained similar to the doctrine Nehru had laid out in the 1950s. During the on-and-off negotiations during this period, Gundevia notes that no bargaining was to be done with any group that "was talking about 'independence' outside the Indian Union,"[171] while still offering a policy of "maximum possible autonomy."[172] The FGN remained in the ethno-separatist gray zone, but was willing to dramatically reduce its direct attacks on Indian forces. The FGN seems to have been intrigued by at least exploring possibilities of negotiation at the same time as escaping the intense, direct repression of the mid/late 1950s. As this tactical overlap emerged, the group's political role shifted from undesirable to business partner. The cease-fire that emerged in 1964 created a sphere of influence situation, in which the FGN would continue to operate, recruit, and even arm itself, but would avoid the kinds of direct, sustained combat that had characterized the mid/late-1950s.

The cease-fire did *not* mean that violence stopped. Indeed, "hostile elements constantly crossed over into East Pakistan and received training in jungle warfare from Chinese experts sent there for the purpose. They returned to their Nagaland jungles with all the sophisticated weapons of war they could carry" and civilian trains in Assam were attacked by FGN forces, as at times were security forces.[173] After the Naga bombing of trains, the peace mission ended, as "GOI announced its intent to continue its talks with the FGN but stuck to its no-negotiating stands in relations to the Mizos."[174] In 1969, for instance, Franke reports that "debates in the Lok Sabha indicated that ISF personnel were killed in the Naga hills on a weekly basis."[175] Pakistan and China are alleged to have provided sanctuary and support to the FGN as it continued to maintain its arms and operations.

Indeed, a history of the Assam Rifles notes that security forces were continually active in the region,[176] while Horam notes that in 1968 a group of Nagas returned from China with "huge amounts of Chinese arms and ammunition."[177] Th. Muivah, who would later become a key leader of the NSCN and NSCN-IM, was deeply involved in Naga relations with the PRC in this period.[178] Strikingly, the "law and order situation was now deteriorating day by day and by 1970 it seemed that it could not get worse."[179] According to my argument and coding, the NNC/FGN should no longer be seen as a business partner by the late 1960s, given that disorder and violence were growing, rather than continuing stability and periphery management. Tactical overlap should have disappeared—but limited cooperation endured even as "armed clashes had become regular features of the Nagaland scene."[180]

FGN engagement with external rivals of India, attacks on security forces, and terrorist strikes did *not* yet lead to a dramatic Indian escalation. These were seen as politically manageable challenges that did not trigger major crises in Indian politics or lead to a wave of sustained public or elite interest in Nagaland. Indira Gandhi continued to renew the cease-fire with the FGN, though direct negotiations tailed off by the end of the decade.[181]

My theory expects tactical overlap to drop by the late 1960s due to the rise in this violence undermining Delhi's goal of a quiet periphery stabilized through indirect rule. The persistence of limited cooperation until 1972 is several years longer than the theory expects, since NNC activities became actively harmful to the tactical interests of the state. The economic tumult of the late 1960s and the dramatic escalation of India-Pakistan tensions in 1970–72, culminating in the independence of Bangladesh, likely distracted Delhi from the Naga conflict. As we will see below, a major change did come in 1972.

A second Naga armed order emerged in 1968. The Revolutionary Government of Nagaland (RGN) split away from the FGN, largely along tribal lines, over-laid with disputes over the failure of negotiations with Delhi, personnel choices within the FGN/NNC, and the assassination of a top Sema leader, Kaito.[182] The RGN was born in competition and conflict with the FGN, and had both its own social base (in the Sema tribe) and deep knowledge of the insurgency.[183] The RGN was, however, substantially weaker than the FGN and needed to find pro-tection from its retaliation.

This context made it both willing and able to help the Indian security forces improve their control of the region amid an increasingly challenging set of NNC activities. Very quickly after the split a tight alliance emerged.[184] As Bhaumik notes, "On paper, the RGN was an underground group, but their fighters could move around freely in the state. The army backed them and used them" against the other Nagas.[185] The government from 1968 would "use the dissidents as a use-ful counterpoise to the unyielding Federal Government of Nagaland";[186] though technically "'underground' men, [they] could move freely and meet State officials any time they wished."[187] Tactical overlap is extremely clear here: RGN was "join-ing hands with the Indian security forces and sleuthing for the capture of Federal Army men."[188]

Politically, "the RGN were now gradually veering round the idea that it was utterly futile to tread the same old path of 'Naga Independence' any longer," while the Indian government "had been closely watching the changes coming over the RGN" leadership and opened negotiations.[189] The state watched the group and its rhetoric and activities to read its intentions and trajectory. As the group reached out and expressed interested in doing business with India, India reciprocated, providing space and support for RGN operations.[190] B. K. Nehru, governor of Nagaland, notes that the Intelligence Bureau paid money to the RGN to the tune of fifty thousand rupees a month, a clear indication of alliance.[191]

This period provides strong overall support for my argument, especially in the 1964–69 period: the NNC was willing to manage the periphery, the Indian government was willing to give them a limited cooperation cease-fire, and when the RGN made itself available as a partner to limit NNC influence, an alliance emerged. The full length of limited cooperation, however, is not supported by my theory: the NNC's terrorist attacks, links with China and Pakistan, and growing use of violence by the late 1960s reduced tactical overlap with Delhi. We should have seen it recategorized as an undesirable group, and met with containment, but it continued to be treated as a business partner until 1972.

War, Incorporation, and the Splintering of the NNC: 1972–88

The 1970s were an eventful decade in Nagaland and its surrounding areas. The 1971 India-Pakistan war ended Pakistan's ability to directly influence the Northeast, while the waning of the Cultural Revolution saw a major reduction in Chinese support for insurgents. The war in Mizoram dragged on, but began to see recurrent periods of limited cooperation as the MNF started talking to the government. The post-1971 war environment was therefore an auspicious opportunity for the Indian government to try something new.

It pursued changes in Nagaland. In 1972, the Indian government unilaterally ended its limited cooperation with the NNC and launched a major offensive. In 1973, the RGN demobilized and was incorporated, ending this armed order. In 1975 the NNC signed the Shillong Accord and demobilized, but splinter elements rejected the deal and created the National Socialist Council of Nagaland (NSCN). The NSCN could continue the fight until its own fratricidal split in 1988, which created the NSCN-IM and NSCN-K factions.

As I noted above, my theory does not predict limited cooperation lasting until 1972, but it does suggest a move toward containment as the NNC's increasingly disruptive activities undermined India's goal of maintaining stability in the Northeast and made working with the NNC operationally unattractive. The specific nature of the crackdown, however, was more extreme than I expect given the NNC's status as an ideological gray zone group. The government decided to radically change course in 1972 following the attempted assassination of the Nagaland chief minister.[192] Fearing that the NNC had far overstepped its bounds, India declared war on the NNC and launched a series of raids and sweeps.

India's aim was to damage the NNC as much as possible through a full-spectrum offensive. Rather than the containment I expect, we instead saw a total war order emerge. In his memoir, B. K. Nehru argued that "the factual position in Nagaland was that the writ of the government of Nagaland did not run in the state. As a result of the 'ceasefire,' the forces at the command of the Governor were unable to do anything to restore their authority."[193] Militarily, "the insurgency was small but difficult to control."[194]

Verghese writes that "the overground was also warned of action if anyone preached secession" as the NFG, NNC, and NFA were banned and limited cooperation ended.[195] Krishna Rao, who served in Nagaland, writes that in 1972 after the attempted assassination of Hokishe Sema, "an agreement that existed on suspension of operations was terminated and the Prevention of Unlawful Activities Act 1967 was enforced in Nagaland by the governor, B. K. Nehru. Vigorous operations were carried out by the Army, some of the gangs were broken up and the situation once again brought under control."[196] The attempted assassination appears to have been the trigger for a dramatic shift to a coercive posture.[197]

The crackdown extended into 1975. The concept of Indian operations was that "the army would embark on large-scale jungle operations chasing the hostiles and making their life miserable till they would be left with only one choice—negotiating for surrender."[198] Intense, sustained combat, rather than the low-level operations we would expect from a containment armed order, marked the 1972–75 period.

This is not an outcome my argument expects; we should have seen containment, and earlier. The move to total war seems to have been a reaction to the collapse of the limited cooperation order's value in the late 1960s and early 1970s, plus the new opportunities to squeeze the NNC/FGN after its loss of access to Pakistani and Chinese support. The FGN became more vulnerable at a time in which it had also become much more troublesome, and "the GOI seemed to be resolved by September 1972 to unilaterally end the case-fire."[199]

Yet, more in line with the theory's expectations for a gray zone group, the government was willing to cut a deal with the NNC after it had been degraded. The 1975 Shillong Accord marked the first time that an official peace deal with an insurgent group occurred in the Northeast. The NNC shifted its ideological position into alignment and agreed to incorporation. There were no real concessions in this case; the central concession of statehood had been granted with the creation of Nagaland state in 1963. In 1975, key NNC leaders moderated their position.[200] The group moved out of the gray zone as it became clear that there was little chance, in their opinion, of achieving further major concessions, much less actual independence. In 1976, the FGN demobilized its arms via the agreed terms of the accord, with a more detailed agreement on demobilization early in 1976.

Yet not everyone agreed that the NNC had nowhere left to go but the mainstream. A set of commanders and political leaders were deeply disillusioned with the NNC's abandonment of the struggle, especially for the paltry gains of the Shillong Accord. As Horam notes, the accord was quite vague and did not deliver anything of direct value.[201] Disillusioned FGN fighters, including the prominent future factional leaders Muivah, Isak Swu, and Khaplang, refused to comply with the accord and by 1980 formed the NSCN. A number of them had received training and weapons from China in the 1950s or 1960s, and they "denounced the Shillong Accord and branded as traitors those who had signed the agreement."[202] Splintering, rather than commitment problems, kept the conflict alive. Phizo, in London, met with Morarji Desai in 1978, but according to the MHA, "As Shri Phizo stuck to his earlier unreasonable and unacceptable stand of independence of Nagaland, no issues relating to Nagaland were discussed."[203]

The new NSCN made good use of sanctuary in Burma and porous borders, as well as a broader sense among many Nagas that the accord had done little to change the basic facts on the ground. The NSCN became the flag-bearer of insurgency in the 1980s. The NSCN settled into a containment order—it launched regular attacks, but avoided large-scale escalation (terror strikes, for instance, or targeted killings of senior politicians). In turn, the Indian government maintained its security posture, with repression and recurrent patrolling, but limited major offensives or crackdowns. As Waterman argues, in this period after the Shillong Accord "counterinsurgents primarily sought to uphold the state-NNC order, allowing the NSCN factions to entrench themselves in order; force was then used to in an attempt to modify this dominance while talks to forge a 'limited cooperation' order were held."[204]

While the splinter NSCN kept anti-state militancy alive, the RGN pushed for incorporation and became a superfluous supporter that demobilized in 1973. It had lost popular support because of its role as an armed ally of the Indian state: "Even in 1970, the Revolutionary Group had lost the confidence of the Naga public and except a few hundred Sema tribe followers, the entire fabric of the much talked about CNP had fallen apart. It was now 1973 and the choice before this shrinking group was either to remain in the jungles and fight a losing battle or surrender."[205] The group was increasingly not useful to the Indian government, with its once-valuable knowledge about the insurgency decaying fast and the public tuning it out. It handed over arms on August 16, 1973, "without striking any political bargains."[206] In return, parts of the RGN were directly incorporated into the BSF,[207] while others entered the police and yet others ended up in political parties.[208]

With the end of the NNC and RGN, Nagaland's armed politics had changed dramatically by the end of the 1970s. The NSCN would carry forward the banner of revolt into the 1980s. MHA documents consistently refer to ongoing conflict in Nagaland during this decade; for instance, the Annual Report for 1986–87 noted that the "NSCN remained active in Nagaland, Naga predominant areas of Manipur and Tirap district of Arunachal Pradesh."[209] Containment dominated the regions throughout this decade as the NSCN pursued a "Nagalim" across state borders.

Containment Turns into Limited Cooperation: 1988–2015

The NSCN broke apart in fratricidal feuding in 1988, with bloody infighting between two key factions that turned into the NSCN-IM and NSCN-K. This feud was partially driven by rumors that the IM faction was going to pursue a negotiated settlement with Delhi.[210] The two groups had distinct tribal bases that allowed both to continue as substantial organizations, though the IM faction was the more powerful. Ongoing containment prevailed in the 1988–97 period. The two Naga groups continued to engage in sporadic ambushes alongside substantial recruitment and fund-raising. There have been allegations that they each became involved in backing political parties and politicians in Nagaland and Manipur, even as they continued to attack the security apparatus.

Yet, with the NSCN factions continuing to live in the gray zone, Delhi remained open to a negotiated settlement. Prime Minister Narasimha Rao met with key IM leaders in 1995, and then Prime Minister Deve Gowda met again with IM leadership in 1997. Both sides were interested in finding a way to resolve the conflict after four decades of violence. In 1997, the NSCN-IM and Government of India signed a cease-fire, though it took several years to agree on the territorial jurisdiction and boundaries of this cease-fire. In 2000–1, the NSCN-K also signed a cease-fire with the government.

It is not clear why exactly these years ended up being the time in which these deals were cut. One plausible account suggests that the explosion of militancy across the Northeast in the 1990s created strong tactical incentives for the GOI to try to cut a deal with the NSCN-IM, since it was a supporter of and inspiration for many of these groups: "Several scholars in explaining the timing of the government's decision have highlighted that the 1990s saw a rush of prairie fires of insurgencies all across the north-east and the hegemony of the NSCN-IM group in assisting these armed groups."[211] Pacifying the periphery became dramatically more pressing in the 1990s: the ULFA revolt that began in the early 1990s, the Bodo insurgency that then erupted in partial response to ULFA, the ongoing violence in Manipur, and the rise of emerging insurgencies in Meghalaya and Karbi Anglong all pushed the Indian security apparatus much harder than during the 1980s, when the Mizo war ended and the Nagas were the premier internal security challenge in the region.

Moving toward some kind of accommodation with the Naga armed groups, even if just a tactical breather, became a much higher priority than continuing to devote resources to a grinding containment. This accounts for the state's growing interest in doing business with the Nagas, shifting them into a business partner relationship compared to being merely undesirable. In 2009, more than a decade after the initial rapprochement, Sudhir Bhaumik, a long-time journalist in the region, argued that "for India, it is a priority to ensure the Naga guerrillas, the toughest in the region, do not renew their armed campaign against India. Durable peace is desirable but not if it means fresh trouble in the neighborhood. So long as a settlement is not reached with the NSCN, India will be happy to keep them confined to their barracks—or fighting each other."[212] Veteran policeman Ved Marwah, who had extensive experience in the Northeast, summarized the mutual value of this order (also in 2009): "The UPA government at the Centre does not want to open another front in Nagaland, nor does the Indian Army; and the NSCN (IM) is quite happy continuing with the status-quo as it is enjoying advantages of both war and peace."[213]

On the other side, both NSCN factions been had fighting for decades with little to show for it. A common interpretation of their decision to explore talks and agree to limited cooperation is that they had decided they needed to moderate their war aims to achieve anything. We lack leadership statements making the case in precisely these terms, however—unsurprisingly, Naga militant leaders publicly interpret the cease-fire as India growing weary and coming to them. Nevertheless, it was the Naga groups who shifted toward both a greater acceptance of the Indian Constitution and a willingness to accept limited cooperation, rather than India offering more generous new terms. The war-weariness mechanism I outline in chapter 2 driving shifts toward limited cooperation seems like a reasonable description of the rise of cease-fire politics in this period, though we will need to wait for more credible descriptions of the internal decision making of these groups. At minimum, this is certainly how the Indian government has viewed the situation: "There is a belief that weaknesses on the Naga side—military defeat, an ageing leadership, and pressure from the grass roots—have pushed the rebels to the negotiating table, and that time is on the government's side to seek a resolution in its own terms."[214]

Interestingly, these cease-fires clearly resembled that of the 1960s—"The terms and conditions of the 'Suspension of Operations' agreement currently offered to armed groups in Northeast India are similar to those of the 1964 ceasefire agreement between the government and NNC."[215] The basic contours of the possible deals on offer short of a formal settlement were similar over time. This makes sense—the basic "rules" for dealing with the political cleavages represented by the NSCN factions were fairly consistent over time, and so were the associated armed orders. Moreover, the terms of the post-1997 deals have not shifted across very different governments at the center, including the coalition government that cut the first NSCN-IM cease-fire, the moderate Hindu nationalist government of Vajpayee from 1998 to 2004, the center-left UPA government of 2004–14, and the hard-line Hindu nationalist government of Modi since 2014. They all resemble both one another and the Naga Peace Mission cease-fire arrived at under the socialist Nehru. Partisan and ideological differences in Delhi have not driven any noticeable shifts in the management of violence in this context—even after the Modi government in 2014, which has ended up aggressively pursuing a peace deal. Modi also signed a demobilizing deal with Bodo armed groups in Assam. The contrast with Modi's approach to Kashmir is quite striking.

The tactical goal of stabilization and periphery management has been accomplished, at the cost of empowering nondemocratic local actors, both state and nonstate, creating "a strange political dynamic, in which the underground began to co-exist with the 'overground.' The mutual sustenance of the 'illegitimate' and the 'legitimate,' on the one hand, undermined the rule of law and weakened the roots of democracy, but on the other, allowed flexibility and co-option that helped the Indian state build its legitimacy in troubled areas like Nagaland and Mizoram."[216] In Kolas's words: "With this approach, the government has effectively legitimized armed actors as 'providers of peace' and custodians of their constituency's political aspirations. The strategy of 'ceasefires and negotiations' has allowed leaders of armed groups to maintain relevance as key political actors, giving militancy a solid foundation in the mainstream of Northeast Indian politics."[217] Waterman agrees: "The emergent forms of order saw a deadlock in peace negotiations and the emergence of complex, ambiguous, and territorially bound rules governing the use of force between state and insurgent actors."[218]

Talks have periodically occurred in and outside of India between the government and the NSCN leaders since 1997. During that time, the factions continued to recruit fighters, raise money through smuggling and extortion, and maintain political and social influence.[219] There were also a number of interfactional clashes and intragroup splits. The Indian security forces continued to patrol and be deployed, but rarely clashed with the Naga armed groups. These state-group relationships were certainly not alliances, but instead ways of managing conflict and reducing violence even in the absence of a political settlement to the conflict.

Thakur and Venugopal offer a fascinating, fieldwork-based study of how limited cooperation works in the Ukhrul district of northern Manipur, an NSCN-IM dominated area. They find that

> the agreement aspires to establish a system whereby the Indian state is clearly the dominant authority, preserving de jure and de facto control of the territory at large, while permitting the NSCN(IM) a peaceful, but carefully controlled, limited existence. In practice, though, the realities on the ground are more relaxed and flexible than those in print. Its provisions are routinely subverted, and the Indian security forces appear to tolerate this. The NSCN(IM) is able to fluidly project coercive authority

well beyond the bounds of its camps, often very openly and without challenge—although it is careful to calibrate that within a set of invisible red lines.[220]

Strikingly, "there are limits even to covert and indirect forms of warfare, and a clear mutual sense of what constitutes permissible conduct. In practice, both sides observe a considerable degree of pragmatic tolerance and self-restraint, although these boundaries are constantly tested."[221] This is a textbook example of limited cooperation.

The field interviews I did in Nagaland and Delhi in 2013 highlighted the mutual compatibility of this order for both state and armed groups: while not ideal for anyone, all could continue to survive and achieve at least minimal goals through these arrangements. At the same time, it was clear that this would not be a permanent solution—the underlying politics remained in play, and maintaining the conflict in suspended animation would eventually not work. These political differences have both changed and remained problematic. Both NSCN factions have slowly shifted away from demands for full independence toward other political statuses for the Naga areas of India. One of the key sticking points has been how to deal with the integrity and political authority of Manipur, since both Naga factions wanted north areas of Manipur incorporated into a "Greater" Nagaland.

In 2015 a shift occurred in both armed orders. The Khaplang group broke its cease-fire, apparently as a result of the IM faction moving more firmly toward a final settlement with Delhi that appeared likely to freeze the Khaplang group out of any final deal. Here interfactional rivalry created incentives to break limited cooperation. Yet as of 2020, the GOI-NSCN-IM dyad remains in limited cooperation, as final terms of incorporation remain unspecified. Media reports indicate that a deal is still under consideration but that serious tensions remain between the group and the state.[222] In the meantime, limited cooperation marches on. By contrast, the NSCN-K is back to war (and has suffered splintering since the death of Khaplang himself), apparently fearing that it would be fully marginalized if the NSCN-IM cut a separate peace while the Khaplang group remained on cease-fire.[223] By fighting, the NSCN-K seems to be aiming for a settlement or bargain that includes its interests as well.[224]

The course of the Naga conflict reveals how fluidly armed groups can move in and out of armed orders over time. The Naga groups have had significant agency, with splits, rivalries, and individual leaders playing huge roles in determining when and how limited cooperation or containment emerged from interaction with the state. The government has been very willing to agree to limited cooperation orders with armed groups—the Northeast is a political periphery that makes potential business partners plentiful. The NNC, NSCN-IM, and NSCN-K all at some point shifted from being undesirable to being business partners once they decided that there were real benefits to working with the state. The specific timing of these shifts was highly contingent, but the broad contours of the conflict clearly align with a gray zone set of political claims and a government that was weakly motivated to try to fully eradicate its armed foes.

The Politics of Violence in India

This chapter shows important patterns in how the Indian state has sought to manage violence. Some armed actors—especially those closely tied to mainstream politics—have received relatively little repression as long as they have operated within the political system. Links to violence have not been an intrinsically disqualifying characteristic, whether for the CPM in West Bengal or the Hindu nationalist movement across much of India. Excessively public and destabilizing forms of violence have triggered government crackdowns, but these have been largely aimed at pushing these actors back to an acceptable level/type of violence and coercion. Though it waxes and wanes, and takes on different manifestations, political violence has become part of the repertoire of politics.

Matters are more complex when it comes to insurgencies. The political stakes have driven dramatic variation in which types of groups are repressed, which are tolerated, and which are worked with. There are of course many variables at play, but the basic pattern is striking: separatist groups in the Northeast have been treated with more political flexibility than the separatists in Kashmir and Punjab. The Maoists of central India exist between these extremes, with protracted, off-the-headlines containment dominating, broken by spells of much more intense conflict. There is a clear political logic to how the state allocates coercion and compromise. Threats vary according to how incompatible groups' demands are with the dominant conceptions of Indian nationalism held by ruling governments. In some of these war zones, militias have emerged or been sponsored that ally tightly with the state; in others (especially in the Northeast), limited cooperation dominates rather than either total war or alliances.

The major change in the last decade is the rise of Modi's BJP. The government's answer to the "Hindu-Muslim question" has shifted dramatically under the BJP, though this represents a culmination of decades of political mobilization. The overt turn toward Hindu nationalist majoritarianism has brought new forms of state repression and political exclusion, especially in 2019 and 2020 as this book is being completed. The three themes I outlined in the last chapter show themselves clearly. First, there is a huge spectrum of state-group relations, from intense crackdowns in Kashmir to enduring cease-fire politics in Nagaland to local collusion with lynch mobs and vigilantes. This variation is evident both qualitatively and quantitatively.

Second, there are deep historical roots to the movements and ideas contending for primacy—we can trace many of them back decades or earlier. This is also true of the challengers to state power, which often have roots in colonial or early postindependence politics. While Indian politics is incredibly dynamic, it is also structured by the past. The parties, insurgents, and state institutions that interact and compete with one another all have deep roots.

Third, there is no plausible way to consider Indian internal security strategy without taking seriously these ideological currents: the state's preferred "idea of India" is what the country's ruling political leadership seeks to advance.[225] Some of these have remained broadly consistent since independence, especially approaches to language, while others have changed, most notably the rise of Hindu nationalism. Since 2014, we have seen a clearly harder line on Kashmir and a much softer line on Hindu nationalist violence, which now takes the form of lynchings, displays of force, and localized vigilantism, ignored or even abetted by police. The Modi government frames its enemies, armed and not, as agents of infestation and subversion. The 2019 abrogation of Jammu and Kashmir's special status, followed by a strikingly intense communications blackout and widespread political detentions, were justified as triggering economic development and political renaissance. Thus far there is little evidence of either, and instead the satisfaction of BJP supporters over this move seems to have been symbolic and ideological—ending the special status of Kashmir, putting Muslims in their place, and providing opportunities for non-Kashmiris to move to Kashmir.

More broadly, the BJP's heavy emphasis on Muslims, Pakistan, and the threat of subversion has fused with a hunt for antinational traitors aimed at dissidents, leftist students and intellectuals, and anyone else identified as enemies of the party's project. The state's weight has been thrown behind this project. BJP politicians openly claim that Hindus must control state power, with no pretense of secularism.[226] These changes have been wrought by a combination of electoral mobilization, state repressive power, and a concerted effort at changing public discourses and "common sense" through the media and educational system. Rather than a stable "reverse centrist spiral" in Indian politics, fundamental questions of nationalist boundaries and hierarchies are in motion as the BJP advances its agenda.[227] The key question for India's politics in the years to come is whether this project changes in response to events, opposition, and elections.

PAKISTAN

Pakistan's history of armed politics shows both highly repressive crackdowns and extensive, deep alliances lasting for years or even decades. There is less of a "gray zone" than in India. Instead, armed orders in Pakistan have more cleanly bifurcated into fairly sustained conflict with insurgents and close cooperation with a variety of pro-state militias and transnational militant groups. Armed electoral politics resemble those in India, but have been far less extensive and clustered primarily in Karachi. The number of armed groups that have cooperated in some capacity with the Pakistani security apparatus is rather stunning, while the severity of crackdowns against some other groups is equally striking.

This chapter argues that the combination of a contested but powerful articulation of Muslim nationalism stretching back to the colonial period with the Pakistan Army's particular version of this project has led to a relatively consistent threat perception and corresponding pattern of armed politics. The state's security managers have viewed ethno-linguistic separatists as ideologically opposed, while having a complex but ultimately more sympathetic view of Islamist armed actors as existing in the gray zone or being ideologically aligned. This leads me to expect a hard line against ethno-linguistic groups and a far more heterogeneous armed politics with self-described Islamists. Tactical overlap between the state and specific armed groups has emerged from cross-border rivalries regarding India and Afghanistan, electoral politics in Karachi especially, and counterinsurgency operations. These tactical incentives have, at times, complicated broader ideological alignments.

Though many analysts and policymakers have been puzzled by what they see as counterproductive Pakistani state and military policies, I argue they flow from a particular set of understandings of the polity and the threats to it. These have indeed often driven counterproductive and destabilizing strategies, but we can still discern a logic undergirding broad patterns of violence management strategy. I also argue that civilian parties sometimes have overlapping threat perceptions, including skepticism about ethno-nationalism and, in some cases, sympathies with Islamist actors, but that the military bears ultimate responsibility for trajectories of armed politics in the country.

This chapter first works through the origins and evolution of regime projects in Pakistan, exploring both colonial and postcolonial conceptualizations of the nation. The chapter seeks to array political actors along Pakistan's "sharia-secularism spectrum," the redistributive dimension, and ethno-linguistic inclusion and hierarchies.[1] It uses these historical trends to outline expectations for internal security policy that are then assessed using the AOSA data and qualitative cases. The chapter thematically explores state responses to linguistic/regional armed groups, strategies toward "Islamist" actors, and electoral violence. It then offers a deeper discussion of patterns of discrimination in targeting of armed groups in Pakistan's Northwest between 2002 and 2015, drawing on joint work with Asfandyar Mir and Sameer Lalwani.[2] It concludes with implications for understanding Pakistani nationalism and security policy.

Building the Idea of Pakistan: The Rise of the Muslim League

The Muslim League emerged later than the Congress, as part of a growing apprehension among Muslims of the consequences of Hindu educational advantages and majority status in the context of British rule. The League went from being an advocacy group for elite north Indian Muslims to an aspiring mass political party seeking some form of parity with the Congress to, eventually, the bearer of a "Muslim nationalism" that sought to carve out an independent nation-state for South Asia's Muslims. The League's byzantine political maneuverings created both intentional and unintentional ambiguities in what it desired from its national project. But it would increasingly embrace demands for some form of Muslim political community, whether fully sovereign or largely autonomous, that would be defined by religion as, at least, an identity marker and, at most, a system of governance. By the onset of World War II and the British crackdown on Congress in 1942, the League had articulated a Muslim nationalism that sharply challenged the Congress' vision.

How did this project answer key questions about language, religion, and ethnicity? By 1947 and the partition of the subcontinent, we would see a distinct distrust and fear of regional linguistic identities, an embrace, despite sustained vagueness, of Islam and the category of "Muslim" as central to a future nation, and a linguistic push for Urdu as integral to nationalism. The League's ideological project was much hazier than that of Congress, and key questions remained unanswered. Yet the politics of the period laid an important structural basis for the politics to come, both in the questions that were answered and those that remained ambiguous.

Formation to Marginalization, 1906–36

The partition of Bengal marked "the event which led Muslims to organize against the Congress."[3] In October 1906 delegation of Muslims asked the Viceroy in Simla for separate and weighted representation of Muslims in the legislative council,[4] and in December 1906 the All-India Muslim League was founded.[5] Shaikh argues that with creation of the League "many [Muslims] sought to restrict, once and for all, Congress' role as spokesman for Hindu, or at least non-Muslim, interests";[6] the Simla delegation "pointed to a vision of society as consisting of two exclusive political groupings—Muslims and non-Muslims."[7] Yet this was not a particularly developed vision, compatible as it was with a wide variety of political structures.

The League built on a rich line of political thought that had tried to identify the distinctive characteristics of South Asian Muslims.[8] Broader international dynamics also became relevant to the subcontinent, as "political ideologies of north Indian Muslims in the 1910s and 1920s were in some cases moulded in response to international developments in the Islamic World."[9] As Jaffrelot argues, the League's nascent "nationalism was a product of a strategy of identity building that an elite group developed in order to escape the Other's domination. While religion was not an exclusive dividing line before the late nineteenth century, it became one at the turn of the twentieth century because of socio-economic, educational and political factors."[10]

Jinnah, then actually a member of Congress, feared that mass politics of the type that Gandhi advanced from 1919 would unleash uncontrollable forces that could not be harnessed by the kind of elite bargaining he favored. Jinnah left the Congress in 1920.[11] The League argued that "Congress was essentially a Hindu, that is to say a non-Muslim, party, fundamentally unqualified to represent Muslim interests."[12]

Yet the League was not particularly active during the 1920s; it faced "political demise,"[13] especially as province-based Muslim parties emerged after the 1919 Montagu-Chelmsford reforms.[14] The end of the Khilafat movement "led to a noticeable political vacuum at the level of all-India Muslim politics" and "the League afterward [following the Khilafat movement] was faced with the salience of regional identities based on ethno-linguistic markers that were now eating away at the foundations of its nationalism."[15] Jinnah spent extensive time in the United Kingdom, while the Congress' internal fractures and lack of major movement in British policy lessened the urgency of its threat to the League's elite Muslim constituency.

This began to change in 1928 due to the Nehru Report discussed in the previous chapter: the INC broke from the prospect of separate electorates and other religiously defined political categorizations.[16] The report was a major statement by Congress, both because of its embrace of multilingualism and its rejection of the Lucknow Pact's vision of interreligious elite collusion. The Congress "largely ignored these [Jinnah's] demands by virtue of a conception of the Indian nation based more on individual citizens than on communities. It recommended the abolition of separate electorates and the maintenance of seats reserved for Muslims only in the provinces where they were in a minority."[17] For Jalal, "It was the perceived threat from the singular and uncompromising 'nationalism' of the Congress to provincial autonomy and class interests which gave the discourse and politics of the Indian Muslims as a subcontinental category a fresh lease of life."[18]

As Shaikh argues, two broad meanings

> have attached to the idea of the Muslim community as it took shape in the context of nineteenth-century colonial India. The first drew attention to the universalist dimensions of the Muslim community by emphasizing its inclusive nature, although it also narrowed its parameters by defining the community in strictly religious terms as faith-based. The second, more exclusive in character, restricted its definition to the sum total of Muslims in India but allowed for the meanings of the community to extend the strict tenets of the faith to encompass the realms of culture and custom.[19]

Jinnah adopted the second approach, but its relationship to the more universalist vision remained ambiguous; as Jaffrelot argues, there was an enduring tension in League ideology between Muslim nationalism and Islamic nationalism. Part of this stress on the Muslim identity cleavage—whatever its specific meaning—was a denial of regional particularity: drawing on Sir Sayyid, "This apparent denial of the validity of a Muslims' regional ties and indeed the rejection of regional expressions of Islam would, in time, come to be closely associated with the religious stance of Pakistan's governing elite."[20] We see this opposition to regionalism emerging, for instance, in the urban Punjab, where urban mobilizations in 1920s "illustrated the power of Islamic symbols to call forth from Muslims a public commitment that defined the existence of a Muslim political community independent of the structure of the colonial state" and, thus, of the Unionist Party's Punjab-centric regionalism.[21]

As we will see below, regionalist resistance to the League posed a massive challenge to Jinnah. Put simply: Why should Muslims in Muslim-majority provinces like Punjab "mobilize behind the League in the service of Muslims in minority provinces?"[22] Indeed, during this period, both Fazl-i-Husain's Unionists and Fazlul Haq's Krishak Praja Party tried to avoid being subsumed into the League's Hindu-Muslim dichotomy.[23] For Gilmartin, "Central to the dynamics of the Pakistan movement were thus the conflicting pulls on Muslims of multiple identities, foremost among which were the provincial and linguistic allegiances— particularly in Punjab and Bengal—that had gained heightened meaning as the British had devolved power to the provinces after 1919."[24]

This was a clearly modern, new ideological construction rather than a call to return to religious practice: "What they stressed was not communal withdrawal and the intensification of religious faith but the consolidation of a distinct Muslim identity shaped by the forces of modern, Western education and intelligible to their new imperial masters."[25] This community vision drove key leaders—but it, and they, deployed a clearly religious discourse that embedded Islam at the center of Pakistani nationalism. Its future meaning would be contested, opening the door to a wide variety of interpretations of how Islam and nation relate: "The building blocks that shaped the idea of Pakistan—community, nation and power—though largely informed by Islam, were all strongly contested. . . . [including] a marked lack of consensus regarding the meaning of Islam."[26]

It is worth noting that the League's emerging political goals did not yet demand an independent state. Indeed, in the 1930s various federal schemes were floated that were potentially compatible with some kind of Muslim homeland within a unified India. "Iqbal's ideas [of 1930] were dismissed as mere poetics in established Muslim political circles," and most leaders focused on the nitty-gritty of political maneuvering and local political rivalry.[27] Nevertheless, this new imagining of a Muslim nationalism (whether to be an independent state or an autonomous subnational entity) was "so extraordinary as to be world-historical in nature," breaking from past precedents.[28]

Jinnah's Return and Battle for Primacy, 1936–42

Political action returned with a fervor after the 1935 Government of India Act. Jinnah made his return to India, preparing to try to bolster this League project in the face of spreading mass politics.[29] The period of the late 1930s saw Jinnah aggressively seek to wrangle provincial bases, especially in Punjab and Bengal, into some kind of loose alignment with the League's broader project. The League's base in minority Muslim provinces was an ever-growing liability in the face of looming majority rule, and so it needed to broaden into the Muslim-majority areas: "Even in the late 1930s, Muslim identity-formation took very different forms in the provincial and national registers."[30] The 1937 provincial elections were a watershed in which the Congress' rise spurred the League to eventually make its demand for some sort of national status in the 1940 Lahore Resolution.

Overcoming regionalism was a challenge in Punjab.[31] The Unionist Party dominated Punjab's politics, and its leader "Sir Fazli Husain rejected outright the idea of building a political party on identification with religious symbols."[32] Indeed, "Husain rejected Muhammed Ali Jinnah's overture to form a united all-India Muslim party before the 1937 elections."[33] As he returned to power, Jinnah faced a delicate balancing act of both trying to win over the Unionists and supporting their (largely city-based) rivals: "In 1936, Jinnah's strongest backing in Punjab came from urban Muslims who had challenged Unionist ideology, Ahar leaders, and 'miscellaneous Urbanites' (as Sir Fazli Husain put it) who saw religious commitment as a foundation for a direct challenge to the structure of imperial power. Many were deeply involved in the symbolic Islamic agitations of the 1930s. Whatever Jinnah's personal religious views, nothing illustrated his political leanings more clearly than his attempted alliance with the Jami'at-I Ulayma-yi Hind in Punjab.[34] Here religious symbolism was used as a wedge to attack the Unionists' cross-religious rural base; Pakistan's future language of politics was being established.

Bengal posed a major challenge. Leftist peasant mobilization was far more pervasive in Bengal than in Punjab, and Bengali linguistic regionalism posed an alternative to the North Indian Muslim elite's conception of politics: "It was in Bengal that the idea of a Muslim nation proved to be most problematic."[35] The Bengali challenge would endure into independence, culminating in the bloody independence of Bangladesh. The League continually found itself bargaining with Bengali leaders, even those who were simultaneously senior League figures, especially A. K. Fazlul Haq, who led the Krishak Praja Party (KPP) in Bengal through 1937.[36] Some in Bengal offered a vision of a more decentralized, differentiated polity not run by north Indian elites. Indeed, through to the run-up to Partition, some Bengalis hoped for an independent Bengal rather than the province's vivisection.

Jinnah launched a political offensive against these provinces by placing Urdu and Islam at the center of an emerging new nationalism. Urdu, the language of the north Indian elite, was identified as the true "Muslim" language of the subcontinent, especially with its linguistic links to Arabic. As Ayres notes, "This concept of national purity, at least insofar as the Pakistan Movement represented it, was very closely linked to the Urdu language as the authorized language of South Asian Islam."[37]

Islam would be the other nationalizing glue: "For the most part, those who fought for Pakistan assumed that Islam would bind together the citizens of the new state regardless of their geographic origins," while "Jinnah and his close associates imagined a singular Pakistan united by the bond of Islam as one nation."[38] Moreover, the two were bound together: "The defence of Islam was also linked to the defence of Urdu."[39] Jinnah took advantage of internal factionalism in Bengal to win over part of the Muslim political elite, preventing the consolidation of a Bengali bloc, while the Punjab's Unionist Party would finally falter in 1946–47 under the weight of communal polarization.

Jinnah's nationalist project did not focus on the content of religious practice: "To overcome the divisive nature of Muslim politics the strategy that emerged was not to define in detail the content of Muslim nationalism but to emphasise the threat from the 'Other.'"[40] It instead used the identity category "Muslim" as the basis for political mobilization, as Jinnah sought "to reshape Muslim politics by using the language of Islamic universalism. By doing so, he hoped to forge an instrument that not only chimed with Muslim sentiment, but would also serve as a powerful tool to mobilize Muslim opinion in favour of his campaign."[41]

This project came more openly into sight, rife as it remained with vagueness and contradictions, with the Lahore Resolution of 1940. The Lahore Resolution called for independent states for India's Muslims. Shaikh and Jalal agree that at least deep into the 1930s Jinnah would settle for some kind of federal arrangement.[42] Lahore did not close off the range of possibilities for what a future India would look like; indeed, its "remarkably clumsy wording left ample—and probably deliberate—scope for vagueness, ambiguity, and equivocation."[43]

Despite this ambiguity, within key sections of the League, above all in the north Indian strongholds of the movement, the 1940s was an energetic period of ideological debate and imagination. Devji, Jaffrelot, and Dhulipala have recently unpacked important ideological antecedents of what became Pakistan, among both clerics and nonclerics.[44] These understandings were not spread evenly throughout the subcontinent's Muslims (especially in Bengal): the earlier literature is right that there was no consensus Muslim League position, either among elites or local activists. The League vision remained, even as it moved toward Partition, fuzzier than the Congress' on key issues.

But the concentration of these political debates and innovations in north India was crucial to the future because these future Muhajir elites would disproportionately lead Pakistan in its early years. Pakistan took on a clear vision as a sanctuary free of Hindu domination. Given the experiences of the League in the colonial era, central to the emerging North Indian Muslim vision of Pakistan was the key place of Urdu as a symbol of South Asian Muslim heritage and pride, a deep suspicion of localized politics that could fracture the unity of the community, and an emphasis on Islam as a political mobilization tool.

Yet this act of innovation could not escape rival ideological visions, whether the practice-oriented Islamist vision of Pakistan or a regionalist vision of a highly decentralized Muslim homeland (or homelands). Therefore, "Jinnah's attempt to recast Indian Muslims as a nation solely on the basis of religious affinity was clearly fraught with contradictions. Not least were the deep ethnic and linguistic divisions that separated Muslims across the sub-continent."[45] These alternative understandings of how to define the polity would haunt both the Muslim League and Pakistan in the years and decades to come.

Regional Politics and Bengal

Both the Muslim League and the Congress sought to overcome regional particularities to build a unified sense of nation across geography. The Congress' move toward multilingualism, however, reduced the internal stresses of this unifying move, though distinct regional sentiments and political identities remained. The League's reliance on Urdu and on a particular north Indian vision of Islam as unifying forces, however, made it much less politically effective in minimizing or accommodating regional cleavages. A somewhat loose but enduring alternative project presented itself at the provincial level, where League nationalism ran into local political identities. Bengal, Punjab, and the Pashtun Northwest were key areas of provincial identity. As we saw above, Jinnah was able to move into both Punjab and Bengal. In the postindependence dispensation, Punjab would be the heartland of the new state (especially its military), while Bengal emerged as an alternative pole of nationalism.

Bengali politics under the colonial period were extremely complex and often fragmented along lines of class, religion, and geography. We cannot speak of a coherent Bengali political project. What we do see, however, is discomfort with Urdu as a dominant language, an interest in the idea of Pakistan involving multiple Muslim homelands, rather than a single, centralized nation-state, and a greater focus on leftist redistribution. This combination placed key Bengali politicians in tension with the League's project. This attitude was reciprocated by Jinnah: "And however important the Muslim-majority provinces were to Jinnah as a bargaining counter in his demand for parity for the League at the centre, his relations with Bengali Muslim politicians were equivocal and as far as possible he kept his distance from them."[46] There were League loyalists, but even many politicians who ultimately aligned with the League had preferences for a decentralized

Pakistan that would allow substantial autonomy to Bengal. Given that Bengalis would form the majority of the new state's population after 1947, this project was of obvious importance for the future.

Grappling with the Political Meaning of Pakistan

India benefited from a comparatively cohesive, well-defined carrier movement in the Congress. Pakistan's Muslim League was much less unified and had struggled to develop or articulate a clear ideology of the polity. Yet the broad markers it lay down would be enormously important, despite their haziness. Defining Pakistan as, in some way, a political community for the subcontinent's Muslims fused together religion and nation. Political appeals to the nation, therefore, had to include appeals to religious solidarity. Over the course of the early postindependence decades, a particular brand of Muslim nationalism advanced by civilians in West Pakistan, the military, and the civil bureaucracy came to dominate the elite politics of Pakistan: "In this exclusionary view of nationhood, recognizing intra-Muslim differences would mean the symbolic undoing of the Pakistan project."[47] Whatever Jinnah's true political goals were, "it is incontrovertible that he saw Hindus and Muslims differently."[48]

This project pitted itself against some of the same regionalist, largely ethno-linguistically defined, forces that had bedeviled League leaders during the colonial period. Alongside this struggle, which would eventually burst into open warfare in Balochistan and East Pakistan, was an enduring set of debates about who counted as a Muslim and the extent to which non-Muslims were included in the Pakistani nation. Contests over the boundaries of and hierarchies within the nation consumed Pakistan's early politics. These two cleavages—of region/language and of religion/nation—have been the dominant areas of ideological contention across Pakistan's history. The early repression of the Communist Party of Pakistan largely eliminated the leftist dimension; though the 1960s and 1970s did see political mobilization over redistribution and the return of a nontrivial Left, this was an anomaly. As Cohen writes, "The leftist vision of Pakistan was incompatible with that of the Establishment . . . the left was systematically suppressed and the Communist Party of Pakistan was banned."[49] The military government of Ayub Khan sought, from 1958, the consolidation of an antileftist, antiseparatist Muslim nationalism to stabilize Pakistan.

Ethno-linguistic mobilization was feared by military and West Pakistani civilian ruling elites, who saw this political cleavage as the greatest threat to the unity of Pakistan. This perception would be turned into action by military crackdowns in Balochistan and East Pakistan, where containment and total war were the default responses to separatist and autonomist movements. While there was limited armed mobilization by groups deploying Islam in the early decades of Pakistan, we see both ideological space for their political claims and some instances of violence (such as by anti-Ahmadi rioters). While it is true that Zia al-Huq's military regime marked a hard turn toward Islamization from 1977, the basic elements that could fuse Urdu-Islam with Pakistan were put in place prior to the late 1970s: Zia's project represented a "fruition of a particular vision of the nation quite apparent from the very start."[50]

Unlike in India, it is difficult to pull apart these cleavages—the confluence of language, religion, and redistribution operated simultaneously in a number of key political disputes, above all the balance between East and West Pakistan. Instead, I approach the evolution of Pakistan's politics through 1972 chronologically, while clearly identifying the consolidation of an ideological project around Ayub Khan and the army and the basis of the threat perception that led to the bloodshed of 1971.

Regionalism, Islam, and Pakistan's Constitutional Battles: Toward Military Rule, 1947–58

Unlike the Congress party-state, the League was a weak and divided institution as it took over the new state of Pakistan.[51] With its leaders heavily drawn from areas now in India, the League lacked the deep roots of patronage and mobilization that had been built by the Congress. It buckled further after the 1948 death of Jinnah, who had so dominated the League from the mid-1930s onward. Liaquat Ali Khan took over power, but without reliable party institutions to build on. Consequently, Pakistan's politics were far more fractured than India's, with a variety of contending projects battling over control of central and provincial power.

Institutionally, Liaquat and his successors (after he was assassinated in 1951) came to rely on the civil bureaucracy to actually run the country. Multiple parties and factions emerged out of the League.[52] Yet Liaquat tried to centralize power: "Pakistan, to Liaquat, depended on the existence of a strong Muslim League and the exclusion of other parties from government power."[53] The conflict this engendered occurred against the backdrop of growing assertiveness by unelected institutions. In 1954, the civil bureaucracy made its power clear by blocking the ongoing Constituent Assembly; a constitution was only agreed on in 1956. It was soon overthrown by a civil-military coup in 1958. This coup followed a decade of the military gaining enormous resources and political influence. The threat from India, legacies of the war over Kashmir, and several crises with India in the early 1950s heightened the perception of danger. These dynamics all occurred against the backdrop of an ongoing effort to generate a constitution through a Constituent Assembly. Unlike in India, the Constituent Assembly in Pakistan became bogged down in disagreements over the ideological project that the new state-nation was to represent—as explored below, the Assembly was wracked by disagreement over questions of language and religion that were at the heart of the country's politics.

The League had emphasized the triplet of Muslim-Urdu-Pakistan, but this approach contained serious problems. Ideologically, there was no elite consensus about the meaning of the idea of Pakistan. There was some clarity on what it was not—it was not Hindu, leftist, or India. These exclusions were hugely important, but not the same as a clear specification of the nation's boundaries and hierarchies. Three types of linked political contestation thus emerged immediately at independence. They could be found in debates over the constitution, in electoral politics, and eventually, in military policies.

First, the actual implications of the "Muslim" part of that unity were highly unclear: "The building blocks that shaped the idea of Pakistan—community, nation and power—though largely informed by Islam, were all strongly contested. . . . [leading to] a marked lack of consensus regarding the meaning of Islam."[54] The Muslim League had never actually articulated a particular interpretation of how state and religion would align. Soon after independence, the Constituent Assembly, and the broader political system, faced disagreement about what would be distinctively Islamic or Muslim about Pakistan. The Objectives Resolution of 1949 tried to accommodate conflicting perspectives on what precisely Islam was doing for Pakistan, but "the range of debate on the Objectives Resolution in the Constituent Assembly demonstrated the lack of consensus among the members."[55]

Despite the lack of specificity, the Objectives Resolution fused Islam to Pakistan at a foundational level, and began a process of shifting Hindus into de facto second-class citizen status.[56] Ispahani argues that "the net effect of the Objectives Resolution was to define the state in Islamic terms."[57] As we will see below, the relatively large Hindu minority population of East Pakistan would make its Bengali Muslims also suspicious in the eyes of many Islamists and West Pakistanis. The terms of the Objectives Resolution and the eventual Constitution of 1956 gave Islam a central, though ambiguous, place in Pakistani politics—claims and demands could be most "legitimately" voiced in terms that justified themselves, in some way, on religious or ethno-religious terms. As Shaikh argues of the new ruling elite, "Their lack of local roots meant that few could do without some form of Islamic legitimation. But such legitimacy came at a price, which involved compromising the secular objectives with which these classes were closely associ-ated."[58] The League's language of politics under empire constrained the contours of legitimate public debate after independence.

The early 1950s also saw an eruption of rioting against Ahmadis. The target-ing of this minority sect was led by *ulema* who wanted the Ahmadis excluded as Muslims by an act of government; when the government refused to their demands, rioting and violence aimed at Ahmadis occurred in 1953.[59] The mili-tary was sent in to repress this violence, but an anti-Ahmadi project among many clerics had begun and would return with a vengeance in the 1970s. As a result of this political mobilization, "the clerics had turned the role of minorities in Pakistan into a wedge issue."[60] The 1950s saw the early primacy of Islam and Muslims over Hinduism and Hindus in the elite imagining of Pakistani national-ism, and the beginning of disputes over the most acceptable forms of religious practice. Under Ayub from 1958, Muslim nationalism would predominate over Islamic nationalism, but with a continual reliance on the symbols and language of Islam as a signifier of Pakistan, and enduring contestation over what precisely the relationship should be. As a general matter, however, "the right of religious minorities, most notably the Ahmadiyya Muslim sect, were given only minimal protection."[61]

Elites, especially bureaucratic and military, in the 1947–71 era "consistently instrumentalized Islam in order to establish and secure Pakistan's existence. However, they also simultaneously sought the authority to define Islam in terms that suited their agendas of modernization and nationalism, which inevitably brought them into conflict with the ulema."[62] This battle was not won by the modernizing elite, as these "*maslaki* parties and their parent movements played a decisive role in establishing Pakistan as the world's first Islamic republic—that is, a nation-state who internal legitimacy derives simultaneously from the consent of the people and an aspirational commitment to authentic Islamic governance."[63]

This religious mobilization and debate was joined by a deep linguistic cleavage along the lines of Urdu versus Bengali, which overlaid West versus East Pakistan. Jinnah's and the League's emphasis on Urdu as a unifying force was driven by a belief that "only through an incorporation of all into a unitary Urdu-speaking nation-state could the country recognize itself as a nation."[64] Yet this meant that "those who objected, or sought an alternative, were stigmatized as 'anti-Pakistan' fifth columns"—fueling regionalist resentment and mobilization.[65] Ultimately, "the contradiction between the country's multiethnic society and the founding Muslim League leadership's nation-state policies politicized and polarized ethnic (especially Bengali) identities and spurred movements for autonomy that sparked military and civilian elite fears of internal fragmentation and put a premium on assimilation."[66] The tensions produced by these enduring cleavages meant that "after independence no consensus emerged on the idea of Pakistan until one was imposed by the military [in 1958], and even it proved elusive."[67]

The 1950s saw this linguistic issue dominate politics, as the threat of Bengali political primacy faced a West Pakistani elite that clung to Urdu for both ideological and self-interested reasons, even to the point of wildly counterproductive policy choices. Multiple factions and projects faced off in this period, leading to a sometimes bewildering series of alliances, rivalries, and events that are far beyond the scope of this book. At the broadest level, however, "the Muslim League leaders. . . . promoted not only Islam but also Urdu as factors of integration in the framework of a unitary state. They wanted to use their new power to contain the ethno-linguistic divisions that had made their life so complicated in the 1930s-1940s."[68] Linguistic regionalism, which had been largely accommodated in India, was not in the cards in Pakistan. As Jaffrelot writes, "A large number of parties were identified with provinces and served as mouthpieces for ethnic movements. Not only did the country's rulers perceive these forces as centrifugal (and even separatist), often disqualifying them as 'anti-Pakistani,' but such groups also fostered the dissipation of the party system."[69]

This attitude came from the very top of the new regime. Jinnah, for instance, told a Bengali crowd in Dhaka in March 1948 that "the State Language of Pakistan is going to be Urdu and no other language. Any one who tries to mislead you is really the enemy of Pakistan. Without one State Language, no Nation can remain tied up solidly together and function."[70] He also opposed the Pakistani Left, going so far as to accuse Pakistan's communists in East Bengal of being foreign agents.[71] Liaquat Ali Khan, his successor, said in the Constituent Assembly that "Pakistan is a Muslim state, and it must have its lingua franca, a language of the Muslim nation."[72] He also "forcefully denied and derided regional demands for autonomy by declaring that Pakistan was only one nation and that 'we must kill this provincialism for all times to come.'"[73] Urdu was particularly attractive because it "could not be identified with any province of Pakistan—which was good for national integration—and had clear affinities with the Middle East where Islam was born."[74] This was clearly a part of a project of national imagining.

This project of pushing Urdu into society was most divisive and dangerous in East Pakistan, with its Bengali linguistic majority. In 1952, Urdu was made the national language as part of a central bureaucratic/West Pakistani elite aim to place Urdu at the center of the new nation: "In the structural opposition inherited from the Hindi-Urdu controversy, the available category of opposition to Urdu implied anti-Muslim, leading to the transference of this opposition onto Bengal."[75] A strand of political thinking among West Pakistani elites included "denying the legitimacy of all claims for political representation, participation, and regional autonomy based on subnational identities."[76]

The place given Urdu by many in West Pakistan triggered an angry response by Bengali political entrepreneurs, who wanted to combine federalism with a multilingual nationalism. They hoped to also turn Bengali demographic power into commensurate political representation. In the provincial elections of 1954, the United Front wiped out the Muslim League in East Pakistan and demanded a more decentralized Pakistan that could accommodate Bengali subnationalism within a united Pakistan. Bengali was incorporated as a national language in May 1954, but east-west tensions endured.[77]

Governor-General Ghulam Muhammad and the ruling elite cracked down on the United Front over remarks made by the East Pakistan chief minister that, they claimed, hinted at reuniting with West Bengal, and the civil bureaucracy became increasingly powerful and centralized, with the president of Pakistan assuming oversized powers. By 1956 West Pakistan had been unified into a single bloc as a form of parity with Bengali-dominated East Pakistan, with Punjab dominating the new entity. The 1956 Constitution that eventually emerged labeled Pakistan an Islamic Republic and built the Objectives Resolution into the constitution that indicated that laws should not be passed that were "repugnant" to Islam.[78] President Iskander Mirza exercised heavy influence over the elected government, symptomatic of an overcentralized political system. In Shah's words, "West Pakistani civilians and military elites refused to recognize subnational identities as legitimate, including the Pashtuns and Sindhis in West Pakistan."[79] In Guha's pithy summary, "Pakistan was created on the basis of religion, but divided on the basis of language."[80]

The power elite in Pakistan also viewed the Left with fear and contempt. Landed or industrial elites faced redistributive demands from peasant movements and parties, especially those based in East Pakistan, and Pakistan had a small communist movement that became a target of political repression. Like language and religion, the question of the Left in the 1950s was linked to East Pakistan: "The UF's alleged Communist bent supplied an additional sense of urgency to the problem" that the West Pakistani elite saw emanating from East Pakistan.[81] For instance, the finance minister in 1954 said that "making any concession to East Bengal would be really making a concession to communism."[82] In McGrath's words, "If there was one point of agreement among the landowners and well-to-do lawyers who made up the League's leadership, it was the fear of communism or other agencies of radical social and economic change."[83] The Communist Party was banned in July 1954 after doing well in East Bengal provincial elections amid allegations that a broader alliance "had conspired with the Pakistan Communist Party to undo the unity of Pakistan."[84] The Left would rise again, to a limited extent, in the 1960s and 1970s, but it was marginal to armed politics, unlike in India, Sri Lanka, or Burma. The successful preemptive suppression of the communists was very effective in blocking this dimension of political mobilization.

Pakistan was a site of intense ideological and political conflict. The deaths of Jinnah and Liaquat Ali Khan "left the [Muslim League] party leaderless and the Parliament deeply divided over the proper role of Islamic law in governmental policy, as well as over the proper division of power between the eastern and western wings of Pakistan."[85] The religious and ethno-linguistic dimensions were particularly conflictual, in ways that were little surprise given the history leading up to independence. The basic conceptual framework of chapter 1 applies well here—while obviously radically simplifying, it captures some of the fundamental contests at the heart of Pakistan's post-1947 politics.

Against the background of this political turmoil rose the Pakistan Army under General Ayub Khan. The military "leadership viewed provincialism as an artifice of politicians' chicanery and as a serious threat to the integrity of Pakistan."[86] Ghulam Muhammad's assertion of power in 1954 gave the interior and defense ministries to future president Iskander Mirza and army chief Ayub Khan; they would be the key figures in the 1958 military coup that put Ayub into power until 1969.[87] The army was focused heavily on building its fighting power against India and looked to both domestic resource extraction and alliance with the United States as the means to this goal.[88] The combination of resources and the perceived threat from India built a relatively cohesive and disciplined organization, in sharp contrast to the shambolic state of Pakistan's political parties.

Over the course of the 1950s, the military under Ayub developed an ideological project that drew on the Muslim League's preindependence politics, the geopolitics of the subcontinent, and the legacies of the British military framework of colonial rule: the military's "perception of reality was hammered into an unchanging strategic doctrine that has profoundly shaped the history and political institutions of the country."[89] The army's project was not Islamist in terms of religious practice, but instead a Muslim nationalism that centered the identity category "Muslim" as central to the Pakistani nation, along with Urdu and a modernizing economic policy. Hindus in East Pakistan were framed as potentially subversive threats, Bengalis relegated to second-class nationhood as an effete and Hinduized ethnic community, and other manifestations of subnationalism seen as fissiparous cleavages that could open the way to an Indian-backed breaking up of the fragile new country.[90] Yet this was not a particularly religiously observant institution; indeed, Ayub himself disliked many of the ulema and thought of Islam as a nationalist tool, not a transnational doctrine. He instead "sought to build a strong central government that would be reinforced by Islam."[91]

In collusion with President Iskander Mirza, the elected government was swept aside in 1958. As Shah argues, "What mattered in shaping the military's institutional response to these perceived threats was how the military interpreted them" and that in 1958, "objectively speaking, there was no catastrophic danger of internal fragmentation or economic collapse at the time of the coup"—it was instead the perception of corrupt, dysfunctional politicians and subnational tensions both in East Pakistan and during the attempted secession of the Khan of Kalat that triggered the military intervention.[92] We will see some similar dynamics in late 1950s–early 1960s Burma. However, Mirza was quickly shoved aside as Ayub and the military became the dominant partner in the military-civil bureaucracy relationship. The army and civil bureaucracy together would dominate Pakistani politics until the disasters of 1971.

Ayub Takes Over (and Falls): Autocracy and "Muslim Nationalism," 1958–71

The new order that Ayub pursued from 1958 until he was forced from office in 1969 combined Muslim nationalism, a particular flavor of economic modernization, and political centralization. In sharp contrast to the Zia regime of 1977–88, Ayub was not an Islamizer. But he was nevertheless deeply skeptical of Bengali and Baloch subnationalism, opposed to the Left, and in favor of political project that could paper over political diversity in Pakistan. This reflected a particular distillation of the various strands available from the League's colonial project. Discipline and social control were fundamental to Ayub's vision of the polity, making him a favorite of Samuel Huntington's 1968 *Political Order in Changing Societies*.[93]

Many things happened in the 1958–71 period, but for the purposes of studying armed politics, the key political action was on the question of subnational mobilization, especially in East Pakistan. There was leftist mobilization in Pakistan, which succeeded in eventually pushing Ayub out, but which was nevertheless met by consistent repression by both him and his successor, military chief Yahya Khan.[94] The 1960s saw the rise of Baloch insurgency. I discuss the specific orders that emerged, and the problems of data that face efforts to study them, in the section on comparative armed orders below. But the political problem that Baloch mobilization, violent or not, represented was the enduring issue of subnationalism and whether, or how, it could be accommodated within a Pakistan that was supposed to be an encompassing homeland for the subcontinent's Muslims. While relatively peripheral to the broader politics of the country, the Baloch question would recur as a challenge to the unity of the state.

Far more central to Pakistani politics was the east-west cleavage. This involved battles over economic redistribution, the distribution of power across regions, and "real" Islam. East Pakistan's economy was systematically ignored by Ayub's development strategy, which focused on industrialization in the west. Bengali remained a national language, but Bengalis were massively underrepresented at the apex of the military and civil bureaucracy, and so regional autonomy continued to be a key demand of many Bengali politicians.

In 1966, the Awami League advanced its Six Point Program, which called for substantial decentralization and a much looser federal structure. Sheikh Mujibur Rahman was a key Bengali politician leading the charge for a radical restructuring of the polity, one that would place far greater power in the hands of East Pakistan. This was a crucial moment in the rise of a clear alternative political project to that of Ayub and the components of the old Muslim League he drew on: it decentered Urdu from Pakistani nationalism and opened space for a broader understanding of what Islam meant for Pakistan.

Ayub had little time for either Islamic clerics or Bengali autonomists. His diaries are a rich source of insight into his ideological worldview. On clerics, for instance, "I told them [a cabinet meeting about JI and political mullahs] that the real trouble was that having attained Pakistan, we shouted so much of running it on Islamic lines without defining what it was that we foolishly passed the initiative on to the mullahs who had always been opposed to Pakistan and the educated Muslim. He, the mullah, got the opportunity of his life to dictate how this state should be run which in the final analysis means that it should be handed over to him as he is the rightful custodian and interpreter of Islam."[95] Ayub wanted Islam as a signifier of Pakistani nationalism, but not Islamic practices or doctrines.

On the question of East Pakistan, Ayub was scathing, framing Bengalis as essentially Hinduized and subverted by Indian influence. He argued that that if Mujib's program was adopted, "the point of no return would be reached and East Pakistan will go under Hinduism and be separated forever."[96] To explain why East Pakistan was so restive, he noted that "when thinking of problems of East Pakistan one cannot help feeling that their urge to isolate themselves from West Pakistan and revert to Hindu language and culture is close to the fact that they have no culture and language of their own nor have they been able to assimilate the culture of the Muslims of the subcontinent by turning their back on Urdu. Further, by doing so they have forced two state languages on Pakistan. This has been a great tragedy for them and for the rest of Pakistan. They especially lack literature on the philosophy of Islam."[97]

Thus, even for the non-Islamist Ayub, Islam and nation were tied together: "Without meaning any unkindness, the fact of the matter is that a large majority of the Muslims in East Pakistan have an animist base which is a thick layer of Hinduism and top crust of Islam which is pierced by Hinduism from time to time."[98] And in a chilling preview of the kind of threat perception that would lead to slaughter in 1971, he told Khawaja Shahabuddin, regarding East Pakistan, "We could not think of a worst combination. Hindus and Bengalis. I told the Khawaja not to lose heart. If worse comes to the worst, we shall not hesitate to fight a relentless battle against the disruptionists of East Pakistan. Rivers of blood will flow if need be, unhappily. We will arise to save our crores Muslims from Hindu slavery."[99] The religious language and framing is striking, showing how deeply the particular fusing of Islam-Urdu-nation at the heart of the Pakistani elite had frozen out more than half the country's citizenry from being seen as "true" Pakistanis and patriots.

Unsurprisingly, the government's response to Bengali autonomist politicians and activists was "repression . . . on the ground that their actions threatened national cohesion."[100] When Ayub was forced out in 1969 because of mass mobilization, he handed power to Yahya Khan, the head of the army. Yahya moved toward greater electoral opening—but this opening promised to allow Bengalis to turn their demographic power into political clout. Many West Pakistanis, now led by Zulfiqar Bhutto and his new Pakistan People's Party (PPP), resolutely opposed this possibility, and the December 1970 election that gave victory to Mujibur Rahman and his Awami League triggered a massive crisis.

Bengali mobilization was a direct threat to the interests of the West Pakistani elite, and to key ideological precepts of the Muslim League: the loose confederation Rahman imagined, including many Hindus in East Pakistan, was not the cohesive, Muslim community of Urdu-speakers that the League elite and its successors had envisioned. Yahya's unwillingness to compromise with Rahman, forced in part by Bhutto's hard-line stance, led to the breakdown of the Pakistani political system. The deep, ethnicized east-west cleavage drove the escalation of conflict into full-scale war.[101] In March 1971, as I discuss in greater detail below, state security forces launched a brutal, total war crackdown on Bengali politicians, Hindu intellectuals, and other suspect categories in East Pakistan. The project of Jinnah's successors faced its ultimate failure in 1971: the intended homeland for South Asia's Muslims had been split in two.

Bhutto and Zia: Islamist Turns after 1971

The most complex pattern of change in the subcontinent can be found in Pakistan. The loss of East Pakistan had two effects. First, it temporarily removed the army from political control, with Zulfikar Bhutto becoming the prime minister. Second, it spurred a reimagination of the idea of Pakistan: with Bangladesh now existing, how could Pakistan claim to be the homeland of the subcontinent's Muslims? The second question overrode the first opportunity: Bhutto—long a fierce advocate of centralizing West Pakistani hegemony—was unable to create a new template for state-society relations, opening a space for the Islamizing Zia to push for a much more religiously grounded understanding of Pakistani nationalism.

The 1971–77 period saw Bhutto try to answer the second question while holding onto power. He first turned to the Left, hoping that socialism combined with a soft Muslim nationalism leveraged against India could trigger economic growth and political stability. A fusion of Islam and socialism was the aspirational package that Bhutto offered. As this agenda faltered—the Left had been largely dismantled in the 1950s and the PPP lacked a firm national grounding to sustain redistributive mobilization—he then tacked to the right and began to curry favor with Islamists.[102] Bhutto had been a key player in the hard line that West Pakistan had taken with the Bengalis of the east, and his views of language were only different than Ayub's in his greater favoritism of his Sindhi political base.[103] Bhutto's project failed badly. The protests following Bhutto's rigged reelection in 1977 spurred a coup that put General Zia al-Huq in charge of Pakistan. The Bhutto years ultimately represented a wasted opportunity to imagine Pakistan anew; Bhutto's posture prior to 1971 as a disastrously miscalculating advocate of West Pakistan's interests and his ideological inconsistency made him a poor leader for setting a new direction from the failed project of Ayub. The basic centralizing and homogenizing impulses of the Pakistan political elite remained in place under Bhutto, though his efforts at building a robust civilian party and a coup-proofing paramilitary force marked a major departure from the developmental authoritarianism of Ayub Khan.

The reign of General Zia al-Huq marks a major change because he moved from the vague Muslim nationalism of Ayub and frenetic inconsistency of Bhutto toward a more consistently Islamist ideological project: "The Islamization of the polity was the central concern of the martial law regime."[104] Zia's agenda was both "strategic and sincere."[105] He saw "Islamization as a process of bringing religious institutions under the control of the state" while also attempting to overcome the "legitimacy crisis" that followed from his seizure of power. It was "regulative, punitive, and extractive" project.[106] Zia both genuinely believed in the primacy of Islam within Pakistani nationalism, *and* used it as a tool to consolidate power in the wake of a brutal coup and the political repression that followed it.

Islam as practice rose in prominence compared to Muslim as category: being Pakistani, in Zia's eyes, meant being a practicing Muslim, particularly a Sunni Muslim. This was not remotely a consensus view in Pakistan, but Zia centralized power in his regime, and his views had a major effect on how the state apparatus deployed religion and framed nationalism. This effort sought to cut through the ambiguities of the past that had clouded the precise relationship between Islam and nation. As Nasr summarizes Zia's agenda, "The Islamization package that General Zia unveiled in 1979, despite its claims of Islamic universalism, was in essence based on narrow Sunni interpretations of Islamic law."[107] Rizvi argues that this marks a shift, providing the "first instance in Pakistan's history when the ruling generals openly declared themselves to be conservative-Islamic in their orientations and cultivated close ties with the political groups of the right, especially those Islam-oriented parties that were prepared to support martial law."

Zia changed textbooks and military training, censored the media while advancing particular narratives through state media production, and introduced a far more explicitly, formally Islamic set of narratives into the public sphere with the imprimatur of state power.[108] This was an ambitious project that reached into both state and society—"Zia pushed out army officers who were too progressive, replaced liberal professors in the universities with members of JI [Jamaat-e-Islami], and promoted both Islamists and orthodox conservatives in the army, the ISI [Inter-Services Intelligence agency], the bureaucracy, and the judiciary."[109] The new constitution, for instance, made Islam a central feature of the definition of the Pakistani nation—not a total break from the past, but a narrowing and hardening of the conflation of Islam and nation. As Ayres argues, under Zia there was "a more forceful push on the state project to produce the people by further emphasizing the idea of the state as Islamic, with a concentration on the austere Deoband tradition patronized by Zia and reinforced by Saudi Wahhabism."[110] Once again, the fear of fissiparous linguistic and regional forces haunted the leader of the state—"Zia's understanding of national cohesion was that Islam was the binding force of the Pakistani nation. He thus advocated the promotion of Arabic and Urdu as a means of overcoming the provincial and 'centrifugal' forces which threatened to rip the nation further apart."[111]

Zia marks a shift away from the Muslim nationalism of Ayub Khan and the developmental authoritarians of the 1950s and 1960s—for Zia, "Islam was at the center of his vision of a rejuvenated Pakistani state . . . Zia was the first Pakistani leader to take Islam seriously."[112] He operated in a context comparatively friendly to appeals to religion, but intentionally chose to emphasize and deploy Islam as a core component of his rule: there was plenty of opportunity for agency that Zia took full advantage of.

A key consequence of this change was far greater ideological space for Sunni Islamist militants and radicals to mobilize within "mainstream" politics.[113] They moved into a gray zone or aligned position, a process with paler echoes in India with the rise of Hindu nationalist armed actors (though these are far more clearly enmeshed in electoral politics). The intensification of the Afghanistan war accelerated preexisting support for mujahideen groups and made them central to Pakistani foreign policy and fused with Zia's regime. This shift thus generated a set of broader consequences, including "far-reaching implications for the role of Islam in the Army,"[114] as, more broadly, "religion acquired new meaning in the political arena and led to the making of political Islam, with extremism, militancy, and radicalism emerging as its various facets."[115] Shiite mobilization in response to Zia's efforts to push this project in turn led the military establishment to see them as a threat, and as a stalking horse for revolutionary Iran; as a result, "Zia's regime began its efforts to contain Shi'i assertiveness by investing in Sunni institutions in general and Sunni seminaries in particular."[116] These various shifts created legacies that would restrict the ability of subsequent leaders to quickly roll back Zia's agenda.

Some things did not change under Zia. Above all, ethno-linguistic minorities continued to be deeply suspect, whether in Balochistan or Sindh (where repression of prodemocracy protesters took place in the early 1980s), in continuity with the past. No room opened for the Left, which continued to be targeted. As Ullah summarizes Zia's views, "Since there was only one Islam and Pakistan was an Islamic state, he could thus portray any expression of ethnic, regional, or political difference as 'antithetical' to Islam. As Zia himself once succinctly put it, 'One God, One Prophet, One Book, one country, one system—no dissension!'"[117] This is in line with the suspicion of dissent and mobilization from the margins found among previous leaders. While Pakistani regimes had been favorable to Islamist armed groups in the past (the proregime militias of 1971 in East Pakistan; the anti-Kabul Islamist rebels of the mid-1970s), it was the 1980s that we see jihadist militancy growing dramatically.

After Zia: Contested Military Stewardship and Muslim Nationalism

Zia's death in 1988 led to a return to a more amorphous Muslim nationalism under both the "democratic decade" and then Pervez Musharraf's military dictatorship and its aftermath. One should not underplay the changes and contestations of the post-Zia era: battles among parties and political actors did sometimes involve different conceptions of what Pakistan should be.[118] The PPP and PML-N had different stances, while Musharraf's 1999–2007 military rule pushed a Muslim nationalism project that tried to consolidate military power and to give space to "modern" Islam, while continuing to favorably view Islamist armed groups against India and in Afghanistan.

Yet Zia's effort to shift what was seen as acceptable and desirable during his rule would have profound consequences for Pakistani society: Zia's legacy "still continues to influence modern Pakistani politics."[119] Government support for and toleration of Islamism and militancy had skyrocketed under his regime. There were several forces that limited radical change.

The first were both prevailing public attitudes and Islamist street and political power. The return of the PPP under Benazir Bhutto and the rise of the Pakistan Muslim League Nawaz (PML-N) under Nawaz Sharif between 1988 and 1999 created important new dynamics, and these parties offered distinguishable ideological visions. Bhutto leaned left with greater sympathy for Sindhi minorities, and Sharif right, more toward Islamist actors, and with a base in the Punjab. However, both had dalliances with Islamist actors—less emphatically in the case of the PPP and Benazir Bhutto, and more openly for the PML, which "presents itself as a party of and for Muslims."[120] As Ullah explores in depth, the Islamist constituency was a source of both support and competition for the PML-N, which strategically used Islamist appeals as one component of its "Muslim democrat" role in Pakistan's party system.[121] Both viewed the Afghan Taliban favorably and voiced strong support for the Kashmir insurgency, which received Pakistani sanctuary. After 2008, these two parties have been joined by Imran Khan's Pakistan Tehreek-e-Insaf (PTI), in power since 2018, which has articulated a vision of an Islamic welfare state (indeed, it "used the 'religion card' against the ruling party, much as Sharif had used it against Benazir Bhutto").[122] The PPP has had the most direct ideological clashes with Islamist actors, including being targeted by the Tehrik-i-Taliban Pakistan (TTP); it has traditionally been "one of Pakistan's most secular and progressive parties."[123] There are clear ideological differences, but the room for them to turn into policy has been constrained.

All of these parties have had to operate in a space in which Islamist mobilization is a recurring threat. After Pakistan's turn to the right after 1971, Islamist parties and organization "have commanded popular sentiment in a manner that both the state and mainstream political parties can ignore [only] at significant political cost," as "military dictatorships and elected governments with weak popular mandates have been particularly dependent on Islamic credentials for popular legitimacy."[124] Indeed, "these shared practices and beliefs are presented as boundaries that protect Muslims from both internal and external threats," with efforts to push back on these articulations facing the tricky rhetorical challenge of trying to both accept some link between Islam and Pakistan without accepting the Islamist message.[125] This helps us understand the complex maneuverings of Pakistan's two major "Muslim democrat" parties (the PPP and PTI) as they sought to both assuage the religious Right while pursuing other, higher priorities like economic development, as well as the struggles of the PPP.

Second, the room to maneuver of civilian parties in internal security was heavily constrained by the military.[126] In the background, even under the democratic periods of 1988–99 and 2008–present, the army has been the ultimate arbiter of security policy. For the topic this book studies—armed orders—the army was the key player in internal and external security choices. Its decisions were the most important in shaping the armed politics of Pakistan. During the post-Musharraf period, in the face of rising militancy, "civilians had effectively lost control of the security forces of Pakistan. But even the military was not fully prepared to act decisively without clear support from the government and civil society."[127]

While post-Zia army chiefs backed away from an Islamizing project, the Zia period left the legacy of "the infusion into the military of deeply conservative Islamic thinking." Indeed, "the use of Islamic symbolism inside cantonments remains a visible reminder of the difficulty of removing the powerful role of religion in the army."[128] As Rizvi has argued, "Islam is integral to Pakistan military ideology," even in its vaguer Muslim-nationalist form.[129] Army chief of staff Janjua and subsequent successors were seen by some as "slowly [beginning] to push back the politicized Islamic elements and [reassert] the age-old tradition keeping Islam and professionalism together and treating the former as a component of the latter," but this was not a radical rollback nor a fundamental challenge to pre-Zia Muslim nationalism.[130] The Islamist turn clearly drew on a deep strand of Muslim League thinking, so it was not a revolutionary vision—but it was a substantial step nevertheless.

Musharraf's military rule from 1999 to 2008 continued this strand of Muslim nationalism, distinguishing between "good" and "bad" versions of Islamist militancy.[131] The military simultaneously sought to delegitimate those groups with radically transnational, antisystemic ideologies and to provide space and support for those groups primarily aimed at India and Afghanistan, and open to some kind of army-dominated politics in Pakistan. Even beyond the Zia era, the armed forces have been "known for their warm yet tactical relations with various religious political parties."[132] I show evidence of this discriminating approach playing out in armed politics later in this chapter. Both Musharraf and civilian parties found themselves challenged when dealing with protesters, armed groups, and social movements claiming to represent Islam: "The authorities in Pakistan find it difficult to crack down on activities that are associated with organizations that operate in the name of Islam and claim to be defending its interest."[133] Musharraf is sometimes compared to Ayub Khan, but his period of rule involved much more openness to doing business with Islamist actors, though like Ayub he was skeptical of provincial and ethno-nationalist claims, especially in Balochistan, where Musharraf triggered another round of conflict with Baloch political actors.

Since Musharraf's fall in 2008, the military has sought to course-correct for an excessive reliance on jihadist groups; below I discuss the turn against the Pakistani Taliban in 2009–14.[134] This has been an important, if slow, shift, and involved efforts to recapture Islam as a discursive ally of the state against its nonstate enemies. Yet the military continues to emphasize Islam as a source of cohesion and to seek ways of managing Islamist groups short of total repression. The security establishment has sought to more effectively corral Islam for its purposes, rather than move entirely away from a fusion of religion and nation.[135] The military also continues to cast suspicion on even unarmed ethno-nationalist movements, most strikingly the Pashtun Tahafuz Movement (PTM), in ways that show important continuities in threat perception.[136] The crackdown against the PTM and allied politicians/activists is an especially striking example of how unarmed actors can be seen as deep political threats even in the absence of a compelling "objective" military threat.

There have been important shifts over time in the security apparatus views of the risks of engaging too openly and ambitiously with political Islam, and we will see below shifts in the 2009–14 period as the rise of Islamist militancy was seen to have run out of control. Nevertheless, key fundamentals of the military's Muslim-nationalist ideological project remain in place even decades after Zia's death, as does a preference for centralization and a deep suspicion of "suspect" ethnic parties and claims. Broadly speaking, we should expect continued repression of ethno-nationalist claim making alongside high-variance approaches to Islamist armed groups.

Patterns of Armed Politics in Pakistan

My interpretation of regime projects in Pakistan shows the historical roots of suspicion toward ethno-linguistic claims and an openness, however ambiguous or complex, to religious claims wrapped in the language of Islam. The almost total lack of leftist insurgency means that I focus primarily on linguistic/regional and Islamist armed actors.[137] These are general tendencies: tactical incentives can interact with them in important ways, and there are outcomes that my argument does not explain well. Nevertheless, the trends broadly follow my expectations.

I begin with broad patterns from the AOSA data. Table 5.1 shows that conflict and cooperation are almost evenly matched: while there has been extensive state repression of armed groups, there have also been many cooperative relationships.

Figure 5.1 distinguishes order-years by group self-identification. Unsurprisingly, we see political clustering: pro-state self-identification tends toward

TABLE 5.1   Armed order-years in Pakistan

TOTAL WAR	CONTAINMENT	LIMITED COOPERATION	ALLIANCE	TOTAL
59 (11.5%)	211 (41.13%)	143 (27.88%)	100 (19.49%)	513

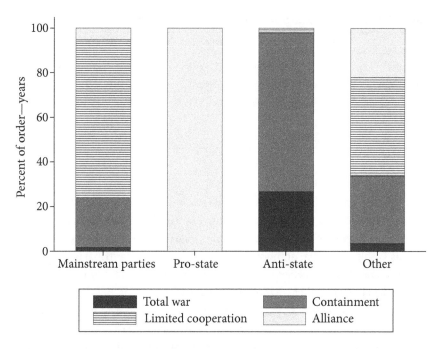

FIGURE 5.1.   Armed orders by self-identification

cooperation, while anti-state aims similarly are primarily conflictual. In contrast to both India and Myanmar, however, there is substantially less limited cooperation with insurgent groups; long-running cease-fires with foes that we see in the Indian Northeast and post-1989 Myanmar are largely absent in the Pakistani case. Instead, alliances and limited cooperation tend to cluster around either pro-state groups or "others" (often transnational groups whose primary focus is on Afghanistan or Kashmir/India). The primary groups involved in alliances are not the armed parties that dominate this category in India (though there are periods of this as well in Pakistan), but instead transnational militants and local militias that work closely with the state against insurgents. There is likely substantial measurement error here, because the boundaries between alliance and limited cooperation are blurry and sources often limited, but the tendency toward close cooperation with pro-state groups is clear. Pakistan's security apparatus has worked with a variety of groups that have been (largely) willing to play by the state's rules while targeting India, Afghanistan, and mutual enemies at home.

Table 5.2 assesses how different combinations of identity/ideology traits map onto armed orders in Pakistan. Linguistic groups are almost exclusively the Muhajir political parties of Karachi, plus one year of the Mukti Bahini in East Pakistan. Linguistic-Tribal are primarily groups in Balochistan. Religious-Tribal

TABLE 5.2 Political cleavages and order-years in Pakistan

	LEFTIST	LINGUISTIC	LINGUISTIC-TRIBAL	RELIGIOUS	RELIGIOUS-TRIBAL	TOTAL
Total war	1 (25%)	2 (3.28%)	23 (23.71%)	13 (6.77%)	20 (12.90%)	59
Containment	3 (75%)	11 (18.03%)	70 (72.16%)	67 (34.90%)	58 (37.42%)	209
Limited cooperation	0	46 (75.41%)	4 (4.12%)	55 (28.65%)	36 (23.23%)	141
Alliance	0	2 (3.28%)	0	57 (29.69%)	41 (26.45%)	100
Total	4	61	97	192	155	509

are primarily groups in northwestern Pakistan that combine Islamist and tribal mobilization, such as the Haqqani network and Gul Hafiz Bahadur group. Religious refers to groups whose mobilization primarily centers on appeals to Islam, such as Lashkar-e-Taiba, unmoored from a highly particular tribal base.

These are obviously very rough categorizations, and in the future scholars can use the data to study other ways of categorizing these groups, but they give a useful sense of the structure of variation that I unpack below. The main linguistic/regional groups able to escape sustained repression (at least some of the time) were the Muhajir armed parties that have tenuously operated in mainstream politics, while the Baloch and Bengali groups have faced very high levels of conflict: for instance, in the 1970s in Balochistan the army "adopted more conventional tactics, using air power, with assistance from the Shah of Iran who lent it helicopters, and cordon-and-clear operations against local tribesmen."[138]

We see the expected repression against the Baloch and Bengalis, but the Muhajir armed groups faced substantially less repression. This is largely, I argue, for tactical reasons: first, the Muttahida Qaumi Movement (MQM) carved out a strong place that made it a necessary partner for a number of civilian regimes (and vice versa) and, second, the MQM-Haqiqi (MQM-H) became a useful tool during periods when the military turned against the MQM. Many of the years of limited cooperation are with the MQM-H to target the MQM, and others involve periods in which the military did business with the MQM and kept the MQM-H on the sidelines. However, even this pattern of relative cooperation has dropped off in recent years, with an intense military crackdown on the MQM in Karachi since 2013.[139]

There is much more extensive state cooperation with groups deploying Islam in some capacity, though substantial variation remains.[140] Alliances especially are most common among groups mobilizing this cleavage. The remarkable array of transnational militant groups mentioned above fall into these categories: cooperation of some sort characterizes more than half of order-years with groups that deploy Islam as central to their message. However, there have been some crackdowns, including substantial periods of total war especially against the Pakistani Taliban and related anti-state groups on the Northwest frontier.[141] The patterns here are on balance far more cooperative than with linguistic/regional groups, but they also show that broad ideological categorizations can nevertheless contain important variation.

These data give a strong sense of political variation in state targeting. For those familiar with Pakistan, the basic patterns should not be a surprise. But the data alone are insufficient to make strong claims. To build on them, I now turn to more specific categories, combining quantitative data, qualitative case expertise, and the theory to explore these dynamics in greater detail; this also allows us to move past the limitations of dyad-year-level aggregation.

Regional Insurgents and State Responses in Pakistan

Table 5.3 outlines the patterns of order-years with groups that we identify as mobilizing linguistic or tribal, but not Islamist, political cleavages. There are many caveats here because the relations between language, ethnicity, tribe, and region differs across and within groups. I refer to them broadly as "regional" armed groups that primarily mobilize identity characteristics and historical narratives specific to a particular region. In practice, this directs us to armed mobilization by Bengalis in East Pakistan, Baloch in Balochistan, and Muhajirs in Karachi. The overall pattern is quite repressive, with 67 percent of dyad-years being conflictual, though also with a substantial amount of limited cooperation with Muhajir armed parties in Karachi.

I focus in this section on the insurgencies in Balochistan and East Pakistan, leaving Karachi for the section on militarized electoral politics below. If we exclude self-identified mainstream political parties (dropping Karachi's Muhajir armed parties, to which I return below, leaving N = 105), conflict of some form shifts into almost all armed order-years—merely 10.48 percent of dyadyears are limited cooperation, with the rest being containment or total war. The comparison to India's ethno-linguistic/tribal Northeast is striking, with limited

TABLE 5.3 Armed orders with regional armed groups

ARMED ORDER	FREQUENCY	FREQUENCY (EXCLUDING POLITICAL PARTIES)
Total war	25 (15.82%)	24 (22.86%)
Containment	81 (51.27%)	70 (66.67%)
Limited cooperation	50 (31.65%)	11 (10.48%)
Alliance	2 (1.27%)	0
Total	158	105

cooperation being far less common than in the Northeast. We will see below that the pattern is flipped for Islamist groups, where 75 percent of dyad-years involve cooperation of some sort.

We need to use real care when using the data: the East Pakistan dyad, between the Mukti Bahini and state, only lasted for a year, while the Balochistan dyads have stretched over decades. Yet it was East Pakistan where we see the most intense and dramatic violence, with the most far-reaching consequences. With this crucial caveat in mind, the data show a strong propensity toward conflict with armed groups mobilizing along linguistic/tribal lines, representing regional identities that fit uneasily with the top-down nationalist project of the military and much of the civilian elite.

How do we go from broad sense of threat to more specific dynamics of conflict? I argued above that a key fear of Pakistan's security managers and political elites has been that linguistic and regional mobilization will undermine the coherence of the state, breaking a Muslim homeland apart in the face of parochial identities. This challenge can be found facing Jinnah and the League even before independence, and led to a quest to use Islam and Urdu as binding agents against these subnational identities. This was a radically different approach than that pursued in India.[142] It had implications for perceptions of armed groups mobilizing regional cleavages. These were primarily Bengali and Baloch, cases in which language, region, and ethnicity/tribe mixed in complex ways to generate distinct regional identities. They would be met with fairly sustained repression, rather than a rapid shift into deal making and accommodation as we saw in India's Northeast.

Bengali mobilization in East Pakistan was one of the core cleavages in 1947–71 Pakistan. The primarily Punjabi elite of West Pakistan, both civilian and military, viewed Bengalis with suspicion and worried about the implications of their demographic size for political control of Pakistan: "Many West Pakistanis were convinced that the Islam practiced in Bengal was 'contaminated' by its long exposure to Hindu social and cultural practices."[143] Bengali political power was curtailed by the 1958 army takeover, but the weakening of Ayub Khan's regime was accompanied by the growth of the Awami League (AL) in East Pakistan. Led by Sheikh Mujibur Rahman, the Awami League demanded radical shifts in the structure of political power in Pakistan, aiming to redress the imbalances that favored West Pakistan. The AL explicitly mobilized around language and regional interests. In turn, elites in West Pakistan sought to protect their dominance, including Ayub Khan, his successor Yahya Khan, and the fast-rising Zulfiqar Bhutto. Mujib was accused of treason, of secessionist sentiment, and of betraying the nation.[144]

This political conflict escalated after Yahya Khan took power from Ayub and decided to hold elections. The military expected a split verdict, in which Bhutto's

PPP, Mujib's AL, and a variety of other parties would be unable to build a dominant political position on their own. Yet when the election results showed consolidated Bengali support for the AL, both the military and Bhutto looked to block Mujib's ascension to power. A political crisis developed.[145] The military alleged that Mujib was conspiring against the state, and a military crackdown ensued. The military explicitly prepared for a "shock action" using "the greatest vigour and determination to create an unmistakable impact."[146] Operation Searchlight of March 1971 was an intense military operation that aimed at rooting out Awami League members, intellectuals, politically suspect Bengali Hindus, and others who were seen as subversive elements.[147] A bloodbath ensued.[148] This is a striking case of state repression preceding large-scale insurgent mobilization; it was not the government striking against a powerful rebel group, but instead an effort to preempt such insurgency, driven by a deeply political perception of threat.

This attack triggered a large-scale Bengali insurgency, which received extensive support from India. The Mukti Bahini emerged as a full-fledged rebellion. I assess this as a total war armed order: 1971 saw a scorched-earth campaign, with the army seeking to root out the insurgents, their supporters and the broader pro-AL social infrastructure in East Pakistan, and the Mukti Bahini hitting the army as aggressively as possible.[149] The army was in alliance orders with a small set of Islamist armed groups that were used to target civilians and militants. These were Urdu-speaking militias, linked to the Jamaat -e-Islami party, that had strong reasons to want to hold at bay Bengali political assertion. There was powerful tactical overlap: the military wanted local intelligence and "deniable" violence, while the "Bihari" militias wanted to pursue a blend of ideological and survival goals. They collaborated in human rights abuses.[150] In particular, the security forces and their allies targeted Hindus, who "were blamed by the military high command for fomenting separatist and pro-Indian views in East Pakistan."[151]

East Pakistan in 1971 tragically encapsulated the key cleavages dominating Pakistani politics, with the state opposing ethno-linguistic mobilization and tilting toward Islamist, Urdu-speaking armed actors. The intensity of the military repression is striking, as is the speed with which repression was chosen over accommodation or negotiation. As I showed earlier, the vision of Bengalis as effete, dangerously close to being Hindus, and inferior to the Punjabis who dominated West Pakistan and the military structured the army's threat perception— indeed, it was the initial crackdown that led to the escalation of the conflict, rather than vice versa. The overwhelming consensus is that this wild and counterproductive overreaction was driven by profound distrust of the Bengali ethnic autonomist movement led by Sheikh Mujibur Rahman.[152] This is only one year of total war, but it is a hugely important one, leading to the creation of Bangladesh and a major interstate war. This was fundamentally a case of politics shaping the onset and nature of violence: "The roots of this debacle lay in the inability of Yahya's martial law regime to see the need for political settlement rather than military action in East Pakistan."[153]

Balochistan is a much different insurgent context. A variety of often opaque insurgent groups have fought for secession or greater autonomy in several rounds of conflict stretching back to the 1950s.[154] The AOSA team had real difficulty establishing details about many of these groups, so the codings are quite general and would benefit from specialized future research; the average confidence of our order coding is quite low (1.9 versus 2.6 for Kashmir, with 3 being high confidence). The general posture of the army has been containment (72 percent), followed by total war (24 percent) and limited cooperation (4 percent). This is a case in which we see extensive conflict, as my theory predicts, but it includes more containment than I would expect. The proportion of total war is reasonably high, and the qualitative details support the proposition that it was intensive repression. Aerial bombing, disappearances, and lack of major political negotiation with armed groups are characteristics of this war, as well as extremely limited access allowed to the media and NGOs.[155] There is little limited cooperation, much less alliance, and only a few cease-fires that lasted a short time.

That said, during long stretches, the army appears to have adopted a containment strategy aimed mainly at keeping a lid on the conflict; we see peaks and valleys in repressive intensity over decades rather than the pedal being mashed to the floor at all times. This is very consistent with the finding from India that even the most loathed (by the state) of armed groups may end up in containment orders for long stretches, as the state marshals its resources for more pressing challenges. There were even periods in which the army de facto gave up fighting Baloch rebels, most notably in the late 1970s, by essentially declaring victory and going home.[156]

This was a highly conflictual set of armed orders, but with the Baloch armed actors often treated more like undesirables than mortal enemies. The most recent round of conflict, since 2006, has borne out this pattern: of the dyad-year orders, roughly 40 percent have been total war, 56 percent limited cooperation, and 2 percent limited cooperation with Baloch armed groups. The Pakistani military has credibly been accused of engaging in severe human rights abuses, including disappearances and the so-called kill and dump strategy.[157] The fragmented and murky insurgency involves several different factions, which have started attacking personnel and facilities linked to the China Pakistan Economic Corridor (CPEC), while themselves committing rights abuses.

There has been little meaningful negotiation or accommodation of these groups, which instead are framed as subversive elements receiving Indian and

Afghan backing: "Instead of redressing Baloch political and economic grievances, the military is determined to impose state control through force."[158] Indeed, the resurgence of the conflict in 2006 involved direct assassination of a major Baloch leader.[159] The political status of the Baloch conflict, like that of East Pakistan's Bengali mobilization, pits "mainstream" nationalism against political demands that are portrayed as irreconcilable, unreasonable, fissiparous, and deeply untrustworthy. As I expect, conflict has predominated; what my theory underpredicts is the substantial amount of containment rather than total war.

"Islamist" Armed Groups: Ambiguities of Alignment

Things change dramatically once we turn to groups that mobilize entirely or in large part around Islam: they fall into the Religious and Religious-Tribal categories of table 5.2. To be clear, the category of "Islamist" group is a heterogeneous one, with a multitude of possible meanings. I focus on nonstate armed groups that explicitly link religious practice to politics, moving beyond the "Muslim nationalism" of the League. Some, like Al-Qaeda, even move past that toward a transnational jihadism beyond the confines of the nation-state. A number of groups on the Northwest frontier have a tribal base that provides another identity dimension to their mobilization.

Islamist groups, as well as unarmed parties and organizations, occupy a complex place in Pakistani politics. Marginal in electoral appeal, they nevertheless present a potential challenge to the state: the Pakistani state and military simultaneously attempt to deploy Islam as a nation-building symbol while trying to maintain autonomy from these Islamist actors.[160] The military has found itself trying to wriggle out of various "rhetorical traps," as armed actors seek to use the same symbols and language as the military to make demands on it.[161]

Figure 5.2 summarizes the distribution of order-year among groups that can be plausibly coded as mobilizing around Islam. This is a very crude coding, to be sure, but it is a useful starting point. We see extensive limited cooperation and alliance, substantially more so than with linguistic-ethnic groups in table 5.3 and (dramatically so after dropping the Muhajir armed parties). This is not universal, however: nearly half of the dyad-years are some form of conflict. Below, I explore how this kind of discrimination within these political cleavages emerges when discussing Pakistan's Northwest: some Islamists step over the line in pushing a transnational Islamist ideology of the polity, and then face the wrath of the ultimately statist military. Others then work with the state against such hard-line groups, generating remarkably complex patterns in areas of counterinsurgency. The overall picture is clear, however—above all, the frequency of alliance is truly striking.

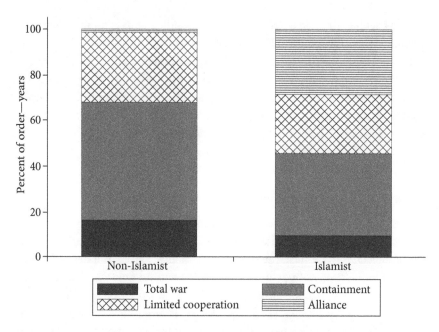

FIGURE 5.2. Armed orders with religiously mobilized groups in Pakistan

We can examine the politics of discrimination within this broad category by examining how groups' stated goals relate to order-years. There is a tight correspondence between their relationship to the security apparatus's stated vision of nationalism and the armed orders that emerge, one that I trace out qualitatively below when studying the rise of the TTP. Goals were a particularly difficult variable to code for this subset of cases, since they are rarely stated as clearly as with secessionist groups, while often autonomy- or reform-seeking groups also use a language that is compatible with either center-seeking goals, religious ambitions, or something else entirely.

Nevertheless, table 5.4 suggests that much of the discrimination among this broad category is also political: some Islamist groups make more ambitious and demanding claims, while others are easier to slot into the security apparatus' preferred political preferences. Alliances are most common with the "ambiguous" category of goals, since these are often nonstate actors that formally pursue political change outside of Pakistan's borders. Limited cooperation and low-level repression (containment) are also common when aimed at groups seeking greater autonomy from central control (often warlords on the Northwest frontier) or "reform" (groups that often mix a domestic and international agenda, like Jaish-e-Mohammed).

When we focus on transnational militant groups whose goals are primarily in India/Indian-administered Kashmir or Afghanistan—the Jaish-e-Mohammed,

Lashkar-e-Taiba, Afghan Taliban, the Haqqani network, and Harkat-ul-Mujahideen—we see exclusively cooperation (table 5.5). There are important ambiguities in coding regarding the splintering of Jaish in the early 2000s (much hinges on how you code the nature of fragmentation in 2002–4, and whether you take seriously the formal banning of the group), but the general pattern is quite extraordinary.[162]

Qualitatively, the Pakistani security apparatus has been an active partner in sponsoring a variety of Islamist armed groups on its territory: for instance, the ISI has helped to "train and equip Islamist fighters and militants who infiltrated and injected themselves into the battle between Kashmiris and the huge Indian military and paramilitary force."[163] As Nawaz reports, even during the crackdown against the TTP I discuss below, "the Afghan Taliban were never a major target of these operations. . . . there was also no operation against the Afghan Taliban in the borderlands of Balochistan,"[164] while "nothing was done to disarm the Punjabi militant groups, including those that operated against India."[165] Indeed, "US intelligence routinely captured transmissions of communications between what they termed officials from Pakistan with the Taliban as well as relatively unhindered movement of the Haqqani party inside North Waziristan."[166] These groups are mainly aimed at Afghanistan and India, but can also act as legitimizers of the military project at home (Lashkar especially). This makes them tactically highly useful as allies to be used against a conventionally stronger India and as tools of leverage within Afghanistan's bloody politics.

There is no question that the Pakistani state does not hold a seamless monopoly over violence—but this does not appear to be worrisome to its security

Table 5.4   Group goals and order-years among "Islamist" armed groups

	AMBIGUOUS/ UNKNOWN	AUTONOMY	CENTRAL CONTROL	REFORM	TOTAL
Total war	9 (4.97%)	17 (17.89%)	6 (60%)	1 (2.5%)	33 (10.12%)
Containment	39 (21.55%)	56 (58.95%)	4 (40%)	26 (65%)	125 (38.34%)
Limited cooperation	51 (28.18%)	22 (23.16%)	0	13 (32.50%)	86 (26.38%)
Alliance	82 (45.30%)	0	0	0	82 (25.15%)
Total	181	95	10	40	326

Table 5.5   Pakistan and four key Islamist militant groups

Limited cooperation	25 (24.51%)
Alliance	77 (75.49%)
Total	102

managers as long as the right kinds of armed groups are involved. It is, of course, not surprising that the state is not locked in total war with groups that are not separatists or center seekers, but the extent and level of cooperation is unthinkable in many other countries, or along other political cleavages within Pakistan. The frequency of alliance show that these are not just bare-bones relationships of convenience but instead have much deeper roots.

Political goals and fears guide the allocation of coercion and compromise in Pakistan. The military's tight embrace of Lashkar-e-Taiba accords with the argument: the group maintains a distance from Al-Qaeda while consistently and publicly signaling its "commitment to the integrity of the Pakistani state and its diverse polity."[167] Combined with its tactical usefulness as a strike arm against India, as shown in Mumbai and Indian-administered Kashmir, this makes it an armed ally of the military. Consequently, Jaffrelot has argued that "as long as the LeT does not attack Pakistan, the army is likely to protect the movement in order to use it again."[168]

The contrast with Al-Qaeda, with operates both in the Northwest and beyond it, is instructive—the Pakistan military has attacked Al-Qaeda and assisted American operations against the group, while largely leaving LeT alone. As with Al-Qaeda, there are Islamist groups that have been repressed; they are currently, to be clear, somewhat underrepresented in the dataset as collection continues. The Pakistani Taliban, Lashkar-e-Jhangvi, and Al-Qaeda have all faced repression; below I examine some of these cases in more detail to explore when the military does crack down on self-identified Islamists. The overall pattern, however, is striking and consistent with my argument about the historically rooted ideological project of the military and much of the civilian establishment.

Armed Party Politics in Karachi

The big exception to the overall trends—armed politics relatively friendly to Islamists and hostile to regional/linguistic groups—comes in Karachi. Here the MQM emerged as an armed political party that both deployed violence and won remarkable electoral power. It began as the All-Pakistan Muttahida Students Organization, an increasingly militant student group in Karachi's violent campus politics, and then launched as the MQM in the 1980s under the leadership of Altaf Hussain.[169] The party quickly became such a key player in Karachi's politics that even the military and national party leaders were forced to do business with it. I code it as either an opposed or gray zone group over time: its explicit ethno-linguistic mobilization made it highly suspect in the eyes of the state, but its embrace of mainstream electoral politics made it more useful as a potential partner. It spawned a splinter, the MQM-H, that became its violent rival while also appealing to Muhajir identity.

Both groups, however, had periods of tactical overlap with the military establishment—sometimes in opposition to one another. The MQM's power in Karachi made it a pivotal player for both civilian politicians and the military as each sought to build coalitions and establish influence in and control over Karachi. This cold political instrumentality forced national elites to tolerate, or actively work with, the MQM for most of its existence—"the military has always seen the ethnic urban Sindh-based party through a tactical lens."[170] It was first valuable as a hedge against Sindhi nationalism in the early 1980s, but then once it generated consistent electoral support it became a key coalitional player in Pakistani politics.[171] This is a case in which narrow instrumental goals are central to understanding armed orders—even when there were severe ideological differences with the various forces in power in the center, the MQM was sufficiently useful in the battle for national power, and itself had enough to gain, that limited cooperation and even alliance was often very valuable. Whether seen as a strange bedfellow or a business partner, the group's power resulted from its ability to stabilize or destabilize Karachi (Pakistan's largest city and key economic hub) and deliver votes and seats in national and provincial elections.

These power politics led to an incredibly complex set of interactions between 1985 and 2014 in which conflict and cooperation hinged on the MQM's value to national political actors, including Benazir Bhutto, Nawaz Sharif, Pervez Musharraf, and the army. In 1992–96, political calculations led to a major crackdown on the MQM, but shifting coalitions rehabilitated the group by 1997. During this time, the MQM-H emerged. It would be fostered by the military as a proxy to be used against the MQM during the period of crackdown in the mid-1990s: we simultaneously see repression against the MQM and cooperation with the MQM-H.[172] Yet after 1997, the MQM-H became a much more marginal player while the MQM largely reestablished itself as a major player in Pakistani politics.

Most strikingly, under Pervez Musharraf's military dictatorship from 1999 to 2008, the MQM was largely left alone by the military in exchange for keeping Karachi quiet and repressing anti-Musharraf dissidents, despite continuing tensions and suspicions. Siddiqa writes that "a negotiated truce between the army and the MQM was implemented in 2002, which resulted in the streamlining of MQM in Sindh's power politics" and "during this period the MQM developed an image of being one of the many political right hands of the military."[173] Thus was tactical overlap at work. Ideologically, the MQM did not consistently push for separatism (contrary to military claims during periods of crackdowns) but did explicitly mobilize ethno-linguistic cleavages, and its leader Altaf Hussain had a habit of rhetorically straying into language that could be interpreted as highly critical of Pakistan and the military's nationalism. I therefore assess it being primarily a business partner in periods of cooperation.

After the MQM lost some of its value after the end of the military rule in 2008 and then became dispensable to the Nawaz Sharif government that came to power in 2013, the military, backed by the PML government, began a major crackdown in 2013 that has since largely broken the MQM.[174] The military's persistent mistrust of the group was no longer constrained by political and strategic calculations: the army did not need a local enforcer in Karachi the way Musharraf did, Sharif did not rely on the MQM for political survival, and the turning tide of the war against the Pakistani Taliban opened up space for a new crackdown against a group that had long been a thorn in the military's side. Unshackled by tactical constraints, the army could pursue its goal of undermining the organization, whether we categorize it as a mortal enemy or an undesirable, and the MQM is now a shell of its former self.[175]

The other Muhajir group that operated in Karachi is the MQM-H, a splinter from the MQM that broke away in the early 1990s and aligned with the Pakistan Army as a kind of armed party-militia against the MQM. The MQM-H was a business partner that largely abandoned any distinct political aims while continuing to, ostensibly, mobilize around the Muhajir identity. It primarily was engaged in limited cooperation, though it did suffer some repression in the early 2000s as part of Musharraf's deal with the MQM. Like the Ikhwans in Kashmir and Tamil paramilitaries in Sri Lanka, this is a case in which groups mobilizing on the same identity cleavage ended up in conflict with one another, driven by factional rivalry.[176]

The Karachi case is more complex than the others, blending aspects of insurgency, militarized electoral politics, intergroup rivalry, and pro-state paramilitarism. The mobilization of regional linguistic identities by the MQM should have made it at least a gray zone, and perhaps opposed, actor in the eyes of the military establishment. Yet it had dual tactical uses: it could help win elections/build coalitions and it could act as a stabilizing force in Karachi in exchange for "forbearance" from the security apparatus.[177] The MQM-H had its own use as well, as a proxy militia to attack the MQM and try to fragment its political space among the Muhajir community. The intricate politics of Karachi made military and armed group incentives far more multifaceted than in a straightforward rural insurgency; if the Muhajir context had existed on a distant periphery rather than being intertwined with regime stabilization and coalition formation calculations, we likely would have seen a much more consistent pattern of repression. This is the case that shows the importance of tactical considerations as a check on ideological categorizations.

Managing Insurgency on the Northwest Frontier

I now pivot to a more detailed examination of a set of comparative cases in a shared context. This section draws directly on joint published work with a pair of excellent coauthors, Asfandyar Mir and Sameer Lalwani, in exploring Islamist insurgency in northwestern Pakistan from 2002 through 2015.[178] As we saw above in the aggregate data, Pakistan has in general been very willing to cooperate with "Islamist" armed groups, but there is important variation that a simple focus on broad ideology cannot capture. Despite key similarities, there is striking variation in how the Pakistani military dealt with armed actors during the rise of the Pakistani Taliban insurgency. This raises the question of how the military sorts through armed groups with broadly similar general ideological stances, moving to a more granular level.

Pakistan's strategy of dealing with these groups has been decidedly mixed. Pakistan has confronted a selection of the groups—like Al-Qaeda, Islamic Movement of Uzbekistan, and the TTP—in sustained campaigns of counterinsurgency. But an equally notable feature of Pakistani strategy has been its accommodation of other groups. Pakistan has provided the Haqqani network with both sanctuary and aid, despite international calls for targeting the group. Other groups, like Hafiz Gul Bahadur's group and Commander Maulvi Nazir's faction, have been managed through live-and-let-live arrangements and formal peace deals. Pakistan has sometimes resorted to deal making in the aftermath of failed military campaigns, showing shifts over time. For example, the Nek Muhammed group was offered a peace deal in 2004 after a failed military offensive, which culminated in the Shakai peace agreement. The Pakistani military has also conducted joint offensives with a number of groups in the region, like the Lashkar-e-Taiba of the Salarzai tribe in Bajaur Agency and the Ansar-ul-Islam in Khyber Agency.

We drew on novel data, moving beyond even the AOSA dataset, on peace deals and military operations to more systematically show the variation in how the Pakistani state's security apparatus has dealt with these actors. We consider only groups with a reported size of more than two hundred foot soldiers, leading to a focus on twenty such organizations.[179] From 2002–13, the Pakistani state—primarily led by the Pakistan Army, but on rare occasions by the provincial government—struck at least twenty-four peace deals with nine of these groups.

The Pakistan Army launched at least fifty-seven large-scale military operations against thirteen of the groups.[180] It carried out joint operations with at least six armed groups during this period.

Several of those targeted in military operations have also been offered peace deals, while others, such as IMU and Al-Qaeda have been targeted with no offer of peace. The Haqqani network, by contrast, received one peace deal and no military offensives were launched against it. The TTP had both the most peace deals and largest number of military offensives against it. In the period under study, the breakaway faction of Turkistan Bhittani and forces of Momin Afridi and Shah Sahib received active support from the army, beyond simply peace agreements. More than 80 percent of the peace deals and military operations have taken place in the Federally Administered Tribal Areas (FATA) region, though violence has been higher in the Khyber Pakhtunkhwa (KP) Province than in FATA.[181] There have also been changes over time within state-group dyads; for instance, the TTP was first offered a series of peace deals, which were then followed by a series of military offensives.

Sorting through Islamist Groups

I argued above that the Pakistan Army's vision highlights Islam as a crucial source of national cohesion, but one that must be directed by the military in its commanding role as guardian of the polity and interpreter of the Constitution. Islamist groups vary in their orientation toward the political role of the military and general approach to the state. As Alyssa Ayres argues, "Whether the country was under civilian or military rule, one common thread has been the insistence with which central leaders, and central institutions, have indulged religious leaders, in some cases some of the most illiberal Islamists available. . . . Pakistan's leaders have coopted Islamism in order to capture and retain control of the discourse of legitimacy."[182] As a consequence, armed and unarmed actors deploying Islamist symbols are often seen as acceptable. But they are increasingly considered ideologically opposed to the extent that they link this rhetoric with challenges to the military and the formal structure of the Pakistani state. In combination, this "strong political centralization and an over-reliance on the military as a means to 'hold' the country together further exacerbated the national emphasis successive rulers placed on the necessity of creating a singular national Islamic culture, with Urdu as the centerpiece."[183]

During the period we focus on, under chiefs of army staff (COAS) Pervez Musharraf, Ashfaq Parvez Kayani, and Raheel Sharif, the army has remained a primarily Muslim-nationalist institution, rather than the transnational Islamist army envisaged by more radical Islamists.[184] Ashfaq Kayani clearly articulated the army's vision of the role of Islam in the national project: "Let me remind you that Pakistan was created in the name of Islam and Islam can never be taken out of Pakistan. However, Islam should always remain a unifying force."[185]

The army has distinguished friendly or tolerable Islamist armed groups from those that are opposed. It appears to have paid close attention to the demands, rhetoric, and symbols of these actors to determine the cleavages they evoke and the goals they pursue. Some Islamists seek to fundamentally alter both Pakistani nationalism and the political role of the military, reflecting much deeper historical cleavages in beliefs about how Islam and nation should be combined.[186] Their vision of a universalist Islamic nationalism decenters traditional state institutions and defines the nation is terms of actual religious practice, not just religious identity. By contrast, other self-described Islamists do not demand major political change and explicitly place themselves within the framework of nationalism acceptable to the Pakistani Army.[187] A number of groups straddle these positions of pure revolutionary opposition and contentment with the status quo: they draw heavily on Islamist rhetoric, symbols, and demands without directly seeking to alter the basic contours of the Pakistani political system. Calls for reform, for instance, neither directly challenge nor support the military elite. However, determining precisely which groups should be categorized in which way turned out to be a messy, bloody, and challenging process over approximately a decade, with numerous unintended and often counterproductive consequences.

At the same time, the army has had important tactical interests in the region. Most relevant to the Northwest are the army's objectives in Afghanistan and in managing the "periphery." The military has attempted to exert influence in Afghanistan since independence and began actively backing Afghan armed actors in 1973. This interest has endured, creating powerful incentives to work with groups that can project power into Afghanistan. Tactical overlap occurs with groups that have some base of support in Afghanistan and substantial military power that can be used against Afghan security forces.

The army also aims to manage the periphery. Pakistan's Northwest is geographically daunting and socially distinct from the country's core, and traditionally both well-armed and out of the direct reach of the Weberian state.[188] The military, as well as civilian governments, have continued a long pattern of indirect rule. Armed groups are useful stabilizers in these areas when they have strong local roots and are able to discipline and control mobilization in a particular area. They are even more valuable when they can be used as a counterbalance against a local enemy of the government.[189]

General Patterns

We measured Pakistani strategic campaigns over time toward each organization in our sample of twenty armed groups.[190] Our broad expectations were generally borne out, according with Christopher Jaffrelot's assessment of "great ambivalence" in military strategy toward armed groups after 9/11.[191]

During the period under study, the Pakistan Army engaged in several alliance relationships in the Northwest, including with the Haqqani network, Turkistan Bhittani group, Tawheed-ul-Islam, Shah Sahib group, and Momin Afridi group. During the period we studied, these groups had no action against them, nor did the army attempt to demobilize them in a way that we can measure. At least at a very crude level, alliances are associated with a combination of ideological and tactical concerns. In addition to holding the Pakistan Army in high esteem, the Haqqanis have been useful to exert influence in Afghanistan and to manage the unstable periphery. Other allies, like the Turkistan Bhittani group, have professed respect for the state and also maintained a rivalry with the TTP, making them valuable local allies. In the military's eyes, these are the "good militants" on the Northwest frontier.

At the other end of the spectrum, groups with opposed ideologies and low tactical utility were treated as mortal enemies, distinguished by the state response of sustained military targeting. For example, we code the TTP, Al-Qaeda, the Nek Muhammad group, and IMU as ideologically opposed to the Pakistan Army. They have generally—but not exclusively—faced a series of sizable military offensives over time. Al-Qaeda stands out for the consistency with which it has been targeted in the post-9/11 period; their senior leadership, including Khalid Habib, Khalid Sheikh Muhammed, Abu Yahya, Al Libi, and other influential cadres, have all been taken off the battlefield by Pakistan, and the military has been supportive of US drone strikes against the group.[192] Assigning a group to the enemy category has not precluded the possibility of attempted peace deals with such groups after unexpectedly severe military setbacks. But crucially, such deals have been very short lived and embedded within a broader trajectory of state suppression efforts that are clearly different than the strategies adopted toward aligned and gray zone actors. Initial policy reactions were of suppression; only after these first offensives failed do we see forms of limited cooperation explored by the military, followed by a return to crackdowns. Strikingly, the military was not prepared for battle even with these kinds of groups, having been oriented toward very different internal threats: the Pakistan Army was "woefully unprepared in terms of training and equipment for this war" after 2001.[193]

Ideological gray zone groups formed the plurality of the sample. This is important because it shows the limits of a simple binary between "good" and "bad" militants: the political spectrum is complex and state policy often involves neither full accommodation nor brutal repression, but instead degrees of toleration and oscillations among containment and limited cooperation. We coded ten groups as slotting into the political role of either business partner or undesirable. These groups were considered to be tolerable and sometimes useful, even as political tensions and major differences in goals existed. State responses toward these actors have been a mix of no action, deals, and sporadic military offensives. Peace deals with business partners have been much more durable than those with ideologically opposed groups, lasting on average longer than twelve months, thereby demonstrating their different strategic significance. Groups offering no utility have been targeted in isolated military operations.

In several of these cases, we saw armed groups shifting their ideological positions by changing their public rhetoric, the goals they espouse, and the symbols they deploy. Such changes move both toward and away from the state: the Abdullah Mehsud and Gul Bahadur groups at points very explicitly renounced maximalist war aims and acknowledged the basic precepts of the Pakistani military's desired polity (though to different degrees), while the Faqir Mohammed group, Lashkar-e-Islam, and TNSM radicalized in opposition to the army. These dynamics were driven by a variety of factors, including behavior of groups in other districts, intragroup factional competition, feuds and rivalries between armed organizations, and the rise and fall of individual leaders. Changes were clearly not purely endogenous to state policy, and in some cases they moved directly against the military's preferences. The army was forced to respond to these shifts, leading to reassessment of political roles and, in turn, state response.

Comparative Case Studies: North and South Waziristan

The medium-N analysis is valuable, but data constraints impose serious limitations. This section complements our analysis by comparing cases to show how these processes play out in greater detail. We can trace patterns of state strategy toward four armed groups: the Haqqani network, the TTP, Mullah Nazir group, and Gul Bahadur group. This small-N research design more carefully measures variables of interest and tracks interactions over time.

This is a case sample which the theory predicts should generate a wide variety of outcomes, based on variation in groups' ideological fit and tactical overlap.[194] They are relatively data-rich cases, allowing for greater confidence in measuring the variables and in their sequencing and interaction over time.[195] They are all within North Waziristan (Bahadur and Haqqanis) or South Waziristan

(TTP and Mullah Nazir), providing a reasonably bounded comparative context that reduces the array of confounding variables.

Haqqani Network: Continuity as Armed Allies

The Haqqani network has been the most consistently cooperative ally of the Pakistani state since 9/11.[196] As early as December 2001, the chief of Pakistan's ISI reportedly met Jalaludin Haqqani in Islamabad.[197] Since then, to the extent that outside observers can tell, the Haqqani network has been largely untouched in its base areas in North Waziristan, with the possible exception of displacement during Zarb-e-Azb in 2014. As of 2020, military operations targeting Al-Qaeda and other foreign militants appear to have generally avoided capturing or even harming Haqqani commanders in their sweeps. At other times, intelligence officers have tipped the Haqqanis off to raids. All available evidence suggests that the Haqqani network is perceived as an armed ally whose goals and behaviors are compatible with the military's project, and the group is seen as a valuable partner for both managing an unstable frontier and striking deep into Afghanistan against rival governments and armed groups.

What are the roots of this alliance? First, the Haqqanis are conspicuous in their support for the Pakistani state. Azaz Syed reports former ISI head Ehsan Ul Haq quoting Jalaludin Haqqani from this period: "Jalalluddin was very positive about Pakistan even at that time when we had announced to support the Americans. He (Haqqani) knew that we (Pakistan) could not do anything for them." Ehsan recalls Haqqani saying, "Don't worry about us. We understand your problems. Please take care of your country, Pakistan, as we think this is our home."[198]

They have never been party to jihadi edicts directed against the Pakistani state by various other armed actors. In fact, they have issued edicts to stop other armed groups from attacking the Pakistani security forces and tried to direct other militants toward fighting American and Afghan—rather than Pakistani—forces. In 2006, for instance, Sirajuddin Haqqani issued a circular saying that jihad against the United States and Afghan government was to continue "till the last drop of blood,'" but fighting against the Pakistan Army was not jihad.[199] Jalaluddin Haqqani, father of Siraj and the leader of the Haqqani network, added that "it [attacking the army] is not our policy. Those who agree with us are our friends and those who do not agree and (continue to wage) an undeclared war against Pakistan are neither our friends nor shall we allow them in our ranks."[200]

Second, as Vahid Brown and Don Rasler note, the Haqqanis are a "strategic asset . . . through which Pakistan can shape and secure its interests along the Durand Line."[201] From the 1990s onward, the army and Haqqanis have shared enemies in Afghanistan's Northern Alliance, with its backing from India, Russia, and the United States. Jaffrelot argues, "For the Pakistan Army, it [the Haqqani network] was a particularly useful resource to combat India's presence in Afghanistan."[202] After 9/11, Jalaluddin Haqqani explicitly highlighted the group's utility: "Let me remind you that on Pakistan's Eastern border is India—Pakistan's perennial enemy. With the Taliban government in Afghanistan, Pakistan has an unbeatable 2,300 km strategic depth, which even President Pervez Musharraf has proudly proclaimed. Does Pakistan really want a new government, which will include pro-India people in it, thereby wiping out this strategic depth? I tell you, the security and stability of Pakistan and Afghanistan are intertwined. Together, we are strong but separately we are weak."[203]

The Haqqanis have their own independent combat and terror capabilities, and they have also provided direct assistance to the Afghan Taliban.[204] The Pakistan Army acknowledges that the Haqqanis play a valuable role as a tool of influence in Afghanistan. This is a long-standing evaluation: "The Haqqani network has proven useful to the Pakistani state for three decades by functioning as a reliable partner which can provide strategic depth (in case of total war with India) and added military capacity in the tribal areas of Afghanistan and Pakistan, and do so with a measure of plausible deniability."[205]

The group's border-straddling networks give it the ability to operate in Afghanistan but find shelter in Pakistan, with a resulting role as a "power broker and the primary facilitator of a cross-border system of violence."[206] It has been "capable and determined,"[207] clearly placing it in the category of tactically useful. Beyond its striking and facilitating power in Afghanistan, the Haqqanis have been able to help broker negotiations, prisoner exchanges, and cease-fires between the military and various militant groups, supporting military indirect rule on the periphery as "effective interlocutors between militants and the Pakistani state."[208]

This combination of ideological affinity and tactical overlap led to an armed order of alliance throughout the time period under study. The Pakistani military "has consistently refused to move against the Haqqani network precisely because the organization is immensely valuable,"[209] and this "continued support and protection" has "exasperated the Obama administration."[210] At least until 2014, the network was "left largely unaffected and free to consolidate its influence across North Waziristan" in a spheres-of-influence arrangement with the central state; in David Rohde's words, the military provided "de facto acquiescence."[211] The military has also allegedly tipped off Haqqanis ahead of US strikes and operations, helping to protect the organization from American efforts to degrade it,[212] in addition to providing it with "an invaluable safe haven."[213] The 2014 Zarb-e-Azb offensive in North Waziristan appears to have, at most, geographically shifted some of the network's activities, but did not repress the organization.

Despite such overt support, the Haqqanis have not been perfectly aligned with the Pakistani state. They represent a prime case of how allies can create principal-agent problems, as they do not perfectly align with all state strategic interests. Through their base of support in North Waziristan, the Haqqanis have indirectly aided and incubated a number of Pakistan's enemies, like elements of the TTP and IMU: indeed, a number of later TTP commanders first gained experience under the Haqqanis.[214] The Pakistani state has never considered this reason enough to alter its state strategy toward the network, in part because the Haqqanis have consistently tried to redirect militants away from Islamabad toward Kabul. State officials have often expressed fears that certain offensive actions, such as an invasion of North Waziristan to specifically target the TTP, could prompt this stalwart ally to defect and join hands with Pakistan's enemies in Afghanistan. This relationship is thus not locked in stone, precisely as the theory would suggest: "When the Haqqani network is no longer seen as reliable and/or relevant to the ISI and its interests Pakistan may have less of an incentive to continue its relationship with the group."[215] Nevertheless, it has shown a remarkable continuity over time in its political role and relationship with state power.

TTP—Shifting Political Roles

The Pakistani Taliban is a much more complex case both because of its looser organizational structure and its evolving ideological position and tactical value over time. The TTP was officially formed in December 2007 out of a collection of armed factions involved in both conflict and cooperation with Pakistan's security forces; this includes the Gul Bahadur group discussed below. A number of these factions originated as "gray zone" actors in the eyes of the state, such as the faction led by Baitullah Mehsud. In the years after 9/11, the military treated them as business partners or undesirables, attempting to either cut deals with them or use sporadic offensives to limit their reach. For instance, in early 2005, a military offensive in South Waziristan was launched that led to a peace agreement that February.[216] The Peshawar corps commander declared that "Baitullah Mehsud is a soldier of peace."[217] This deal eventually broke down, but the army's efforts to construct it show that these groups were seen as tolerable and manageable. By the summer of 2007, however, such attempts were bearing increasingly little fruit and the factions that were to constitute the TTP were signaling growing opposition to the state.[218] This process of ideological radicalization took on greater speed after the Lal Masjid siege in July 2007: it "would alter B. Mehsud's priorities. He turned his weapons against the Pakistani state and to this end organized the TTP under the auspices of Al-Qaeda."[219]

Baitullah Mehsud spearheaded the new TTP coalition, which eventually merited recategorization as an opposed group as it continued to escalate its direct, public challenge to the state. The creation of the TTP in late 2007 marked a major change in ideological position for this coalition of militants. Their growing radicalization and explicitly anti-state attitude moved it into the ideologically opposed category, although this shift along the spectrum was not immediate or seamless, especially because splintering and internal dissension made it hard to know exactly who spoke for the group. Here we focus on the core TTP led by Baitullah Mehsud, Hakimullah Mehsud, and, more recently, Mullah Fazlullah.

A statement by Baitullah's spokesman Maulvi Omar on December 13, 2007, stated that the sole objective behind creating TTP was to unite the Pakistani Taliban to wage a "defensive jihad" against the Pakistani forces, carrying out military operations in the Northwest.[220] Baitullah confirmed this statement in an interview in January 2008, criticizing the Pakistan Army for "playing the different tribes and regions off of one another. In area X it is in peace talks or has a truce in place, and then in area Y it is in a state of war. Then the roles change, and it is in combat against area X and talking peace with area Y." He referred to the "Pakistani army's war in the tribal areas as an American war."[221]

Given this political position, the TTP posed a formidable challenge to the Pakistani military. Jason Burke further notes that the group's "rhetoric and ideology were informed by a socially revolutionary agenda" at the local level, mobilizing against local power holders.[222] President Musharraf declared Baitullah Mehsud "public enemy number one" as early as January 2008. The TTP launched an "unprecedented spate of attacks on the Pakistani military itself through the autumn of 2007 and into 2008," constituting a "direct assault on the core of the Pakistani political and security establishment."[223] Our argument suggests that the army should have quickly categorized it as ideologically opposed and responded accordingly. There is clear evidence that by 2009, "the army became aware of the challenge the entire Islamist sphere (including what it heretofore considered as "good Islamists") posed to its authority and Pakistan's territorial integrity."[224]

A series of military operations ensued in 2007–9, including Zarga Khel in North Waziristan, Operation Tri-Star in South Waziristan, Operation Eagle Swoop, Operation Labbaik, and Operation Eagle Swoop II. These were not very successful: as in its battles with the Nek Mohammed group in 2004, the army was poorly prepared and knocked back on its heels. As a result of recurrent military setbacks, the military sought peace deals to minimize losses in 2008 and early 2009.[225]

These occasional efforts at deal making clearly show that the argument does not seamlessly explain the case: change was a protracted and noisy process, and therefore this is not a simple success for the theory. Part of the explanation was a temporary conciliatory policy between late November 2008 and early 2009: the TTP became a strange bedfellow as the army sought to pacify the periphery during an India-Pakistan crisis. The November 26, 2008, Mumbai attacks led to heightened tensions between India and Pakistan, with the Indian government pledging a surgical response inside Pakistan.

Though we did not code it as a major ideological shift, the TTP briefly became a strange bedfellow, with limited cooperation being useful to the army for stabilizing restive areas of the Northwest to free up military capacity for a confrontation with India. This was accompanied by a rhetorical shift by the army, which—in a dramatic turnaround—declared TTP to be patriotic Pakistanis. A senior official of the ISI told a group of senior journalists that "we have no big issues with the militants in Fata. We have only some misunderstandings with Baitullah Mehsud and Fazlullah. These misunderstandings could be removed through dialogue."[226] This may also have been related to efforts to encourage splintering by TTP factions (such as the Bahadur group, discussed below) by seeking peace deals as a tool for fragmentation.[227]

This turned out to be cheap talk. Though the cease-fire between the Pakistan Army and TTP lasted until the tensions with India eased, conflict resumed soon after the crisis died down. The TPP used the respite as an opportunity to further consolidate its gain in both FATA and Swat. Ongoing—and by 2009 escalating—offensives suggest that the army did not see enduring space for a deal with the TTP, unlike with the various gray zone groups with which it was negotiating (including Mullah Nazir, Bahadur, and Abdullah Mehsud) during the same period. There was "fighting on an unprecedented scale" with the TTP that suggests a much more resolved effort to crack down on the group. These operations focused on "clearing the TTP strongholds of Ladha, Makin, and Sararogha."[228]

The slow transformation in political role from perceived business partner to mortal enemy that occurred between 2005 and 2009 culminated in a state strategy to suppress the TTP, initiated by the launch of Operation Rah-e-Rast—in which the army sought to "regain its control over South Waziristan"—in May 2009.[229] In October, thirty thousand combat forces went into South Waziristan Agency in Operation Rah-e-Nijat (Path to Salvation).[230] The TTP was a consistent target of the military from 2009 onward, as would be expected with regard to a perceived mortal enemy. Interestingly, during these operations the army worked with several groups that had either always opposed the TTP or that splintered from it.

Civilian governments attempted negotiations again in 2013, after the drone strike killing of Hakimullah Mehsud, highlighting how civil-military divisions can undermine our army-focused argument.[231] Nevertheless, after these talks failed, the military returned to targeting the TTP aggressively. COAS Kayani was "most reluctant" to accept TTP demands and his successor Raheel Sharif was "even more determined."[232] As 2014 progressed, "the army intensified its strikes" and then launched Operation Zarb-e-Azb into North Waziristan.[233] As noted above, the Haqqanis do not appear to have been damaged in any serious way by this assault, but the TTP was, showing the military's ability to discriminate in its targeting. Interestingly, when power feuds over succession within the TTP led a group of Mehsuds to defect in the wake of Hakimullah's death, they moderated their ideological position and became business partners of the military against the remaining Fazlullah-led core TTP.[234]

Not every period matches the theory's expectations, particularly late 2008/ early 2009 and early/mid-2013, when there were efforts at limited cooperation. Civil-military complications, residual ambiguity about how to classify the TTP, and the byzantine splintering of the group all add complexity to the case that we acknowledge. Nevertheless, the basic trajectory was very different from that of otherwise similar state-group dyads and is generally in line with the basic theoretical predictions. The military was happy to tolerate or do business with TTP precursor factions until they explicitly turned against the state and made demands that simply could not be granted without shattering the military's political project. Once that shift in symbols, discourses, and patterns of behavior occurred, the army slowly but surely recategorized the group and launched sustained, often brutal, attacks against it.

Life and Death in the Gray Zone: Mullah Nazir and Hafiz Gul Bahadur

The Haqqanis are a clear illustration of an armed ally political role, while the TTP broadly represents a mortal enemy. This section addresses two gray zone groups, led by Mullah Nazir (in South Waziristan) and Hafiz Gul Bahadur (in North Waziristan). We consider them together because they both represent gray zone groups and have often operated in close proximity to one another. Both (although particularly Bahadur) occupy a more ambiguous space with regard to the Pakistani military than either the TTP or Haqqanis.[235] They reveal the complexity of armed politics in Pakistan, where simply being an armed group has no fixed political meaning. Their experiences also demonstrate the limits to cooperation when militant organizations do not line up with the army's ideological project. With both groups, there was a general trajectory of limited cooperation (though with several shifts in the case of Bahadur): "Pakistan cultivated Mullah Bahadur and Maulvi Nazir in an attempt to counter the anti-state elements of the TTP generally and Baitullah and Hakimullah Mehsud in particular."[236]

We begin with the somewhat more straightforward case of the Mullah Nazir group. He became the head of a militant group in Wana in 2004,[237] tightly linked to the Afghan Taliban and with a base in the Ahmadzai Wazir tribe.[238] Nazir had a deep distaste for Uzbek militants operating in South Waziristan and expelled them; they ended up aligned with Baitullah Mehsud. Mullah Nazir preferred to focus on Afghanistan rather than attacking the Pakistani state, driving further divisions between himself and the emerging TTP of Baitullah.[239] Brief attempts at rapprochement between Nazir and Baitullah in 2009 and 2011 failed almost immediately. But he did not actively and publicly support the Pakistani state or serve as its strike arm in Afghanistan, unlike groups such as LeT and the Haqqanis. This autonomy included maintaining links with Al-Qaeda, an enemy of the state.[240] Classifying his group as a gray zone actor is therefore appropriate, as it straddled the lines of alignment and opposition.

Nazir's rivalry with Baitullah led to clashes with the TPP from early 2008, making him tactically very valuable to Pakistan's military, which was beginning to mobilize against Baitullah's organization during this period. We expect him to be viewed as a business partner armed group and thus be targeted for limited cooperation, and this is exactly what happened. In the years prior to Nazir's death by an American drone in 2013, "Pakistan's military and Nazir's faction were operating under a non-aggression pact, and violent incidents between the two were rare."[241] Indeed, "the Pakistan Army sought to bolster Nazir against Baitullah Mehsud, who was protecting the Uzbeks."[242] Seth Jones and C. Christine Fair argue that "the Pakistani government likely provided support to Mullah Nazir for a number of reasons, including to help balance against the Tehreek-e-Taliban-e-Pakistan in South Waziristan and to ensure some Pakistani oversight over Nazir's group."[243]

Though Nazir's links to Al-Qaeda likely limited a full embrace, the military and Nazir group had mutual interests in denying territory to the TTP and trying to splinter Baitullah and Hekimullah's group.[244] Nazir was killed by the United States in 2013 because of his close links to the Afghan Taliban and Al-Qaeda, but his successor, Bahawal Khan, appears to have continued a collusive relationship with Pakistan's military.[245] As with the Mehsud splinter of the TTP, the Mullah Nazir group has continued to operate as a warlord force on the frontier, demonstrating that a fragmented monopoly of violence is not politically problematic for the Pakistani military as long as the right kinds of groups fracture that monopoly. It also shows that the army's political support remains limited if the group does not profess ideological precepts acceptable to the Pakistani state.

Gul Hafiz Bahadur's group has had a more labyrinthine trajectory. Like the Mullah Nazir group, Pakistani forces cut deals with Bahadur to limit the TTP's reach in the FATA.[246] Yet Bahadur was actually briefly part of the TTP in 2007–8, and in 2014 he broke his cease-fire with the military in the run-up to Operation Zarb-e-Azb. As with Nazir's links to Al-Qaeda, this track record of both affiliation and competition with the TTP puts the Bahadur group squarely in the gray zone. Bahadur emerged from the same militant milieu as many other leaders, based in North Waziristan and with experience in Afghanistan and connections to the Haqqanis and Afghan Taliban. As with Baitullah Mehsud and other groups that later formed the TTP, he began to clash with the Pakistani military in the mid-2000s. The Haqqanis helped to broker a cease-fire between his group and the military, "which had been fighting an on-again, off-again war for almost two years," in 2006.[247] Bahadur both fought against and signed peace agreements with the army in 2006 and 2008.

Bahadur was a deputy in the TTP when it formed in December 2007. Yet unlike Baitullah Mehsud, he was uncomfortable with foreign militants and broke from the TTP in 2008 when Afghan Taliban leader Mullah Omar opposed its formation as a distraction from the battle in Afghanistan. In doing so, he staked out a position as "a pragmatist, maintaining constructive relations with a host of militants in North Waziristan and beyond while avoiding confrontation with the Pakistani state that might initiative a powerful crackdown."[248] According to Jaffrelot, Bahadur "dissented [from TTP line]—partly because of the old rivalry between Wazirs and Mehsuds, partly because the Pakistani Army had wooed him, playing on this rivalry, partly because Wazirs resented the role of the Uzbeks in the TTP—but then fell back in line in 2009."[249] He subsequently aligned with Mullah Nazir and groups emphasizing the war in Afghanistan over that against the Pakistani state.[250]

These perambulations continued into early 2009, when Bahadur agreed to join a coalition with Mullah Nazir and Baitullah Mehsud to try to unify the factions of the Northwest frontier (under pressure from Mullah Omar to try to rationalize the militancy). This alliance, however, quickly fell apart over enduring disagreements about how to deal with the Pakistani state. As a result, from 2009–14 Bahadur "hedged his bets and seems to have largely allowed Pakistani troops to pass through North Waziristan" and "quickly distanced himself from the TTP and its leadership. . . . Bahadur focuses exclusively on US and NATO forces in Afghanistan."[251] Limited cooperation, via a cease-fire, with Bahadur was useful to the army as a way of minimizing its military challenges and constraining the spread of the TTP. Though party to another abortive united front effort in late 2011 and early 2012, Bahadur and the TTP could never settle the key question of "whether or not to attack the Pakistani state."[252]

This limited cooperation continued until 2014, when Bahadur declared an end to his cease-fire with the Pakistani government. It had held for half a decade prior collapsed. As a result, it appears that Bahadur's group may have been targeted in the Zarb-e-Azb offensive of 2014–15, which possibly resulted in his death.[253] It is not clear what triggered Bahadur's decision to break from the limited cooperation and forthrightly reject the military's authority, which should have led the army to recategorize him as a mortal enemy. Until further data becomes available, it is difficult to know what drove his decision to adopt a radically different ideological stance.[254]

These findings help us put into perspective the Pakistani military operations in North Waziristan, which escalated in 2014, and the future of military policy on the strategically crucial Northwest frontier. Operation Zarb-e-Azb in 2014 was rhetorically hailed by Pakistani leaders as a full-fledged assault on nonstate militancy. Yet the evidence from our case studies strongly suggests a continuing pattern of selective violence toward—and tacit (at minimum) cooperation with some—armed groups. We have already discussed the case of the Haqqani network. A breakaway faction of the TTP, the Punjabi Taliban group led by Asmatullah Muawiya, seems to have been accommodated after moderating its ideological positions in 2014, even though the group was previously involved in lethal attacks, including one on the Sri Lankan cricket team.

The military has brought a kind of tenuous, heavily armed stability to the Northwest frontier, though at high human cost and without fully eliminating the TTP insurgency. Pushing back the TTP was a major accomplishment for the state, and it was not achieved through hearts-and-minds counterinsurgency. The military worked with a variety of armed actors to isolate, split, and target the Pakistani Taliban—the process of reestablishing the writ of the state was not the same as establishing a state monopoly of violence. Instead, it was fundamentally about sidelining actors that offered a direct ideological and military challenge to the political status quo. It took much a higher bar to trigger this kind of direct crackdown than we see in the Balochistan or East Pakistan cases—to "select into" being an unacceptable Islamist actor seems rather more challenging than with regional groups (including unarmed groups). Indeed, we have seen harsh repression of the unarmed PTM in many of the same areas where the military initially cut deals with or ignored the rise of the TTP and its predecessor factions.

A fractured monopoly of violence has been perfectly compatible with the Pakistani military's political project: the key question is who is allowed to carry guns, not whether anyone is. Even attacking the regime or perpetrating some degree of violent opposition is not equivalent to being ideologically beyond the pale; the army has done business with a number of groups that it has also clashed with. As long as organizations continue to operate within the military's broad vision of the polity, and offer something of value to its instrumental interests, there is political space to continue bargaining even with those that are simultaneously imposing costs on the army.

This kind of discrimination is likely to endure into the future. There have been meaningful changes in the last decade, most strikingly the weakening of the TTP and rhetorical shifts in how militants in general are framed. Yet Pakistan's military has shown a willingness to directly defy, or to work around, international efforts to force more broad-reaching repression of militants, instead prioritizing domestic political goals and interests.[255] The Afghan Taliban have remained recipients of sanctuary, while the Lashkar-e-Taiba and Jaish-e-Mohammed have not, as of this writing, faced a sustained campaign of intense repression.

It is certainly possible that this will change as coercive pressure, whether from India, America, or the international community, finally becomes intolerable and makes the tactical value of these groups insufficient to overcome the costs. Yet the most likely pathway to ending this broader state of affairs is a military-backed project of "mainstreaming" these militants into electoral politics, seeking to weave them into the fabric of normal politics: they would become superfluous supporters, rather than decisively purged out of the political system. Indeed, Chacko argues that since 2014, "the authorities have engaged in selective "mainstreaming" of certain state-allied militant groups."[256] This outcome would shift the landscape of Pakistan's armed politics, but leave potentially dangerous ideological strands firmly embedded into political life.

6

BURMA/MYANMAR

Burma/Myanmar has been the site of large-scale civil conflict and state repression since its independence in 1948. This chapter explores the political origins of these dynamics. In an odd way, despite the labyrinthine complexity of Myanmar's wars, they are simpler than in India or Pakistan. An ethnically Bamar-dominated and religiously heavily Buddhist nationalist project, with colonial roots, dominated the fragile state after independence, solidifying political cleavages along lines of language, religion, and ethnicity. These divisions, which had elements of fluidity and malleability in the 1940s and 1950s, were dramatically hardened and exacerbated by the military dictatorship of General Ne Win, who took power in 1962.

This fusion of hard-line exclusionary nationalism with authoritarian military rule drove a pervasive regime perception of enemies. For tactical reasons, there have been important shifts toward limited cooperation with armed groups since 1989, but the military's dominance of internal security policy has continued and brought an enduring focus on centralization and Buddhist-Bamar dominance. This project softened a bit after Ne Win was pushed aside by a military junta, but even after democratization, majoritarian nationalism continues to be a powerful political force among both civilian and military ranks, against a backdrop of enduring military suspicion of civilians, ethnic minorities, and federalism.

Numerous armed orders have emerged over time, but prior to 1989, conflict dominated over cooperation. After 1989, we have seen a shift toward much more cooperation, though little actual conflict resolution. Unlike in the other chapters, here I consider postindependence projects largely alongside armed orders: in contrast to India, Pakistan, and Sri Lanka, large-scale and sustained insurgency broke out essentially at independence. It would be artificial to try to present the evolution of postindependence regime projects without directly engaging with this ongoing, pervasive violence. The colonial period thus becomes particularly important for giving insight into how the country's leaders perceived the political landscape at independence.

The chapter starts with these colonial dynamics. It shows how the period of British rule fostered a new Burman (also called Bamar) nationalism that set itself in opposition to both colonialism and to ethnic minorities that were seen as collaborators with these forces. This project took on a visceral and violent reality during the bloody years of World War II, when Burmese nationalists backed by Japan fought with ethnic minorities supported by the British and Americans. This process built a carrier movement known as the Anti-Fascist People Freedom League (AFPFL) with a strongly anticolonial, majoritarian nationalist political project. While articulating a broader Burmese nationalism, this project favored the Bamar ethnicity and Buddhist religion as the top of a hierarchy of priority, laying the basis for ongoing political conflict.

I then explore what happened when the British departed and large-scale civil war erupted. I combine armed order data and case examples with the broader historical narrative. Because war and independence occurred at the same time, this chapter weaves together the armed orders with the broader politics, identifying the key shifts over time and their implications for armed politics. The argument does well in key areas, but it also runs into important limits, most notably in fully explaining the major shift toward limited cooperation and tenuous-but-new cease-fire politics from 1989 to the present. It concludes with a discussion of what my claims and findings can tell us about the tumultuous politics and future of contemporary Myanmar.

Colonial Politics and the Making of Modern Burma

Rather than being led by the elite likes of Jinnah, Nehru, or Senanayake, the most powerful nationalist movement in Burma was dominated by young students with weak links to the colonial ruling classes. This was a result of the dislocations of the Anglo-Burmese wars, the importation of Indian businessmen and civil servants, British strategies of indirect rule that favored ethnic minorities on the periphery, and the power of European business interests in

Rangoon. An aggressive surge from below sought to radically alter the fundamentals of political authority in the country.

The emergent project was carried forth by the *Thakins* of student movements in the 1930s, by armed groups in the 1940s, and then by the AFPFL from 1945. As Martin Smith writes, "The origins of the main national parties, from the CPB to Ne Win's BSPP, are deeply rooted in anti-colonial/anti-fascist resistance."[1] We have to look before 1948 to understand subsequent patterns of armed politics in Burma: "The historical role in the fight for independence holds the key for contemporary political identity, rhetoric, and the contest over legitimacy, and national symbols."[2] This was the fundamental period that forged a new ideological project that placed the Bamar ethnicity/Burmese language alongside Buddhism as key pillars of an ascendant nationalism. Two important alternatives also emerged: a Communist Party that eventually turned to insurgency, and a set of ethnic minorities pursuing a more decentralized, federal polity that could hold Bamar reassertion at bay.

Overcoming the Indignities of Empire: Mobilization and Articulation, 1920–40

A major set of nationalist mobilizations began in the late 1910s and early 1920s. Controversies over footwear in Buddhist pagodas began to show a "link between Buddhism and Burmese nationalism,"[3] while student boycotts targeted British colonial governance.[4] The 1920s also saw efforts to mobilize rural populations.[5] Unlike in 1920s India, however, efforts at bridging the urban-rural divide were unsuccessful.

While urban politicians had to rely on local political figures, parties did not develop that could incorporate both sectors of the population: political feuds in the mid-1920s "brought to an end the first attempt to fashion a nationalist political movement bridging across the gap separating urban and rural leadership. The groups corresponded roughly to the Western-oriented [largely urban] faction and the traditionalist *pongyi*-led [largely rural] elements of the population."[6] From 1920, instead, "a fateful pattern was developed for using the university and the schools as instruments of political opposition."[7] The Saya San rebellion of the early 1930s was a clear instance of rural rebellion,[8] but most of what we might consider "nationalist" politics was centered in the political "pressure cooker" of Rangoon.[9] Efforts at mobilizing rural populations tended to rely heavily on appeals to Buddhism, which were not welcomed by Burma's many non-Buddhists.[10] Militarization was pervasive: "By the mid-1930s, every major nationalist or religious organization had established its own *tat* (army)."[11]

In the 1920s and 1930s, we see three key patterns emerging in Burmese politics. The first was political and organizational fragmentation. Splits over participation in the colonial government stretched back to the early 1920s and recurred in the 1930s.[12] As Moscotti notes, "The amorphous political groupings that were the vanguard of Burmese nationalism centered around a few key individuals who adapted their political programs to the situations in which they operated."[13] There was no Indian National Congress equivalent, nor a cozy elite bargain like that between the British and the Ceylon National Congress (CNC) in Ceylon.

Second, nationalism among many in these movements came to be signified by Buddhism and the Burmese language. Charney argues that the Burmese language "became more closely linked to ethnic identity, just as Buddhism, no longer the state religion, had also become a mark of being Burmese."[14] This movement was consolidated into opposition to special roles for ethnic minorities, like the Karen and Kachin (much less Indians, who were seen as foreign interlopers). British strategy aimed to separate and protect them.[15] For many Burmese nationalists in early 1920s "minority representation in special constituencies meant "divide and rule" tactics and the negation at the very outset of the newly awakened nationalist interest in political liberalism and co-operation under a common citizenship."[16] Unsurprisingly, Karen political organizations were opposed to this approach, foreshadowing future splits and violence.[17] The nationalist General Council of Burmese Associations (GCBA), for instance, "worked to broaden the scope of the nationalist movement, but crucially failed to win support from the ethnic minorities," before collapsing into splintering of its own.[18] We can see echoes here of the Sinhalese-Tamil cleavage in colonial and postcolonial Ceylon.

Third, the most aggressive manifestation of the nationalist movement abandoned constitutional politics in favor of student and urban radicalism. This nationalist agenda was ultimately to be led by a group that called itself Dobama Asiayone (We Burmans Association); many of its members referred to themselves as Thakins (or masters).[19] It was founded in 1930 after Indo-Burman rioting, and over the course of the early 1930s moved "gradually to the forefront of the nationalist campaign."[20] It planted a flag for a particular understanding of Burmese nationalism: "The Dobama's early successes in popular mobilization came in its campaign aimed at repudiating foreign influences in language, clothing, and literature and at affirming the traditions of indigenous Burmese language and clothing."[21] This movement, while loosely organized, "proved to be the source of the nationalist leadership, which assumed control in the final surge leading to Burma's independence."[22] This grouping "was destined in time to fill the political vacuum" left by the failure of constitutional politics in Burma:[23] unlike the hard-fought 1937 election in India, Burma's election campaign of 1936 "aroused little popular enthusiasm."[24]

The grouping offered a simultaneous message of inclusion and exclusion. On one hand, "they called those who cooperated with colonial rule 'Their Burma' (*thudo bama*) as opposed to 'Our Burma' (*do bama*), and regarded them as enemies to be defeated along with colonial rule."[25] This perception became fused with an intense focus on the Burmese language and an appeal to the Buddhist religion: on language and religion, the ideological polity tilted toward a more exclusive and narrow vision of "true" nationalism. It was framed a message of empowerment for a Burman majority that had seen itself marginalized under British rule.

Along the redistributive dimension, these student radicals were influenced by some form of Marxism. However, "as a whole [these were] essentially . . . nationalist rather than . . . Communist organizations, although [they were] revolutionary in spirit. Marxism tended to buttress [their] all-out opposition to capitalist imperialism."[26] The Dobama "contained a strong Communist element" led by Thakin Than Tun.[27] The Burma People's Revolutionary Party was formed in 1939, which "was to be the nucleus of the future Socialist Party,"[28] while, also in 1939, the Communist Party of Burma (CPB) was founded.[29] These leftist actors would split in the coming years over how rigorously to adhere to the Marxist-Leninist line. As Nakanishi notes, splits and British crackdowns made "it difficult to consolidate leadership" into a single overarching party organization.[30]

Tinker notes that it was this political grouping, however loose, that would become the leadership of the new independent Burma: "The national leaders of the future were creating some clamour on the fringe of Burmese politics; their first platform was the Rangoon University Students' Union,"[31] and they "were, in the future, to become Cabinet Ministers."[32] For such a large country, it is remarkable how concentrated the future leadership was: "All of Burma's major political leaders for the next four decades emerged on the national scene during these years [1937–47], held commanding positions in the state or army, and gained the kind of administrative experience necessary for the challenges ahead."[33]

In 1940, the Freedom Bloc, "an ultranationalist organization . . . amalgam of the Sinyetha Party, affiliated political *pongyi* groups, minor elements of the defunct Ngabwinsaing Party, and the Dobama Asiayone, except for those extremists who insisted on following the orthodox Communist line of policy," emerged to demand independence.[34] One of its major figures was future AFPFL leader Aung San, who argued that "attempted socialist action in Burma prior to the achievement of nationalist ends was sheer adventurism."[35] As Smith notes, "The historic success of the Thakin movement to was bring together and organize in ten short years the different and largely unpoliticized sections of the community, including students, peasants, and workers."[36] Yet it did not reach far beyond the ethnic Burman core and made Burmese language and Buddhist religion integral to its ideological project. The combination of left-wing politics and ethno-majoritarianism was a powerful one in 1930s Burma—but only in the Burman heartland.

The War: 1940–45

World War II provided a set of fundamentally new political opportunities: "The political groups best able, by virtue of their superior daring, nationalist principles, and adaptability, to take advantage of the new situation were the components of the Dr. Ba Maw-Thakin Party 'Freedom Bloc.' Under circumstances of continued peace, such a group could have risen to political dominance only after decades of political struggle, if indeed it could have done so at all."[37] Beyond the Freedom Bloc, for a whole generation of Burmese "the Second World War was without doubt the major formative political experience."[38] Instead of operating through colonial channels as in the other cases in this book, a group of young radicals—who became known as the "Thirty Comrades"—made contact with the Japanese and formed the Burmese Independence Army (BIA) in late 1941 as a proindependence, anti-British army backed by Japan. After the successful Japanese invasion of 1942, the BIA claimed the mantle of Burmese nationalism.

Yet other projects were at work during the war. First, the Communist Party of Burma took Moscow's line of resistance to the Japanese, and "in wartime conditions the CPB thus gained much valuable organizational experience."[39] Like India's communists, the CPB saw the Japanese as a fascist force that needed to be resisted, following the anti-Axis line from Moscow. Second, members of the Karen and Kachin worked with the British and Americans against the Japanese, acting as guerrillas and intelligence operatives.[40] Smith argues that "out of these diverse wartime experiences markedly different perceptions were to surface."[41] The Karen saw the BIA as a violent, oppressive force for Burman ethno-chauvinism. For the BIA and the noncommunist elements of the broader Thakin movement, "the Karens were clearly regarded as potential fifth-columnists" by Burmese nationalists during ethnic massacres of the war,[42] seeing "all Karens as British collaborators, as the enemy."[43] During this period, "the BIA became an armed Burman ethno-nationalist force and . . . closely associated the Karens in general with the British."[44]

In 1943, Aung San began reaching out to the Allies in preparation for a change in sides.[45] In summer of 1944 the Anti-Fascist People's Freedom League (AFPFL) was formed in secret, drawing heavily on the successor force to the BIA. The AFPFL turned on the Japanese in the waning months of the war in 1945. This change of alignment allowed the AFPFL to lay claim to victory once the Allies defeated Japan, despite its collaboration with the Japanese for most of the war.

The AFPFL—despite dramatic twists and turns—became the carrier movement that ruled Burma at independence in 1948.

The AFPFL's Tenuous Primacy: 1945–48

The end of the war pitted British hopes for a return to the pre-1940 status quo against the AFPFL's ability to summon protests and strikes, against a background of mobilized private armies.[46] Eventually the AFPFL pushed the British into the London Agreement of 1947, which promised independence and established elections for a Constituent Assembly. Burma became independent in 1948. In the waning days of the war and its aftermath, "the Freedom League [AFPFL] alone acquired the essential internal cohesion, the mass following, and the capabilities of physical resistance needed to champion the nationalist cause."[47] Its "prime architects and leaders" were Aung San and the communist leader Than Tun.[48] Than Tun would leave the AFPFL when the CPB split away, but initially acted as link between "essentially nationalist Thakins (Aung San and Nu), the Socialist organizers of the peasant and worker association (led by Thakins Mya and Ba Swe), and the more doctrinaire Communist underground (Thakins Thein Pe in India and Soe in Burma)."[49]

The AFPFL dominated the 1947 Constituent Assembly elections and would then run Burma almost continually from 1948 to 1962: "At its center was a closely knit cadre of Thakins, long united by personal acquaintance and by experiences gained in a common struggle."[50] However, it faced serious ideological and factional conflict in 1946 and 1947, even before the full-scale insurgencies of 1948–49. In this period three distinct types of aspirational carrier movements that would become major players in independence entered into competition with one another: the AFPFL's Socialist Party core; the Communist Party of Burma (CPB); and ethnic minorities, above all the Karen National Union (KNU). The CPB and KNU represented political paths not taken in the colonial era, but both would endure in the post-1948 period as key players in Burma's extraordinarily violent armed politics.

The heart of the AFPFL was Aung San's Socialist Party.[51] The CPB, however, was also a powerful organization within the front. Its leadership had deep roots in the Thakin movement of the 1930s, but they had nevertheless disagreed with Aung San and the Thirty Comrades over the priority to be given to Marxism-Leninism and whether to ally with the Japanese. The period of CPB involvement in the AFPFL only lasted until October 1946. Disagreement arose with Aung San and his supporters about how much, and how, to cooperate with the British.[52] The Socialists "had replaced CPB officials in nearly all key positions" within the

AFPFL,[53] showing their desire to hold the CPB at bay within the front. By 1946, "Aung San had now built up a formidable power base inside both the Socialist Party and the AFPFL, as well as his private army, the PVOs."[54] The CPB's Than Tun, who had been deeply involved in the AFPFL, was forced out of the leadership,[55] and CPB left the front in late 1946.[56]

In October 1946, "the trouble-making Communists, including both the Than Tun and the Thein Pe factions, were completely and finally excluded from the council of the AFPFL, amid widespread recriminations."[57] Aung San and the Socialists had largely seized control of the AFPFL, which was the main negotiating partner with the British: "From this point on the Socialist Party nominees ... dominated the AFPFL and held virtually all the key positions in the first post-independence government."[58] Aung San also loosely controlled the Pyithu Yebaw Ahphwe (People's Volunteer Organization, PVO), "a private army, with district formations throughout the country, all operating under a central headquarters controlled by Aung San."[59]

The AFPFL's Socialist core plunged forward after purging the CPB, signing a deal with the British government in January 1947. However, Aung San's assassination in July 1947 presaged instability to come. He was succeeded by U Nu, the future prime minister, and the Socialists continued to dominate the carrier movement that took over from the British. U Nu had his own particular views, but the AFPFL generally continued to advance its vision of a resurgent Burma that returned rightful power to ethnic Burmans, incorporated the periphery, and advanced a leftist economic approach.[60] There were some overtures again to the CPB after the Aung San assassination, but they soon fell apart due to U Nu's suspicion that the CPB would try to take over the AFPFL from within amid large-scale strikes and protests driven by the communists.[61] The Socialists would become the new ruling regime, but they were unable to fully incorporate the PVO private army, which splintered after Aung San's death. Both the CPB and KNU would pose powerful armed challenges to the AFPFL project.

The CPB was thus left out of the scramble for power. It had split already in 1946, with Thakin Soe's "Red Flag" CPB departing while advocating an armed revolutionary line.[62] The remaining, "White Flag," CPB's purge from the AFPFL later in 1946 clearly showed that it would be going it alone in the new Burma, as an opposition to the Socialist Party's more moderate line. The CPB followed a Marxist-Leninist ideology that pushed for greater resistance to the British,[63] a highly centralized state, large-scale nationalization of industry, and a class-based analysis of social cleavages: "The CPB's shift from a legal opposition party to an underground insurgent organization began in April 1947 when it carried out a half-hearted boycott of the elections to the Constituent Assembly."[64] By April 1948, the CPB would wholeheartedly adopt a line of armed resistance, laying the basis for four decades of insurgency.[65]

The main ethno-separatist carrier movement during this period was the KNU. The British and AFPFL sparred over the future of the Frontier Areas where the Chin, Kachin, and Shan dominated.[66] A rough status quo was maintained for those areas in the 1947 Panglong Agreement, but without a final resolution of their relationship to the looming new state. Even here, Aung San and others alarmed ethnic minorities: Aung San "was reported to have declared bluntly that the Kachins must decide 'whether they wanted to remain with their own kin or align themselves with British imperialism,'" in a clear echo of the Burmese nationalist movement's distrust of the minorities for their links to the British.[67]

The Karen faced geographical dispersion that made political bargaining even more complex:[68] "The most glaring of all the 1947 Constitution's many failings was its muddled attempt to resolve the Karen question."[69] Splits within the Karen forged the KNU, which represented "those Karens who saw no future for themselves in a united and independent Burma."[70] Like portions of the Ceylon Tamil community, the coming of independence heralded a massive shift in political power within the new state. For the KNU, being forced into an ethno-majoritarian Burma, led by the people who had violently attacked the Karen during World War II, was a nightmare that needed to be avoided at all costs. The KNU began arming and reaching out to the British (and private British citizens) for support.

As 1947 turned into 1948, therefore, the Socialist Party seized the reins of state, but with a variety of armed competitors for power. The colonial period had birthed the ideas and organizations that underpinned the new political arena. From this context, armed politics was endemic to Burmese politics. In Callahan's words, "As the British colonial state disintegrated overnight, there emerged a dizzying array of nonstate organizations of violence, wherein coercion was the currency of politics and the weakened state became only one of numerous entities with claims on violence, territory, resources, and people,"[71] while for Charney "the Burmese had achieved independence without a revolution, which prevented the emergence of internal solidarity or the squeezing out of rival groups and ideologies."[72] This was the stuff out of which postcolonial Burmese politics were constructed.

After Independence: Politics and Violence in Burma

Burma had an extraordinarily tumultuous entry into independence. Armed politics erupted at birth and persisted. This is why it does not make sense to pull apart threat perceptions and armed orders after independence—they occurred simultaneously, without the sequencing we see in India, Pakistan, and Ceylon/Sri

Lanka. The lack of sequencing also weakens the inferences we can make about the effects of ideological projects, since the immediate military challenges of widespread insurgency limited space for choice beyond hard necessity. The AFPFL government, under U Nu, faced communist revolt and sooner thereafter Karen separatist insurgency, accompanied by various other ethnic insurgents and local private armies. Burma's new regime was immediately plunged into an extraordinary array of armed orders stretching across most of the country. In its earliest days, basic functional challenges preoccupied political and military leaders.

By the early 1950s, however, there was enough state coercive capacity to start making political choices about how to deal with armed groups. Once the regime acquired this breathing room, we start to see more interesting strategic choices and ensuing orders and order terminations. The prime minister for most of 1948–62 period, U Nu, pursued a complex blend of strategies, mixing a Burman nationalism with extensive amnesties and cease-fires with ethnic groups, and continuing to hold out space for the armed Left to integrate itself into "mainstream" politics while also attacking them with the military.

U Nu's position was viewed as veiled ethno-majoritarianism by many ethnic groups—while nevertheless being seen as too soft by the military. The army had consolidated under Ne Win as a predominantly ethnic Burman institution forged in brutal counterinsurgency against ethnic and communist insurgents. It developed a political worldview that drew heavily on colonial-era Burman nationalism, with a new layer of authoritarian contempt for civilians and suspicion of its insurgent adversaries. After the army seized power in 1962, we see a new, more radical ideological project at the helm of state that pulled together both historical and contemporary influences into a highly nationalist, exclusionary, and ruthless war machine.

This is reflected in a shift in patterns of armed order—there was a change in 1962 from a fairly high variance to a very narrow band of variation, with alliances, limited cooperation, incorporation, containment, and total war largely collapsing into a new wave of military hostilities, including a greater incidence of total war orders. Burma's fragmented, fluid armed landscape of the 1950s consolidated into a highly resolved, repressive central state squaring off against an array of mortal enemies. Decades of war resulted, with remarkably few cease-fires, much less peace deals, until the late 1980s. After 1989, we saw a dramatic shift toward limited cooperation. I will argue that this was largely tactical, a response to war weariness and splintering among armed groups combined with the new pressures facing the Myanmar military amid democratization challenges. This pattern of variation over time is visible in figure 6.1 below.

Table 6.1 provides a more specific breakdown of the temporal patterns in armed orders in Myanmar. The break after 1989 is extremely striking, marking

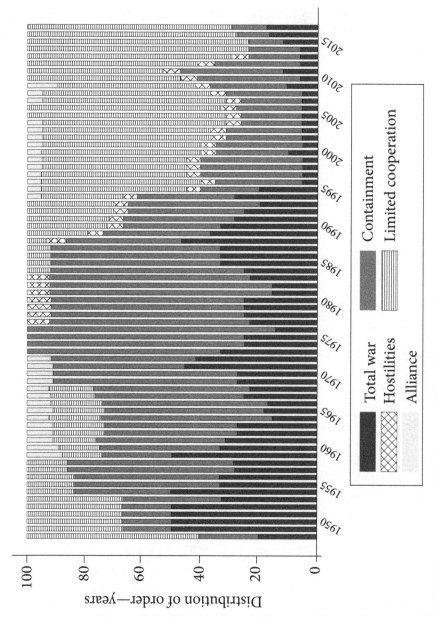

FIGURE 6.1. Armed politics in Burma/Myanmar, 1948–2017

Table 6.1 Order-years in Myanmar over time

	1948–61	1962–88	1989–	TOTAL
Total war	36 (37.89%)	87 (26.44%)	68 (12.32%)	191 (19.51%)
Containment	35 (36.84%)	206 (62.61%)	154 (27.90%)	395 (40.35%)
Military hostilities	0	7 (2.13%)	25 (4.53%)	32 (3.27%)
Limited cooperation	21 (22.11%)	18 (5.47%)	290 (52.54%)	332 (33.91%)
Alliance	3 (3.16%)	11 (3.34%)	15 (2.72%)	29 (2.96%)
Total	95	329	552	979

an era of cease-fire politics alongside ongoing conflict. Prior to 1989, however, the story is largely one of conflict, including substantial proportions of total war. We can disaggregate the pre-1989 period into the U Nu and Ne Win regimes. Under U Nu, the civil war raged amid de facto state collapse soon after independence. But there was also a substantial amount of limited cooperation, largely with private armies linked to the AFPFL and its politicians. This high-variance set of orders narrowed drastically from 1962 into a grim, grinding set of conflicts in which total war or containment absolutely dominated (nearly 90 percent of dyad-years).

During the 1988–90 period, Ne Win was removed from office by the military in the face of growing pressures for democratization in the Bamar heartland, the Communist Party of Burma splintered into several successors that abandoned communism, and ethnic insurgents came under pressure both from constituents and foreign countries to explore alternatives to ongoing fighting. This combination of primarily tactical dynamics led to a substantial shift toward cease-fires and limited cooperation from 1989. Conflict continued, however, and few armed groups—even those engaged in long-term limited cooperation—demobilized. Of the twenty-one cease-fires in Myanmar we have coded (which surely undercounts the first period, to be clear), all but two are from 1989 or later. This does not include a pair of amnesties and efforts at talks in 1963 and 1980, which were efforts by the Ne Win government to negotiate the surrenders of insurgent groups, rather than any kind of mutual agreement about limiting violence.

It is impossible to understand these patterns without taking politics seriously. The historical construction of a Bamar-Buddhist ideological project gave new rulers a set of preferences and fears that informed patterns of repression and accommodation. This project took on a more refined and concentrated form under Ne Win before slightly expanding in concessions after 1989. Armed groups

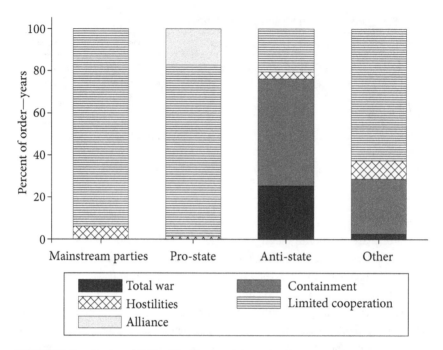

FIGURE 6.2.   Group self-identification and armed orders

themselves had agency as well, as I will explore below: both ideological radical-ization and war weariness contributed to decisions about how hard to fight and when to accept cease-fires. But in this case, agency has been quite constrained by the intensely limited political concessions on offer from the military. There has been much less "slack" available than for at least some groups in both India and Pakistan.

The very restricted space for armed politics beyond insurgency and coun-terinsurgency can be seen in figure 6.2. While acknowledging that self-identification in this case can be particularly tricky, since especially post-1989 lines blur in whole variety of ways, it is still striking how overwhelmingly we cat-egorize groups as anti-state rebels, even among groups pursuing limited coopera-tion. This gets to the political dynamics of the conflict—many groups have been willing to do business with the military since 1989, but their underlying political posture has not radically shifted.

Regime targeting of armed groups shows comparatively little of the careful discrimination we saw in India and Pakistan: language, religion, and redistribu-tive cleavages all primarily saw repression prior to 1989, and then equally expe-rienced the shift toward cooperation after 1989. This is because these cleavages were largely fused in the eyes of majoritarian nationalism: ethnic minorities were a suspect category, while leftist insurgents were seen as irreconcilables under Ne

Win. There is certainly some variation worth noting, however. The most intense counterinsurgency appears to have been aimed at the center-seeking CPB. While ethnic groups received very consistent repression prior to 1989, there was more containment than with the CPB. Among minority groups, the incorporation of accepted "national" ethnic groups into the nation—on the Tatmadaw's (the Burma Army's) terms—was seen as ultimately desirable, while, by contrast, anti-Rohingya sentiment (among both military and civilians) has led them to be framed as fundamental outsiders to the Myanmar nation. Table 6.2a examines order-years by groups' stated goals before 1989, while table 6.2b does so after 1989, keeping in mind the limits of cleanly categorizing goals.

There is evidence of an even harder line against center-seeking groups in the pre-1989 period, primarily the Communist Party of Burma, than against autonomy- and independence-seeking ethnic groups. But the basic pattern shows little cooperation across group goals. After 1989, there is some continued hard fighting against separatists, but a broader shift among proautonomy groups (the vast

TABLE 6.2a Group goals and order-years before 1989

	UNKNOWN/ AMBIGUOUS	INDEPENDENCE	AUTONOMY	CONTROL	CRIMINAL
Total war	4 (10.53%)	57 (35.85%)	25 (16.03%)	37 (88.10%)	0
Containment	34 (89.47%)	94 (59.12%)	101 (64.74%)	3 (7.14%)	9 (28.12%)
Military hostilities	0	0	0	1 (2.38%)	6 (18.75%)
Limited cooperation	0	8 (5.03%)	26 (16.67%)	1 (2.38%)	7 (21.88%)
Alliance	0	0	4 (2.56%)	0	10 (31.25%)
Total	38	159	156	42	32

TABLE 6.2b Group goals and order-years, 1989–2016

	UNKNOWN/ AMBIGUOUS	INDEPENDENCE	AUTONOMY	CONTROL	REFORM
Total war	6 (24%)	26 (50%)	32 (7.64%)	1 (3.57%)	0
Containment	0	19 (36.54%)	129 (30.79%)	2 (7.14%)	0
Military hostilities	0	0	0	24 (85.71%)	1 (12.5%)
Limited cooperation	5	5 (10%)	257 (61.34%)	1 (3.57%)	7 (87.5%)
Alliance	14 (56%)	0	1 (0.24%)	0	0
Total	25	50	419	28	8

majority of dyad-year observations) into containment or limited cooperation orders. The goals and self-identification of groups are quite hard to parse out in a number of these cases, so this is just suggestive data. But it gives a clear sense that there has been comparatively little political discrimination in coercion and compromise: most armed groups were harshly repressed before 1989, and after 1989 the state has been willing to pursue narrow tactical cease-fires with a wide variety of groups, especially those that have abandoned overt independence seeking.

What does order termination look like in Myanmar? We code twenty-six terminations, of which fourteen are military collapses, six are incorporation, five are absorption, and one is disarmament. Of the numerous armed groups operating in Myanmar, the fact that only six incorporation outcomes have occurred is quite striking. Moreover, these incorporations are generally of small groups, including several splinters of larger organizations. The absorption cases simply continue the fight within a new organization, so they largely involve the transformation of an order rather than strictly speaking its end. This is further evidence of the "suspended animation" nature of armed politics in Myanmar: even during periods of relatively low conflict, armed groups are remaining heavily armed and uninterested in the terms of demobilization on offer from the government. As with limited cooperation, there is more incorporation after 1989. Strikingly, only one clear incorporation case occurred before 1989, though the haziness of much of the empirical record makes this undoubtedly an undercount (especially for the 1950s).

The rest of the chapter explores the politics driving these patterns after independence. I find that there is substantial support for my argument, but also very real limitations and problems. The underlying structure of Bamar-Buddhist nationalism has helped to drive a highly conflictual and repressive set of orders. This underlying threat perception led to counterproductive but sustained military crackdowns and a striking lack of meaningful political accommodation. These are hard to explain without taking seriously ideological projects. But the major shift in armed politics in and after 1989 is only partially explained by my theory, with a set of tactical and international considerations driving political changes more than ideological transformations. The current state of Myanmar's armed politics reflect this uneasy blend of tactical calculations that favor widespread limited cooperation alongside deep political conflicts that prevent demobilization or peace building.

State Breakdown and Militarized Reconstruction

While Partition took an extraordinary human toll, Burma suffered an even deeper collapse in basic governance at independence. Callahan succinctly summarizes the situation: "The British colonial state disintegrated overnight, there emerged a dizzying array of nonstate organizations of violence, wherein coercion was the currency of politics and the weakened state became only one of numerous entities with claims on violence, territory, resources, and people."[73] The colonial state had been battered by the Japanese occupation, and the British return had not led to either an institutional renewal or to a broader political consensus about the meaning of Burmese nationalism. As table 6.1 shows, the period from 1948–61 would see a striking range of variation in armed orders, though primarily tilted toward conflict.

The AFPFL, and its Socialist Party core, represented a primarily ethnic Bamar majoritarianism, combined with leftist views on redistribution and the economy. It was viewed with deep suspicion by several of the ethnic minority groups, above all the Karen National Union (KNU), which feared that it would pursue a centralizing, homogenizing strategy. The CPB, now on the outside of the ruling coalition, opposed the regime as too rightist and pliant to the British. It had already begun mobilizing for violence prior to independence. These two dimensions of conflict— left-right and majority-minority—would intersect in labyrinthine ways in 1948–49 to break apart the army and plunge the country into widespread violence.

Within months of independence, the U Nu-led government in Rangoon faced a growing insurgency led by the CPB, which had broken from/been expelled by the Socialists prior to independence. The communist insurgency sought to topple the regime in its moment of prime weakness, and to replace it with a socialist state that it believed could truly break from the colonial past. Even as it began to mobilize for war against the CPB in early 1948, ethnic tensions within the military between the Karen and Burmans escalated. The KNU and its armed wing began to clash with state forces, Burman civilians, and progovernment militias over the course of 1948. Rangoon faced insurgency along both communist and ethnic dimensions.

These emerging insurgent forces were not the only armed groups on Burma's soil. The PVOs, which had answered loosely to Aung San, were dispersed across the Burman heartland without a consolidated chain of command. As Callahan notes, the "PVO was the first in a series of well-armed, nonstate, and at times anti-state armies made up mainly of those kicked out of the state's coercive apparatus or those who had abstained from joining the army for political reasons."[74] Various "pocket armies" operated in local contexts, often linked to AFPFL political leaders. The Socialist Party and its allies within the army developed militias, known as the Sitwundan, as counterinsurgent forces that could balance Karen dominance of the military in 1948. They would become "yet another party army," one that was linked to the ethnic Burman wing of the army.[75]

The collapse of the military as a cohesive force made these militias and private armies particularly important. This collapse occurred for structural reasons, in the clash of "two very different visions of who the enemy was for each camp" between the Karen and Burman wings of the army.[76] Two ideologies of the polity squared off—the Karen hoped for a decentralized Burmese state that resembled the "two Burmas" policy of the British, while the Burman nationalists aimed to knit the country together under a shared state and identity that would privilege the Burmese language and restore the majority to its rightful place of pride. The escalation of violence between Karen and Burmans in late 1948 eventually triggered a series of military defections by Karen units to the KNU and its armed wing. U Nu responded by replacing the Karen head of the army with Ne Win, banning the KNU's armed wing, and patching together a motley collection of remaining army units, Sitwundan militias, police, students, and others.[77] The Socialist Party played a key role in the counterinsurgent offensives of the late 1940s, using its local armies to hold territory and fight rebels, as the army rebuilt itself following the Karen defections.[78]

This incredibly tumultuous environment created little space for political decision making beyond basic military necessity. The government was engaged in hostilities with the CPB and KNU by the end of 1948, with an escalation of this violence in 1949 that pushed it to the edge of collapse. There was little space to do anything other than try to generate the capability to hold off insurgent forces wherever they were most threatening. My theory has little to say beyond the obvious—the government targeted the groups that were most threatening to its survival. Containment and total war dominated relations with the CPB (which had been joined by various PVO bands) and KNU, while alliances and limited cooperation orders characterized Rangoon's relationship with militias and private armies linked to the Socialist Party.[79]

Consolidation and State Making under U Nu, 1950–62

This period of desperation and military urgency ended in 1950. Burma continued to be wracked by insurgency, and the government lacked a monopoly of violence. But Rangoon had held on, and the military and party-linked militias consolidated a loose state control in ever-greater swathes of the country: "These Socialist Party forces pacified most of the country by incorporating local bosses, dacoit bands, and thugs into units loyal enough to the Union government that the elite-level political struggle in Rangoon stabilized in favor of the AFPFL."[80]

Space opened for armed politics that was not a pure function of military necessity. U Nu was the central decision maker for most of the 1950s. However, Ne Win and his army grew increasingly coherent and politically minded;

a "soft coup" put him in charge from 1958–60, and then an unambiguous coup in 1962 ended the era of civilian politics. This section considers two simultaneous processes—first, U Nu's efforts to manage and end orders with a wide range of groups, and second, the consolidation of military political preferences under Ne Win that laid the basis for the new politics of 1962 and after. Ironically, even as U Nu's strategies reduced the objective military threat to the state, the military per-ceived *increasing* levels of political threat from U Nu's complex blend of repres-sion and (limited) accommodation. As a result, from 1962 "any notion of Aung San's 'unity in diversity' or 'federal' democracy was abandoned; instead security became the government's major concern."[81] For the next twenty-five years Ne Win "followed a very simple, twofold strategy: he concentrated on building up a highly centralized system of administration from the centre in Rangoon while, in areas of rural insurgency, carrying out relentless counterinsurgency programmes in a bid to crush armed opposition once and for all."[82]

U Nu is a complicated figure, and his policies show much higher variance than any of the other national leaders considered in this chapter. He did not lead a disci-plined cadre party, and his prominence was in part a result of the vacuum created by Aung San's assassination. U Nu's ideological position drew on the AFPFL's ver-sion of Burmese nationalism, most strikingly in his decision to make Buddhism the official state religion in 1961, which helped to trigger the Kachin insurgency. The inability of U Nu to forge a fundamentally new vision of Burmese nationalism was enormously dangerous: "Burma achieved independence under the auspices of Burman nationalism, but, in the late 1940s and early 1950s, it might have still been possible for the new country to create a multi-ethnic nation. Unfortunately, the conditions under which Burma gained its independence made it impossible for reconciliation and co-operation to occur between the again dominant Burmans and the other ethnic groups."[83] Yet he was not a hard-line nationalist, supporting at least the idea of the 1947 Panglong Agreement that Aung San had negotiated with Shan, Kachin, and Chin ethnic leaders. U Nu was also open to rapproche-ment with the Left—while the AFPFL had fallen out with the CPB, it was not an ideologically right-wing regime, and it favored democratic incorporation of the Left (though, to be clear, on the government's terms).

U Nu found the AFPFL party armies largely unproblematic beyond the nui-sance and unwanted attention their excesses could create. They were tactically useful and politically unthreatening, leading to "alliances [that] represented unprecedented political accommodation between Rangoon elites and upcoun-try political bosses, guerrillas, and black marketers."[84] Though we lack system-atic, fine-grained data on individual private armies and AFPFL-linked armed groups, the general pattern appears to be one of fairly firm alliances between the government and these actors: the government needed to extend its reach into the periphery, and in exchange these groups were given room to maneuver.[85]

In Boudreau's words, "Outside large Central Burmese cities, autonomous organizations, pocket armies and warlords resisted integration into national political parties, and needed to be courted, conquered or mollified."[86] The Sitwundan was another example of a "party army that found the space to operate inside state institutions."[87] More broadly, in the 1950s "state practice accommodated protest."[88]

Policy toward the communists and ethnic minorities blended amnesties and openness to negotiation with serious ongoing military offensives. The first column of table 6.1 shows substantial heterogeneity in armed orders during this period. The CPB was not formally outlawed until 1953 despite its direct onslaught against the state; even after banning, the government signaled its willingness to parley on terms that CPB lay down arms and follow the model of the Communist Party of India.[89] Starting in 1950, "more and more cadres began supporting the attempts to negotiate with the government in Rangoon. Hundreds of CPB cadres simply surrendered."[90] Thus, as Lintner summarizes, "Although the government did not legalize the CPB, its policy towards the Communists since the inception of armed struggle in 1948 had been a combination of military pressure and attempts to solve the problem by political means."[91]

U Nu refused to directly negotiate with CPB, but the Peace Committee was "allowed . . . to speak publicly on the CPB's behalf" alongside mass peace demonstrations.[92] Nakanishi notes that "in 1958 he [U Nu] proclaimed an amnesty for insurgent groups including the Red Flag and White Flag Communist Parties, which was followed by legalization of the People's Volunteer Organisation Party."[93] This followed successful CPB surrenders in 1957.[94] The military continued to exert pressure, but there was political space for negotiations and defections.

A similar strategy was pursued against the KNU and other ethnic separatist rebels. Intense warfare in the late 1940s pushed the KNU back from its high-water mark, and by 1956 "the insurgencies had been contained."[95] Amnesties in 1950 and 1956 were quite effective.[96] The KNU was forced to regroup on the periphery, as did the New Mon State Party (NMSP). U Nu allegedly promised Mon, Rakhine, and Pao leaders their own states as terms of a deal,[97] using his "consummate political skills."[98] The 1958 amnesty also had a major effect on the ethnic insurgents, with "a flood of insurgent surrenders around the country."[99] These were not at the level of organizations, however: this was not a period of full-scale incorporation and deal making. Instead, surrenders occurred at the individual and factional level.

U Nu's blend of continued hostilities with recurrent amnesties was reasonably effective at pushing back the threat of state collapse and increasingly isolating insurgents on the periphery, while not troubling progovernment private armies. As Smith notes, "with the key exception of the Karen insurgency, the 1958 mass surrenders should have marked the beginning of a new era of tranquility in the war-divided country."[100]

It is important, however, to remain clear about the nature of counterinsurgency and state policy under U Nu and subsequent leaders. U Nu still offered a vision of the polity centered on Bamar nationalism, combining Buddhism with the Burmese language as key elements of an imagined Myanmar, with the ethnic minorities holding a de facto lower status in a unitary state. Since the late 1940s, total war was a common phenomenon, with the Tatmadaw pursuing scorched-earth COIN both in heartland areas (against the CPB) and on the ethnic minority peripheries. This began under U Nu's government, which blended the heavy hand with amnesties and some deal making with armed groups. During the 1948–62 phase, the key challenges were launched by the KNU and the Communist Party of Burma, as well as a plethora of smaller groups. In the late 1950s and early 1960s, groups in Kachin and Shan states turned to revolt in the face of U Nu's centralizing tendencies and military repression. U Nu's emphasis on Buddhism, especially the declaration of Buddhism as a state religion in 1961, for instance, was the trigger for the Kachin revolt, which continues to this day.

Extraordinarily hard-fought campaigns were waged, as both the CPB and KNU were serious insurgencies. Once the state consolidated around the hard, insular shell of the Tatmadaw, these forces were driven back. Against this broadly repressive background, however, there were two distinctive aspects of the U Nu period compared to what would come next under Ne Win's military dictatorship. First, U Nu's government was largely willing to work with "pocket armies" linked to the AFPFL until the mid-1950s: as in India or 1990s Karachi, militarized electoral groups were acceptable as long as they stayed within the loose bounds of mainstream politics.[101] Ne Win would discard with these groups, but they were very important in the 1950s. Second, U Nu pursued a broader range of armed orders with armed groups, often using third-parties as interlocutors, providing amnesties, and engaging in a high-variance array of strategies to try to stabilize Burma. This strategy had some success in limiting the reach of the CPB and pushing the Karen back from their high-water mark of 1949. Yet, ultimately, U Nu's moves toward centralization and pushing for Buddhism as state religion, reflecting the broader AFPFL project, undercut his creative stabilization initiatives by triggering new Shan and Kachin revolts that helped provide the justification for his overthrow by the military in 1962.

The Rise of the Army and the Origins of the 1962 Coup

U Nu's regime was threatened by two political developments in the Burman heartland, rather than by rebels. First, the AFPFL developed deep internal cleavages, eventually splitting into rival factions. In 1958, the "Clean" and "Stable" factions of the AFPFL emerged, and part of U Nu's response was to make common cause with leftist politicians who were seen as stalking horses for the communists by the Burma Army.[102] This would open the space for a military intervention from 1958–60, which would be solidified into a full-scale military regime under General Ne Win starting in 1962.

Second, the army had become a consolidated and reasonably autonomous force with its own ideas about politics over the course of the 1950s. It was deeply concerned about both accommodation with the Left and ethnic minorities, against both of which it had waged bitter warfare. An analogy to 1950s Pakistan is interesting: in both cases, armies that faced serious threats, had access to resources, and operated in an environment of weak civilian institutionalization and cohesion began seeking a greater political role while fearful (often far in exaggeration of "objective" political facts) of fissiparous ethnic mobilization and leftist challenges from below. The military would take advantage of the crisis within the AFPFL to stake its own claim to rule.

During the 1950s, "the army was becoming a state within the state, but few Burmese paid much attention to it."[103] Interestingly, this was occurring precisely as the objective military threat to the state was *declining*. A series of 1956 offensives meant that in much of the country "rebels were also surrendering or accepting government offers of equal rights and new land,"[104] while "the Communist and Karen insurgencies were more or less over by the mid-1950s,"[105] and the army's own documents note that insurgent threat had receded.[106] However, the way that U Nu had defanged many of these insurgencies was deeply alarming to the military: it saw the amnesties, and the peace commission set up to woo the CPB, as inimical to the unity and security of Burma: "Gen. Ne Win and the Tatmadaw hardliners undoubtedly viewed the growing collusion between insurgent organisations and their above-ground supporters with mounting concern. Indeed with the flood of rebel surrenders that year, it became increasingly difficult to distinguish between members of the insurgent and parliamentary opposition parties."[107]

This threat perception had deeper historical origins. Some of the young Burman activists and soldiers who mobilized against the British and, for a period, with the Japanese during the 1930s and 1940s became leaders in the new Burma Army. After the Karen mutinies of the late 1940s, they rapidly rose in the ranks to end up running the military. Ne Win, for instance, had been a member of Dobama Asiayone and then part of the Burma Independence Army (BIA), before being incorporated into the new postcolonial army. Ne Win and his cohorts saw the ethnic minorities, especially those who had worked with the British like the Kachin and Karen, as fifth columnists and suspect. While the army had leftist sympathies (and Ne Win had been open to parleying with the communists in the late 1940s), its years of intense fighting with the CPB had solidified its identification of these groups as ideologically opposed. The experience of counterinsurgency more broadly created a set of organizational perceptions: "None of the threats faced in the 1950s could be blamed on easily identifiable, geographically containable populations, which led battalion commanders and military planners almost inevitably into broader programs aimed at reordering, reeducating, and redefining the population throughout the country."[108]

Thus, fear that U Nu would integrate former rebels "infuriated military leaders, who had risked their lives on battlefields fighting these very rebel forces";[109] indeed, "Army die-hards saw these moves as opening the door to the communists."[110] In 1958, a military publication offered its "first extended articulation of the army leadership's profound distrust of the population, democracy, and especially the 'misconstrued' constitutional provisions guaranteeing freedoms of speech and association."[111] This was the "tatmadaw's reading of the first decade of postcolonial rule," and it was a grim verdict shot through with looming praetorianism.[112] The split within the AFPFL and resulting political crisis opened the door to the army: "The split in the ruling party was undeniable, but the insurgents hardly posed a threat any longer, and few were able to discern any serious decline in the overall law and order situation in the country."[113]

A soft coup occurred, with Ne Win becoming caretaker prime minister from 1958 to 1960. He argued in Parliament that this was necessary because "the rebels were increasing their activities, and the political pillar was collapsing. It was imperative that the Union should not drown in shallow waters as it nearly did in 1948–49. So it fell on the armed forces to perform their bounden duty to take all security measures to forestall and prevent a recurrence."[114] A number of the military officers who now ran the government had been involved in the military since the 1940s BIA, showing continuity in the nature of the Burma Army leadership over time.

The military committed to showing it could govern Burma. In addition to managing much of the civil bureaucracy, it launched a series of offensives against its insurgent foes and worked on incorporating the various private armies that continued to operate in Burma.[115] The army did reach out to the KNU just before handing power back to civilians over in early 1960, but there was no offer of a separate state or other major concessions, so the Karen rejected the offer.[116] During this period, Shan rebellion flared up in November 1959.[117]

When U Nu returned to power in 1960, he continued to try to mix accommodation and repression. His pledge to make Buddhism the state religion had earned him support from many in the Buddhist political heartland, but was deeply alienating to non-Buddhists.[118] As Jones notes, "After 1960, amidst continued civilian power struggles, U Nu courted Bamar support by establishing Buddhism as the state religion, sparking protest from non-Buddhist minorities. Shan, Mon, and Rakhine leaders demanded greater regional autonomy, while other minority leaders openly discussed secession."[119] The Kachin Independence Army (KIA) launched its insurgency in February 1961, as insurgency in the Shan State also escalated.[120] These ethnic groups were Panglong signatories whose members had become deeply frustrated with "progressively more centralized and Burmanised form of government in Rangoon."[121] We see here how ideological projects can also help to *generate* revolts as well as shaping state responses, making them foundationally important for understanding a country's politics.

U Nu responded by returning to the other part of his strategy—talks and accommodation. As he began this process, Ne Win and the high command, having returned to the barracks in 1960, "watched with unease as ethnic leaders around the country, both above and underground, began to call for a new political dialogue. Many Tatmadaw hardliners felt the very basis of the Panglong Agreement was now being called into question" in favor of a new federal structure.[122] U Nu moved toward possible federalism, embarking on a Nationalities' Seminar in February 1962 to discuss new ways of structuring the state.[123] For Lintner, "a political solution to the ethnic crisis seemed to be in sight."[124]

Yet "any such solution was anathema to Ne Win and the Tatmadaw leaders who, in over a decade of constant fighting under their slogan 'One Blood, One Voice, One Command,' had come to see themselves as the lone protectors of the Union's national integrity and the Federal Movement as merely another guise for the insurgents' demands."[125] Just before U Nu was supposed to give a speech on the matter, the military launched a direct coup. Ne Win justified it by saying that "federalism is impossible; it will destroy the Union," while Aung Gyi said that "we had economic, religious and political crises with the issue of federalism as the most important for the coup."[126] The army feared that U Nu would give ground to ethnic groups (despite the more likely outcome that accommodation would actually *demobilize* insurgency), leading to secession and disintegration—and so it took power.

Enemies on All Fronts: Ne Win in Power, 1962–88

Just as Ayub Khan had focused on a subset of the existing strands in the idea of Pakistan, Ne Win emphasized the centralizing and Burmanizing aspects of U Nu's rule, while downplaying his willingness to at least loosely accommodate some ethnic and leftist political forces. Rather than the blend of repression and accommodation under U Nu, we see in table 6.1 a clear shift toward far more consistent and unrelenting counterinsurgency by Ne Win's regime: the varying armed orders of 1948–61 shrink into some form of conflict almost across the board from 1962 to 1988. As Smith writes, "At a stroke Burmese's political land-scape was transformed and, in many ways, simplified."[127]

Ne Win did offer peace talks in 1963, but they quickly failed when it became clear that the military viewed them as a route to surrenders by the armed groups. The regime quickly incorporated the private armies that remained from the AFPFL era, creating a robust monopoly of state violence in regime-controlled regions of the country. From this point on, almost any nonstate armed mobilization—as well as unarmed mobilization—in pursuit of decentralization, federalism, or autonomy was seen as ideologically opposed by the state's coercive core. The gray zone that U Nu had often worked within disappeared into a stark vision of support or opposition. And this was a cohesive ideological project at the top of the regime: "Burma's new rulers were a group of close friends" with deep historical ties.[128]

This makes sense in terms of the theory I laid out in chapter 1: the military's organizational roots in the 1930s nationalist movement and 1940s BIA had instilled a deep distrust of the ethnic minorities and decentralization of power away from the Burman majority, fears of internal disunity opening space for for-eign influence, and a comfort in taking political action without formal demo-cratic processes. As South writes, "The Tatmadaw moved to capture this state, in order to defend a particular idea of the nation, the origins of which lie in the colonial era and the Second World War."[129] The new Revolutionary Council was totally dominated by the military.[130] The onslaught against insurgent forces was hugely costly, in both blood and money: "Burma's endless counter-insurgency war imposed a massive burden on the Tatmadaw."[131] This was not a natural, obvious outcome: the Tatmadaw *chose* war over accommodation with ethnic minorities.

Indeed, Ne Win explicitly articulated the central role of racial thinking to his nationalism: "By equating non-Burman ethnicity with disloyalty, it views those ethnic identities as something that non-Burmans must overcome in order to become part of the nation. Presumably they can accomplish this by adopting "Myanmar" (Burman) culture. However, even if a non-Burman manages to suc-cessfully deny and leave behind his or her culture, statements like this from Ne Win made it clear that their membership in the national group was still suspect and conditional."[132]

The 1960s through 1970s were dominated by counterinsurgency and the increasing prominence of the so-called four cuts military strategy, which aimed to brutally slice connections between insurgents and the population. There was some variation between total war and containment that seems to largely have mapped onto military expediency and tactical tides. As shown in figure 6.1 and table 6.2a, this was a period of repression and violence as Ne Win's military sought to wipe out armed challengers to its rule. Other than an ephemeral peace parley in the early 1980s, meaningful political accommodation was not on the agenda. Ne Win combined this domestic repression with a wide-ranging xenophobia and emphasis on autarky that left Burma strikingly isolated.[133] China supported the CPB, and Thailand backed a number of ethnic rebel groups along its border with Burma, but the regime's long wars with these armed groups predated the high point of external support they received.

There was one exception to this pattern of general crackdown and combat: the military did engage in limited cooperation with the Ka Kwe Ye militias in Shan State during the late 1960s/early 1970s.[134] It saw them as useful tactical assets in fighting the CPB and Shan insurgents in the extremely inaccessible terrain of Shan State, while the militias in question were only loosely political and thus not threatening. They fell squarely into the business partners political role. But this limited cooperation came to an end once it became clear that the militias were not particularly reliable or useful: the militia program was shut down around 1973 after it became apparent that they did not add much value, and actually were causing some problems: "The growing strength of the militias, and the possibility that the Tatmadaw could not control them, was a concern to its leaders."[135] Other than this period, the 1962–88 wars saw bloody efforts at violence monopolization by a highly militarized, unitary state, with "militias" being created and controlled by security forces, rather than existing as autonomous organizations interacting and cooperating with the state.[136]

1989 and the (Partial) Remaking of the Myanmar Periphery

This basic security posture continued until the late 1980s. Yet, as we saw in the data in table 6.1, 1989 marks a major shift in armed politics in Myanmar: cease-fires originated with the splinters of the CPB and then spread to several other major groups. After 2009, even more cease-fires occurred—though others collapsed—during a peace process push. The Tatmadaw has found a set of business partners in groups like the UWSA, KNU, and, from 1994–2011, KIA. What explains the move toward much more extensive limited cooperation? We lack much evidence from within the regime over these last thirty years, so these are highly caveated claims. But it appears that a confluence of factors drove both ideological and tactical shifts, leading a number of groups to be recategorized as business partners. However, as of 2020 we have not seen any major movement on incorporation, and substantial conflicts have continued in several parts of the country. There has not been a transformational change in the core political cleavages nor any evidence of a fundamental rethinking within the military. A combination of recalculated tactical incentives with enduring ideological goals and political disagreements help to explain the largely "frozen" nature of armed politics in the country over the last thirty years.

On the government's side, in 1988–90 a series of crises rocked the regime. Ne Win was shunted aside by a new military junta in the face of surging prodemocracy demonstrations led by the National League for Democracy (NLD) of Aung San Suu Kyi.[137] The junta sought to stabilize the Burman heartland, redeploying forces to Rangoon and cracking down on protesters. It now faced tactical reasons to try to limit its liability on the periphery amid international condemnation and economic crisis. These created powerful incentives to limit fighting in the ethnic minority areas that were the focus of long-standing counterinsurgency operations.

The military benefited enormously from the 1989 collapse of the Communist Party of Burma (CPB) into a series of ethnic factions. The CPB had been run by a core of ethnic Bamar communists, but its foot soldiers and many of its commanders were from the ethnic minority communities. Sick of an endless war, and seeing little chance of revolutionary victory—especially as Chinese support had waned—these groups launched a mutiny against the aging leadership.[138] The successors were ethnically defined and abandoned any radical political claims: communism disappeared as an ideology and the CPB's armed group successors were close to apolitical. Their primary political demands focused on ethnic autonomy in some way, whether formalized or de facto. At first, the military regime did not know how to respond and continued to claim that the CPB was involved in the prodemocracy protests.[139] However, it was also reaching out to the remnants as it explored the possibilities for a deal.

This combination created the crucial initial opening for cease-fire politics. The army's Military Intelligence reached out to the CPB successors and crafted a loosely institutionalized deal. This took pressure off both sides—there was strong new tactical overlap that was greatly facilitated by the unambitious war aims of the CPB's remnants. Vague ethnic autonomy was much preferable to revolutionary communism, even if it was, at best, still a gray zone demand in the military's eyes (which continued, and continues, to prefer a highly centralized political system). As Lintner summarizes, "It was hardly surprising that the deals made with the ex-CPB mutineers were business-oriented and did not include any provisions for regional autonomy or peace talks."[140]

It is worth quoting Thant Myint-U's reconstruction of the logic of this shift:

> The Communist insurgency was no more, but in its place were four for-
> midable replacement armies, all uncertain of what to do next. This took
> place over the same months in which the junta in Rangoon, after crush-
> ing pro-democracy demonstrations, was trying desperately to survive.
> This government's coffers were empty. . . . the key to the junta's survival
> would be a historic understanding reached with the ex-Communist
> armies.[141]

This transformation is a partial fit for my theory. The tactical imperatives were
clearly new and help explain the shift, and there was a clear reduction in ideological (as well as military) threat resulting from the CPB's collapse. It is extremely
hard to tell what the new junta's underlying project was and whether it differed
in meaningful ways from Ne Win's vision of the nation; detailed internal data are
simply not available. The junta certainly was interested in escaping the political
bind it found itself in, but that is not the same as a major ideological rethinking of
nationalism—it is not clear how the demand for informal ethnic autonomy was
truly seen by the regime leaders.

Ideologically, a number of armed groups abandoned or moderated their
war aims, opening political space for at least cease-fires—for instance, the CPB
mutineers had smashed portraits of Marx, Engels, Lenin, and Mao and burned
communist literature, signaling an abandonment of the old approach.[142] The
cease-fires often let a group continue to operate in its home turf, creating tactical overlap with the regime: "The ex-Communist forces could do business as
they pleased."[143] The collapse of the CPB saw a major decrease in the ideological
ambition of its heavily armed successors in the country's north—the United Wa
State Party/United Wa State Army (UWSP/UWSA), for instance, was "driven by
poverty and war-weariness" into the cease-fire and its nominal goal became to
"achieve the formation of a Wa state directly under control of the central government in Rangoon and not administered through Shan State" while accepting that
"the UWSP will not seek independence."[144] This was a far cry from the explicitly
revolutionary ambitions of the CPB.

The collapse of the CPB and adoption of cease-fires by its successors placed
new military pressures on other armed groups like the KIA and KNU that had
been fighting for decades, and "several war-weary groups subsequently signed
ceasefires with SLORC (State Law and Order Restoration Council, i.e., the
military regime) from 1989–1991. The army was then concentrated against
the hold-outs, generating further ceasefires. By 1996, 14 ceasefires had been
agreed, covering most major resistance organizations."[145] Thailand also began
a realignment with the military following the end of the Cold War, putting

pressure on groups like the NMSP to cut a deal with the regime. While intense conflict continued, such as with the KNU, others, including the KIA and New Mon State Party, decided to join the CPB successors in trying their hand at cease-fire politics. Eventually, between 1989 and 2009, dozens of groups signed cease-fire agreements with the military.[146] The Tatmadaw's strategy—as costly as it was—had grimly succeeded in pushing back the armed groups into a long, slow retreat. With Ne Win's departure from the scene, the new geopolitical environment, and the pressures of war on these groups, a juncture emerged in which new possibilities could be explored. Limited cooperation became the dominant order across much of the periphery: "While these cease-fires did not lead to substantial political dialogue, they allowed rebels to retain their arms and govern pockets of territory."[147]

These cease-fires reworked political order on the periphery.[148] The basic state approach endured: on the one hand, offering cease-fires, on the other, continuing to oppose federalism and using lethal force against groups unwilling to sign a deal. As a result, "one can see the existence of fluid political and social orders in the country's borderlands."[149] Even the KNU, battered by shifts in the balance of military power, the change in Thailand's orientation toward Myanmar, and internal disputes over the advisability of continuing to fight, eventually signed a cease-fire in 2012.[150] Intertwined with these political-military shifts were economics: "Ethnic-minority rebels largely signed cease-fires out of war weariness, poverty, and a desire for development. Accordingly, their subsequent incorporation into a national system of rule was primarily pursued through economic means: development spending; joint business ventures; and the re-routing of economic flows to benefit the regime."[151] Kevin Woods refers to this system of limited cooperation as "ceasefire capitalism," describing how "different territories, and the authority figures that exert control over them, overlap to create conditions where national military and state officials share power with non-state authority figures, such as ceasefire political organizations, insurgent groups and paramilitaries. These different (non-) military-state authority figures all partake to some degree in governance activities in ceasefire zones, resulting in a complex mosaic of political territory not neatly separated out."[152]

This approach would be integral to the general movement toward controlled regime transition over the next two decades: "The balance of power between regime and opposition forces shifted fundamentally in the former's favour, enabling it to diminish (though not destroy) the threats that had prompted its intervention and withdraw on its own terms. This outcome stemmed from the transformation of Myanmar's geopolitical and economic context, which supported the regime's strategies to centralize power and reduce centrifugal challenges, giving it the confidence to resume Myanmar's forced march to 'disciplined democracy.'"[153] Regime politics in the center were intertwined with the tenuous, partial pacification of the periphery.

Though elements of the theory are importantly supported by the shift of 1989, there was nevertheless not a major apparent ideological rethinking in the regime. The argument is in better shape when exploring how tactical overlap emerged between the state and armed groups, and why armed groups shifted their ideological positioning. The key mechanisms of armed group-side change identified in chapter 2 can be found in the Myanmar cases—internal fragmentation, international pressures, and war weariness all contributed to the KIO and KNU coming to the table, for instance. When it comes to ideology, despite not fully explaining the shift in 1989, a focus on nationalism and ideological project continues to explain why there has been no *resolution* to these conflicts with ethnic minority groups. The cease-fire wave was supposed to lead eventually to a general political settlement. But in the late 2000s and early 2010s, strains began to show.[154] Over the next decade, the KIA cease-fire collapsed when younger cadres pushed back against an elite they viewed as complacent, the army has become locked in open warfare with a new alliance of insurgents, and the UWSA continues to flex its power to keep the Tatmadaw off the China border.[155]

Even those cease-fires that remain in place have, for the most part, not turned into peace deals and incorporation. This is different than India's Northeast, where at least some meaningful deals have occurred. Where incorporation has occurred, it has involved smaller groups agreeing to surrender and act as arms of the security apparatus (often as Border Guard Forces), without political concessions of any meaningful sort.[156] These groups, whether incorporated or acting as depoliticized armed allies, have served clear tactical purposes for the military: "The BGFs [Border Guard Forces] and the newly formed militias served as proxy forces for the Tatmadaw to exercise influence in areas not under their direct control, and enhanced their ability to apply indirect pressure on EAOs [ethnic armed organizations]."[157]

Alliances have also occurred at times when the Tatmadaw and an armed group fought against another armed group. This has happened, for instance, with the Democratic Karen Buddhist Army (DKBA) against the KNU after its split from the KNU in 1994:[158] after the DKBA broke away, "the insider intelligence and additional troops that DKBA provided were instrumental in the counterinsurgency's success at overrunning the Manerplaw headquarters of the KNU in 1995."[159] Similarly, Bai Quoxian's splinter faction of the Myanmar National Democratic Alliance Army fought against the MNDAA in Kokang in 2009, before becoming incorporated as a Border Guard Force.[160] These groups have mostly abandoned ambitious politics, sliding into a role as local pawn of the regime, though political changes even in these dyads can weaken the relationship—the DKBA, for instance, distanced itself from the regime in the early 2010s.[161]

What is driving this pattern? Despite initial signs of flexibility, the military has continued to push for a unitary, nonfederal state, been willing to break cease-fires when armed groups were insufficiently politically compliant, and has committed very high levels of violence in ongoing conflicts.[162] The military, and many Bamar civilian politicians (including those, like Aung San Suu Kyi, who were part of the democratic opposition), continued to pursue a particular idea of what the nation should be and how it should be managed and controlled by the state, contributing to the failure to move beyond limited cooperation.[163] As Myint-U argues, "The peace process did nothing to address questions of identity, and how Burma should see itself as a multiracial and multicultural country."[164] On the other side, the extraordinary complexity and fragmentation of the armed group landscape contributed to the failure of the peace process as well.

My argument unfortunately helps us understand the brutal ethnic cleansing of the Rohingya in upper Rakhine state in 2017. The Rohingya occupy a particular place in the nationalist imaginary of the military and many civilians—they are seen by many as outsiders, not legitimately part of any conception of nation of Myanmar.[165] This is one reason that they are consistently referred to as "Bengali," framing them as from Bengal rather than "authentically" from Rakhine state. This links them to the Indian influx under British colonialism that was so intensely resented by Bamar nationalists of the 1920s through the 1940s, and which contributed to the Ne Win regime's targeting of the remaining Indian community after taking power in 1962. Rohingya militancy waxed and waned over time, and there were recurrent rounds of state repression against Rohingya populations.[166] During the 1990s, the junta began promoting the ideas of a fixed "135 National Races" that authentically belonged to the broader Myanmar nation—these *taingyintha* "were at the very center of the state narrative."[167] This conceptualization excluded the Rohingya, seen "as immigrants and not natives deserving special protection and special rights."[168]

Rohingya militancy emerged again in a new form after clashes between Buddhist ethnic Rakhine and Rohingya in the early 2010s, which was driven by part by Myanmar's nascent democratization.[169] The Arakan Rohingya Salvation Army (ARSA) began launching small-scale attacks, and its strike against security forces in August 2017 was the trigger for a massive state crackdown and ethnic cleansing. The rise of ISIS and fears of Muslim/Islamist infiltration into Myanmar combined with a long-standing Bamar nationalist disdain for the Rohingya to both heighten threat perceptions and to justify extraordinary measures against an objectively small military threat: "Public opinion in Burma saw ARSA not as a ragtag outfit trying to defend the rights of an oppressed minority but as militants who were the local leading edge of a global Islamic threat."[170] The state response involved direct targeting of civilians, spurring a mass exodus of hundreds of thousands into Bangladesh. This action, rather than simply representing a narrow cabal of military elite, was supported among many in the public. Aung San Suu Kyi also defended these measures, consistent with her track record as being a Bamar nationalist.[171]

This is a grim example of why it is worth taking political ideas seriously in the study of conflict: the military power of ARSA was quite marginal, especially compared to groups like the UWSA, but it was seen as a subversive, alien threat that required an extremely bloody, exclusionary response. It is unclear how a theory built around material or military power would predict the ferocity and breadth of the Tatmadaw's response to the ARSA attack. Historically contingent politics and threat perceptions are instead essential to understand why the tragedy of 2017 arose in the form it did.

My argument helps us understand why there have been decades of conflict in Myanmar. Rather than an accommodationist nationalism that could make serious concessions to ethnic minorities, the project that took power in 1948 represented a sons of the soil majoritarianism from below that saw these forces as fissiparous and seditious. Along with a powerful communist movement that was seen as an irreconcilable revolutionary force, these ethnic insurgent forces were met with a heavily repressive security response, especially under Ne Win from 1962 to 1988. The Rohingya were increasingly excluded from this nationalism, helping to explain the bloody course of state policy toward them over decades, culminating most dramatically in 2017.

Understanding why this was the path taken requires taking seriously the colonial period of movement construction: the regime that emerged, first under U Nu and then Ne Win, carried with it a set of goals and fears that differed from a number of alternative nationalist projects that we saw elsewhere in the region, as well as alternatives being advanced by others in Burma. Bamar nationalism resembled Sinhala Buddhist nationalism, with its overriding focus on overcoming colonial humiliation and restoring the majority population to its rightful place. As in Sri Lanka, however, this project tipped from a restorative goal of equitable distribution of power into a dark discourse of ownership and dominance that then spurred peripheral revolt and decades of violence.

In the last three decades, Myanmar has seen very important shifts in its armed politics. But there has not been a fundamental ideological rethinking of Myanmar nationalism, especially by its powerful military, which continues to control security policy. Even the civilian governments of Thein Sein and Aung San

Suu Kyi have embraced key aspects of this majoritarian project. The post-1989 shift was more tactical than fundamental, reciprocated by hard-pressed armed groups facing the challenge of multidecade insurgency and the collapse of the communist ideological challenge to the center. This helps us understand why the breakthrough into cease-fire politics has not been followed by a movement into widespread incorporation. The potential for ongoing conflict will remain in the future unless a serious rethinking of the terms of the nation occurs.

SRI LANKA

Sri Lanka has been the site of two forms of insurgency: a pair of ultra-Left revolts by the Janatha Vimukthi Peramuna (JVP) in 1971 and 1987–90 and a far more protracted Tamil separatist insurgency from the mid-1970s until 2009 that emerged out of a history of anti-Tamil pogroms. From its status at independence as one of the most stable former British colonies in Asia, Sri Lanka (known as Ceylon until 1972) experienced an extraordinary amount of violence and conflict. From the early 1970s onward, we see clear and measurable armed politics. Even prior to the 1970s, however, we see more amorphous networks of party-linked thugs who led riots.

Unlike Burma, there was a lag after independence before the onset of intense and protracted armed politics, nor was there was a descent into military authoritarianism. But like Burma, and in contrast to both India and Pakistan, the dominant project that quickly emerged was a sons of the soil majoritarianism: rural Sinhalese masses and their more elite leadership sought rightful representation in the new political arena that could overcome underrepresentation under British colonial rule. Though there were reasonable demands for redistribution in this movement, crucial to Sinhalese nationalist ascendance was a hard-line majoritarianism that heightened perceived threats from ethnic minorities and limited space for meaningful political accommodation. This helped to breed elite backing for Sinhalese anti-Tamil rioters, increasingly exclusionary state policies, and, eventually, the radical Tamil insurgency of the Liberation Tigers of Tamil Eelam (LTTE).

Sri Lanka is a far smaller country than the others studied in this book and lacks their often-extraordinary diversity of armed politics. Yet the conflicts it has experienced show the value of taking history seriously rather than assuming similarities across governments' threat perceptions. We see in this case a potential alternative path that may have avoided many of the pressures that the Sinhalese nationalist turn induced: though poorly articulated and ultimately swept away, a "Ceylonese" nationalism was advanced in the late 1940s and early 1950s that might have, with more skilled political leadership, built a different dominant nationalist frame than the ultimately victorious Sinhalese Buddhist majoritarianism.[1] History offered multiple possible directions; the one that emerged out of political competition drove the ethnic conflict that emerged.

In part because of this ideological project's capture of the state, we see a highly bifurcated pattern of armed orders in Sri Lanka. On one extreme, there was intense conflict (including a comparatively high level of total war) against unambiguously insurgent groups during the LTTE and the JVP uprisings. On the other, there were a long-standing set of alliances with "flipped," essentially depoliticized Tamil paramilitaries reliant on the state for survival. There were some stretches of limited cooperation and even a short period of "strange bedfellows" alliance between the government and LTTE, but these were tenuous and short lived. The business partners and undesirables of post-1989 Burma, India's Northeast, or Pakistan's Northwest are largely missing here; there was not much of an "in-between" armed politics. Tamil mobilization, even in its more moderate forms and periods, was strongly opposed by the bulk of the dominant Sinhalese political sphere. We see repression even prior to armed politics, and then overwhelmingly conflictual armed orders once conflict arose. The JVP revolts are extremely straightforward: my argument has little of interest to say beyond the obvious. Both were open revolutionary attacks that posed a severe and pressing military threat to government survival. They were treated accordingly, with intense repression and mutual total war. The JVP orders provide little support for or against my theory, since they are consistent with multiple existing arguments.

In this chapter, I first provide an overview of nationalist politics during the colonial period, primarily the emerging, but fragmented, contest between "Ceylonese" and Sinhalese Buddhist nationalism. I then identify the major shift that occurred after independence and the rise of the Sinhalese nationalist movement as the dominant project driving governments, both as a result of their own initiative and the pressures they faced from the electorate from 1948 until 1972. From the early 1970s onward, electoral competition between Sinhalese parties, while intense and hard-fought, was nevertheless centered around a broad consensus on the Sinhalese language and Buddhist religion as central to "authentic" nationalism. The left-right dimension was not very relevant to armed politics. Having established how the political system moved into this structure, I then explore the armed orders that emerged during the Tamil revolt from the mid-1970s until 2009, mapping out the escalation of the conflict into total warfare. The chapter concludes with implications for understanding Sri Lanka's present and future politics.

Colonial Ceylon and Nationalism from Below

Ceylon had a very different pattern of colonial politics than in what became India, Pakistan, or Burma/Myanmar. There was no mass agitation, large-scale violence, or intensive party building. The Ceylon National Congress (CNC) was the primary vessel of mainstream politics. It combined hard-nosed elite rivalries with loose organization and did not develop a particularly clear ideological project as a result. The relatively collaborative relationship with the British and lack of mass mobilization reduced the CNC's incentives for formulating and institutionalizing a nationalist vision. Instead, it offered a hazy "Ceylonese" nationalism that avoided specificities, veered into Sinhalese majoritarianism among many of its leaders as electoral incentives shifted in the 1930s, and was unmoored from actual political mobilization, which remained highly localized and factional in the colonial period.

The CNC was therefore not a carrier movement with the drive and vision of the Muslim League, INC, or the AFPFL. It became the new ruling party of independent Ceylon, under the name of the United National Party (UNP), in 1948, and thus it is a key focus of this chapter. Yet, more quickly and fundamentally than in the other cases, the CNC's rival carrier movements moved to the center stage of the postcolonial political arena. Its fragmented, elitist organizational structure allowed distinct factions to primarily occupy themselves with internecine feuding. It therefore simultaneously voiced an amorphous Ceylonese nationalism, allowed Sinhalese chauvinists within its ranks, and avoided taking hard positions on the structure of the island's future polity.

The most important alternative was the Sinhalese Buddhist nationalist movement that developed from the 1880s, arguing for a restoration of status and power to the Sinhalese majority. This movement had a variety of organizational manifestations and never coalesced into a single institution, but it laid the ideological foundation for a new form of majoritarian nationalism that became politically prominent from the 1950s onward. Crucially, this movement successfully established a language of politics that centered around Sinhalese Buddhist ownership of the land and a clear linkage between this identity cleavage and islandwide nationalism more broadly. On the other side of the ethnic ledger, Tamil political organizations also developed; though they did not adopt a separatist position until decades after independence, they represented an alternative path of greater decentralization and multilingualism.

Elite Politics, Sinhalese Assertion, and British Colonial Rule through 1916

British colonial rule in Ceylon was consolidated in 1815 after the Second Kandyan War. British policy in the colony focused on protecting the interests of planters and European economic elites, but it also began to cultivate elite leaders, especially an emerging stratum of English-speakers of diverse ethnicities. Within the bureaucracy, Tamils became increasingly represented because of the more expansive presence of English education in Tamil areas.[2] As a result of this fairly cozy arrangement, in late nineteenth and early twentieth century "formal politics in Sri Lanka were remarkably passive, even stagnant or immobile."[3]

This stasis at the level of formal politics did not mean that ideological innovation was not occurring, however. The rise of efforts at Christian proselytizing led to a Buddhist response that constructed a new understanding of Sinhalese nationalism: this ideology of the polity would never capture the commanding heights of colonial politics, but it created a new and powerful language of politics that rose to prominence once mass enfranchisement changed the political arena.[4] In the 1890s and early twentieth century, Anagarika Dharmapala was the "foremost among those who made religion a mobilizing marker,"[5] as "he promoted a grandiose Buddhist history of Sri Lanka, inspired fear by suggesting colonial rule threatened Buddhism with extinction, and claimed that Christians, Hindus, and the British were all responsible for Buddhism's decadence."[6] Though, as I show below, this movement did not create an enduring, institutionalized carrier movement, it "played a major role in preparing the Sinhalese ideationally for the ethnocracy that lay in store."[7]

Where did this Sinhalese Buddhist project come from? While it drew on existing myths about the deep history of the Sinhalese on the island,[8] it also was inspired by the example of other Asian nationalisms, particularly the Japanese.[9] This made it a distinctly modern, not ancient, nationalist ideology, one that sought to reconfigure the past and link up with contemporary cases to forge a new project that could restore the Sinhalese Buddhist fusion to a place of primacy. Over time, its spread would thwart "all attempts by moderates in both communities to forge a common 'Ceylonese' or 'Sri Lankan' identity in the twentieth century."[10]

But in the short run, Dharmapala did not create a party like the Congress or League. Other movements would instead adopt particular aspects of this platform, such as for liquor temperance. For the most part, however, "No consistent attempt, much less a systematic one, was made to channel the enthusiasm and discontent it generated into a political force of real significance."[11] The rise of Sinhalese Buddhist assertion did not immediately lead to clashes over language or the future of the Tamil minority. In the 1910s, however, it seemed to be beginning to align with elite politics: "The two strands of agitation discussed earlier, the Buddhist and the 'constitutionalist', showed every sign of a fruitful convergence" that could mesh mass and elite politics.[12] Yet anti-Muslim riots in 1915 fractured this convergence: the British "came to regard them [the riots] as part of an organized conspiracy against the British by the Sinhalese" and aggressively cracked down on Sinhalese Buddhist activists.[13]

The 1915 riots were a crucial juncture for Ceylon's political development. Sustained elite-mass linkages did not develop around a single project, the British worked hard to prevent the rise of a unified independence movement, and the specter of communal violence began to haunt politics. As we see below, the Ceylon National Congress would take up the mantle of mainstream political aspiration, but it did not seek, or attain, even partial hegemony over the meaning of Ceylon nationalism. Instead, it was "the Sinhalese nationalism of the early twentieth century . . . which laid the foundation of the present nation-state."[14] Organizationally, this "tradition-oriented nationalist sentiment was primarily concerned with religious and cultural matters and grew separately from the political independence movement shepherded by the Ceylon National Congress . . . although originating in the same social and ideological discontents and sharing hostility toward colonial rule, the two streams of sentiment developed markedly different characteristics."[15]

The Looming Shadow of Majority and Minority: The CNC and the Donoughmore Constitution

Ceylon's mainstream politics were highly constitutional and nonconfrontational after the British crackdown following 1915's riots: "Compared to the *storm und drang* of the Indian movement, the Ceylon independence movement in the 1920s and 1930s appeared to be staid and dull, even phlegmatic at times."[16] Yet as Ceylon embraced mass suffrage and political mobilization began to quicken, new ideas and cleavages were formed that are essential for understanding postindependence politics: "Those years of democratic transition saw the making of minorities and the consolidation of a majority identity."[17]

The Ceylon National Congress emerged as the primary vehicle of Ceylonese politics. It was dominated by Sinhalese, but of a largely elite, English-speaking social background. The party never developed either robust institutions or a dominant leader. This fragmented organizational structure allowed for distinct nationalist projects to be nestled within it, from the hazy "Ceylonese nationalism" of D. S. Senanayake to the emerging Sinhalese Buddhist chauvinism of S. W. R. D. Bandaranaike. A basic structure of the future nation was not articulated or institutionalized in the pivotal period between 1919 and the coming of World War II.

The CNC, formed in 1919, faced three challenges. First, it would become seen as a Sinhalese party despite "early visions of an 'integrated' Ceylonese identity."[18] It initially had both Tamil and Sinhalese members (and it also included both Buddhist and Christian Sinhalese), but in the early 1920s British governor-general Manning pursued a strategy of ethnic division: his policy "was directed at creating enduring divisions with the elite while organizing the estrangement of minorities from the Ceylon National Congress, the only elitist political association that attempted to draw its membership from all communities."[19]

The "frailty of the proclaimed unity of Sinhalese and Tamils was quickly demonstrated, however" in a 1921 rupture over whether to have a reserved Tamil seat in the Legislative Council from Western Province.[20] Moreover, the CNC was faced by intra-Sinhalese caste competition that led to "intense efforts to consolidate intra-ethnic unity among the Sinhalese"; these were not wholly successful but nevertheless raised alarms among non-Sinhalese minorities.[21] As Ceylon moved toward greater popular participation, "these developments [the rise of Sinhalese Buddhist nationalism] had occurred on the whole separate from the movement among the English-educated elite for the liberalization of the political system. But from the 1920s on pressure began to mount to combine the two movements."[22] The Donoughmore Constitution of 1931 introduced universal mass suffrage that put Tamils at a severe political disadvantage, while also eliminating communal representation. Part of this constitutional setup was driven by the British, but also "the elitist politicians, in their demand for constitutional reform, considered the perpetuation of the principle of communal representation an affront to their liberal capacity."[23]

The CNC consequently "promoted the belief that the creation of a Ceylonese nation, as opposed to a Sinhalese one, was a political necessity and was therefore an advocate of 'responsive' cooperation with the minority communities."[24] But this change toward mass suffrage and away from formal communal representation heightened Tamil fears that were exacerbated by both the new Sinhalese majority and the formation of an all-Sinhalese board of ministers in the 1930s. Members of the CNC were not averse to using Sinhalese nationalist symbols and tropes.[25] In Tambiah's words, "Although the Dharmapala brand of Buddhist nationalist thrust seemed to become muted, or even pushed off the stage, the Ceylonese elitist politicians in fact conducted throughout a revealingly two-sided discourse, simultaneously 'communalist' and parochial and 'constitutionalist' and secular."[26]

The year 1936 was important for the unfolding of communal politics: "The 1936 elections consolidated the recapture of power by Sinhala Buddhist politicians" and "quite deliberately, no provision was made for communal representation, although the minorities were almost unanimous in urging that it be retained."[27] Consequently, "universal suffrage was among the main determining factors in the revival of 'religious' nationalism, that is to say nationalism intertwined with Buddhist resurgence and the cultural heritage associated with Buddhism."[28]

G. G. Ponnambalam was the key representative of Sri Lankan Tamils in this period, eventually founding the All-Ceylon Tamil Congress in 1944.[29] Ponnambalam advanced increasingly worried calls for some form of ethnic parity. Tamil representatives outlined an ideology of the polity that included substantial space for power-sharing and ethnic equality, though they too sometimes veered into an exclusionary racial chauvinism of Tamil superiority. The dominant Tamil response would not shift into separatism for decades to come, but it did chart out a path not taken during the colonial (and postcolonial) period.

Second, the CNC faced the challenge of the Sinhalese nationalists, even as it struggled to convince Tamils of its good intentions. Sinhalese CNC leaders played a crucial role in restraining Sinhalese chauvinism. Organizationally, "F. R. Senanayake and D. B. Jayatilaka between them kept a tight rein on religious enthusiasm. Their approach was in every way a contrast to Dharmapala's and they set the tone from about 1918 up to Jayatilaka's retirement from active politics in 1942."[30] DeVotta agrees: "Leading Sinhalese elites of the day, especially F. R. Senanayake and D. B. Jayatilaka, worked assiduously to counterbalance Buddhist nationalism and keep it out of the political arena, and this ensured that nationalists influenced by Dharmapala were marginalized for nearly a generation."[31] Even when facing the potential power of harnessing an unvarnished Sinhalese nationalism, during this period "the ideological orientations of the national political leadership, deeply steeped as they were in British traditions, had prevented the utilization of this mobilizational groundswell for explicit political purposes."[32]

The CNC mostly held the line against totally unambiguous Sinhalese chauvinism. But it did not prevent its own members from building up a Sinhalese nationalist movement, and its leaders' unwillingness to engage in mass mobilization left it only weakly able to penetrate and mobilize the Sinhalese rural masses who were most marginalized by the primacy of English as language of state. The main organizational manifestation of this ideological project was the Sinhala Maha Sabha (SMS), which was founded by S. W. R. D. Bandaranaike, among others, in 1934–35. Bandaranaike was a CNC member and from a privileged family background, but "by the early 1930s Bandaranaike had decided that nationalism based on the cultural revival among the Sinhalese-speaking Buddhists was the only solution to Ceylon's apparent acquiescence in the imperial connection."[33] Though a CNC member, he "devoted his time and energy to the development of links with the political periphery—the rural areas and the vernacular intelligentsia—through the SMS."[34]

There is some dispute about whether the SMS had stronger organizational roots than the CNC; to the extent it was popular, this was among Sinhalese speakers in rural areas who were frozen out of advancement by the dominance of English.[35] Regardless, it had long-lasting importance as the vanguard of a developed ethno-majoritarian ideological project that explicitly sought a Sinhalese Buddhist restoration and a nationalism that spoke primarily in terms of the Sinhala language and Buddhist religion: "The Sabha was never an organized political party, and its effect was more in conceptual formulation than in behavioral manifestation. Yet the political conceptualizations prepared by the Sabha may be considered the foundation upon which Bandaranaike, the political entrepreneur, and Sinhalese language nationalism, the political movement, raised their triumphant edifices in the 1950s."[36]

The SMS "spoke in the name of Sinhalese nationalism" and was an "exclusively and self-consciously Sinhalese political organization."[37] It was unabashed in its demand for turning Ceylonese nationalism into Sinhalese nationalism. This ideological drive was viewed with great discomfort by CNC elites, who tried to keep their distance: "Its potentially divisive effect in a plural society such as Sri Lanka deterred the moderate leadership in the Board of Ministers from giving it their support with any enthusiasm. For the members of the Sinhala Maha Sabha could not conceive of a Sri Lanka politically that was not essentially Sinhalese or Buddhist in character."[38] Bandaranaike, by contrast, mobilized a "broader array of less privileged, less prosperous groups" than other Sinhalese factional elites.[39] He "had long dabbled in Sinhalese chauvinism and by late 1936 or early 1937, he appears to have decided that it should be a central—and possibly *the* central—theme in his career."[40] Specifically, by end of 1937 "he had reluctantly concluded that *Ceylonese* nationalism 'is scarcely possible.'"[41]

The SMS and its even looser predecessors were held at bay by the CNC in the 1920s and 1930s. Yet, even though "the Sabha played a minor role in preindependence politics,"[42] it was the "progenitor" of the Sri Lanka Freedom Party (SLFP) in the 1950s, which brought this project to electoral dominance.[43] Bandaranaike's "success in penetrating and mobilizing rural Sri Lanka was demonstrated convincingly in the 1950s."[44] The roots of this postindependence politics can be found in the ideational innovations of the colonial era: "Once Sinhala 'nationalism' gained momentum, its very conceptualization, phenomenological basis, and practical realization were inseparable from the identity and historical pride provided by the Buddhist legacy, the cultural capital that Buddhist projects provided, and the languages in which Buddhist literature were couched and transmitted."[45]

Finally, the CNC faced endemic organizational factionalism. Its easy access to political power and collusion with the British limited its incentives to engage in the kind of hard-nosed ideological articulation and competition that were necessary elsewhere. Consequently, "with no proper political parties or definite programmes, the political oligarchy fought amongst themselves for power."[46] This lack of clear leadership or institutional structures made it possible for Bandaranaike to play his own game with the SMS, and undermined efforts to carve out an aspirationally hegemonic nationalist project that could be pushed down into local politics. Russell argues that "the problem that beset the Sinhalese moderates, in fact, was much the same as that which afflicted the minority coalition: that is, there was no unity or homogeneity of purpose among the leaders. . . . the struggle for undisputed leadership among the moderates in the Sinhalese political elite was almost as acute as the struggle which existed between the moderates and extremists."[47]

This elite fragmentation meant that the CNC was not an effective organizational weapon like the INC.[48] Moreover, elite-mass linkages were weak: "The Congress and the independence movement remained the almost exclusive preserve of the middle class throughout the colonial period. In marked contrast to the independence struggle led by the Indian National Congress, into which Gandhi injected characteristics of a mass popular movement early in the present century, the Ceylonese independence movement failed to establish roots or engender enthusiasm among the masses."[49] Bandaranaike took advantage of both weaknesses, even as he remained a CNC member: "The development of the Sinhala Maha Sabha inevitably led to an estrangement between Bandaranaike and the Sabha on the one hand and, on the other, most of his fellow ministers and the Ceylon National Congress to which they were at least tenuously attached."[50] The later challenges elites faced in managing mass politics had much to do with this historical legacy: "The isolation of the national level left most leading politicians less alert than they might have been to the possibility of new social forces emerging in a system which was open enough to invite this."[51]

The UNP and Ceylon's Tame Transition

The CNC continued its leading position through World War II, and Ceylon became independent in 1948. This period was free of the extraordinary violence and dislocation occurring elsewhere. But it also revealed the range of ideologies of the polity that could plausibly be pursued after independence. Jayatilaka's retirement and death would "open the way for a new generation of militant nationalists (many of whom were members of the Sinhala Maha Sabha and the Buddhist Theosophical Society) to make their distinctive but divisive impact on the life of the country."[52] The already leaky firewall erected by the CNC against Sinhalese nationalism was breaking down, and Russell argues that the SMS "considerably strengthened its position" during the war.[53]

In 1943, debates about the national language of Ceylon offered a preview of possible future compromises and conflicts: "The original resolution of 1943 [for Sinhala-only, which was then amended to include Tamil] . . . signifies the first political attempt at the institutionalization of language-based group interests."[54] This move toward Sinhalese as language of nation—led in part by future president J. R. Jayewardene—was supported by many CNC leaders, reflecting the straightforward problem of rural Sinhala marginalization under colonial rule.[55] For many, the push toward Sinhala was not primarily about intra-island cleavages but instead an assertion against British rule. The *swabasha* movement aimed to limit the constraints imposed by English, but many of its advocates had not considered the ways in which it would affect Tamils or the forces it would empower.[56] In retrospect, DeVotta argues, an English link language policy, as developed in India, "might better have served the country," but at the time this was seen as an unreasonable concession to the British.[57]

A compromise, which included Bandaranaike, was reached to also call for Tamil as a national language.[58] The new Soulbury Constitution included guarantees preventing discrimination against minorities.[59] Yet outside elite council circles, much Sinhalese opinion "was for the establishment of the unequivocal supremacy of the Sinhala language."[60] This previewed how "language became a powerful factor, the symbol of all other ethnic symbols," in the emerging political sphere.[61]

D. S. Senanayake was the island's most important politician in the 1940s. He formed a new party, the United National Party (UNP), in 1946 that could lead an independent Ceylon.[62] Senanayake was the bearer of a multiracial, but rather vague, Ceylonese nationalism,[63] but this "placed himself in opposition to an increasingly influential current of opinion—represented by Bandaranaike and his Sinhala Maha Sabha—which viewed the Sri Lanka polity as being essentially Sinhalese and Buddhist in character and which rejected the concepts of a secular state and a multiracial polity."[64] To draw on the conceptualization of ideological projects from chapter 1, the competing projects differed on the weight they would put on the Buddhism along the religious dimension and Sinhala on the linguistic dimension.

This tension within the CNC and the UNP was not resolved prior to independence: Bandaranaike joined the UNP, seeing it as a loose coalition rather than disciplined party organization.[65] Within the UNP, he became a subordinate to D. S. Senanayake, "a role in which he found little comfort."[66] The party "swiftly developed into a catch-all organization" with limited central control.[67] In the run-up to the 1947 elections that were to lay the basis for the new postindependence government it "was in ghastly disarray."[68] Indeed, "the party's failure to win even a bare majority of the seats was highly embarrassing" in 1947.[69] It was able to form a government by linking up with G. G. Ponnambalam's All-Ceylon Tamil Congress, which suffered a split by S. J. V. Chelvanayakam's more radical Federal Party (FP) over disputes about the future of ethnic relations on the island. The FP was "very much a voice in the wilderness until the general elections of 1956."[70]

Ceylon in 1947–48 thus appeared likely to see continued peace and prosperity: "There seemed little or no evidence of the religious turmoil and linguistic conflicts which were to burst to the surface in the mid-1960s."[71] D. S. Senanayake, despite the organizational mess that was the UNP, advanced a nationalist project "based on a double compromise: the softening of Sinhalese dominance by the establishment of an equilibrium of political forces, the keynote of which was moderation, and an emphasis on secularism."[72] Yet, "this Sri Lankan nationalism had a crucial flaw. It was basically elitist in conception, and it had little popular support extending beyond the political establishment."[73] Bandaranaike and, above all, the forces he sought to harness held a very different vision of the future nation. It was this clash of a hazy but inclusive nationalism with a much narrower but more carefully and deeply articulated vision that structured Sri Lanka's politics for the next half-century.

The Political Foundations of the New Ceylon

In contrast to its later trajectory, the early decades of Ceylon's independence did not involve substantial armed group mobilization. The main form of violence were anti-Tamil riots and pogroms that occurred as the wave of Sinhalese nationalism swept into power, reconfiguring the country's political mainstream. The only state–armed group relationship that meets my criteria for "armed politics" prior to the mid-1970s is the 1971 JVP uprising and government response. Its radically antisystemic revolutionary posture was unsurprisingly seen as ideologically opposed, and the group was targeted for total war, leading to its defeat within a couple of months.

More significant than this conflict (which would recur in a far more violent and challenging form in 1987) was the shift in ideological project among Ceylon's ruling elite by the early 1970s, and the reaction it engendered among Tamils. From the loose Ceylonese nationalism of the late colonial UNP/CNC we see movement toward a hard-line Sinhalese majoritarianism mobilized by S. W. R. D. Bandaranaike and his new Sri Lanka Freedom Party (SLFP) from the early 1950s onward. It cast Tamil mobilization as deeply inimical and suspicious, a form of separatism and internal subversion. The reconfiguring of the ideology of the polity that the SLFP pioneered, and that the United National Party (UNP) then emulated for electoral advantage, had huge consequences in the 1970s, both triggering and shaping responses to Tamil armed militancy.

After Independence

Ceylon was widely viewed as the least troubled and most promising of South Asia's new states. Marked by a nonviolent, collaborative transfer of power under the aegis of a moderate ruling party, there was little overt sign of the troubles to come. The UNP under D. S. Senanayake appeared to have a clear path forward. Indeed, the main threat the UNP perceived was from Sri Lanka's Left, which mobilized workers in and around Colombo for redistribution and, in some cases, revolution.

D. S. Senanayake and the UNP did not make radical changes to the politics of Ceylon; indeed, "they seemed oblivious to the political perils involved in making the process so bland as to be virtually imperceptible to those not directly involved."[74] Language policy, despite a formal commitment to lessen the primacy of English, did not move dramatically.[75] This was a major miscalculation, as DeVotta argues: "In adopting this gradualist approach, however, they misgauged the sentiments and frustrations of the Sinhalese lower and middle classes."[76]

Unaware of the gathering storm, the UNP continued to advance a nationalist project "based on a double compromise: the softening of Sinhalese dominance by the establishment of an equilibrium of political forces, the keynote of which was moderation, and an emphasis on secularism."[77] Similarly on religion, the UNP in 1948 "adopted a secular and liberal approach in which no religion was favoured."[78] Yet, "this Sri Lankan nationalism had a crucial flaw. It was basically elitist in conception and it had little popular support extending beyond the political establishment."[79] The same was true of its Marxist rivals, who focused on class cleavages and, at this point, advocated secularism. The disenfranchisement of Indian Tamils working in the upland plantations made rural Sinhalese voters even more important.[80]

The Rise of the SLFP, Riots, and the Primacy of Sinhalese Nationalism

The grassroots mobilization of the rural Sinhalese masses and intelligentsia by Bandaranaike and other political and religious entrepreneurs during the colonial period came to the fore in the 1950s: "Beneath the surface, these religious, cultural, and linguistic issues were gathering momentum and developing into a force too powerful for the existing social and political set-up to accommodate or absorb."[81] Initial signs of this tide emerged when S. W. R. D. Bandaranaike broke from the UNP and formed the Sri Lanka Freedom Party (SLFP), which advocated a more explicitly Sinhalese conception of "real" nationalism. The SLFP was held at bay in the 1952 elections, following D. S. Senanayake's death. Dudley Senanayake, his son, led the UNP to an overwhelming victory.

However, the SLFP and its Mahajana Eksath Peramuna (MEP) electoral alliance swept to a massive victory in 1956 on the cause of the Sinhalese language and Sinhalese nationalism. A new project seized the commanding heights of state power. Of this Sinhalese nationalist constituency, De Silva writes of "its deep sense of grievance, its social and economic discontent, its resentment at being neglected by both the Left and the UNP."[82] Bandaranaike spent 1951–56 activating and politicizing the forces of Sinhalese nationalism, who felt excluded, marginalized, and looked down on by elites during the 1952 election.[83] They found new political space in independent Ceylon: "Their grievances were not new. . . . what was new was the insistence of their appeals and the organization of issue-oriented voluntary associations for sustained pressure."[84]

The forces of Bandaranaike's Sinhalese assertion unified to capture power in 1956: "The nationalists and extremist *bhikkus* (Buddhist monks) were determined to merge forces and clamor for Sinhala to be made the sole official language."[85] Language and religion were fused in this nationalist vision: "The two elements—Buddhism and Sinhala—were so closely intertwined that it was impossible to treat either one in isolation."[86] In their eyes, and the eyes of those politicians either swept along with or targeted by them, "the concept of a multiracial polity was no longer politically viable" in the face of a "rejection of the concept for a Sri Lankan nationalism."[87] The UNP abandoned its earlier pledges, and began "outbidding" over the issue of Sinhalese nationalism.[88] This was not a contingent result of individual leaders' agency; instead, Bandaranaike's government "had its roots in the recent past, especially in the temperance movement in the early twentieth century."[89] Without understanding this history, there is no way to make sense of subsequent governments' perceptions and fears.

The election of 1956 was the beginning of almost two decades of SLFP dominance, despite the assassination of S. W. R. D. Bandaranaike by a disgruntled monk in 1959, attacked for his efforts to construct a language deal with S. J. V. Chelvanayakam of the Federal Party in 1957. Ironically, the forces Bandaranaike had intentionally set in motion swept him away, as any moves toward moderation were now framed as selling out and abandonment of the Sinhalese cause. The politics of the 1950s included several major riots, which turned into pogroms against Tamils. Local specialists in violence linked to politicians were deeply implicated in these riots, with government forces that did not protect minorities. I do not include these as armed orders because of their lack of organizational coherence—they rose and quickly fell, but they give a clear sense of the changing political tides and the willingness of those in power to look the other way at, or openly encourage, lethal nonstate violence.

The ideological project that came to dominate the country's politics was largely driven by pressure from below; this was not the top-down nationalist innovation of elites in India or Pakistan. The particular electoral geography of the country provided powerful mechanisms of influence for rural Sinhalese political entrepreneurs as they sought to break the power of the multilingual Colombo elite. In turn, ambitious politicians had to shift their positions to accommodate this new movement. The top-down projects of India and Pakistan represent a quite different pattern; while they too had to deal with mass sentiment, they set the agenda to a greater extent. The ethnic demography of Ceylon made appeals to Sinhalese sentiment electorally sufficient to win power, in contrast to the more fragmented landscapes of India and Pakistan.

S. W. R. D. Bandaranaike's widow, Sirimavo Bandaranaike, led Ceylon in 1960–65 and 1970–77. In the interregnum, Dudley Senanayake tried to counteract the Sinhalese nationalist tide by attempting deals with Tamil political leaders. His UNP was in power from 1965 to 1970, but its efforts to arrange a deal on language policy with Tamils ran into the limits to reconciliation, just as S. W. R. D. Bandaranaike's had, that were "set by the new balance of forces established by the Bandaranaikes, husband and wife, in the decade 1956–65."[90] The UNP's initial efforts to shift course in 1965 from the trajectory set by the Bandaranaikes met with "the most virulent campaign of ethnic hostility ever waged in Sri Lanka in recent times. The Opposition unleashed a barrage of racialist propaganda, in which the SLFP, as the unabashed advocate of the Sinhalese-Buddhist domination of the Sri Lankan polity, was joined by the Communist Party and the LSSP."[91] Efforts to push district councils were defeated by mass mobilization by the SLFP, which claimed that they would be a precursor to federalism, as well as by intra-UNP skepticism. Even when politicians sought to escape the SLFP's project, they were constrained by public opinion and political contention.

There was a left-right component to SLFP-UNP competition. Part of the SLFP's strategy was to fuse socialism with Sinhalese nationalism; it became the center-left party and the UNP the center-right party. The SLFP deployed this combination to attack the UNP during its 1965–70 period in power, seeking to simultaneously undermine the Dudley-Chelvanayakam pact of 1965 over language and the UNP's efforts to liberalize the economy. By contrast, the UNP was a center-right party focused on trying to spur economic growth by limiting state intervention. Mrs. Bandaranaike's return to power in 1970 was at the head of a left coalition that included other leftist parties. Yet this left dimension did not drive a politics of cross-ethnic class mobilization, but instead a fusion of the linguistic-religious definition of the nation with redistributive demands within that nationalist imagining.

Oscillations around Sinhalese Buddhist Nationalism, 1970–present

The section below outlines the armed politics that emerged from this combustible combination: the Sinhalese nationalist project accelerated a Tamil separatist movement that turned to violence by the late 1970s. The governments that came and went from 1970 until the bloody end of the Tamil revolt in 2009 somewhat varied in the intensity of their hawkishness and, especially, in their orientation on the left-right distributive dimension, but the basic preference for Sinhalese and Buddhism remained central to the ruling parties' positions. This was institutionalized in the constitution of 1972, and then again given symbolic centrality in the new 1978 constitution: "The Republic of Sri Lanka shall give to Buddhism the foremost place." The political revolution of 1956 proved highly sticky, especially after the defeat of Dudley Senanayake's efforts to resist the tide from 1965 until 1970.

Mrs. Bandaranaike won election in 1970, and with her return pushed hard for the Sinhalese Buddhist project. She aggressively moved to shift state policy toward Sinhalese dominance. Her decisions in 1971 to shift university admissions in favor of Sinhalese and in 1972 to make Buddhism the state religion were clear triggers for escalating ethnic conflict, which would break out into war in the late 1970s. An ideological project was generating hugely important, and tragic, policies. This movement into ethno-nationalism increasingly framed Tamils as interlopers, aliens, and guests. In Horowitz's classic work on ethnic conflict, the Sinhala-Tamil cleavage is a recurrent example of how insecure majoritarianism can generate stunningly dire threat perceptions that seem wildly out of proportion to any "objective" measure of threat.[92]

Armed politics with Tamil groups did not begin until the early/mid-1970s, and I consider them below, but the underlying threat perception that became institutionalized in both dominant parties identified Tamil linguistic demands as a pathway to national disintegration, treason, and Indian subversion. In the eyes of the rulers of the state and their coalition, Tamil demands could and should not be easily accommodated; those who tried to break with that approach were punished both by the electorate and other elites. This logic of outbidding is well known, but what it needs to operate is an understanding of how this political "common sense" emerged and of the ideological work necessary to shift the language of politics so dramatically, even in the face of the UNP's initial disinterest in such a project. The roots of this major political movement lay in the politics of colonial Ceylon and the inability of the CNC to generate local linkages in rural Sinhalese areas that could both discipline and respond to the resentments and grievances of this constituency. This ideological shift in the 1950s centered Ceylon's politics around the Sinhalese-Tamil cleavage, building a deep distrust of Tamils into the political mainstream. Future Tamil mobilization, both peaceful and violent, would be viewed through this lens of suspicion and threat.

Mrs. Bandaranaike's victory in 1970, following the failure of the 1965 Senanayake-Chelvanayakam pact in the face of intense SLFP pressure, was a decisive signal that efforts to accommodate Tamil demands for greater representation continued to be a potentially fatal electoral liability.[93] The UNP and SLFP from this point on continued to try to appeal to the Sinhalese constituency, even while articulating differences on the economic dimension. This does not mean total consensus or unanimity, but the broad contours of political debate were set: Tamil separatism was seen as a pressing threat and institutional options for changing the political system were opposed as the thin end of a secessionist wedge. This ran into growing Tamil mobilization in the 1970s that began to more forthrightly demand either federalism or full-blown independence. The Tamil United Liberation Front (TULF) and other Tamil political organizations were seen by Sinhalese as making unreasonable demands far out of proportion to their rightful share of national resources; they in turn perceived a majoritarianism that sought to convert a Sinhalese majority into total dominance.

In the face of this emergent political context, the Vaddukodai Resolution of 1976, advanced by the TULF, the main Tamil political opposition, marked a break from the previous demands for federalism by identifying the goal of a "Tamil Eelam": Mrs. Bandaranaike's government "left the FP [Federal Party] and the Tamils with no alternative but to turn their backs on the single federalized island entity."[94] Mrs. Bandaranaike lost resoundingly to J. R. Jayewardene in 1977, and he would run a UNP government until he was succeeded by Ranasinghe Premadasa in 1988. Jayewardene leaned relatively right compared to Mrs. Bandaranaike, both on economic policy and foreign policy. But his basic attitude toward the ethnic question was not radically different; indeed, in the 1940s and 1950s he had been a committed advocate of Sinhala-only language policy. His UNP government did move in a conciliatory direction in the late 1970s, but this was "too little, too late," as Tamil radicals had by this point begun to outflank Tamil politicians trying to balance mainstream politics and separatism.[95]

The ideological project that consolidated itself in both parties deepened the Sinhalese-dominated parties' views of the Tamils as a rebellious ethnic category, laying the basis for the hard-line responses to Tamil militancy that emerged over the course of the 1970s and especially the early 1980s. DeVotta argues that "adherents to this nationalist ideology insist on expanding and perpetuating Sinhalese Buddhist supremacy within a unitary state; creating rules, laws, and structures that institutionalize such supremacy; and attacking those who disagree with this agenda. For those who have bought into it, this ideology is sacrosanct and hence nonnegotiable, and consequently all who question or oppose it are considered enemies of the state."[96]

The Tamil militants, as well as Tamil politicians after Vaddukodai, were identified as ideologically opposed to the project of the country's ruling parties. There would be shifts in political party positioning in the decades to come, with occasional efforts to negotiate driven by military defeats I discuss below, but the underlying political structure of the Sinhalese nationalist project remained in place, facing off against what became an equally hard-line Tamil nationalist project under the LTTE. After 1994, the SLFP would hold the presidency until 2015, so it would be the dominant party of state following a long period of UNP dominance.

The J. R. Jayewardene government from 1977 to 1989 was the first to directly battle Tamil armed groups in a sustained way; the militancy of the early/mid-1970s was fairly sporadic and loosely organized. It escalated, as we will see below, over the course of the 1980s. In 1989, another UNP president, Ranasingha Premadasa, took power. He was then assassinated in 1993 by the LTTE. Chandrika Bandaranaike Kumaratunga of the SLFP—daughter of S. W. R. D. and Sirimavo Bandaranaike—was president from 1994 until 2005, when she was succeeded by Mahinda Rajapaksa, also of the SLFP. It was Rajapaksa who carried out the final phase of the war against the LTTE, destroying it in 2009. Kumaratunga and Rajapaksa differed in a variety of ways, but both they and their coalitions broadly represented the rural, revisionist Sinhalese Buddhist upsurge of the 1950s and its ideological project. I discuss their tactical and military choices below, but the broad political story is simple: after a period of UNP dominance, the SLFP took control of the presidency (even as the prime ministership was briefly in UNP hands from 2001 to 2004) until 2015. We should not expect major ideological changes in the decades of major warfare; if anything, there was further hardening of resolve in the face of LTTE suicide bombings and attacks on civilians.[97]

Armed Politics in Sri Lanka

Sri Lanka has experienced three major bouts of political violence—the ultra-Left JVP attacked the state in 1971 and then from 1987 to 1990, while a set of

Tamil militant groups (ultimately dominated by the LTTE) waged war from the early/mid-1970s until 2009. The distribution of armed orders varies depending on what types of groups (and group-periods) we focus on. Sri Lanka presents the simplest empirical case of the four countries examined: it is the smallest, with the fewest armed groups. Table 7.1 focuses on the overall pattern of armed politics, and then shows subsets between all armed groups and groups during periods in which they are clearly identified as anti-state insurgents.

Table 7.2 shows armed politics between the government and ethnic minority Tamil armed groups. These include the Liberation Tigers of Tamil Eelam (LTTE; early known as the Tamil New Tigers), People's Liberation Tigers of Tamil Eelam (PLOTE), Tamil Eelam Liberation Organization (TELO), and Eelam People's Revolutionary Liberation Front (EPRLF), among others. Most of these originated as anti-state militants, but over time we saw side switching and the rise of new pro-state groups, like the Eelam People's Democratic Party (EPDP) and Tamil Makkal Viduthalai Pulikal (TMVP).

Figure 7.1 shows time trends in the proportion of order-years for the category of self-identified Tamil rebel groups. From 1987 on, this primarily captures the LTTE, as other Tamil groups disappeared or became pro-state paramilitaries. There is some measurement error here because of shifts within years and because

TABLE 7.1   Armed politics in Sri Lanka

	ALL ORDERS	INSURGENTS
Total war	31 (15.12%)	30 (32.61%)
Containment	54 (26.34%)	49 (53.26%)
Limited cooperation	24 (11.71%)	11 (11.96%)
Alliance	96 (46.83%)	2 (2.17%)
Total	205	92

TABLE 7.2   Tamil armed groups in Sri Lanka

	ALL	INSURGENT DYAD-YEARS ONLY
Total war	28 (14.74%)	27 (33.75%)
Containment	43 (22.63%)	41 (51.25%)
Limited cooperation	23 (12.11%)	10 (12.5%)
Alliance	96 (50.53%)	2 (2.5%
Total	190	80

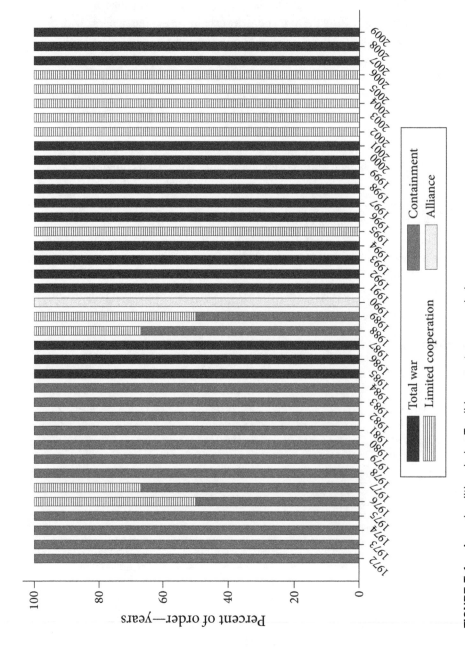

FIGURE 7.1. Armed politics during Tamil insurgent group-periods

of lack of clarity on specific relationships in the late 1970s (sometimes "limited cooperation" appears to really be "neglect"), but the basic trends are clear—increasingly intense conflict into the 1980s, then an unusual period of less severe conflict and even some cooperation during and just after the Indian intervention of 1987, followed largely by total war, broken with periods of cease-fire, until the destruction of the LTTE in 2009.

In examining state-groups relations within this broad cleavage, we see a serious bifurcation. Of the armed order-years in which the state was interacting with a clearly anti-state insurgent Tamil group (as opposed to Tamil groups during periods acting as paramilitary parties), 33.75 percent were total war, 51.25 percent containment, and 12.5 percent the more ambiguous military hostilities coding. This leaves only 15 percent of any kind of cooperative dyad-years among this type of group; a far cry from India's handling of ethno-linguistic separatists or Myanmar's construction of a cease-fire regime along the ethnic periphery after 1989. This was a vicious and intense war. And the blame is to be shared: while the Sri Lankan state bred the revolt through unaccommodating policies and intense repression, the LTTE emerged as a radical and unyielding force, unafraid to use human shields or target civilians, and refusing to cut a deal short of sovereignty.[98]

However, insurgency was not the only behavior of Tamil armed groups. When we include a set of long-standing government relationships with "flipped" Tamil militant groups and pro-state paramilitaries, alliance ends up being the dominant armed order. The PLOT, TELO, TMVP, and EPDP spent long stretches as allies or business partners with the Sri Lankan government; the decades of war combined with multiple dyadic alliances to create a large proportion of alliance order-years. They were used as "Tiger-hunters," providing intelligence, deniable violence, and at times, standing as political parties intended to serve as a political counterweight to the LTTE (whether real or nominal). But the core political dynamic was conflict between the LTTE and the state. This is another area where we need to be discerning when using the quantitative data. Though alliance dominates a breakdown of post-1990 order-years, this is not because of a highly cooperative *overall* conflict environment, but instead because of the number of small Tamil paramilitaries.

Along the fundamental Tamil-Sinhala linguistic-religious cleavage, there were mainly either enemies or allies. Because of this bunching on the extremes of the spectrum, the Tamil war resembles India's battles in Kashmir and Punjab, Pakistan's in East Pakistan, and Burma before 1989 more than India's Northeast, Pakistan's Northwest, or post-1989 Myanmar. There were a few periods of limited cooperation that I explore below, but they were largely lulls in the broader war brought on by military stalemate or international pressure. The genuine odds of a meaningful political solution were very low from 1983 on. This was a pitiless and very bloody war, with decades worth of large-scale human rights abuses and civilian displacement.

The JVP Wars: Unambiguous Military Threat

The JVP was founded as a political organization in the late 1960s amid much left-wing ferment. Led by Rohana Wijeweera, the JVP advocated a revolution that would sweep away both the vestiges of colonial rule and the feudal democracy it perceived as having taken root since. The party was dominated by Sinhalese, rather than being a cross-ethnic leftist coalition, and had an ambiguous relationship with Mrs. Bandaranaike's United Front—it campaigned for her in 1970 but also viewed the UF and Ceylon's Left as essentially sellouts who were not pursuing the truly revolutionary path.[99] The early 1970s JVP drew heavily on students and the rural underemployed youth, promising to shatter a repressive and unequal status quo.[100]

The JVP's ideological posture was therefore radically antisystemic, including deep hostility toward electoralist left-wing parties that were incorporated into parliamentary politics. By early 1971, the JVP had clearly decided to rebel, believing that the electoral Left could never deliver a meaningful revolutionary change to Sri Lanka's politics. Rather than reacting to state policy, it planned a revolt.[101] It is little surprise that Mrs. Bandaranaike's government viewed the JVP with suspicion and took preemptive action to shut the organization down once it learned of the JVP's plan to attack the state. The JVP launched its revolt and several months of total war ensued, resulting in the JVP's decimation and the end of this period of armed politics in Ceylon. My theory has little of distinctive value to say about the JVP in 1971: it is the kind of unambiguous, direct military threat that is easily explained by a straightforward logic of regime survival. There was not much space for discretion or interpretation in the government's response: if it did not repress, it would be overthrown.

The JVP was unbanned in the late 1970s under Jayewardene, and it pursued a mainstream electoral path without violence, including competing hard in elections in the early 1980s.[102] After the "Black July" anti-Tamil riots of 1983, the JVP was banned by the government, which claimed it was involved in the pogrom. There is little evidence of this: instead, it is widely believed that Jayewardene banned the JVP on a pretext, one of the scapegoats for the riots that in reality had deep involvement by the ruling UNP.

The JVP was pushed underground and began preparing for another possible revolt, although there was little active violence until 1987. In 1987, as the Tamil war escalated, the Sri Lankan government was coerced into the Indo-Lanka

Accord with the Indian government, and the Indian Peacekeeping Force (IPKF) arrived on the island, the JVP saw its opportunity and began targeting UNP members and security forces. It accused the government of selling out to India while exploiting the poor. Its violence grew into 1988 and hit a grim crescendo in 1989, with large-scale human rights abuses on both sides.[103] This round of insurgency was another politically unambiguous, militarily threatening assault on the central state, though in this case largely caused by the Jayewardene administration forcing it underground. Given Sri Lanka's small geography and the group's ultraradical war aims, total war occurred at the height of both insurgencies. The JVP pursued leftist goals of total revolution, infused with Sinhalese Buddhist nationalism: it sought to reshape the entire economy and political system of Sri Lanka, with its base in Sinhalese students and impoverished rural areas.

My theory has little beyond the obvious to say about these cases—despite some openness to the left by SLFP governments, the JVP posed an obvious military threat that left little to interpret or choice in how to respond. In a small country, the JVP's efforts to mobilize the rural Sinhalese masses, infiltrate the army, and seize Colombo left very little room for political voice. Intense state crackdowns, including extra-judicial killings, torture, and disappearances, occurred in 1971 and 1989, while the JVP targeted security force families, assassinated with wanton abandon, and used extreme coercion against civilians.[104]

It is worth noting, however, that there is also a substantial amount of containment in the JVP's codings. This is not just a total war case. After the destruction of the JVP in 1971, containment lasted for a number of years despite it barely existing at all, and that primarily in jail. Prior to its full insurrection in 1987, we also see containment following its banning (on a pretext) in 1983. During the most unambiguous periods of direct challenge, those that are understood to be actual civil war, total war was the order of the day. The other periods involved the hazy edges of what counts as armed politics, especially during the 1970s, and so containment appears to have been the dominant approach. This is consistent with a simple military threat story: when the JVP was marginal, it was not targeted with much force; when it posed a serious military attack, it faced severe repression. Since the early/mid-1990s, the JVP has been a mainstream political party, generally at the extremes of the Sri Lankan political system, but unarmed.[105]

Trajectories of Tamil Militancy

The emergence of Tamil militancy offers a much clearer opportunity to see where my theory works, since it involved more potential state political discretion in response over a much longer period of time. Rather than a sudden upsurge of direct, regime-threatening violence, the armed mobilization was much slower, more gradual, and reactive to government policies; Tamil political mobilization evolved in the face of the Sinhala nationalist upsurge of the 1950s. Anti-Tamil pogroms and the failure of two attempted bargains between Sinhalese and Tamil leaders left many Tamils seeing little hope of maintaining influence within the Sri Lankan political system, especially when Mrs. Bandaranaike pushed aggressively for key policy and symbolic changes in the early 1970s. I have traced out the details of Tamil insurgency elsewhere, so here focus on the big picture trends.[106]

Phase One: Containment to Total War, 1972–90

The first glimmerings of armed militancy began in the late 1960s and early 1970s with small bands of Tamil youth.[107] The gathering insurgency emerged at a relatively low level, especially in the 1970s—bank robberies, for instance. This could have been handled in a variety of ways by the Sri Lankan government, from rapid accommodation of political concerns to full-throated crackdowns. In parallel to the emerging militancy came a hardening of the goals of nonviolent Tamil politicians, who began to turn toward explicitly demanding a separate state. Compared to the JVP uprisings, the range of political choice was much broader, both because of the lack of Tamil militants' ability to overthrow the regime and because plausible responses included autonomy and federalist solutions.[108]

This is where the time spent above on the historical emergence and consolidation of Sinhala Buddhist nationalism pays off analytically. With the rise of the Sinhala Buddhist SLFP under S. W. R. D. Bandaranaike, the political sphere was seriously constrained by "outbidding": efforts to make some accommodation with Tamil political demands were undermined by the rival Sinhalese party.[109] Over time, both parties adopted a fairly firm stance against major political concessions that would undermine the unitary nature of the state and concede a high degree of autonomy to Tamil areas in the north and east of the island.

Mrs. Bandaranaike and then Jayewardene pursued a broadly repressive and unaccommodating policy during the 1970s and early 1980s, including toward the nonviolent Tamil political class. The space for accommodation, whether of violent or nonviolent actors, was limited by the accepted contours of politics: for those desiring a unitary state that favored Sinhala language and Buddhism, granting serious autonomy or embracing federalism was seen as the first step toward separatism and the continued onslaught on the (perceived) small and isolated Sinhalese community. Once Tamil politicians declared their goal to be a separate state, government resolve to crack down increased and the police, and then later on the Sri Lankan Army, began to pursue intensifying sweeps.

The limitations on Tamil civilian participation in politics—some imposed by the state, then others self-imposed—drove the Tamil population out of the mainstream political arena.[110]

This fueled growing escalation of the armed conflict and the sidelining of the older Tamil politicians and parties, who became seen as increasingly irrelevant in the face of spiraling violence. Tamil militants, especially those of the Liberation Tigers of Tamil Eelam (LTTE), lethally targeted Tamil moderates and advocates of nonviolence, embracing violence as a means to both dominate the Tamil community and carve out a separate state free of Sinhalese dominance. Anti-Tamil riots in 1983, in retaliation for the killing of Sri Lankan soldiers in an LTTE ambush, marked the point of clear no return:[111] the war heated up further, India became more actively involved in supporting Tamil armed groups to push pressure on Colombo to cut a deal with them, and the LTTE would rise to dominance and become the sole Tamil insurgent group on the Tamil side by 1990.[112]

From 1983 until 1987, five main Tamil groups fought the Sri Lankan government. We see a blend of total war and containment as an overmatched Sri Lankan security apparatus lethally flailed in Tamil regions, with the trend moving toward total war. The limited space for political concession shrunk further, and Jayewardene became increasingly autocratic in his rule both in Tamil and Sinhalese areas. The Sri Lankan state doubled-down on repression while lacking the capacity to monopolize violence, and the Tamil insurgency began to fracture into competing groups with varying levels of ambition.

Armed orders grew more complicated in 1986–90, however, as the conflict attracted growing Indian attention and pressure for a settlement.[113] At this point the LTTE also launched a series of fratricidal attacks on other Tamil groups to try to achieve hegemony over the Tamil militant space, even as they were all receiving sanctuary and support from the Indian government. In 1987, the Indians coerced the Sri Lankan government to accept the Indo-Lanka Accord, which would create a devolved political system backed by the Indian Peacekeeping Force (IPKF). The fact that it took Indian threats to make devolution a reality gives a sense of how resistant the Sinhalese Buddhist ideological project was; as we will see, it was largely abandoned after the Indians left.

The Indian intervention was the crucial moment that drove the bifurcation in Tamil armed groups' alignment I noted in the quantitative data above. The LTTE carried on the banner of rebellion, refusing to accept the Indo-Lanka Accord and turning violently against the IPKF. A pitched war would develop between the Indian military and the Tigers in northern and eastern Sri Lanka from 1987 until the Indian withdrawal of 1990. Yet, most of the other Tamil groups either went dormant or became supportive of the IPKF. The EPRLF, for instance, was the key local partner of the IPKF, able to provide local information and a nominal legitimizing face for the Indian presence among Tamils. The tactical overlap between the IPKF and EPRLF was clear: the EPRLF needed protection, and the IPKF needed a local partner. The EPRLF would later be essentially wiped out after the Indian departure.[114]

It was during this period that the JVP attacked the Sri Lankan government, using the Indo-Lanka Accord and presence of the Indian troops as key justifications to pursue a revolution. Colombo became increasingly desperate to get rid of the Indians.[115] After Ranasinghe Premadasa became president, succeeding Jayewardene, he pursued a rapprochement with the LTTE. In a remarkable, though brief, alignment of tactical incentives, the LTTE and Sri Lankan government reached a rapprochement in 1989–90 because of their mutual desire to see the Indians gone.[116] We actually see an alliance order in early 1990, even more cooperation than what I expect from a strange bedfellows political role: the government allegedly airlifted guns to the Tigers to help them get rid of the Indians.[117] This is a striking, if unusual, case of deep ideological divisions being overcome by extremely pressing shared tactical goals, which rose to the fore as a determinant of alignment choices.

How do we make sense of this period? The Tamil insurgents were clearly identified as a threat early on, though their small size and limited activities in the 1970s did not trigger a major response. The default response was repressive, in containment orders that deployed primarily police forces to try to root them out. The militant groups' growth, the escalation of violence (spurred in large part by the anti-Tamil riots of "Black July" 1983), and Indian intervention took things to the next level, with total war.[118] The Tamil mobilization was not met with proactive concessions or efforts to forge lasting cease-fires; the question was instead primarily how to successfully repress. This period sees both the rise and fall of India's alliance with the LTTE, and its endurance until 1990 with anti-LTTE Tamil groups like the EPRLF that worked with the IPKF from 1987 to 1990.

Phase Two: Total War Interspersed with Limited Cooperation, 1990–2006

The second phase began with the departure of the IPKF and the rapid return of war between the state and the LTTE. The IPKF withdrew in 1990, buffeted by domestic skepticism of their mission in India and the bloody stalemate with the LTTE. Their ally, the EPRLF, was largely wiped out by the Tigers, and other Tamil groups either defected to the LTTE or fled into the arms of the Sri Lankan state, while the LTTE killed off or drove into exile other dissidents.[119] The split within the Tamil militant milieu solidified at this point: pro- and anti-Tiger policy was the divide of the day.

With the Indian withdrawal, the narrowly tactical, anti-Indian basis of Prema-dasa's brief period of cooperation in 1989–90 with the LTTE disappeared, and the relationship returned to total war. Very intense combat ensued, including a blend of conventional and insurgent tactics by the Tigers and their sustained campaign of assassinations (including of President Premadasa, with whom they had pre-viously worked).[120] We can see this shift after the IPKF departure in the AOSA data: 79 percent of order-years (11/14) between the government and Tamil New Tigers/LTTE were containment (the others total war) before 1990, while after 1990 we see 68 percent (13/19) of dyad-years being total war, and the remaining years being limited cooperation during cease-fire negotiations. The intensity of the conflict noticeably grew.

How do we make sense of this trend? Why didn't the two parties agree to a deal that would prevent costly ongoing conflict? The ruling Sinhalese parties had little interest in a major reconfiguration of the political system. As DeVotta argues, "The nationalist ideology dictates that the LTTE are intransigent, incor-rigible, and not to be trusted; the military must therefore eradicate the organiza-tion if Sri Lanka's territorial integrity is to be safeguarded."[121] In turn, the Tigers had emerged as a highly radical actor territorially and militarily dominant in substantial areas of the north and east, with a track record of direct attacks on civilians and brutal terrorism. Both deeply distrusted the other: the Tigers saw the government as a purely majoritarian force that would never allow meaningful Tamil rights, while Colombo saw the Tigers as an irreconcilably separatist force.

As the data above show, total war became the dominant form of conflict from 1990 onward. Yet we also see some periods of limited cooperation. What explains these breaks from the overall conflict trajectory? Limited cooperation primar-ily occurred during cease-fires in 1994–95 and 2002–6. Cease-fires emerged as way to explore the possibilities for resolving the war when the battlefield bal-ance made it impossible for either side to accomplish clear gains by fighting. The Tigers and government traded offensives in 1991–94 and 1995–2001 that showed the LTTE's formidability, but also the government's ability to keep fight-ing despite dramatic reverses. Both sides showed a very high level of resolve. In 1995, after a demoralizing spate of assassinations, the government of new president Chandrika Bandaranaike Kumaratunga tried a cease-fire that failed within months and laid the basis for the incredibly violent "Eeelam War III" from 1995 to 2001.[122]

In 2002, after the LTTE had launched devastating attacks on Sri Lanka's main airport but been unable to recapture the Jaffna peninsula, and 9/11 made the international community increasingly less sympathetic to the Tigers, both sides agreed to try again under Norwegian mediation.[123] But there was still a deep political divide on core issues that undermined meaningful negotiations. During the 2002–6 period, the LTTE appears to have hoped to create facts on the ground through their military power, governance capabilities, and de facto international recognition. The Colombo government appears to have hoped to find a way out of the costly war with an international "safety net" to buffer against disaster, but deep intragovernment divisions existed between the SLFP president and UNP prime minister, with the former more skeptical of the possibility of doing business with the LTTE. The peace process quickly fell apart, just as the efforts in 1994–95 failed.[124]

When the SLFP's Mahinda Rajapaksa was elected as president in 2005, the government pursued a final war. The Tigers appear to have been overly confident about their ability to withstand the larger, better trained, and politically unconstrained Sri Lankan security forces. Alongside these two core combatants were a set of Tamil armed parties that acted as paramilitaries working with the state and also often standing for election, though rarely with great success. Their primary raison d'être was military, not electoral. They had been targeted by the LTTE and sought protection from the state as a survival strategy. The Eelam People's Democratic Party of Douglas Devananda and the PLOTE, for instance each had specific areas of operations, acting as Tiger hunters for a Sinhala-dominated Sri Lankan Army and police forces. A newer version, the TMVP, led by LTTE defector Colonel Karuna, had a similar profile, with a base in eastern Sri Lanka that helped the army target the Tigers once conflict recurred in 2005–6.[125] These long-standing relationships explain why we see so much cooperation in the left column of table 2—like the Ikhwans in Kashmir, these Tamil groups abandoned an autonomous political position, living under state protection.

These represent another set of cases in which groups mobilized around particular cleavages do not actually make corresponding political demands and instead abandon political claim making. Despite being ethnic Tamil armed groups, the pro-state paramilitaries were neutered as political actors, making them ideologically acceptable despite their ethnic profile. Rather than becoming strange bedfellows, pursuing a highly strained tactical cooperation with an ideologically opposed central state, they instead took on the profile of armed allies, and then eventually superfluous supporters once they were no longer needed.[126] We saw a similar pattern with the Kashmiri Ikhwans—side-switching militants whose politics largely disappeared in favor of a desperate bid for survival.[127]

Phase Three: War to the Death, 2006–9

The third phase was total war to the death in 2006–9, culminating in the physical annihilation of the LTTE as an organization and the thoroughgoing militarization of state presence in Tamil areas of the north and east. There was no accommodation given; the Rajapaksa government clearly believed that there was no point to trying to parley with the Tigers, and brute force became the best option.[128] Mahinda Rajapaksa was the inheritor of the SLFP mantle: hugely popular among rural Sinhalese, and unabashed in his belief that Tamil separatism had to be stamped out lest the distinctive ethnic-religious character of Sri Lanka be eroded. The government took advantage of the growing international isolation of the Tigers, their inability to keep up with the increasing size and firepower of the Sri Lankan security forces, and a set of new tactics that favored the attrition of scarce Tiger manpower over the rapid capture of territory.

The final three years of the war were extraordinarily bloody, and appropriately are coded as total war in the AOSA dataset.[129] The government took advantage of the intelligence provided by the TMVP split of 2004 and dramatically improved its fighting power to address the often-frustrating failures 1990s. The war ended in 2009 with the total military defeat of the LTTE and the group's disappearance as a functioning militant organization.

The argument above challenges no conventional wisdoms about Sri Lanka's ethnic war: the supremacy of Sinhalese Buddhist nationalism as an ideological project is central to most accounts of the origins and rise of both Tamil insurgency and the nature of the war that then developed. What is the value added? First, this chapter provides new data on armed politics to map out the trajectories of the conflict in more systematic detail. Second, and much more important, putting this case in explicit comparative perspective makes clear the importance of studying history and ideology in understanding armed politics: "Reference to ideology explains why conflict resolution in Sri Lanka has been intractable and why a settlement to the civil war based on meaningful devolution is unlikely."[130] The trajectory of Sri Lanka was not structurally foreordained by state capacity, geography, or ethnic demography; we see other cases even within the same postcolonial region with very different outcomes.

The Sri Lankan case, in comparative perspective, offers compelling evidence of how ideological projects can shape threat perceptions and state strategies. In recent years, political scientists have sometimes embraced "bloodless" explanations of civil conflict, with a focus on strategic and material incentives.[131] Without dismissing the importance of these dynamics, Sri Lanka offers a serious caution. A rich set of fears and perceptions structured how the dominant Sinhalese Buddhist ruling coalition understood the nature of the problem posed by the Tamil minority. We can see the origins of these beliefs in the historically contingent project that emerged out of decades of "sons of the soil" nationalist mobilization from below. Other projects, whether "Ceylonese" nationalism or an India-style "state-nation" project, would have identified and responded to the Tamil mobilization quite differently.[132] There were paths not taken that could have led to radically different outcomes.

Sinhalese Buddhist nationalism identified Tamils as the primary threat to the unity of the nation, given their alleged links to India and expansionist goals, combined with the fragility of Sinhala language and Buddhism. This threat perception can be identified in Bandaranaike's movement well before independence, and decades prior to armed Tamil mobilization. It is thus little surprise that once militant groups emerged, the dominant response was coercive. Even when small and weak, the Tamil militants were seen as highly threatening. It is of course important to be clear that the Tigers themselves also became an extremely radical actor with much blame on their own shoulders. That said, there were plausibly different political paths Sri Lankan governments could have taken prior to the LTTE's dramatic takeoff in 1983. Once a threat perception was established, it became embedded in political parties and mass politics, and thus highly "sticky."

It is worth, however, noting three exceptions to this pattern of conflict. The first was the two cease-fires with the Tigers. This was a result of mutual exhaustion. There is nothing specific in my theory that would expect this, beyond the tactical value of each side getting some breathing room. These cease-fires did not come close to achieving major political outcomes. Second, there was a very brief alliance order between the LTTE and government in 1989–90 against the Indians. My argument certainly accounts for greater cooperation in this period, as a way of getting rid of the IPKF (a shared goal), but it predicts limited cooperation rather than alliance: the LTTE should have been treated as a strange bedfellow rather than an armed ally. Third, and similarly, the tight alliance with the Tamil paramilitaries involved a deeper cooperation than my argument predicts. These latter two leaves us with a set of changes that are in the direction the theory expects, but with much greater vigor than the argument expects; in other cases, we saw more containment than expected, but here we see more alliance than expected.

What might we take away from this argument about the future of Sri Lankan politics? The deeply rooted primacy of a particular nationalist ideology does not appear to have gone away. What DeVotta wrote in 2007 still has resonance: "The institutionalization of the Sinhalese Buddhist nationalist ideology means that a political solution to Sri Lanka's ethnic conflict is unlikely; meaningful devolution, whereby Sri Lanka's Tamils could coalesce with their ethnic counterparts and gain equality and self-respect, is also not in the offing—irrespective of how the conflict ends or the preferences of the international community."[133] The 2015–19 government, created by a coalition of minority Tamils and Sinhalese rivals to the Rajapaksas, held out the possibility of a meaningful shift in Sri Lanka's politics, but, while it did create broader democratic space, it did not generate these kinds of structural changes.[134]

Indeed, 2019's presidential election returned the Rajapaksas and their Sinhalese Buddhist constituency to power after this brief interregnum. The electoral campaign expanded its focus of suspicion from Tamils to also include Muslims, in the wake of the bloody Easter 2019 terrorist attacks on hotels and churches. The new government's approach appears to favor ongoing repression and surveillance to ensure that no new insurgency ever arises; in this case, the goal of the state will be to avoid having to return to two-sided armed politics by constant surveillance and a heavy security footprint in Tamil (and Muslim) areas. The basic structure of political life that emerged by the mid-1950s, and was consolidated from 1970, seems unlikely to change in the near future.

RETHINKING POLITICS AND VIOLENCE

This book has two goals. The first is to persuade the reader that there is important variation in armed orders. The second is to make the case for taking regime ideologies seriously as helping to shape these armed politics across space and time. If the reader has been convinced, there is little point in repetition; if, by now, the reader remains unmoved, a final effort at persuasion is unlikely to change much. Instead, this chapter identifies new research directions and policy implications that flow from these claims. Some of the promising future research agendas emerge from failures of the argument, unexpected findings, and loose ends, so this chapter acts as a postmortem even as it also looks forward. After considering promising research directions, I turn to ways that my argument can help us understand pressing contemporary policy challenges. Both research and policy analysis can benefit from broadening how we think about violence, order, and state power.

Future Research Directions

The study of civil war and political violence has expanded dramatically in the last three decades—what is there new to say? The armed politics approach provides an opportunity to move past the increasingly saturated core of existing research into new directions that can integrate with other areas of study, encourage a reexamination of common assumptions, and offer new questions. I first begin with questions that arise from the limits of this book, and then move on to building on areas of greater success.

Moving Past the Failures of the Argument

There are two major areas in which my argument comes up short, pointing toward better future work. First, the mechanisms of armed group agency I discuss in the book are substantially less developed than its theorization of regime perceptions and interests, and they surely only capture a subset of the myriad calculations armed actors make. This is a very challenging area for simple theory: the case studies reveal an incredibly complex, shifting set of reasons for changes in groups' ideological position and willingness to cooperate. The mechanisms I identify in chapter 2—war weariness, intramovement fragmentation, and international pressures—certainly made important and regular appearances in the empirical work, but only capture some of the action.

What are some possible next steps? Individual leaders seem to be particularly important; since many armed groups are fairly small and weakly institutionalized, individual preferences and personalities may play a larger role than in governments. Bringing more of the arguments about leaders in international relations literature into the civil war context,[1] and broadening research on leadership decapitation's consequences to a wider range of outcomes, could prove fruitful as a way of understanding variation in the political flexibility of armed actors.[2] A similarly vexing problem is theorizing the consequences of armed group rivalry. While there has been extensive work on how fragmentation and competition affect armed groups, such competition can seem to induce both more and less violence across contexts. As we see in Myanmar, Northeast India, and northwestern Pakistan, competition can moderate some groups while radicalizing others.[3] We need a more sophisticated understanding of the conditions under which each outcome is most likely: when does splintering drive groups toward the state, and when instead does it drive them away?

Finally, we need more research on the constraints that civilian constituencies place on armed group malleability, and why the nature of this civilian-group relationship may vary.[4] One of the recurring claims in the case literature is that armed groups' choices about ideological positioning can be constrained—or enabled—by civilian preferences. Yet these civilian political goals vary in their importance to different organizations; some groups are much more involved in civilian governance and consultation than others.[5] Moreover, preferences are themselves incredibly challenging to measure given the contexts in which they occur—running credible surveys or systematic interviews/focus groups about how civilians feel about armed groups can be difficult.[6]

Second, this project has focused on reasonably cohesive regimes. Pakistan is the trickiest case in this book, given its deep civil-military divides, but the primacy of the military allows us to largely focus on it as the dominant security manager. But in other cases of armed politics, regimes are more fragmented, riven by factionalism and competing security apparatuses, and deeply influenced by international actors. In contemporary Iraq and the Democratic Republic of Congo, for instance, "the state" is not always a particularly clear and unitary organization; rather, different actors can nestle and operate within the shell of state institutions. Tilly's conceptualization of the state as an "arena" for competing actors is more relevant to these kinds of cases than the more Skocpolian notion of state as cohesive political actor (though one directed by the goals of the movement that controls it) that this book leans toward.[7]

Future research will need to grapple with how to theorize and measure armed politics when the state is not a single actor in the security arena.[8] Systematically theorizing how components of a disaggregated state relate to different armed groups is a daunting proposition. One possibility is to simply multiply the number of orders each group can be involved in, since it may relate with different components of the state in different ways.[9] But this overlooks the complex relationships among state factions themselves. It may make more sense to explicitly begin from a more fully and systematically networked conceptualization of the state and armed groups that captures the byzantine relationships that can emerge in these contexts (I return to network approaches below).

Comparing across contexts can highlight similarities and differences in armed orders between fragmented-state and cohesive-state environments.[10] I have assumed that fragmented states are different, but perhaps this assumption is wrong or at least overly strong: life in Lebanon's armed politics may bear some important resemblances to Pakistan's, despite other differences. Within fragmented-state contexts, scholars can see whether the armed orders framework is tractable in some form, or if an entirely different conceptualization is needed.

Whatever findings emerge from this research will be valuable, whether they "lump" or "split" contexts. A fundamental challenge facing the field is that we see radically diverse forms of political violence and state repression: from shattered states like the Central African Republic to militarized regimes like Burma's fighting robust insurgents to dominant regimes imposing their will on unarmed society as in contemporary China. We need to know which theories and concepts apply where and when in order to move forward.

Taking Ideas Seriously

The strengths of the book also point toward promising future directions. There is at least plausible evidence that different governments understand political goals and nationalist boundaries differently, and that this variation influences their approaches toward armed groups.[11] In some cases this impact is clearer than others, and it is difficult to say with high confidence how to weigh these factors relative to others—throughout I have sought to caveat my claims. Nevertheless, it is reasonable to suggest that ideological projects can both predate and shape patterns of armed politics.

It is easy to think of ideas, discourse, and rhetoric as a smokescreen thrown up to hide "real" interests, or as epiphenomenal to them. And that can certainly be correct: only the truly naïve would simply map rhetoric onto reality. But this book shows that we need to take actors at least somewhat seriously when they articulate what they believe about how to create boundaries around and priorities within a polity.[12] There is a hard core of functional needs that armed organizations (states or not) need to achieve in order to continue to exist. But that core is fairly thin. Beyond it, political life becomes remarkably indeterminate— what, precisely, is the desired goal of political action? ISIS has its answers; Trotsky and Lenin theirs; Nehru his; the Pakistan Army its. We should obviously not assume that their political visions can explain all of their behaviors, but should also not assume that they are simply a cunning pretext for natural, obvious other goals.

As the empirical chapters showed, there was a wide range of possible alternative definitions of the nation that could have been pursued in South Asia; it mattered enormously which won out in the scramble for political power. We can reconstruct plausible counterfactual paths not taken that would be equally compatible with the objective military, political, and military realities facing a government. South Asia's politics would likely have unfolded very differently had Hindu nationalism reigned supreme in 1947 India or Bengali regionalism been fully represented in 1950s Pakistan. Threat perceptions are, in turn, inextricable from these broader political projects.

This book therefore offers a corrective to the vision of politics in much of the political violence literature: in influential accounts, ethnic groups or strongman factions battle for control of resources and patronage within the hollow shell of the state.[13] There is no ideology, no politics beyond that of greed and survival. This is sometimes a perfectly reasonable approximation of the situation: a number of the post–Cold War civil wars in Africa are characterized by scholars as meeting this model.

But in many hard-fought civil wars—much less the far broader scope of armed politics I explore in the book—we see highly ideological actors fighting for goals that do not seem obviously driven by straightforward greed or free-standing material interests. Whether the extraordinarily intense battles in 1918–23 Central and Eastern Europe and 1930s Spain, the intense left-right polarization that contributed to waves of war in the developing world during the Cold War, or the rise of actors like ISIS, it is impossible to make sense of how actors developed their preferences, organized their forces, and fought or laid down arms without understanding what they fought for and what they feared. Walter goes so far as to argue that we should characterize broad historical periods of civil wars by the ideological dimensions along which they were fought.[14]

Just as the "thugs as combatants" approach to explaining insurgent mobilization has fallen by the wayside in favor of more sophisticated arguments, the next goal should be developing richer accounts of how armed organizations (state and nonstate) perceive the political world and decide on their goals within it.[15] There has already been exciting progress in recent years, ranging from intra-group socialization to the targeting of violence to legacies of violence for political alignments.[16]

Where can research go next? Exploring ideology can involve an extraordinarily broad range of tools: big data text analysis, ethnography, interviews, primary sources and archives, careful examinations of public statements, surveys, and cross-national coding of armed group goals can all provide leverage on this question. It is important in such work to construct politically plausible counterfactuals that identify courses not taken and that can at least partially disentangle ideological arguments from potential alternatives. It is unlikely that any ideational theory will be a dominant "master variable": as in this book, tactical imperatives, international interventions, electoral politics, and a huge variety of other dynamics are always at work. Instead, it is likely that ideological variables will be most useful in helping to explain the sources of actors' political preferences and perceptions, which then set the stage for strategic interactions and responses to events. This suggests a research agenda that seeks to complement, rather than replace, existing arguments.

Rethinking Conflict Stabilization

The empirical evidence suggests that we need to broaden our understanding of how conflicts stabilize, end, or transform. Existing research is rich and impressive, but the dominant arguments do not tell us much about what happens in places where the international community has a limited role: key arguments in the literature highlight the role of third-party mediators and international peacekeeping.[17] But these cannot apply to South Asia, because the independent variable they focus on does not vary much: the international community has largely been locked out of a mediating or peacekeeping role in the countries I study here. Strikingly, there are reasons to believe that South Asia's experience may come to resemble the world's more generally as the era of peace-building interventions after the Cold War seems to be waning.[18] Furthermore, this evidence suggests that many conflicts stabilize or peter out into ambiguity and murkiness; these trajectories do not support a straightforward distinction between ongoing war versus a demobilizing peace settlement.

Instead, we see cease-fires and limited cooperation orders (and some alliances) that can last for years or even decades, groups disarming without formal deals, and even a few successful peace processes despite an almost total absence of international involvement. There are a number of ways that the guns can fall silent in state–armed group interactions—and there are plenty of interactions that never actually involve violence between these two actors in the first place.[19] Scholars need to move beyond a focus on formal, institutionalized peace processes that inevitably lead to demobilization because these are not the only relevant solutions to conflict.[20] If we think of state-group orders as representing a spectrum, then we should think of a similarly diverse range of pathways to some form of conflict stabilization and termination.

The most striking finding is that limited cooperation can be used to reduce the costs of violence without having to deal with the incredibly difficult process of full-scale demobilization. This is especially common, it seems, in conflicts with actors operating in a gray zone ideological space: for instance, secessionist and autonomist groups in India, post-1989 ethnic armed groups in Myanmar that reduced their war aims, and a number of Islamist armed actors in Pakistan. These groups can be quite "tolerable" as business partners, and both sides may get what they want out of the arrangement. By contrast, center-seeking and mortal enemy secessionists are much less likely to see such deals, since the political space for even a live-and-let-live bargain is more restricted.

Ideological projects can therefore help us understand which armed orders are the most likely cases for enduring cooperation short of demobilization (possibly as a waystation to demobilization, possibly not), and which are unlikely to end short of military defeat. The common analogy that guides existing work is a security dilemma in which conflict erupts if there is not a third-party to provide information and credible punishment for defection.[21] But sometimes states and groups instead cut deals, avoid one another, and even do business together. While there are plenty of wars that existing literature explains well, we need to accommodate gradations of cooperation and conflict, from those situations in which mutual coexistence is impossible to those in which tight alliances emerge.

Such a move requires new data that measure outcomes distinct from formal deals or cease-fires, new theories that can better capture the conditions under which mutual armament is compatible with absence of actual violent conflict within a state's formal borders, and a loosening of political science's strong, if often unspoken, normative attachments to peacekeeping, formal institutions, and the primacy of the central state. This does not mean developing an alternative normative attachment to local warlords, development aid as bribery, or collusive arrangements that freeze out civilians. But it does mean taking seriously the full range of variation in how conflicts end, wane, or evolve, instead of artificially restricting it.

This approach may help to answer a set of interesting questions. When is disarmament (as distinct from incorporation) seen as acceptable to both sides, and how are such arrangements negotiated? How do civilians view long-standing limited cooperation agreements in conflict zones—when are they seen as a reasonable way to carve out autonomy, as selling out by armed groups or the state, or as a kind of grim collusion from above that freezes out their voices? When do armed group leaders trust the government enough to accept incorporation without international involvement?[22] Why does limited cooperation sometimes collapse—what new information or political dynamics emerge after the onset of cooperation that break these deals apart? How do groups decide to shift toward electoral participation, and when do they decide to continue carrying arms into electoral politics?[23] What tensions exist in alliance orders, and when do they culminate in incorporation or a reduction in cooperation? Internal conflict is not going away, while the possibilities for serious international intervention to build peace may be diminishing, so thinking carefully and broadly about pathways to stabilization is essential for both scholarly and policy purposes.

The Weight of History

A recurring theme in this book is that politics is far from fluid: once institutions and meanings become relatively (though never totally) fixed, the room to maneuver shrinks, the range of plausible outcomes narrows, and the possibilities for radical change correspondingly restrict. Though it shares much with Straus's important work on ideas and state violence, which highlights the agency of postcolonial leaders, this book roots nationalist projects even deeper in colonial politics, which further limits their malleability.[24] There has been a strong historical turn in political science research, taking on very different forms, and this sensibility can be productively imported to political violence.[25]

If the section above offered some hope—that there are real possibilities to avoid open war even without a state monopoly of violence—this section is less hopeful. An implication is that the space for fluidity in conflict contexts can be highly limited, contributing to protracted and bloody wars reflecting deeply held political goals that make compromises undesirable despite the costs of conflict. The thinkable and politically plausible choices available to actors may be far more circumscribed in some contexts than others, and understanding this variation is likely to require deep contextual knowledge.[26]

This, unfortunately, helps us understand long-lasting wars and conflicts that seem to involve wildly disproportionate violence, especially state repression. While there is no doubt that military and demographic variables play a key role in how regimes decide to fight, they alone may be insufficient for understanding why intense crackdowns and enduring rebellions occur even when conceivable peace deals are on the table.[27] These dynamics are "strategic," but only because they reflect a cost-benefit assessment deeply shaped by ideological considerations.[28]

The staggering violence of anticommunist purges in 1965–66 Indonesia was propelled by both Islamist and secular anticommunist discourses that painted communists as alien and outsiders to the nation.[29] The Assad regime has faced the straightforward demographic challenge of being a minority-rule regime, but has adopted a strikingly vicious strategy accompanied by a rhetoric of disease and cleansing. Rather than seeking accommodation, deescalation, or third-party assurances to find a solution to the basic strategic problem of minority rule, the regime instead accepted extraordinary cost and risk in pursuit of total victory. As we saw in chapter 6, Ne Win could have very plausibly tried to cut a deal with the various ethnic armed groups dotting the Burmese periphery, but resolutely avoided doing so. Ideological projects are emphatically not the only explanation for any of these outcomes, but they help us understand why plausible alternative paths were not taken.

This is true in contexts other than civil war. The violence deployed by Bangladeshi political parties toward one another, revolving as they come in and out of power, cannot be easily disentangled from their different approaches to the meaning of Bangladeshi nationalism and the meaning of the 1971 liberation war. These parties certainly also face commitment problems, the complexities of patronage politics, and principal-agent challenges in controlling their members, so clashing nationalisms is certainly not all that is driving conflict—but there is no way to understand Bangladeshi politics without taking into account this underlying ideological dispute.[30]

Such projects may not be easy to change. Even after decades of democracy, anticommunist rhetoric and a war of narratives about 1965 persist in Indonesia. Ne Win's departure led to a tactical softening, but certainly not abandonment, of the Burmese military project. The Assad regime has largely won its civil war, regardless of the staggering cost. Bangladesh's ruling party has consolidated its rule and targeted those offering rival narratives. Just as there is a risk of scholars being naïve in taking ideological statements as prima facie true, so too there is a risk in scholars being naïve by not taking sufficiently seriously what regimes say about who they see as their enemies and what they plan to do to them. These statements reflect decades of politics, the creation of carrier movements and regimes, public opinion and public legitimation tactics, and a whole variety of other processes that can solidify a particular vision of politics along key ideological dimensions. This does not mean change is impossible, and I have pointed to such cases throughout the book, but it should temper optimistic assumptions about the speed and ease of shifts in government threat perceptions. Research can improve by historicizing the regimes, rebels, and other armed actors that constitute the political landscape.

Violence and "Mainstream" Politics

The evidence from this book shows that armed political parties, private armies, militias, and nominal rebels can be deeply involved in mainstream political life. Even when there is little or no active violence, these actors can be both present and influential. Riots, lynching, ethnic cleansing, assassinations, disappearances, and more mundane acts of day-to-day coercion can all be part of "normal" politics.[31] Even hardened insurgents can use violence and other resources to try to tip the political balance in their favor, whether intervening in elections, killing candidates, or covertly throwing support behind particular parties.[32]

Seemingly placid, uneventful politics can rest on huge apparatuses of state monitoring, repression, and social control. Regimes seek to garrison the political arena, using violence and its threat to hold at bay ideas, actors, and social forces that they perceive as threatening to undo the government's project. State building has two faces: on the one hand, shiny manifestations of quality bridges and effective governance; on the other, the midnight knock on the door and vast, murky zones of emergency powers, deniable violence, and both legal and illegal repression. It is little surprise that the most intensive campaigns of mass killing have been enacted by capable, robust, and ideologically driven regimes.[33]

Scholars need to think carefully, and critically, about how seemingly straightforward politics are undergirded by or intertwined with violence and coercion. Exploring these linkages is not easy—it requires empirical research into intentionally hidden phenomena, and a willingness to look bluntly at the ways in which the most mundane, bland, and straightforward processes may in fact involve deeply unsettling and normatively troubling state and armed group behavior. Distinctions in academic research between the developed and "developing" world, or between "normal" and "contentious" politics, are problematic. For instance, seemingly normal politics often is only possible because dissidents, radicals, and trouble-makers are eliminated or barred from political life. The contours that normalcy takes, for better and worse, are deeply shaped by who is kept out. There is a risk of taking for granted the shape of political arenas, rather than studying how precisely they are forged in the first place.[34]

This means systematically studying how armed groups get involved in elections, governance, and everyday political life, how governments use repression or its threat to shape what is categorized as mainstream politics, and the ways in which governments and armed groups openly or tacitly work together across a wide range of topics.[35] Criminal groups can be a natural extension of this focus, with street gangs, drug cartels, and organized crime sometimes shaping how governance and normal politics play out on the ground.[36]

States and Power

The traditional understanding of state power in political violence research draws explicitly or implicitly on a stylized Weberian approach—strong states have a legitimate monopoly of violence within their borders.[37] These tend to be accompanied by robust institutions that reach across territory and penetrate diverse social groupings. Indeed, as I discuss below, many policy prescriptions for dealing with violence and civil war recommend strengthening state capacity, demobilizing armed groups, and seeking establish a Weberian institutional state structure.[38]

This book suggests caution about assuming that this is what state power necessarily looks like. We need to stop assuming that state power is necessarily linked to violence monopolization, "legitimate" or not. First, states make choices about how to apply coercion—even objectively strong governments repress unevenly. In the United States, with its large and overlapping assemblages of internal security forces, right-wing militias seem to attract consistently less political attention than other armed actors on US soil, even when armed and expressing violent intent. Regimes that lack armed groups in their territory also decide which suspected dissidents and "unreliable" elements to place their repressive focus on.[39] The history of law enforcement many countries is one of varying attention, ranging from de facto neglect of urban peripheries to a heavy focus on protecting politically dominant social and economic groupings.[40]

It is extremely rare to have a stable, evenly distributed application of state attention. Even if a government does not view any armed (or unarmed) groups favorably, it is likely to still choose to focus on some over others. We need to understand what drives variation in those choices; as this book suggests, there is a deeper politics involved that can lead to some surprising outcomes even by repressive governments that do not actively favor any armed groups. Threat perception remains essential to understanding how state power is deployed, and why we see patterns of discrimination.

Second, more dramatically, governments may not perceive any political threat from armed groups—and under some circumstances may actually view them favorably. A monopoly of violence is not everywhere and always a top priority, nor does it seem to be essential in the eyes of security apparatuses that are, by any reasonable objective criteria, quite powerful. Militias, transnational militants, armed political parties, and networks of agents provocateurs and regime-friendly thugs can all be both useful assets without being seen to delegitimize the regime.[41] Such actors need not be intrinsic signs of state weakness; as Day and Reno provocatively suggest, the ability to do business with, and co-opt or defang, nonstate armed groups may in fact be a valuable tool of *expanding* state power.[42] A singular focus on a particular manifestation of state power—as bureaucratic monopoly—may lead us to miscode regimes as "weak" when in fact they are simply playing a different game than scholars think they should be.[43]

This implies an understanding of state power as best seen in action and strategy rather than its structural characteristics: the same bundle of state coercive capacity can be used in a wide variety of ways. State capacity is one of the most enduringly vexed concepts and measures in the social sciences.[44] In the murky realm of security and violence, it becomes even more so. While efforts to systematically measure variation in coercive capacity are important and should continue, there is also value to sometimes sidestepping these debates in favor of comparing how states actually use coercion and cooperation.

This does not mean capacity is irrelevant: I focused on states with relatively cohesive security institutions, and then explored variation within this context. The existence of medium-capacity security apparatuses in these cases obviously mattered, so this is a complementary claim rather than a full alternative approach.[45] The outcomes in India, for instance, surely would have looked different if there was a fragmented central regime and factionalized security services. But state capacity did not speak for itself. Thinking about states through the lens of strategies rather than structures has its uses and may allow the field to move away from debates about strong versus weak states that do not always capture how violence and order are actually produced.

Beyond Dyads: Toward Networks of Interaction

Theoretically, I began to integrate extradyadic dynamics by arguing that tactical overlap often develops as a result of the behavior of some third actor (for instance, insurgents working with states because of a shared enemy), while fragmentation and rivalry can affect ideological positioning. The empirical work here relies on dyadic data, whether in the quantitative dataset or the case studies. The cases regularly make reference to other groups and armed orders, but largely through mechanisms about tactical overlap or ideological distance. This dyad-year approach has serious limits, which I acknowledged repeatedly:

we can end up with numerous observations that are being driven in part by interactions with other actors. It can also "clutter" the data with many observations over the course of a decades-long dyad; an alternative approach would be to focus on "spells" of the same order, but doing so would miss the over-time changes in other variables that occur even as the same order holds.[46] For these reasons, among others, I used the quantitative data as evidence that the armed politics approach can be operationalized and to provide descriptive evidence on patterns of order, while relying on tight dialogue with qualitative evidence to move toward causal claims.

These are useful steps, but future work would benefit from a more explicit network orientation, both theoretically and empirically. There has been important work on armed group interactions, but it tends to be limited to explicit civil war contexts and periods of violence. This matters because other armed actors may play a central role in the calculations of both states and insurgents, and theoretically relevant interactions may occur even in the absence of violence. Bringing network tools into the broader world of armed politics is a promising way to extend both research agendas.[47] Thinking about armed politics more as a field of multisided, mutually interdependent interactions rather than as a simple collection of dyadic interactions is certainly closer to the reality of the situation that we see in a number of the cases. Building data that can capture this complex array of relationships, and theory that can generate clear, comprehensible predictions for patterns, is a major challenge, but one that would improve our understanding of multi-actor armed interactions.

Integrating the Study of Political Violence

These directions all lead toward a broader intellectual agenda. The study of civil war has been enormously productive. But it should not exist in its own self-reproducing silo. This book joins a broader wave of research showing that violence and its absence exist on a spectrum. Civil wars emerge from prewar interactions, they can end in a wide variety of ways, during their existence they influence and are influenced by many other political processes, from elections to political economy, and they have echoes of and affinities with non–civil war politics. Yet distinct literatures exist on electoral violence, state repression, revolutions, and state building and state capacity.[48]

Too often research projects anchored within one of these approaches artificially truncate the relevant independent variables, dependent variable, or both, leading to explanations and data that only capture a subset of the actual phenomenon being studied. This was clear in the armed politics data from South Asia—standard datasets of armed conflict were missing substantial swathes of theoretically relevant data, even when we restrict our focus to clearly insurgent groups. A fundamental, and defensible, conceptual choice drove this: for civil war datasets, "conflict" must involve ongoing battle deaths. But if we have a theory of strategic interaction between actors in which violence is only one possible outcome, it is not obvious why we should restrict observations to only years in which that battle death threshold is hit. Unless our theories no longer apply in years of twenty-four or fewer battle deaths, we should want to know just as much about the years of nonviolent interaction.[49]

This suggests the value of reorienting research toward a broader, more encompassing study of political violence, writ large. This book shows one way to engage with traditional civil war research while bringing new questions, approaches, and methods into dialogue with canonical literature. We should array a wide spectrum of potential organizational and individual behaviors as potential choices, and develop theories that can account for them in this full spectrum of possibilities. The armed politics approach moves toward this goal: it is intentionally agnostic about the nature and goals of the actors, flexible about their relationship with the state, and able to accommodate changes over time. Perhaps the most valuable contribution of this book would be helping analysts and scholars think more broadly about integrating research on conflict, violence, and political order under a shared analytical aegis.

Implications for Policy

This project is more useful for helping us think about conflict than it is in offering highly specific recommendations. A few key themes emerge, however, that can help shape ways of thinking about and managing armed politics.

Diverse Pathways to Order

This book suggests that policymakers and analysts may need to accept a much messier, more protracted, and more ambiguous set of outcomes than they have traditionally preferred. Clear conflict termination with demobilization and the creation of a consolidated and legitimate state monopoly of violence, backed by international guarantors and capacity building, is certainly a worthwhile goal to pursue.[50] But the evidence from South Asia shows that this is far from the only possible endgame. We actually saw some successful peace deals in the AOSA data, despite the lack of international guarantees and involvement—the Mizo National Front, for instance, negotiated and then implemented a highly successful peace deal with the government. This is good news, because the standard international tool kit for conflict management does not apply to most of the region, with governments deeply skeptical of a major international role. Yet the number of orders that end in clear incorporation nevertheless remains fairly small.

It is not hard to see why a stable, accommodative, and just monopoly of violence is so desirable. The problem is that achieving this outcome may be so difficult that falling back onto a deeply imperfect, but manageable, armed politics could be preferable. States are far more prolific jailers and killers than nonstate armed groups; handing Leviathan even more power should not be the default inclination of peace building. It is important to remember that the push for state capacity building can in fact accelerate conflict. The Myanmar military's push toward its borders in recent years, amid efforts at state-favoring cease-fires, has led to flare-ups of violence with armed groups, compared to periods of quiet when the state was not attempting to flex its military muscles.[51] Peace processes may have built into them particular biases that may favor one actor over another, with the state generally being the beneficiary of this bias.

Rather than a peaceful demobilization, most armed orders that ended did so in military collapse. This is a grim but important fact: as Toft and Luttwak have argued, sometimes military victory may be the most durable and decisive outcome.[52] Even relatively low-intensity conflicts are extremely punishing for small and badly outgunned groups. High-intensity conflicts, like that against the LTTE in Sri Lanka, can see a state summon huge amounts of coercive capacity and a willingness to do whatever it takes to prevail on the battlefield. It is difficult, however, to be enthusiastic about this as a general policy prescription for conflict management: it opens the door to impunity for severe human rights abuses, unnecessary civilian suffering, and the many unexpected consequences of conflict. While it is important to be clear-eyed about how orders actually end in order to provide realistic analysis, bloody total warfare is certainly not a solution.

There can be viable alternatives to either demobilization or military crackdowns. Such arrangements may be more organic and thus enduring than imposed or artificial peace efforts, and potentially involve lower costs than protracted warfare. Limited cooperation and alliances can often persist for long periods of time. Cease-fires, live-and-let-live deals, and active collaboration can all limit conflict and protect civilians from the worst excesses of open warfare. Both domestic and international actors should be more comfortable with this admittedly ambiguous set of outcomes—they may not be the best outcome, but they can be very importantly better than the worst.[53]

Yet it is essential to be clear about the downsides of embracing these in-between orders. Working with armed groups can involve deep trade-offs—such orders can be tenuous, often entrench corrupt or abusive armed groups and state authorities beyond the reach of institutional or popular accountabil-ity, limit the reach of state bureaucracies, and do not necessarily transition into stable and legitimate political order.[54] These are serious downsides that are often necessary to make state-group cooperation work: the nature of the deal frequently freezes out other actors and allows impunity for various kinds of normatively troubling behavior. These orders nevertheless need to at least be on the agenda for consideration: compared to the common alternatives of a brutal war to the death or pushing for implausible peace deals, such orders should be taken seriously as a way to reduce harm even if unable to achieve more expansive goals.

The contemporary politics of Iraq are illustrative: Kurdish armed groups, a fragmented Iraqi state, and a collection of Shiite militias is far from ideal, but the alternative of attempting to destroy or incorporate all of these armed groups under the aegis of an increasingly powerful and centralized regime would be sufficiently unpopular that it might very well spark more severe violence. The last thing the ethnic minorities of Myanmar want is to be fully exposed to the tender mercies of the military. Even from the perspective of outsiders, it is not remotely obvious that trying to promote centralization, state building, and vio-lence monopolization is the moral or wise choice in Myanmar. And for many huddled in northern Syria's refugee camps as of this writing, a messy and frac-tured distribution of control over violence may be far preferable to what would accompany the return of the Assad regime.

The point is not to valorize militias, warlord politics, or collusive bargains. It is simply to insist that formal peace settlements and state violence monopo-lization are not always necessary for stabilization or peace—and that under some circumstances they may be normatively preferable to building a state monopoly of violence.[55] A robust Weberian state tends to be a lovely thing for those on whose behalf it works, but can be a grim, blood-stained jail for those in its gunsights.

Rethinking Goals and Roles in Conflicts

These claims are especially important because there are reasons to believe that the global environment is moving toward increasingly limited space for ambitious international interventions. Recent studies have argued that the post–Cold War era of international intervention may have come to an end—instead, we see a greater focus on state sovereignty by rising powers, combined with limited Western interest in protracted interventions to build peace and state capacity in areas of conflict.[56] The United States is likely to remain focused on a blend of great power competition with light-footprint, special forces-oriented engagement in countermilitancy operations.[57] India, China, and Russia show little interest in expansive views of international involvement in internal conflicts, and Europe faces serious constraints on engaging in deep, costly engagements abroad. Indeed, proxy wars seem like the emerging front for transnational influences on internal conflict, rather than expanded peace building.

Under these conditions, the role of the international community will largely be one of nudges, support, resources, and facilitation; other than in particularly permissive political environments for intervention, outside players are unlikely to be the central actor in political reconstruction. Succeeding in achieving international goals will require substantially reduced expectations about international leverage and deep contextual knowledge about the worldviews and organizational capacities of both state and armed groups. It also requires accepting that the best practices developed in El Salvador, Kosovo, or Nepal may simply be irrelevant to Syria, Kashmir, or Thailand's Deep South.[58]

For both domestic governments and armed groups themselves, one analytical takeaway is that the perfect should not be the enemy of the good. Regimes often make unrealistic demands of armed groups. Sometimes this is mere pretext in pursuit of total domination, but it can instead reflect a greater self-confidence about the balance of power and interests than is reasonable.[59] Some armed groups are uninterested in negotiation, but many others are possible partners for deal making, either as a steady-state equilibrium or as the opening bid of a longer process of demobilization.

Pursuing these kinds of deals can require managing intense domestic political criticism for being soft on militancy or facilitating violence and corruption. Sometimes these criticisms are correct; the dark side of deal making can overwhelm its potential advantages. But when it is more desirable to limit violence, resisting domestic backlash is essential. Doing so successfully can involve everything from open defense of working with armed groups to the cultivation of ambiguity about what exactly is happening. This is an area in which normative values may often clash with one another and choices can quickly become very difficult: for instance, transparency should be a top priority, yet it can also sometimes undermine potential cooperation that would reduce conflict.[60] For governments that do embrace limited cooperation and alliance, careful attention is needed to limit the downsides, whether impunity, corruption, or the fusion of "normal" politics with violence and coercion.

The same very much applies to the potentially dangerous game of cultivating or working with violent actors within "mainstream" politics. Understanding the actual role of armed groups in areas without a monopoly of state violence requires a broad view of how armed groups can operate: they may also be political parties, like the CPM in West Bengal, Shiv Sena in Mumbai, and MQM in Karachi; or private armies run by local elites, as in parts of the Philippines; or de facto wings of the state security apparatus, like the Tamil paramilitaries of Sri Lanka. International interveners and government policymakers need to account for this diversity of functions as they navigate this terrain—there may be very complex and murky relationships among groups and between groups, governments (at various levels), and elites and social groups. Whether aiming to work with or undermine such groups, it is essential to have a realistic understanding of the functions they serve and the actors with whom they are aligned in any given context.

What can armed groups draw from these findings? They generally face far more constrained options than governments: other than a few unusually powerful nonstate actors, they tend to be weaker, poorer, and less linked to international flows of revenue and diplomacy than the governments with which they interact. Many groups, especially political parties and militias, have intrasystemic goals that limit their ambitions. The constraints on them are less binding, if still important, since they face fewer obstacles to achieving their political aims. But for those with more far-reaching goals, the findings here ought to be sobering: at least in the region I studied, collapse was the dominant outcome among groups that ended, victory was vanishingly rare, and incorporation tended to occur only after protracted negotiations, and often on terms that favored the government.[61] For groups considering violent mobilization, especially those that would fall into gray zone or opposed ideological categories, this should induce some caution; for those currently at war, it suggests hard truths about the odds of achieving more maximal ends.

There are some useful insights, however, that can provide the basis for crafting strategy. Negotiation can in fact deliver something of value despite huge power asymmetries. Deal making short of a full settlement or demobilization (such as cease-fires, alliances, or long-term limited cooperation) can preserve a degree of autonomy and independence that is likely better than alternatives. Many armed groups (especially political parties with coercive capacity) find niches within the political system that allow them to advance their interests, and even highly ambitious anti-state groups can survive for long periods of time. In this kind of environment, there are no silver bullets, but there are ways of successfully navigating even structurally daunting armed politics. This nevertheless often requires compromise and honest appreciation of the possible, engagement with civilian constituencies that can allow the group to maneuver most effectively, and a keen appreciation of the "red lines" that would invite the most severe state repression. The stakes are so high for armed groups precisely because their margin for error is so slim.

Understanding Government Threat Perceptions

It is a cliché that we need to understand history and context to make sense of conflict zones. But that does not just mean getting the facts right. It also means taking seriously (which is fundamentally different than justifying or agreeing with) the motivating ideologies and goals of conflict actors. This book puts heavy weight on the perceptions of governments and their security apparatuses. There is no doubt that ideological claims can mask more mundane military/functional, economic, or electoral incentives as well, but keeping ideological projects in mind is valuable in two key ways.

First, it can help us understand behavior that seems "objectively" disproportionate or even counterproductive, as well cases of inadequate repression. The Pakistani case is a clear example of the latter: various Western policymakers and analysts have been deeply frustrated over time by the unwilling of the military to crack down on various groups.[62] The Indonesian military and military-backed militias' slaughter of communists in 1965–66 is a case of the former—a campaign of repression that was wildly out of proportion to the communists' military power.[63] Without excusing or rationalizing either, understanding their threat perceptions as they were, rather than how outside analysts think they should be or wish they were, helps us understand—*not* justify—the patterns of behavior we see. Both militaries had threat perceptions that seemed to point to particular courses of action, based on assessments on the most pressing political threats to their desired nationalist project.

Second, focusing on historically rooted ideological projects provides insight into the conditions under which governments will be receptive to international pressure, whether inducements or coercion. The Myanmar military and many civilians in governments have proven highly resistant to international efforts to induce the safe return of Rohingya refugees purged by the military in 2017. Aung San Suu Kyi has actively defended the operations—and received substantial domestic political support for doing so.[64] Without in any way justifying any of this, it is the case that both military and civilian behavior is less surprising if we understand the way the Rohingya have been framed within the dominant nationalist narratives of independent Burma. Moreover, the homogenizing, authoritarian orientation of the powerful military has shown little evidence of dramatic change over the decades.

The ideological projects of governments play a central role in how they understand politics and respond to armed actors. These are deeply contextual and historically contingent, but can still be systematically compared along key dimensions, especially language, religion, and redistribution. This blend of context and comparison provides a flexible framework for identifying possible state strategies toward armed groups across the full of spectrum of conflict and cooperation. Pulling together ideological variables with a new approach to armed politics can help us make sense of the complex political landscapes of the twenty-first century.

Notes

INTRODUCTION

1. For recent overviews, see Shalaka Thakur and Rajesh Venugopal, "Parallel Governance and Political Order in Contested Territory: Evidence from the Indo-Naga Cease-fire," *Asian Security* 15, no. 3 (September 2, 2019): 285–303, https://doi.org/10.1080/14799 855.2018.1455185; Alex Waterman, "Counterinsurgents' Use of Force and 'Armed Orders' in Naga Northeast India," *Asian Security* 17, No. 1: 119–37, https://doi.org/10.1080/1479 9855.2020.1724099.

2. For earlier explanations of this approach, see Paul Staniland, "States, Insurgents, and Wartime Political Orders," *Perspectives on Politics* 10, no. 2 (2012): 243–64, https:// doi.org/10.1017/S1537592712000655; Paul Staniland, "Armed Politics and the Study of Intrastate Conflict," *Journal of Peace Research* 54, no. 4 (July 1, 2017): 459–67, https://doi. org/10.1177/0022343317698848. These were inspired in large part by Catherine Boone, *Political Topographies of the African State: Territorial Authority and Institutional Choice* (Cambridge: Cambridge University Press, 2003). Excellent recent work that explores dynamics of side switching or long-term cease-fires includes Sabine Otto, "The Grass Is Always Greener? Armed Group Side Switching in Civil Wars," *Journal of Conflict Resolution* 62, no. 7 (August 1, 2018): 1459–88, https://doi.org/10.1177/0022002717693047; Kolby Hanson, "Good Times and Bad Apples: Rebel Recruitment in Crackdown and Truce," *American Journal of Political Science*, https://doi.org/10.1111/ajps.12555; Sabine Otto, Adam Scharpf, and Anita R. Gohdes, "Capturing Group Alignments: Introducing the Government and Armed Actors Relations Dataset (GAARD)," *Research & Politics* 7, no. 4 (October 1, 2020): 2053168020971891, https://doi.org/10.1177/2053168020971891.

3. For a broader range of work on state–armed group relationships, see Rachel Kleinfeld and Elena Barham, "Complicit States and the Governing Strategy of Privilege Violence: When Weakness Is Not the Problem," *Annual Review of Political Science* 21, no. 1 (2018): 215–38, https://doi.org/10.1146/annurev-polisci-041916-015628; Kenneth John Menkhaus, "Governance without Government in Somalia: Spoilers, State Building, and the Politics of Coping," *International Security* 31, no. 3 (2007): 74–106; William Reno, *Warlord Politics and African States* (Boulder, CO: Lynne Rienner, 1998); William Reno, *Warfare in Independent Africa* (New York: Cambridge University Press, 2011); Dipali Mukhopadhyay, *Warlords, Strongman Governors, and the State in Afghanistan* (Cambridge: Cambridge University Press, 2014); David Keen, *The Economic Functions of Violence in Civil Wars* (Oxford: Oxford University Press for the International Institute for Strategic Studies, 1998); Otto, "The Grass Is Always Greener"; Lee J. M. Seymour, "Why Factions Switch Sides in Civil Wars: Rivalry, Patronage, and Realignment in Sudan," *International Security* 39, no. 2 (October 1, 2014): 92–131, https://doi.org/10.1162/ ISEC_a_00179; Costantino Pischedda, "Wars within Wars: Why Windows of Opportunity and Vulnerability Cause Rebel Fighting in Internal Conflicts," *International Security* 43, no. 1 (August 1, 2018): 138–76, https://doi.org/10.1162/isec_a_00322; Kathleen Gallagher Cunningham, *Inside the Politics of Self-Determination* (Oxford: Oxford University Press, 2014); Paul Staniland, "Between a Rock and a Hard Place: Insurgent Fratricide, Ethnic Defection, and the Rise of Pro-State Paramilitaries," *Journal of Conflict Resolution* 56, no. 1 (February 2012): 16–40, https://doi.org/10.1177/0022002711429681; Stathis

N. Kalyvas, "Ethnic Defection in Civil War," *Comparative Political Studies* 41, no. 8 (August 1, 2008): 1043–68, https://doi.org/10.1177/0010414008317949; Megan A. Stewart, "Civil War as State-Making: Strategic Governance in Civil War," *International Organization* 72, no. 1 (2018): 205–26, https://doi.org/10.1017/S0020818317000418; Leonard Wantchekon, "The Paradox of 'Warlord' Democracy: A Theoretical Investigation," *The American Political Science Review* 98, no. 1 (February 2004): 17–33.

4. Peter L Bergen, ed., *Talibanistan: Negotiating the Borders between Terror, Politics, and Religion* (New York: Oxford University Press, 2013); Zahid Hussain, *Frontline Pakistan: The Struggle with Militant Islam* (New York: Columbia University Press, 2007). Though I focus in this book on state-group dynamics, the framework is applicable to relationships among armed groups as well; groups may fight, ally, or cooperate with one another, not just with the state. Fotini Christia, *Alliance Formation in Civil Wars* (Cambridge: Cambridge University Press, 2012); Kristin M. Bakke, Kathleen Gallagher Cunningham, and Lee J. M. Seymour, "A Plague of Initials: Fragmentation, Cohesion, and Infighting in Civil Wars," *Perspectives on Politics* 10, no. 2 (2012): 265–83, https://doi.org/10.1017/S1537592712000667; Peter Krause, *Rebel Power: Why National Movements Compete, Fight, and Win* (Ithaca: Cornell University Press, 2017); Tricia Bacon, "Is the Enemy of My Enemy My Friend?," *Security Studies* 27, no. 3 (July 3, 2018): 345–78, https://doi.org/10.1080/09636412.2017.1416813; Leonard Wantchekon, "The Paradox of 'Warlord' Democracy: A Theoretical Investigation," *American Political Science Review* 98, no. 1 (February 1, 2004): 17–33.

5. Edward Aspinall, *Islam and Nation: Separatist Rebellion in Aceh, Indonesia* (Stanford, CA: Stanford University Press, 2009), outlines the intricacies of GAM-state armed orders over time.

6. This resembles what Staniland, "States, Insurgents, and Wartime Political Orders," refers to as "passive cooperation." See also Reno, *Warlord Politics* and *Warfare in Independent Africa*, and Jesse Driscoll, "Commitment Problems or Bidding Wars? Rebel Fragmentation as Peace Building," *Journal of Conflict Resolution* 56, no. 1 (February 1, 2012): 118–49, https://doi.org/10.1177/0022002711429696.

7. Paul Richards, *No Peace No War: Anthropology Of Contemporary Armed Conflicts*, 1st ed. (Athens : Oxford: Ohio University Press, 2004).

8. Paul Staniland, "Militias, Ideology, and the State," *Journal of Conflict Resolution* 59, no. 5 (August 1, 2015): 770–93, https://doi.org/10.1177/0022002715576749.

9. Seth G. Jones and Christine C. Fair, *Counterinsurgency in Pakistan* (Santa Monica, CA: Rand Corporation, 2010).

10. In 2014, this shifted to alliance in the face of the rise of the Islamic State.

11. John Sidel, *Capital, Coercion, and Crime: Bossism in the Philippines* (Stanford, CA: Stanford University Press, 1999).

12. Christia, *Alliance Formation in Civil Wars*; Stephen M. Walt, *The Origins of Alliances* (Ithaca: Cornell University Press, 1987).

13. Staniland, "Armed Politics"; Sabine C. Carey, Michael P. Colaresi, and Neil J. Mitchell, "Governments, Informal Links to Militias, and Accountability," *Journal of Conflict Resolution* 59, no. 5 (August 1, 2015): 850–76, https://doi.org/10.1177/0022002715576747; Philip G. Roessler, "Donor-Induced Democratization and the Privatization of State Violence in Kenya and Rwanda," *Comparative Politics* 37, no. 2 (January 1, 2005): 207–27, https://doi.org/10.2307/20072883; Milli Lake, "Building the Rule of War: Postconflict Institutions and the Micro-Dynamics of Conflict in Eastern DR Congo," *International Organization* 71, no. 2 (April 2017): 281–315, https://doi.org/10.1017/S002081831700008X.

14. Matt Bradley and Raja Abdulrahim, "U.S., Iranian-Backed Shiite Militias Share Uneasily in Battle for Iraq's Tikrit," *Wall Street Journal*, March 29, 2015, sec. World, https://www.wsj.com/articles/u-s-iranian-backed-shiite-militias-share-uneasily-in-battle-for-iraqs-tikrit-1427672890.

15. Staniland, "Between a Rock and a Hard Place."

16. Catherine Boone, "Politically Allocated Land Rights and the Geography of Electoral Violence The Case of Kenya in the 1990s," *Comparative Political Studies* 44, no. 10 (October 1, 2011): 1311–42, https://doi.org/10.1177/0010414011407465; Susanne Mueller, "The Political Economy of Kenya's Crisis," in *Voting in Fear: Electoral Violence in Sub-Saharan Africa*, ed. Dorina Akosua Oduraa Bekoe (Washington, DC: United States Institute of Peace, 2012), 145–80.

17. Ian Douglas Wilson, *The Politics of Protection Rackets in Post-New Order Indonesia: Coercive Capital, Authority, and Street Politics*, 1st ed. (London: Routledge, 2015); Gerry van Klinken, *Communal Violence and Democratization in Indonesia: Small Town Wars* (London: Routledge, 2007); Yuhki Tajima, *The Institutional Origins of Communal Violence: Indonesia's Transition from Authoritarian Rule* (New York: Cambridge University Press, 2014); Sana Jaffrey, "Leveraging the Leviathan: Politics of Impunity and the Rise of Vigilantism in Democratic Indonesia" (PhD diss., University of Chicago, 2019).

18. Robert Gerwarth and John Horne, *War in Peace: Paramilitary Violence in Europe after the Great War* (Oxford: Oxford University Press, 2013).

19. C. Christine Fair, "Lessons from India's Experience in the Punjab, 1978–1993," in *India and Counterinsurgency: Lessons Learned*, ed. Sumit Ganguly and David P Fidler (London: Routledge, 2009), chapter 8; Sameer P. Lalwani, "Size Still Matters: Explaining Sri Lanka's Counterinsurgency Victory over the Tamil Tigers," *Small Wars & Insurgencies* 28, no. 1 (January 2, 2017): 119–65, https://doi.org/10.1080/09592318.2016.1263470; Bertil Lintner, *The Rise and Fall of the Communist Party of Burma (CPB)* (Ithaca: SEAP Publications, 1990).

20. Sidel, *Capital, Coercion, and Crime.*

21. Karen Barkey, *Bandits and Bureaucrats: The Ottoman Route to State Centralization* (Ithaca: Cornell University Press, 1994). Charles Tilly, *Coercion, Capital, and European States, AD 990–1992* (Cambridge, MA: Blackwell, 1992). For sophisticated recent studies that explore more complex relationships within and between states, see Rachel A. Schwartz, "Civil War, Institutional Change, and the Criminalization of the State: Evidence from Guatemala," *Studies in Comparative International Development* 55, no. 3 (September 1, 2020): 381–401, https://doi.org/10.1007/s12116-020-09312-7; Rachel Sweet, "Bureaucrats at War: The Resilient State in the Congo," 19, no. 475, African Affairs (2020): 224–50.

22. For major contributions to defining and measuring civil conflict, see James D. Fearon and David D. Laitin, "Ethnicity, Insurgency, and Civil War," *American Political Science Review* 97, no. 1 (February 2003): 75–90; Nicholas Sambanis, "What Is Civil War? Conceptual and Empirical Complexities of an Operational Definition," *Journal of Conflict Resolution* 48, no. 6 (December 2004): 814–58; Nils Petter Gleditsch et al., "Armed Conflict 1946–2001: A New Dataset," *Journal of Peace Research* 39, no. 5 (September 1, 2002): 615–37, https://doi.org/10.1177/0022343302039005007; Janet I. Lewis, "How Does Ethnic Rebellion Start?," *Comparative Political Studies* 50, no. 10 (September 1, 2017): 1420–50, https://doi.org/10.1177/0010414016672235; Kristine Eck and Lisa Hultman, "One-Sided Violence Against Civilians in War: Insights from New Fatality Data," *Journal of Peace Research* 44, no. 2 (2007): 233–46.

23. Reno, *Warfare in Independent Africa*, maps out a variety of ways armed groups have operated in Africa, showing that this insight is in no way limited to South Asia. Similarly, see Roessler, "Donor-Induced Democratization and the Privatization of State Violence in Kenya and Rwanda"; Dorina Akosua Oduraa Bekoe, ed., *Voting in Fear: Electoral Violence in Sub-Saharan Africa* (Washington, DC: United States Institute of Peace, 2012); Catherine Boone, *Property and Political Order in Africa: Land Rights and the Structure of Politics* (New York: Cambridge University Press, 2014); Philip Roessler, *Ethnic Politics and State Power in Africa: The Logic of the Coup-Civil War Trap* (Cambridge: Cambridge University

Press, 2016); Christopher R. Day and William S. Reno, "In Harm's Way: African Counter-Insurgency and Patronage Politics," *Civil Wars* 16, no. 2 (April 3, 2014): 105–26, https://doi.org/10.1080/13698249.2014.927699; Jeremy Weinstein, *Inside Rebellion: The Politics of Insurgent Violence* (Cambridge: Cambridge University Press, 2007).

24. On levels of analyses in civil conflict, see Stathis N. Kalyvas, "The Ontology of 'Political Violence': Action and Identity in Civil Wars," *Perspectives on Politics* 1, no. 3 (2003): 475–94; Christia, *Alliance Formation in Civil Wars*; Evgeny Finkel, *Ordinary Jews: Choice and Survival during the Holocaust* (Princeton, NJ: Princeton University Press, 2017); Sarah Elizabeth Parkinson, "Organizing Rebellion: Rethinking High-Risk Mobilization and Social Networks in War," *American Political Science Review* 107, no. 03 (2013): 418–32, https://doi.org/10.1017/S0003055413000208; Anastasia Shesterinina, "Collective Threat Framing and Mobilization in Civil War," *American Political Science Review* 110, no. 3 (August 2016): 411–27, https://doi.org/10.1017/S0003055416000277.

25. Among others, see Erica Chenoweth and Maria J. Stephan, *Why Civil Resistance Works: The Strategic Logic of Nonviolent Conflict* (New York: Columbia University Press, 2011). Adria Lawrence, *Imperial Rule and the Politics of Nationalism: Anti-Colonial Protest in the French Empire* (Cambridge: Cambridge University Press, 2013); Kathleen Gallagher Cunningham, Marianne Dahl, and Anne Frugé, "Strategies of Resistance: Diversification and Diffusion," *American Journal of Political Science* 61, no. 3 (2017): 591–605, https://doi.org/10.1111/ajps.12304; Ches Thurber, "Social Ties and the Strategy of Civil Resistance," *International Studies Quarterly*, accessed November 13, 2019, https://doi.org/10.1093/isq/sqz049; Nimmi Gowrinathan and Zachariah Mampilly, "Resistance and Repression under the Rule of Rebels: Women, Clergy, and Civilian Agency in LTTE Governed Sri Lanka," *Comparative Politics* 52, no. 1 (October 1, 2019): 1–20.

26. Erica Chenoweth and Adria Lawrence, eds., *Rethinking Violence: States and Non-State Actors in Conflict* (Cambridge, MA: MIT Press, 2010).

27. On how regimes treat dissident movements, see Marie-Eve Reny, *Authoritarian Containment: Public Security Bureaus and Protestant House Churches in Urban China* (Oxford, New York: Oxford University Press, 2018); Lisa Blaydes, *State of Repression: Iraq under Saddam Hussein* (Princeton: Princeton University Press, 2018) Lisa Blaydes, *State of Repression: Iraq under Saddam Hussein* (Princeton, NJ: Princeton University Press, 2018); Christian Davenport, "State Repression and Political Order," *Domestic Political Violence and Civil War* 1, no. 1 (2013): 1–23, https://doi.org/10.1146/annurev.polisci.10.101405.143216; Christian Davenport et al., "The Consequences of Contention: Understanding the Aftereffects of Political Conflict and Violence," *Annual Review of Political Science* 22, no. 1 (2019): 361–77, https://doi.org/10.1146/annurev-polisci-050317-064057.

28. Among many others, see Stathis N. Kalyvas, *The Logic of Violence in Civil War* (Cambridge: Cambridge University Press, 2006); Stathis N. Kalyvas, "The Landscape of Political Violence," *The Oxford Handbook of Terrorism*, March 14, 2019, https://doi.org/10.1093/oxfordhb/9780198732914.013.1; Roger Dale Petersen, *Resistance and Rebellion: Lessons from Eastern Europe* (Cambridge: Cambridge University Press, 2001). Elisabeth Jean Wood, *Insurgent Collective Action and Civil War in El Salvador*, Cambridge Studies in Comparative Politics (New York: Cambridge University Press, 2003); Zachariah Cherian Mampilly, *Rebel Rulers: Insurgent Governance and Civilian Life during War* (Ithaca: Cornell University Press, 2011); Eli Berman et al., *Small Wars, Big Data: The Information Revolution in Modern Conflict* (Princeton, NJ: Princeton University Press, 2018); Jason Lyall, Graeme Blair, and Kosuke Imai, "Explaining Support for Combatants during Wartime: A Survey Experiment in Afghanistan," *American Political Science Review* 107, no. 04 (2013): 679–705, https://doi.org/10.1017/S0003055413000403; Dara Kay Cohen, *Rape during Civil War* (Ithaca: Cornell University Press, 2016); Jessica A. Stanton, *Violence and Restraint in Civil War: Civilian Targeting in the Shadow of*

International Law, Reprint ed. (New York: Cambridge University Press, 2016); Laia Balcells, *Rivalry and Revenge: The Politics of Violence during Civil War* (Cambridge: Cambridge University Press, 2017); Abbey Steele, *Democracy and Displacement in Colombia's Civil War*, 1st ed. (Ithaca: Cornell University Press, 2017); Ana Arjona, *Rebelocracy: Social Order in the Colombian Civil War* (Cambridge: Cambridge University Press, 2016); Asfandyar Mir, "What Explains Counterterrorism Effectiveness? Evidence from the U.S. Drone War in Pakistan," *International Security* 43, no. 2 (November 1, 2018): 45–83, https://doi.org/10.1162/isec_a_00331; Robert A. Blair, Sabrina M. Karim, and Benjamin S. Morse, "Establishing the Rule of Law in Weak and War-Torn States: Evidence from a Field Experiment with the Liberian National Police," *American Political Science Review* 113, no. 3 (August 2019): 641–57, https://doi.org/10.1017/S0003055419000121; Mara Revkin, "What Explains Taxation by Resource-Rich Rebels? Evidence from the Islamic State in Syria," *Journal of Politics* 82, No. 2 (April 2020): 757–64, https://doi.org/10.1086/706597.

29. Roessler, *Ethnic Politics and State Power in Africa*; Scott Straus, *Making and Unmaking Nations: War, Leadership, and Genocide in Modern Africa* (Ithaca: Cornell University Press, 2015); Vincent Boudreau, *Resisting Dictatorship: Repression and Protest in Southeast Asia* (Cambridge: Cambridge University Press, 2004); Stuart J. Kaufman, "Symbolic Politics or Rational Choice? Testing Theories of Extreme Ethnic Violence," *International Security* 30, no. 4 (2006): 45–86; Barbara F Walter, *Reputation and Civil War: Why Separatist Conflicts Are so Violent* (Cambridge: Cambridge University Press, 2009); Reno, *Warfare in Independent Africa*.

30. For important recent work on ideology and armed conflict more broadly, see Straus, *Making and Unmaking Nations*; Barbara F. Walter, "The Extremist's Advantage in Civil Wars," *International Security* 42, no. 2 (November 1, 2017): 7–39, https://doi.org/10.1162/ISEC_a_00292; Francisco Gutiérrez Sanín and Elisabeth Jean Wood, "Ideology in Civil War Instrumental Adoption and Beyond," *Journal of Peace Research* 51, no. 2 (March 1, 2014): 213–26, https://doi.org/10.1177/0022343313514073; Amelia Hoover Green, *The Commander's Dilemma: Violence and Restraint in Wartime* (Ithaca: Cornell University Press, 2018); Staniland, "Militias, Ideology, and the State"; Jonathan Leader Maynard, "Ideology and Armed Conflict," *Journal of Peace Research* 56, no. 5 (September 1, 2019): 635–49, https://doi.org/10.1177/0022343319826629; Kanchan Chandra and Omar García-Ponce, "Why Ethnic Subaltern-Led Parties Crowd Out Armed Organizations: Explaining Maoist Violence in India," *World Politics* 71, no. 2 (April 2019): 367–416, https://doi.org/10.1017/S004388711800028X; Sarah Parkinson, "Practical Ideology in Rebel Groups," *World Politics* (forthcoming); Stefano Costalli and Andrea Ruggeri, "Indignation, Ideologies, and Armed Mobilization: Civil War in Italy, 1943–45," *International Security* 40, no. 2 (October 1, 2015): 119–57, https://doi.org/10.1162/ISEC_a_00218.

31. Sheri Berman, *The Social Democratic Moment: Ideas and Politics in the Making of Interwar Europe by Sheri Berman* (Cambridge, MA: Harvard University Press, 1998); Stephen E. Hanson, *Post-Imperial Democracies: Ideology and Party Formation in Third Republic France, Weimar Germany, and Post-Soviet Russia* (New York: Cambridge University Press, 2010).

32. Shivaji Mukherjee, "Why Are the Longest Insurgencies Low Violence? Politician Motivations, Sons of the Soil, and Civil War Duration," *Civil Wars* 16, no. 2 (April 3, 2014): 172–207, https://doi.org/10.1080/13698249.2014.927702.

33. A discussion of the state of the literature on nonstate armed groups can be found in Sarah E. Parkinson and Sherry Zaks, "Militant and Rebel Organization(s)," *Comparative Politics* 50, no. 2 (2018): 271–90, https://doi.org/10.2307/26532682.

34. The armed politics framework also cannot account well for violence by weakly institutionalized or localized networks of rioters and specialists in violence. These are

enormously important, but this book's approach is most useful for better organized, enduring armed nonstate institutions and their relationships with state power. Recent work on these dynamics includes Nicholas Rush Smith, *Contradictions of Democracy: Vigilantism and Rights in Post-Apartheid South Africa* (New York: Oxford University Press, 2019); and Sana Jaffrey, "Leveraging the Leviathan: Politics of Impunity and the Rise of Vigilantism in Democratic Indonesia" (PhD dissertation, University of Chicago, 2019).

35. The basic methodological approach of the book, layering different kinds of comparisons and forms of evidence, follows from Henry E. Brady and David Collier, eds., *Rethinking Social Inquiry: Diverse Tools, Shared Standards* (Lanham, MD: Rowman & Littlefield, 2004); James Mahoney, "After KKV: The New Methodology of Qualitative Research," *World Politics* 62, no. 1 (January 14, 2010): 120–47; Alexander L. George and Andrew Bennett, *Case Studies and Theory Development in the Social Sciences* (Cambridge, MA: MIT Press, 2005).

36. Paul Pierson, *Politics in Time: History, Institutions, and Social Analysis* (Princeton, NJ: Princeton University Press, 2004).

37. On similarity and difference across the subcontinent, see Adnan Naseemullah and Paul Staniland, "Indirect Rule and Varieties of Governance," *Governance* 29, no. 1 (2016): 13–30, https://doi.org/10.1111/gove.12129; Adnan Naseemullah, "Riots and Rebellion: State, Society and the Geography of Conflict in India," *Political Geography* 63 (March 1, 2018): 104–15, https://doi.org/10.1016/j.polgeo.2017.06.006; Shivaji Mukherjee, "Colonial Origins of Maoist Insurgency in India: Historical Institutions and Civil War," *Journal of Conflict Resolution* 62, no. 10 (November 1, 2018): 2232–74, https://doi.org/10.1177/0022002717727818; Abhijit Banerjee and Lakshmi Iyer, "History, Institutions, and Economic Performance: The Legacy of Colonial Land Tenure Systems in India," *American Economic Review* 95, no. 4 (September 1, 2005): 1190–1213.

CHAPTER 1. THE POLITICS OF THREAT PERCEPTION

1. For a comparison of FBI responses to the KKK, New Left, and Black Panthers, see David Cunningham, *There's Something Happening Here: The New Left, the Klan, and FBI Counterintelligence* (Berkeley: University of California Press, 2004).

2. Jan-Werner Müller, *Contesting Democracy: Political Ideas in Twentieth-Century Europe*, Reprint ed. (New Haven, CT: Yale University Press, 2013); Alexander S. Kirshner, *A Theory of Militant Democracy: The Ethics of Combatting Political Extremism* (New Haven, CT: Yale University Press, 2014).

3. Peter J. Katzenstein, *Cultural Norms and National Security: Police and Military in Postwar Japan* (Ithaca: Cornell University Press, 1996), 71–77.

4. Sheri Berman, *The Social Democratic Moment: Ideas and Politics in the Making of Interwar Europe by Sheri Berman* (Cambridge, MA: Harvard University Press, 1998).

5. Jonathan Leader Maynard, "Ideology and Armed Conflict," *Journal of Peace Research* 56, no. 5 (September 1, 2019): 635–49, https://doi.org/10.1177/0022343319826629.

6. See, among others Scott Straus, *Making and Unmaking Nations: War, Leadership, and Genocide in Modern Africa* (Ithaca: Cornell University Press, 2015); Daron Acemoglu and James Robinson, *Economic Origins of Dictatorship and Democracy* (New York: Cambridge University Press, 2006); Carles Boix, "Economic Roots of Civil Wars and Revolutions in the Contemporary World," *World Politics* 60, no. 3 (2008): 390–437; Lars-Erik Cederman, Andreas Wimmer, and Brian Min, "Why Do Ethnic Groups Rebel? New Data and Analysis," *World Politics* 62, no. 1 (2010): 87–119. Davenport introduces a multidimensional approach to threat dimension in which multiple aspects of politics can shape government responses in Christian Davenport, "Multi-Dimensional Threat Perception and State Repression: An Inquiry into Why States Apply Negative Sanctions," *American Journal of Political Science* 39, no. 3 (1995): 683–713, https://doi.org/10.2307/2111650.

7. Straus, *Making and Unmaking Nations*; Deborah J. Yashar, *Contesting Citizenship in Latin America: The Rise of Indigenous Movements and the Postliberal Challenge* (Cambridge: Cambridge University Press, 2005); Niraja Gopal Jayal, *Citizenship and Its Discontents* (Cambridge, MA: Harvard University Press, 2013).

8. Alfred Stepan, Juan Linz, and Yogendra Yadav, *Crafting State-Nations: India and Other Multinational Democracies* (Baltimore: Johns Hopkins University Press, 2011); Anthony W. Marx, *Faith in Nation: Exclusionary Origins of Nationalism* (New York: Oxford University Press, 2003).

9. For the United States in comparative perspective, see Robert C. Lieberman et al., "The Trump Presidency and American Democracy: A Historical and Comparative Analysis," *Perspectives on Politics* 17, no. 2 (June 2019): 470–79, https://doi.org/10.1017/S1537592718003286.

10. Maya Tudor and Dan Slater, "Nationalism, Authoritarianism, and Democracy: Historical Lessons from South and Southeast Asia," *Perspectives on Politics*, forthcoming; Straus, *Making and Unmaking Nations*.

11. For instance, Pradeep K. Chhibber, *Ideology and Identity: The Changing Party Systems of India*, Reprint ed. (New York: Oxford University Press, 2018), offers an important mapping of ideological space that he argues is specific to India. While his account is richer, mine can at least partially accommodate it by pointing to variation along the left-right and religious dimensions.

12. Ben Kiernan, *The Pol Pot Regime: Race, Power, and Genocide in Cambodia under the Khmer Rouge, 1975–79*, 3rd ed. (New Haven, CT: Yale University Press, 2008); Michael Walzer, *The Paradox of Liberation: Secular Revolutions and Religious Counterrevolutions*, Reprint ed. (New Haven, CT: Yale University Press, 2016); Ramachandra Guha, *India after Gandhi: The History of the World's Largest Democracy*, 1st ed. (New York: Ecco, 2007).

13. For foundational work seeking to explore differences between ethnic and ideological conflicts, see Chaim Kaufmann, "Possible and Impossible Solutions to Ethnic Civil Wars," *International Security* 20, no. 4 (spring 1996): 136–75; Nicholas Sambanis, "Do Ethnic and Nonethnic Civil Wars Have the Same Causes? A Theoretical and Empirical Inquiry (Part 1)," *The Journal of Conflict Resolution* 45, no. 3 (2001): 259–82.

14. Thomas Blom Hansen, *The Saffron Wave: Democracy and Hindu Nationalism in Modern India* (Princeton, NJ: Princeton University Press, 1999), 27.

15. See, among many others, Vincent Boudreau, *Resisting Dictatorship: Repression and Protest in Southeast Asia* (Cambridge: Cambridge University Press, 2004); Evgeny Finkel, "The Phoenix Effect of State Repression: Jewish Resistance during the Holocaust," *American Political Science Review* 109, no. 2 (May 2015): 339–53, https://doi.org/10.1017/S000305541500009X; Evgeny Finkel, Scott Gehlbach, and Tricia D. Olsen, "Does Reform Prevent Rebellion? Evidence From Russia's Emancipation of the Serfs," *Comparative Political Studies* 48, no. 8 (July 1, 2015): 984–1019, https://doi.org/10.1177/0010414014565887; Christian Davenport, "State Repression and Political Order," *Annual Review of Political Science* 10, no. 1 (2007): 1–23, https://doi.org/10.1146/annurev.polisci.10.101405.143216; Marie-Eve Reny, *Authoritarian Containment: Public Security Bureaus and Protestant House Churches in Urban China* (Oxford: Oxford University Press, 2018).

16. Scott Straus, ed., *Remaking Rwanda: State Building and Human Rights after Mass Violence*, 1st ed. (Madison: University of Wisconsin Press, 2011); Filip Reyntjens, "Rwanda: Progress or Powder Keg?," *Journal of Democracy* 26, no. 3 (July 13, 2015): 19–33, https://doi.org/10.1353/jod.2015.0043.

17. Ronald Grigor Suny, *The Revenge of the Past: Nationalism, Revolution, and the Collapse of the Soviet Union*, 1st ed. (Stanford, CA: Stanford University Press, 1993).

18. Robert Gerwarth and John Horne, "Bolshevism as Fantasy: Fear of Revolution and Counter-Revolutionary Violence, 1917–1923," in *War in Peace: Paramilitary Violence in Europe after the Great War* (Oxford: Oxford University Press, 2013), 44.

19. Gerwarth and Horne, "Bolshevism as Fantasy," 42. They find that similar dynamics occurred in Britain and, especially, France (where communists, Jews, and Free Masons were fused together), but that these "governments took a calmer view and distinguished carefully between home-grown labour militancy and native socialism on the one hand, the actual threat from Russian communism on the other"; by contrast, "anti-Bolshevik myths" and "fantasies" drove a much harder-line reaction in central Europe and northern Italy, spurring intense counterrevolutionary armed mobilization (51).

20. Straus, *Making and Unmaking Nations*, 56.

21. This approach is frequently found in the study of African civil wars, which see extremely weak regimes beset on all sides (including from within) by challengers in an environment rich in economic resources to be looted or captured. See Philip Roessler, *Ethnic Politics and State Power in Africa: The Logic of the Coup-Civil War Trap* (Cambridge: Cambridge University Press, 2016); William Reno, *Warfare in Independent Africa* (New York: Cambridge University Press, 2011). A skeptical take can be found in Marielle Debos, *Living by the Gun in Chad: Combatants, Impunity, and State Formation* (London: Zed Books, 2016). This may accurately describe many of these wars, but such an approach has limited resonance in many other parts of the world.

22. Sheri Berman, *The Social Democratic Moment: Ideas and Politics in the Making of Interwar Europe by Sheri Berman* (Cambridge, MA: Harvard University Press, 1998); and especially Sheri Berman, *The Primacy of Politics: Social Democracy and the Making of Europe's Twentieth Century* (Cambridge: Cambridge University Press, 2006), 11.

23. This broadens the range of possible moments of ideological entrepreneurship from Straus's focus on initial postindependence regimes and moments of regime change from one-party rule to democracy, though it can include both (cf. Straus, *Making and Unmaking Nations*, 63). We both note that turnover in parties can matter, but is less systematically important.

24. Ian Lustick, *Unsettled States, Disputed Lands: Britain and Ireland, France and Algeria, Israel and the West Bank-Gaza* (Ithaca: Cornell University Press, 1993), 123.

25. Steven R. Levitsky and Lucan A. Way, "Beyond Patronage: Violent Struggle, Ruling Party Cohesion, and Authoritarian Durability," *Perspectives on Politics* 10, no. 4 (2012): 869–89, https://doi.org/10.1017/S1537592712002861.

26. We should see much less change in ideological project when coups amount to a "reshuffling" of the elite deck.

27. Alfred C. Stepan, *The Military in Politics: Changing Patterns in Brazil* (Princeton, NJ: Princeton University Press, 1974).

28. Harold A. Crouch, *The Army and Politics in Indonesia* (Ithaca: Cornell University Press, 1978); Ulf Sundhaussen, *The Road to Power: Indonesian Military Politics, 1945–1967* (Oxford: Oxford University Press, 1982); Katharine E. McGregor, *History in Uniform: Military Ideology and the Construction of Indonesia's Past* (Singapore: NUS Press, 2007); Geoffrey B. Robinson, *The Killing Season: A History of the Indonesian Massacres, 1965–66* (Princeton, NJ: Princeton University Press, 2018).

29. Pablo Policzer, *Rise and Fall of Repression in Chile* (Notre Dame, IN: University of Notre Dame Press, 2009), 49, 50.

30. On the American case, see Robert C. Lieberman et al., "The Trump Presidency and American Democracy: A Historical and Comparative Analysis," *Perspectives on Politics* 17, no. 2 (June 2019): 470–79, https://doi.org/10.1017/S1537592718003286; John Sides, Michael Tesler, and Lynn Vavreck, *Identity Crisis: The 2016 Presidential Campaign and the Battle for the Meaning of America* (Princeton, NJ: Princeton University Press, 2018).

31. James C. Scott, "Revolution in the Revolution: Peasants and Commissars," *Theory and Society* 7, no. 1/2 (March 1979): 97–134; Ranajit Guha, *Elementary Aspects of Peasant Insurgency in Colonial India* (Durham, NC: Duke University Press, 1999).

32. Straus, *Making and Unmaking Nations*, 65.

33. Straus, *Making and Unmaking Nations*, 65.

34. Benjamin Smith, "Life of the Party: The Origins of Regime Breakdown and Persistence under Single-Party Rule," *World Politics* 57, no. 3 (2005): 421–51; Levitsky and Way, "Beyond Patronage."

35. Jeffrey Ira Herbst, *States and Power in Africa: Comparative Lessons in Authority and Control* (Princeton, NJ: Princeton University Press, 2000).

36. Christophe Jaffrelot, *The Hindu Nationalist Movement in India* (New York: Columbia University Press, 1996); Milan Vaishnav, ed., *The BJP in Power: Indian Democracy and Religious Nationalism* (Washington, DC: Carnegie Endowment for International Peace, 2019).

37. On the functional challenges of state formation and maintenance, see classic work by Theda Skocpol, *States and Social Revolutions: A Comparative Analysis of France, Russia, and China* (Cambridge: Cambridge University Press, 1979); Joel S. Migdal, *Strong Societies and Weak States: State-Society Relations and State Capabilities in the Third World* (Princeton, NJ: Princeton University Press, 1988); Charles Tilly, *Coercion, Capital, and European States, AD 990–1992* (Cambridge, MA: Blackwell, 1992); Jeffrey Ira Herbst, *States and Power in Africa: Comparative Lessons in Authority and Control* (Princeton, NJ: Princeton University Press, 2000); Dan Slater, *Ordering Power: Contentious Politics and Authoritarian Leviathans in Southeast Asia* (Cambridge: Cambridge University Press, 2010).

38. This is the state-centric equivalent of Gutiérrez Sanín and Wood's critique of the insurgency literature: "The absence of ideology in these works reflects a presumption that all insurgent groups are essentially alike: whatever the differences in rhetoric, groups and their members respond similarly to such incentives and thus ideological differences are irrelevant." Francisco Gutiérrez Sanín and Elisabeth Jean Wood, "Ideology in Civil War: Instrumental Adoption and Beyond," *Journal of Peace Research* 51, no. 2 (March 1, 2014): 215, https://doi.org/10.1177/0022343313514073.

39. Straus *Making and Unmaking Nations*.

40. Jayal, *Citizenship and Its Discontents*, 19.

41. Ali Riaz, *Bangladesh: A Political History since Independence*, Sew ed. (London: I. B. Tauris, 2016); Salil Tripathi, *The Colonel Who Would Not Repent: The Bangladesh War and Its Unquiet Legacy* (New Haven, CT: Yale University Press, 2016).

42. William Gould, *Hindu Nationalism and the Language of Politics in Late Colonial India* (New York: Cambridge University Press, 2004).

43. See Duncan McCargo, *Tearing Apart the Land: Islam and Legitimacy in Southern Thailand* (Ithaca: Cornell University Press, 2008) on the Thai case.

44. Philip Selznick, *Leadership in Administration: A Sociological Interpretation* (Evanston, IL: Row, Peterson, 1957).

45. Christian Davenport, Sarah A. Soule, and David A. Armstrong, "Protesting While Black? The Differential Policing of American Activism, 1960 to 1990," *American Sociological Review* 76, no. 1 (February 1, 2011): 152–78, https://doi.org/10.1177/0003122410395370; Desmond S. King and Rogers M. Smith, "Racial Orders in American Political Development," *American Political Science Review* 99, no. 1 (2005): 75–92.

46. As Hansen Thomas Blom Hansen, *The Saffron Wave: Democracy and Hindu Nationalism in Modern India* (Princeton, NJ: Princeton University Press, 1999), 62, summarizes Zizek, "Ideology can perfectly well coexist with widespread cynicism, jokes, irony, and all the other features normally taken as proof of the impotency of ideology, as long as people act according to the ideological grammar." See also Sarah Parkinson, "Practical Ideology in Rebel Groups," *World Politics* (forthcoming).

47. Ronald R. Krebs, *Narrative and the Making of US National Security* (New York: Cambridge University Press, 2015), 21.

48. James C. Scott, *Domination and the Arts of Resistance: Hidden Transcripts* (New Haven, CT: Yale University Press, 1990), https://www.jstor.org/stable/j.ctt1np6zz.

49. Krebs *Narrative and the Making of US National Security,* 4–5; James Scott, *Weapons of the Weak: Everyday Forms of Peasant Resistance* (New Haven, CT: Yale University Press, 1985); Benedict J. Tria Kerkvliet, *The Power of Everyday Politics: How Vietnamese Peasants Transformed National Policy* (Ithaca: Cornell University Press, 2005); Ranajit Guha, *Elementary Aspects of Peasant Insurgency in Colonial India* (Durham, NC: Duke University Press, 1999).

50. Gopal Jayal, *Citizenship and Its Discontents,* 20.

51. There is a particularly strong relationship between violent and nonviolent politics for political organizations viewed as enemies. Enemies often—though certainly not always—emerge as *armed* groups precisely because they are not able to mobilize non-violently. The regime's efforts to control the political system target even unarmed enemy groups with antisubversion laws, surveillance, crackdowns, and exclusion from mainstream politics (Sullivan 2014). Unarmed enemies either disintegrate under the harsh glare of state repression (by far the most common outcome) or take up arms in an effort to pursue their goals outside of mainstream politics, as in Jeff Goodwin, *No Other Way Out: States and Revolutionary Movements, 1945–1991* (Cambridge: Cambridge University Press, 2001). Preemptive regime targeting can foster violent mobilization, blending the distinction between armed and unarmed groups.

52. See Stephen Kotkin, *Stalin: Waiting for Hitler, 1929–1941,* Illustrated ed. (London: Penguin Press, 2017), on Stalin's particular threat perception.

53. On militias, see Corinna Jentzsch, Stathis N. Kalyvas, and Livia Isabella Schubiger, "Militias in Civil Wars," *Journal of Conflict Resolution,* April 7, 2015, 0022002715576753, https://doi.org/10.1177/0022002715576753; on electoral violence, Sarah Birch, Ursula Daxecker, and Kristine Höglund, "Electoral Violence: An Introduction," *Journal of Peace Research* 57, no. 1 (January 1, 2020): 3–14, https://doi.org/10.1177/0022343319889657.

54. Loren Ryter, "Pemuda Pancasila: The Last Loyalist Free Men of Suharto's Order?" *Indonesia,* no. 66 (1998): 45–73, https://doi.org/10.2307/3351447; Benedict Richard O'Gorman Anderson, *Violence and the State in Suharto's Indonesia* (Ithaca: SEAP Publications, 2001).

55. Javier Auyero, *Routine Politics and Violence in Argentina: The Gray Zone of State Power,* 1st ed. (Cambridge: Cambridge University Press, 2007). See also *The Ambivalent State: Police-Criminal Collusion at the Urban Margins* (Oxford: Oxford University Press, 2019); Enrique Desmond Arias and Daniel M. Goldstein, eds., *Violent Democracies in Latin America* (Durham NC: Duke University Press Books, 2010).

56. Peter Krause and Ehud Eiran, "How Human Boundaries Become State Borders: Radical Flanks and Territorial Control in the Modern Era," *Comparative Politics* 50, no. 4 (July 1, 2018): 479–99, https://doi.org/10.5129/001041518823565632.

57. An overview can be found in International Crisis Group, "Oil and Borders: How to Fix Iraq's Kurdish Crisis," Crisis Group, October 17, 2017, https://www.crisisgroup.org/middle-east-north-africa/gulf-and-arabian-peninsula/iraq/55-settling-iraqi-kurdistans-boundaries-will-help-defuse-post-referendum-tensions.

58. On the interwar Germany case, see James M. Diehl, *Paramilitary Politics in Weimar Germany* (Bloomington: Indiana University Press, 1977). See Richard J. Evans, *The Coming of the Third Reich,* Reprint ed. (New York: Penguin Books, 2005); and Evans, *The Third Reich in Power,* Reprint ed. (New York: Penguin Books, 2006), on the role of paramilitarism within the Nazi movement and the power struggles following its seizure of power.

59. This is, in reality, obviously a continuous variable along a spectrum of overlap. For simplicity's sake, I use high/low language; in the case studies, I rely heavily on shifts in direction.

60. There are certainly other domains in which armed groups may be useful, but broadening this variable too far would allow me to explain away all anomalous cases.

61. Christia, *Alliance Formation in Civil Wars*. See also Sabine Otto, "The Grass Is Always Greener? Armed Group Side Switching in Civil Wars," *Journal of Conflict Resolution* 62, no. 7 (August 1, 2018): 1459–88, https://doi.org/10.1177/0022002717693047; Fotini Christia, *Alliance Formation in Civil Wars* (Cambridge: Cambridge University Press, 2012); Kristin M. Bakke, Kathleen Gallagher Cunningham, and Lee J. M. Seymour, "A Plague of Initials: Fragmentation, Cohesion, and Infighting in Civil Wars," *Perspectives on Politics* 10, no. 2 (2012): 265–83, https://doi.org/10.1017/S1537592712000667; Peter Krause, *Rebel Power: Why National Movements Compete, Fight, and Win* (Ithaca: Cornell University Press, 2017); Tricia Bacon, "Is the Enemy of My Enemy My Friend?" *Security Studies* 27, no. 3 (July 3, 2018): 345–78, https://doi.org/10.1080/09636412.2017.1416813; Lee J. M. Seymour, "Why Factions Switch Sides in Civil Wars: Rivalry, Patronage, and Realignment in Sudan," *International Security* 39, no. 2 (October 1, 2014): 92–131, https://doi.org/10.1162/ISEC_a_00179; Costantino Pischedda, "Wars within Wars: Why Windows of Opportunity and Vulnerability Cause Rebel Fighting in Internal Conflicts," *International Security* 43, no. 1 (August 1, 2018): 138–76, https://doi.org/10.1162/isec_a_00322; Kathleen Gallagher Cunningham, *Inside the Politics of Self-Determination* (Oxford: Oxford University Press, 2014).

62. Paul Staniland, "Armed Groups and Militarized Elections," *International Studies Quarterly* 59, no. 4 (December 1, 2015): 694–705, https://doi.org/10.1111/isqu.12195.

63. Philip G. Roessler, "Donor-Induced Democratization and the Privatization of State Violence in Kenya and Rwanda," *Comparative Politics* 37, no. 2 (January 1, 2005): 207–27, https://doi.org/10.2307/20072883.

64. Idean Salehyan, *Rebels without Borders: Transnational Insurgencies in World Politics* (Ithaca: Cornell University Press, 2009); Daniel Byman, Peter Chalk, Bruce Hoffman, William Rosenau, and David Brannan, *Trends in Outside Support for Insurgent Movements* (Washington, DC: RAND, 2001), http://www.rand.org/pubs/monograph_reports/MR1405/.

65. Henning Tamm, "The Origins of Transnational Alliances: Rulers, Rebels, and Political Survival in the Congo Wars," *International Security* 41, no. 1 (July 1, 2016): 147–81, https://doi.org/10.1162/ISEC_a_00252; Henning Tamm, "Rebel Leaders, Internal Rivals, and External Resources: How State Sponsors Affect Insurgent Cohesion," *International Studies Quarterly* 60, no. 4 (December 1, 2016): 599–610, https://doi.org/10.1093/isq/sqw033.

66. Some armed allies may decide to demand incorporation rather than collusion/alliance, as I discuss below.

67. Roessler, "Donor-Induced Democratization"; Sabine C. Carey, Neil J. Mitchell, and Will Lowe, "States, the Security Sector, and the Monopoly of Violence: A New Database on pro-Government Militias," *Journal of Peace Research* 50, no. 2 (March 1, 2013): 249–58, https://doi.org/10.1177/0022343312464881; Kristine Eck, "Repression by Proxy How Military Purges and Insurgency Impact the Delegation of Coercion," *Journal of Conflict Resolution* 59, no. 5 (August 1, 2015): 924–46, https://doi.org/10.1177/0022002715576746; William Reno, *Warfare in Independent Africa* (New York: Cambridge University Press, 2011).

68. On armed groups' political roots and social embeddedness, see Jeremy Weinstein, *Inside Rebellion: The Politics of Insurgent Violence* (Cambridge: Cambridge University Press, 2007); Aisha Ahmad, "The Security Bazaar: Business Interests and Islamist Power in Civil War Somalia," *International Security* 39, no. 3 (January 1, 2015): 89–117, https://doi.org/10.1162/ISEC_a_00187; Paul Staniland, *Networks of Rebellion: Explaining Insurgent Cohesion and Collapse*, 1st ed. (Ithaca: Cornell University Press, 2014); Laia Balcells,

Rivalry and Revenge: The Politics of Violence during Civil War (Cambridge: Cambridge University Press, 2017); Janet I. Lewis, *How Insurgency Begins: Rebel Group Formation in Uganda and Beyond* (Cambridge: Cambridge University Press, 2020), https://doi.org/10.1017/9781108855969.

69. This assumption is sometimes wrong, but it seems like a plausible approximation of how governments think about nonstate violence.

70. This is a contrast to the civil war termination literature, which focuses heavily on formal peace deals and explicit agreements about demobilization. For instance, Barbara F. Walter, *Committing to Peace: The Successful Settlement of Civil Wars* (Princeton, NJ: Princeton University Press, 2002); Aila M. Matanock, *Electing Peace: From Civil Conflict to Political Participation* (Cambridge: Cambridge University Press, 2017).

71. James D. Fearon, "Rationalist Explanations for War," *International Organization* 49, no. 3 (summer 1995): 379–414.

72. Alex Weisiger, *Logics of War: Explanations for Limited and Unlimited Conflicts*, 1st ed. (Ithaca: Cornell University Press, 2013).

73. Though not my focus in this book, similar dynamics are extremely common with unarmed movements as well. Regimes often move preemptively to eliminate prospective threats. Christopher M. Sullivan, "Political Repression and the Destruction of Dissident Organizations: Evidence from the Archives of the Guatemalan National Police," *World Politics* 68, no. 4 (October 2016): 645–76, https://doi.org/10.1017/S0043887116000125.

74. Straus, *Making and Unmaking Nations*; Robert Powell, "War as a Commitment Problem," *International Organization* 60, no. 01 (2006): 169–203, https://doi.org/10.1017/S0020818306060061; Weisiger, *Logics of War*.

75. Christia, *Alliance Formation in Civil Wars*.

76. Auyero, *Routine Politics and Violence in Argentina*.

77. Adnan Naseemullah and Paul Staniland, "Indirect Rule and Varieties of Governance," *Governance* 29, no. 1 (2016): 13–30, https://doi.org/10.1111/gove.12129.

78. Reno, *Warfare in Independent Africa*.

79. Kenneth A. Oye, ed., *Cooperation under Anarchy* (Princeton, NJ: Princeton University Press, 1986); Helen Milner, "The Assumption of Anarchy in International Relations Theory: A Critique," *Review of International Studies* 17, no. 1 (1991): 67–85; Barry R. Posen, "The Security Dilemma and Ethnic Conflict," *Survival: Global Politics and Strategy* 35, no. 1 (1993): 27–47, https://doi.org/10.1080/00396339308442672, provide foundational ways to think about the relationship between anarchy within and between states.

80. Expectations of external intervention, beliefs about the likely collapse of a central regime, and access to illicit resources and local social control during low-level wars are important factors that can keep rebels involved in long twilight wars of containment.

CHAPTER 2. HOW ARMED ORDERS CHANGE

1. On the evolution of these categories over time, see Lisa Blaydes, *State of Repression: Iraq under Saddam Hussein* (Princeton, NJ: Princeton University Press, 2018).

2. Paul Staniland, "Armed Groups and Militarized Elections," *International Studies Quarterly* 59, no. 4 (December 1, 2015): 694–705, https://doi.org/10.1111/isqu.12195. For an overview of the electoral violence literature writ large, see Sarah Birch, Ursula Daxecker, and Kristine Höglund, "Electoral Violence: An Introduction," *Journal of Peace Research* 57, no. 1 (January 1, 2020): 3–14, https://doi.org/10.1177/0022343319889657.

3. Aila M. Matanock and Paul Staniland, "How and Why Armed Groups Participate in Elections," *Perspectives on Politics* 16, no. 3 (September 2018): 710–27, https://doi.org/10.1017/S1537592718001019; Dorina Akosua Oduraa Bekoe, ed., *Voting in Fear: Electoral Violence in Sub-Saharan Africa* (Washington, DC: United States Institute of

Peace, 2012); Birch et al., "Electoral Violence"; Paul Staniland, "Violence and Democracy," *Comparative Politics* 47, no. 1 (2014): 99–118; Abbey Steele and Livia Schubiger, "Democracy and Civil War: The Case of Colombia," *Conflict Management and Peace Science* 35, no. 6 (November 1, 2018): 587–600, https://doi.org/10.1177/0738894218787780.

4. Roessler, "Donor-Induced Democratization." Stephanie M. Burchard, *Electoral Violence in Sub-Saharan Africa: Causes and Consequences* (Boulder, CO: FirstForumPress, 2015); and Bekoe, ed., *Voting in Fear*, explore these dynamics as well.

5. John Sidel, *Capital, Coercion, and Crime: Bossism in the Philippines* (Stanford, CA: Stanford University Press, 1999); William Reno, *Warfare in Independent Africa* (New York: Cambridge University Press, 2011); Ali Riaz, *Bangladesh: A Political History since Independence*, Sew ed. (London: I. B. Tauris, 2016).

6. Scott Straus and Charlie Taylor, "Democratization and Electoral Violence in Sub-Saharan Africa, 1990–2008," in *Voting in Fear: Electoral Violence in Sub-Saharan Africa*, ed. Dorina Akosua Oduraa Bekoe (Washington, DC: United States Institute of Peace, 2012), 15–38; Susan D. Hyde and Nikolay Marinov, "Which Elections Can Be Lost?" *Political Analysis* 20, no. 2 (April 1, 2012): 191–210, https://doi.org/10.1093/pan/mpr040; Emilie M. Hafner-Burton, Susan D. Hyde, and Ryan S. Jablonski, "When Do Governments Resort to Election Violence?" *British Journal of Political Science* 44, no. 1 (2014): 149–79, https://doi.org/10.1017/S0007123412000671, all explore how the tightness of elections can influence violence. See also Gareth Nellis and Niloufer Siddiqui, "Secular Party Rule and Religious Violence in Pakistan," *American Political Science Review* 112, no. 1 (February 2018): 49–67, https://doi.org/10.1017/S0003055417000491; Gareth Nellis, Michael Weaver, and Steven C. Rosenzweig, "Do Parties Matter for Ethnic Violence? Evidence from India," *Quarterly Journal of Political Science* 11, no. 3 (October 30, 2016): 249–77, https://doi.org/10.1561/100.00015051.

7. Staniland, "Armed Groups and Militarized Elections."

8. Staniland, "Violence and Democracy."

9. Byman et al., *Trends in Outside Support for Insurgent Movements*; Salehyan, *Rebels without Borders*; Kenneth A. Schultz, "The Enforcement Problem in Coercive Bargaining: Interstate Conflict over Rebel Support in Civil Wars," *International Organization* 64, no. 2 (2010): 281–312; Nathan Constantin Leites and Charles Wolf, *Rebellion and Authority: An Analytic Essay on Insurgent Conflicts* (Chicago: Markham, 1970); Henning Tamm, "The Origins of Transnational Alliances: Rulers, Rebels, and Political Survival in the Congo Wars," *International Security* 41, no. 1 (July 1, 2016): 147–81, https://doi.org/10.1162/ISEC_a_00252; Henning Tamm, "Rebel Leaders, Internal Rivals, and External Resources: How State Sponsors Affect Insurgent Cohesion," *International Studies Quarterly* 60, no. 4 (December 1, 2016): 599–610, https://doi.org/10.1093/isq/sqw033; David B. Carter, "A Blessing or a Curse? State Support for Terrorist Groups," *International Organization* 66, no. 1 (2012): 129–51, https://doi.org/10.1017/S0020818311000312.

10. Steve Coll, *Ghost Wars: The Secret History of the CIA, Afghanistan, and Bin Laden, from the Soviet Invasion to September 10, 2001* (New York: Penguin, 2004), provides a useful overview.

11. Thant Myint-U, *The Hidden History of Burma: Race, Capitalism, and the Crisis of Democracy in the 21st Century*, 1st ed. (New York: W. W. Norton, 2019).

12. Barnett R. Rubin, *The Fragmentation of Afghanistan: State Formation and Collapse in the International System,* 2nd ed. (New Haven: Yale University Press, 2002).

13. Morgan Kaplan, *Persuading Power: Insurgent Diplomacy and the International Politics of Rebellion* (PhD diss., University of Chicago, 2016).

14. Thérése Pettersson, Stina Högbladh, and Magnus Öberg, "Organized Violence, 1989–2018 and Peace Agreements," *Journal of Peace Research* 56, no. 4 (July 1, 2019): 589–603, https://doi.org/10.1177/0022343319856046.

15. Kristin M. Bakke, Kathleen Gallagher Cunningham, and Lee J. M. Seymour, "A Plague of Initials: Fragmentation, Cohesion, and Infighting in Civil Wars," *Perspectives on Politics* 10, no. 2 (2012): 265–83, https://doi.org/10.1017/S1537592712000667; Peter Krause, *Rebel Power: Why National Movements Compete, Fight, and Win*, 1st ed. (Ithaca: Cornell University Press, 2017).

16. International Crisis Group, "Averting an ISIS Resurgence in Iraq and Syria," accessed October 7, 2020, https://www.crisisgroup.org/middle-east-north-africa/eastern-mediterranean/syria/207-averting-isis-resurgence-iraq-and-syria.

17. This most closely resembles the dyadic structure of much of the data on armed group-state interactions, both in this book and in prominent civil war datasets (i.e., Pettersson et al., "Organized Violence, 1989–2018 and Peace Agreements").

18. These arrangements keep both actors armed, and thus attenuate the commitment problems that plague efforts at full demobilization and disarmament, a challenge at the heart of Barbara F. Walter, *Committing to Peace: The Successful Settlement of Civil Wars* (Princeton, NJ: Princeton University Press, 2002); and Aila M. Matanock, *Electing Peace: From Civil Conflict to Political Participation* (Cambridge: Cambridge University Press, 2017). This is a way of sidestepping the instability that can accompany peace deals. See also Sarah Zukerman Daly, *Organized Violence after Civil War: The Geography of Recruitment in Latin America* (Cambridge: Cambridge University Press, 2017).

19. Kristian Stokke, "Building the Tamil Eelam State: Emerging State Institutions and Forms of Governance in LTTE-Controlled Areas in Sri Lanka," *Third World Quarterly* 27, no. 6 (September 1, 2006): 1021–40, https://doi.org/10.1080/01436590600850434.

20. As Sambanis and Schulhofer-Wohl note, such gaps complicate many empirical measurements of what counts as a civil war. By "filling in" these periods with armed orders, this book tries to address that challenge. Nicholas Sambanis and Jonah Schulhofer-Wohl, "Sovereignty Rupture as a Central Concept in Quantitative Measures of Civil War," *Journal of Conflict Resolution* 63, no. 6 (July 1, 2019): 1542–78, https://doi.org/10.1177/0022002719842657.

21. For an overview of how militias specifically can fill these roles, see Corinna Jentzsch, Stathis N. Kalyvas, and Livia Isabella Schubiger, "Militias in Civil Wars," *Journal of Conflict Resolution* 59, no. 5 (August 1, 2015): 755–69, https://doi.org/10.1177/0022002715576753. and the articles in that special issue.

22. Paul Staniland, "Between a Rock and a Hard Place: Insurgent Fratricide, Ethnic Defection, and the Rise of Pro-State Paramilitaries," *Journal of Conflict Resolution* 56, no. 1 (February 2012): 16–40, https://doi.org/10.1177/0022002711429681.

23. On armed group relations with civilians, see, among others, Zachariah Cherian Mampilly, *Rebel Rulers: Insurgent Governance and Civilian Life During War* (Ithaca: Cornell University Press, 2011); Ana Arjona, Nelson Kasfir, and Zachariah Mampilly, eds., *Rebel Governance in Civil War* (Cambridge: Cambridge University Press, 2015); Ana Arjona, *Rebelocracy: Social Order in the Colombian Civil War by Ana Arjona* (Cambridge: Cambridge University Press, 2015); Megan A. Stewart, "Civil War as State-Making: Strategic Governance in Civil War," *International Organization* 72, no. 1 (2018): 205–26, https://doi.org/10.1017/S0020818317000418.

24. On splits and splintering, see Kathleen Gallagher Cunningham, Kristin M. Bakke, and Lee J. M. Seymour, "Shirts Today, Skins Tomorrow Dual Contests and the Effects of Fragmentation in Self-Determination Disputes," *Journal of Conflict Resolution* 56, no. 1 (February 1, 2012): 67–93, https://doi.org/10.1177/0022002711429697; Evan Perkoski, "Internal Politics and the Fragmentation of Armed Groups," *International Studies Quarterly* 63, no. 4 (December 1, 2019): 876–89, https://doi.org/10.1093/isq/sqz076.

25. Paul Staniland, *Networks of Rebellion: Explaining Insurgent Cohesion and Collapse*, 1st ed. (Ithaca: Cornell University Press, 2014); Kathleen Gallagher Cunningham, *Inside*

the Politics of Self-Determination (Oxford: Oxford University Press, 2014); Peter Krause, *Rebel Power: Why National Movements Compete, Fight, and Win* (Ithaca: Cornell University Press, 2017); Fotini Christia, *Alliance Formation in Civil Wars* (New York: Cambridge University Press, 2012); Costantino Pischedda, "Wars within Wars: Why Windows of Opportunity and Vulnerability Cause Inter-Rebel Fighting in Internal Conflicts," *International Security* 43, no. 1 (August 1, 2018): 138–76, https://doi.org/10.1162/isec_a_00322; Ariel Ahram, *Proxy Warriors: The Rise and Fall of State-Sponsored Militias* (Stanford, CA: Stanford Security Studies, 2011); Wendy Pearlman, *Violence, Nonviolence, and the Palestinian National Movement* (Cambridge: Cambridge University Press, 2011); Sabine Otto, "The Grass Is Always Greener? Armed Group Side Switching in Civil Wars," *Journal of Conflict Resolution* 62, no. 7 (August 1, 2018): 1459–88.

26. For a supply-demand conceptualization of side switching, see Stathis N. Kalyvas, "Ethnic Defection in Civil War," *Comparative Political Studies* 41, no. 8 (August 1, 2008): 1043–68, https://doi.org/10.1177/0010414008317949.

27. M. R. Narayan Swamy, *Tigers of Lanka, from Boys to Guerrillas*, 7th ed. (Colombo: Vijitha Yapa, 2006).

28. Christia, *Alliance Formation in Civil Wars.*

29. On dynamics after military victory in a civil war, see Monica Duffy Toft, "Ending Civil Wars: A Case for Rebel Victory?," *International Security* 34, no. 4 (April 1, 2010): 7–36, https://doi.org/10.1162/isec.2010.34.4.7; Laurie Nathan and Monica Duffy Toft, "Civil War Settlements and the Prospects for Peace," *International Security* 36, no. 1 (2011): 202–10.

30. Stathis N. Kalyvas, *The Logic of Violence in Civil War* (Cambridge: Cambridge University Press, 2006).

31. Stephen E. Hanson, *Post-Imperial Democracies: Ideology and Party Formation in Third Republic France, Weimar Germany, and Post-Soviet Russia* (New York: Cambridge University Press, 2010).

32. Scott Straus, *Making and Unmaking Nations: War, Leadership, and Genocide in Modern Africa* (Ithaca: Cornell University Press, 2015); William Gould, *Hindu Nationalism and the Language of Politics in Late Colonial India* (Cambridge: Cambridge University Press, 2004). The extent of such constraints will certainly vary by regime and context: totalitarian personalist regimes will likely provide much more space for dramatic shifts than single-party states or democratic regimes. All that is necessary for this argument to have value is that there is, on average, a meaningful "lag" induced in government ideological positioning due to concerns over legitimation, resistance, and mass public opinion.

33. On the rigidities of and constraints on many counterrevolutionary regimes, see Theda Skocpol, *States and Social Revolutions: A Comparative Analysis of France, Russia, and China* (Cambridge: Cambridge University Press, 1979); Daron Acemoglu and James Robinson, *Economic Origins of Dictatorship and Democracy* (New York: Cambridge University Press, 2006).

34. This is a classic case of path-dependence: what occurred in the past constrains plausible options in the present. See James Mahoney and Kathleen Ann Thelen, eds., *Explaining Institutional Change: Ambiguity, Agency, and Power* (Cambridge: Cambridge University Press, 2010); Paul Pierson, *Politics in Time: History, Institutions, and Social Analysis* (Princeton, NJ: Princeton University Press, 2004); Ruth Berins Collier and David Collier, *Shaping the Political Arena: Critical Junctures, the Labor Movement, and Regime Dynamics in Latin America* (South Bend, IN: University of Notre Dame Press, 2002).

35. On incremental institutional change, see James Mahoney and Kathleen Thelen, "A Theory of Gradual Institutional Change," in *Explaining Institutional Change: Ambiguity, Agency, and Power*, ed. James Mahoney and Kathleen Thelen (Cambridge: Cambridge University Press, 2010), 1–37.

36. See, for instance, Shuja Nawaz, *Crossed Swords: Pakistan, Its Army, and the Wars Within* (Oxford: Oxford University Press, 2008); Shuja Nawaz, *The Battle for Pakistan: The Bitter US Friendship and a Tough Neighbourhood* (New York: Vintage Books, 2019); Duncan McCargo, *Tearing Apart the Land: Islam and Legitimacy in Southern Thailand* (Ithaca: Cornell University Press, 2008); Duncan McCargo, "Mapping National Anxieties," *RUSI Journal* 154, no. 3 (June 1, 2009): 54–60, https://doi.org/10.1080/03071840903097654.

37. P. N. Abinales, *Making Mindanao: Cotabato and Davao in the Formation of the Philippine Nation-State* (Quezon City: Ateneo de Manila University Press, 2000); P. N. Abinales and Donna J. Amoroso, *State and Society in the Philippines* (Lanham, MD: Rowman & Littlefield, 2005).

38. On revolution and its threat, see Skocpol, *States and Social Revolutions*; Charles Tilly, *From Mobilization to Revolution* (Reading, MA: Addison-Wesley, 1978); Jeff Goodwin and Theda Skocpol, "Explaining Revolutions in the Contemporary Third World," *Politics & Society* 17, no. 4 (December 1, 1989): 489–509, https://doi.org/10.1177/003232928901700403; Jeff Goodwin, *No Other Way Out: States and Revolutionary Movements, 1945–1991* (Cambridge: Cambridge University Press, 2001); Acemoglu and Robinson, *Economic Origins*; Dan Slater, *Ordering Power: Contentious Politics and Authoritarian Leviathans in Southeast Asia* (Cambridge: Cambridge University Press, 2010); Evgeny Finkel and Scott Gehlbach, *Reform and Rebellion in Weak States* (Cambridge: Cambridge University Press, 2020); Paul Staniland, "Leftist Insurgency in Democracies," *Comparative Political Studies*, July 8, 2020, https://doi.org/10.1177/0010414020938096.

39. For studies of ruling regimes' behavior after regime change, see, among many others, Skocpol, *States and Social Revolutions*; Stephen M. Walt, *Revolution and War* (Ithaca: Cornell University Press, 1996); Michael Albertus, *Autocracy and Redistribution: The Politics of Land Reform*, 1st ed. (New York: Cambridge University Press, 2015); Vincent Boudreau, *Resisting Dictatorship: Repression and Protest in Southeast Asia* (Cambridge: Cambridge University Press, 2004; Philip A. Martin, "Commander-Community Ties after Civil War," *Journal of Peace Research*, October 1, 2020, 0022343320929744, https://doi.org/10.1177/0022343320929744.

40. For empirical measurement of revolutions, see Jeff D. Colgan, *Petro-Aggression: When Oil Causes War* (Cambridge: Cambridge University Press, 2013). Since revolutions are only one subset of a broader class of major regime changes (such as decolonization), this is only a starting point, but shows that it is possible to systematically measure major dramatic ruptures in political authority.

41. On legacies of past conflict or coups, see foundational work by James D. Fearon and David D. Laitin, "Ethnicity, Insurgency, and Civil War," *American Political Science Review* 97, no. 1 (February 2003): 75–90; John B. Londregan and Keith T. Poole, "Poverty, the Coup Trap, and the Seizure of Executive Power," *World Politics* 42, no. 2 (1990): 151–83, https://doi.org/10.2307/2010462; Paul Collier et al., *Breaking the Conflict Trap: Civil War and Development Policy* (Washington, DC: World Bank, 2003).

42. For background, see Ali Riaz, *Bangladesh: A Political History since Independence*, Sew ed. (London: I. B. Tauris, 2016); Willem van Schendel, *A History of Bangladesh*, 1st ed. (Cambridge: Cambridge University Press, 2009).

43. Haroon K. Ullah, *Vying for Allah's Vote: Understanding Islamic Parties, Political Violence, and Extremism in Pakistan* (Washington, DC: Georgetown University Press, 2013), 164.

44. See Milan Vaishnav, ed., *The BJP in Power: Indian Democracy and Religious Nationalism* (Washington, DC: Carnegie Endowment for International Peace, 2019).

45. For accounts of how group competition and social embeddedness can induce or block particular trajectories, see Pearlman, *Violence, Nonviolence, and the Palestinian National Movement*; Krause, *Rebel Power*; Anoop K. Sarbahi, "Insurgent-Population Ties

and the Variation in the Trajectory of Peripheral Civil Wars," *Comparative Political Studies* 47, no. 10 (September 1, 2014): 1470–1500, https://doi.org/10.1177/0010414013512602.

46. On internal disputes over groups' positions leading to conflict, see Stephen John Stedman, "Spoiler Problems in Peace Processes," *International Security* 22, no. 2 (autumn 1997): 5–53; Andrew Kydd and Barbara F. Walter, "Sabotaging the Peace: The Politics of Extremist Violence," *International Organization* 56, no. 2 (spring 2002): 263–96; Ethan Bueno de Mesquita, "Conciliation, Counterterrorism, and Patterns of Terrorist Violence," *International Organization* 59, no. 1 (winter 2005): 145–76; Cunningham, *Inside the Politics of Self-Determination*; Michael Woldemariam, *Insurgent Fragmentation in the Horn of Africa: Rebellion and Its Discontents* (New York: Cambridge University Press, 2018).

47. For approaches to understanding state repression in general, see Evgeny Finkel, "The Phoenix Effect of State Repression: Jewish Resistance during the Holocaust," *American Political Science Review* 109, no. 2 (May 2015): 339–53, https://doi.org/10.1017/S000305541500009X; Christian Davenport, "State Repression and Political Order," *Annual Review of Political Science* 10, no. 1 (2007): 1–23, https://doi.org/10.1146/annurev.polisci.10.101405.143216; Christopher M. Sullivan, "Undermining Resistance: Mobilization, Repression, and the Enforcement of Political Order," *Journal of Conflict Resolution*, February 2, 2015, https://doi.org/10.1177/0022002714567951; Shivaji Mukherjee, "Why Are the Longest Insurgencies Low Violence? Politician Motivations, Sons of the Soil, and Civil War Duration," *Civil Wars* 16, no. 2 (April 3, 2014): 172–207, https://doi.org/10.1080/13698249.2014.927702.

48. See Thomas C. Schelling, *Arms and Influence* (New Haven: Yale University Press, 1966) and Kalyvas, *Logic of Violence in Civil War*, for discussions of effective coercion.

49. For discussions of selective vs. indiscriminate violence, see, among many others, Kalyvas, *Logic of Violence in Civil War*; Jason Lyall, "Does Indiscriminate Violence Incite Insurgent Attacks? Evidence from Chechnya," *Journal of Conflict Resolution* 53, no. 3 (June 1, 2009): 331–62, https://doi.org/10.1177/0022002708330881; Laia Balcells, *Rivalry and Revenge: The Politics of Violence during Civil War* (Cambridge: Cambridge University Press, 2017); Abbey Steele, *Democracy and Displacement in Colombia's Civil War* (Ithaca: Cornell University Press, 2017); Lee Ann Fujii, "The Puzzle of Extra-Lethal Violence," *Perspectives on Politics* 11, no. 2 (2013): 410–26, https://doi.org/10.1017/S1537592713001060; Evgeny Finkel, *Ordinary Jews: Choice and Survival during the Holocaust* (Princeton, NJ: Princeton University Press, 2017). For the purposes of this book, I conceptualize selective violence as the ability of a government to consistently, even if imperfectly, repress members and sympathizers of a group without large-scale victimization of civilians unconnected to the group. This is a lower bar than the definition of selective emphasized by Kalyvas, but for the purposes of group-state interactions, it seems reasonable.

50. For structural factors that also affect war duration, see James D. Fearon, "Why Do Some Civil Wars Last so Much Longer than Others?" *Journal of Peace Research* 41, no. 3 (May 2004): 275–301; David E. Cunningham, "Veto Players and Civil War Duration," *American Journal of Political Science* 50, no. 4 (October 2006): 875–92.

51. Barbara F. Walter, *Committing to Peace: The Successful Settlement of Civil Wars* (Princeton, NJ: Princeton University Press, 2002), offers the most influential theoretical account of the challenges facing such processes.

52. Stedman, "Spoiler Problems in Peace Processes"; Kydd and Walter, "Sabotaging the Peace"; Kelly M. Greenhill and Solomon. Major, "The Perils of Profiling: Civil War Spoilers and the Collapse of Intrastate Peace Accords," *International Security* 31, no. 3 (2007): 7–40.

53. On conditionality in violence, see Jeff Goodwin, *No Other Way Out: States and Revolutionary Movements, 1945–1991* (Cambridge: Cambridge University Press, 2001);

Kalyvas, *Logic of Violence in Civil War*; Matthew Adam Kocher, Thomas B. Pepinsky, and Stathis N. Kalyvas, "Aerial Bombing and Counterinsurgency in the Vietnam War," *American Journal of Political Science* 55, no. 2 (2011): 201–18, Benjamin Lessing, *Making Peace in Drug Wars: Crackdowns and Cartels in Latin America* (Cambridge: Cambridge University Press, 2017). In this context, I view indiscriminate violence as involving targeting of groups that is not response to actual group political statements or behavior. It often overlaps with civilian targeting.

54. See, for instance, David Brenner, *Rebel Politics: A Political Sociology of Armed Struggle in Myanmar's Borderlands* (Ithaca: Southeast Asia Program Publication, 2019) on civilians' skepticism of cease-fire politics in the Karen and Kachin areas of Burma.

55. For insights on protracted warfare and the bargaining problems associated with it, see James D. Fearon, "Rationalist Explanations for War," *International Organization* 49, no. 3 (summer 1995): 379–414; Robert Powell, "War as a Commitment Problem," *International Organization* 60, no. 01 (2006): 169–203, https://doi.org/10.1017/S0020818306060061; Barbara F. Walter, *Reputation and Civil War: Why Separatist Conflicts Are so Violent* (Cambridge: Cambridge University Press, 2009); Alex Weisiger, *Logics of War: Explanations for Limited and Unlimited Conflicts*, 1st ed. (Ithaca: Cornell University Press, 2013); Shivaji Mukherjee, "Why Are the Longest Insurgencies Low Violence? Politician Motivations, Sons of the Soil, and Civil War Duration," *Civil Wars* 16, no. 2 (April 3, 2014): 172–207.

56. Henning Tamm, "Rebel Leaders, Internal Rivals, and External Resources: How State Sponsors Affect Insurgent Cohesion," *International Studies Quarterly* 60, no. 4 (December 1, 2016): 599–610, https://doi.org/10.1093/isq/sqw033; Staniland, *Networks of Rebellion*; Claire Metelits, *Inside Insurgency: Violence, Civilians, and Revolutionary Group Behavior* (New York: New York University Press, 2010); Pearlman, *Violence, Nonviolence, and the Palestinian National Movement*; Krause, *Rebel Power*.

57. For a glimpse of how intricate the strategic interactions involved can be, see Bueno de Mesquita, "Conciliation, Counterterrorism, and Patterns of Terrorist Violence"; Tricia Bacon, "Is the Enemy of My Enemy My Friend?" *Security Studies* 27, no. 3 (July 3, 2018): 345–78, https://doi.org/10.1080/09636412.2017.1416813; Christia, *Alliance Formation in Civil Wars*.

58. Cunningham, *The Politics of Self-Determination*. See also Bethany Ann Lacina, *Rival Claims: Ethnic Violence and Territorial Autonomy under Indian Federalism* (Ann Arbor: University of Michigan Press, 2017), on how governments respond to demands, which in some cases can trigger revolts.

59. Paul Staniland, "Between a Rock and a Hard Place Insurgent Fratricide, Ethnic Defection, and the Rise of Pro-State Paramilitaries," *Journal of Conflict Resolution* 56, no. 1 (February 2012): 16–40, https://doi.org/10.1177/0022002711429681.

60. Christia, *Alliance Formation in Civil Wars*.

61. Donald L Horowitz, *Ethnic Groups in Conflict* (Berkeley: University of California Press, 1985); Mia Bloom, *Dying to Kill: The Allure of Suicide Terror* (New York: Columbia University Press, 2005); Neil DeVotta, *Blowback: Linguistic Nationalism, Institutional Decay, and Ethnic Conflict in Sri Lanka* (Stanford, CA: Stanford University Press, 2004).

62. Krause, *Rebel Power*; Cunningham, *Inside the Politics of Self-Determination*; Pearlman, *Violence, Nonviolence, and the Palestinian National Movement*.

63. Barbara F. Walter, "The New New Civil Wars," *Annual Review of Political Science* 20, no. 1 (2017): 469–86, https://doi.org/10.1146/annurev-polisci-060415-093921; Barbara F. Walter, "The Extremist's Advantage in Civil Wars," *International Security* 42, no. 2 (November 1, 2017): 7–39, https://doi.org/10.1162/ISEC_a_00292.

64. A related literature has explored how external actors can shape ethnic bargaining; Rupen Cetinyan, "Ethnic Bargaining in the Shadow of Third-Party Intervention,"

International Organization 56, no. 3 (2002): 645–77, https://doi.org/10.1162/002081802 760199917; Alan J. Kuperman, "The Moral Hazard of Humanitarian Intervention: Lessons from the Balkans," *International Studies Quarterly* 52 (March 2008): 49–80, https://doi.org/10.1111/j.1468-2478.2007.00491.x; Erin K Jenne, *Ethnic Bargaining: The Paradox of Minority Empowerment* (Ithaca: Cornell University Press, 2007).

65. Paul Staniland, "Organizing Insurgency: Networks, Resources, and Rebellion in South Asia," *International Security* 37, no. 1 (2012): 142–77, https://doi.org/10.1162/ISEC_a_00091.

66. The Liberation Tigers of Tamil Eelam are a classic case: they refused to agree to India's demands that they moderate their stance and demobilize as part of the 1987 Indo-Lanka Accord.

67. For analyses of the complex politics of international involvement in civil wars, see Jonah Schulhofer-Wohl, *Quagmire in Civil War* (Cambridge: Cambridge University Press, 2020), https://doi.org/10.1017/9781108762465; Andrew Mack, "Why Big Nations Lose Small Wars: The Politics of Asymmetric Conflict," *World Politics* 27, no. 2 (January 1975): 175–200; Jason Lyall and Isaiah Wilson III, "Rage against the Machines: Explaining Outcomes in Counterinsurgency Wars," *International Organization* 63, no. 1 (winter 2009): 67–106; Kate Cronin-Furman, "Human Rights Half Measures: Avoiding Accountability in Postwar Sri Lanka," *World Politics* 72, no. 1 (January 2020): 121–63, https://doi.org/10.1017/S0043887119000182; Milli Lake, "Building the Rule of War: Postconflict Institutions and the Micro-Dynamics of Conflict in Eastern DR Congo," *International Organization* 71, no. 2 (April 2017): 281–315, https://doi.org/10.1017/S002081831700008X; Michael W. Doyle and Nicholas Sambanis, *Making War and Building Peace* (Princeton, NJ: Princeton University Press, 2006).

CHAPTER 3. ARMED ORDERS AND IDEOLOGICAL PROJECTS IN SOUTH ASIA

1. See, among others, Nicholas Sambanis, "What Is Civil War? Conceptual and Empirical Complexities of an Operational Definition," *Journal of Conflict Resolution* 48, no. 6 (December 2004): 814–58; Nils Petter Gleditsch et al., "Armed Conflict 1946–2001: A New Dataset," *Journal of Peace Research* 39, no. 5 (September 1, 2002): 615–37, https://doi.org/10.1177/0022343302039005007; Lars-Erik Cederman, Kristian Skrede Gleditsch, and Halvard Buhaug, *Inequality, Grievances, and Civil War* (New York: Cambridge University Press, 2013); Thérése Pettersson, Stina Högbladh, and Magnus Öberg, "Organized Violence, 1989–2018 and Peace Agreements," *Journal of Peace Research* 56, no. 4 (July 1, 2019): 589–603, https://doi.org/10.1177/0022343319856046; Idean Salehyan, "Best Practices in the Collection of Conflict Data," *Journal of Peace Research* 52, no. 1 (January 1, 2015): 105–9, https://doi.org/10.1177/0022343314551563; Joakim Kreutz, "The War That Wasn't There: Managing Unclear Cases in Conflict Data," *Journal of Peace Research* 52, no. 1 (January 1, 2015): 120–24, https://doi.org/10.1177/0022343314541845.

2. On progovernment militias, see Sabine C. Carey, Neil J. Mitchell, and Will Lowe, "States, the Security Sector, and the Monopoly of Violence: A New Database on proGovernment Militias," *Journal of Peace Research* 50, no. 2 (March 1, 2013): 249–58, https://doi.org/10.1177/0022343312464881. On "two-sided" conflicts, see Kristine Eck and Lisa Hultman, "One-Sided Violence Against Civilians in War: Insights from New Fatality Data," *Journal of Peace Research* 44, no. 2 (2007): 233–46.

3. Paul Staniland, "Armed Politics and the Study of Intrastate Conflict," *Journal of Peace Research* 54, no. 4 (July 1, 2017): 459–67, https://doi.org/10.1177/0022343317698848.

4. On these politics, see S. Mahmud Ali, *Understanding Bangladesh* (New York: Columbia University Press, 2010); Ali Riaz, *Bangladesh: A Political History since Independence,*

Sew ed. (London: I. B. Tauris, 2016); Willem van Schendel, *A History of Bangladesh*, 1st ed. (Cambridge: Cambridge University Press, 2009).

5. For instance, there is a rich literature on whether and how peace deals arise and what happens to them. We find that peace deals are far from the only way that dyads nonviolently end, but can also explore their fate within the sample of AOSA cases.

6. These narratives and data can be found on my website upon publication: http://www.paulstaniland.com.

7. For some of these analyses, I discuss (sometimes in footnotes) multiple versions of the India data, with and without Indian state-level dyads. State-level dyads reflect the federal structure of the Indian state, in which specific states are often the prime COIN force as long as the conflict is below a certain level (this is most relevant to the Naxalites in the 1980s and 1990s), as well as "militarized politics" contexts in which state governments can themselves cooperate or clash with political parties (West Bengal, Bihar, Kerala, Maharashtra). Including these state dyads alongside the more standard national government-group dyad can duplicate the same group's presence and introduces cross-case lack of comparability, since I did not research this level of specificity in the other countries. Including them, however, does not radically change the results of any of the India or cross-national analyses—it primarily serves to increase the number of alliance orders. I return to this subset in more detail when discussing India.

8. The armed order spectrum can be seen as a way of adapting the classic spectrum of individual roles introduced in Roger Dale Petersen, *Resistance and Rebellion: Lessons from Eastern Europe* (Cambridge: Cambridge University Press, 2001), to the level of organizational interaction.

9. Dropping Indian state-level dyads, where we find many armed parties, moves limited cooperation to 45 percent, alliance to 42 percent, and containment to 12 percent—alliances become somewhat less common outside of the subnational state context.

10. Ahsan I. Butt, *Secession and Security: Explaining State Strategy against Separatists* (Ithaca: Cornell University Press, 2017).

11. For a study of transnational alliances, see Henning Tamm, "The Origins of Transnational Alliances: Rulers, Rebels, and Political Survival in the Congo Wars," *International Security* 41, no. 1 (July 1, 2016): 147–81, https://doi.org/10.1162/ISEC_a_00252.

12. Subir Bhaumik, *Troubled Periphery: Crisis of India's North East* (Los Angeles: Sage, 2009) provides a valuable overview of the dynamics of external support in the Northeast.

13. Barbara F. Walter, *Reputation and Civil War: Why Separatist Conflicts Are So Violent* (Cambridge: Cambridge University Press, 2009).

14. For an overview of challenges to armed group resilience at different levels of analysis, see Jeremy Weinstein, *Inside Rebellion: The Politics of Insurgent Violence* (Cambridge: Cambridge University Press, 2007); William Reno, *Warfare in Independent Africa* (New York: Cambridge University Press, 2011); Paul Staniland, *Networks of Rebellion: Explaining Insurgent Cohesion and Collapse*, 1st ed. (Ithaca: Cornell University Press, 2014); Sarah Elizabeth Parkinson, "Organizing Rebellion: Rethinking High-Risk Mobilization and Social Networks in War," *American Political Science Review* 107, no. 3 (2013): 418–32, https://doi.org/10.1017/S0003055413000208; Ana Arjona, *Rebelocracy: Social Order in the Colombian Civil War* (Cambridge: Cambridge University Press, 2016).

15. For important research that focuses on the value of an international role in peace processes, see Barbara F. Walter, *Committing to Peace: The Successful Settlement of Civil Wars* (Princeton, NJ: Princeton University Press, 2002); Virginia Page Fortna, *Peace Time: Cease-Fire Agreements and the Durability of Peace* (Princeton, NJ: Princeton University Press, 2004), and *Does Peacekeeping Work?: Shaping Belligerents' Choices After Civil +War* (Princeton, NJ: Princeton University Press, 2008); Aila M. Matanock, *Electing Peace: From Civil Conflict to Political Participation* (Cambridge: Cambridge University Press, 2017).

16. For a discussion of alternatives to the standard playbook of international peace building, see Séverine Autesserre, *Peaceland: Conflict Resolution and the Everyday Politics of International Intervention* (Cambridge: Cambridge University Press, 2014).

17. This appears as a double-count, so I only count it once.

18. For approaches to measuring ideology, see Stephen E. Hanson, *Post-Imperial Democracies: Ideology and Party Formation in Third Republic France, Weimar Germany, and Post-Soviet Russia*, 1st ed. (Cambridge: Cambridge University Press, 2010); Sheri Berman, *The Social Democratic Moment: Ideas and Politics in the Making of Interwar Europe by Sheri Berman* (Cambridge, MA: Harvard University Press, 1998); Lisa Wedeen, *Authoritarian Apprehensions: Ideology, Judgment, and Mourning in Syria*, 1st ed. (C+hicago: University of Chicago Press, 2019); Keith T. Poole and Howard Rosenthal, "A Spatial Model for Legislative Roll Call Analysis," *American Journal of Political Science* 29, no. 2 (1985): 357–84, https://doi.org/10.2307/2111172.

19. Partha Chatterjee, *Nationalist Thought and the Colonial World: A Derivative Discourse?* (London: Zed Books, 1986).

20. William Gould, *Hindu Nationalism and the Language of Politics in Late Colonial India* (New York: Cambridge University Press, 2004).

21. Ramachandra Guha, *India after Gandhi: The History of the World's Largest Democracy*, 1st ed. (New York: Ecco, 2007).

22. Christophe Jaffrelot, "The Roots and Varieties of Political Conservatism in India," *Studies in Indian Politics* 5, no. 2 (2017): 205–17.

23. Alfred Stepan, Juan Linz, and Yogendra Yadav, *Crafting State-Nations: India and Other Multinational Democracies* (Baltimore: Johns Hopkins University Press, 2011); Alyssa Ayres, *Speaking Like a State: Language and Nationalism in Pakistan* (Cambridge University Press, 2009).

24. For a discussion of the strands within Congress, see Vivek Chibber, *Locked in Place: State-Building and Late Industrialization in India* (Princeton, NJ: Princeton University Press, 2003).

25. Steven I. Wilkinson, "Which Group Identities Lead to Most Violence? Evidence from India," in *Order, Conflict, and Violence*, ed. Stathis Kalyvas, Ian Shapiro, and Tarek Masoud (New York: Cambridge University Press, 2008), 271–300; Lawrence Saez, Giovanni Capoccia, and Eline de Rooij, "Where State Responses Fail: Religious Extremism and Separatism in India (1952–2002)," *Journal of Politics*, 74, no. 4 (2012): 1010–22.

26. Christo+phe Jaffrelot, *The Hindu Nationalist Movement in India* (New York: Columbia University Press, 1996).

27. Christophe Jaffrelot, "The Fate of Secularism in India," in *The BJP in Power: Indian Democracy and Religious Nationalism*, ed. Milan Vaishnav (Washington, DC: Carnegie Endowment for International Peace, 2019), 51–62.

28. Ayesha Jalal, *The Sole Spokesman: Jinnah, the Muslim League, and the Demand for Pakistan* (Cambridge: Cambridge University Press, 1985), offers a classic history of Jinnah and the Muslim League. For a more recent assessment, see Venkat Dhulipala, *Creating a New Medina: State Power, Islam, and the Quest for Pakistan in Late Colonial North India* (Cambridge: Cambridge University Press, 2015).

29. Christophe Jaffrelot, *The Pakistan Paradox: Instability and Resilience* (New York: Oxford University Press, 2015).

30. Farzana Shaikh, *Making Sense of Pakistan* (New York: Columbia University Press, 2009). *Pakistan: Nationalism Without a Nation?* (New Delhi: Manohar, 2002), provides a range of perspectives about the nature of Pakistani nationalism.

31. A classic study is David Gilmartin, *Empire and Islam: Punjab and the Making of Pakistan* (Berkeley: University of California Press, 1988).

32. Stephen P. Cohen, *The Idea of Pakistan* (Washington, DC: Brookings Institution Press, 2004).

33. Alyssa Ayres, *Speaking Like a State*.

34. Maya Tudor, *The Promise of Power: The Origins of Democracy in India and Autocracy in Pakistan* (Cambridge: Cambridge University Press, 2017).

35. Myron Weiner, *Sons of the Soil: Migration and Ethnic Conflict in India* (Princeton NJ: Princeton University Press, 1978).

36. James Manor, *The Expedient Utopian: Bandaranaike and Ceylon* (Cambridge: Cambridge University Press, 2009).

37. Neil DeVotta, *Blowback: Linguistic Nationalism, Institutional Decay, and Ethnic Conflict in Sri Lanka* (Stanford, CA: Stanford University Press, 2004); K. M De Silva, *A History of Sri Lanka*, Rev. & updated ed. (New Delhi: Penguin Books, 2005); K. N. O. Dharmadasa, *Language, Religion, and Ethnic Assertiveness: The Growth of Sinhalese Nationalism in Sri Lanka* (Ann Arbor: University of Michigan Press, 1992).

38. Donald L. Horowitz, *Ethnic Groups in Conflict* (Berkeley: University of California Press, 1985).

39. For an account of the rise of Tamil nationalism, see A. Jeyaratnam Wilson, *Sri Lankan Tamil Nationalism: Its Origins and Development in the Nineteenth and Twentieth Centuries* (New Delhi: Penguin, 2001).

40. On ethnic status, see Horowitz, *Ethnic Groups in Conflict*; Roger Dale Petersen, *Understanding Ethnic Violence: Fear, Hatred, and Resentment in Twentieth-Century Eastern Europe* (Cambridge: Cambridge University Press, 2002); Professor Lars-Erik Cederman, Kristian Skrede Gleditsch, and Halvard Buhaug, *Inequality, Grievances, and Civil War* (New York: Cambridge University Press, 2013).

41. John F. Cady, *A History of Modern Burma* (Ithaca: NCROL, 1958); Albert D. Moscotti, *British Policy and the Nationalist Movement in Burma, 1917–1937* (Honolulu: University Press of Hawaii, 1974).

42. Michael W. Charney, *A History of Modern Burma* (Cambridge: Cambridge University Press, 2009).

43. Mary P. Callahan, *Making Enemies: War and State Building in Burma* (Ithaca: Cornell University Press, 2003).

44. Martin J. Smith, *Burma: Insurgency and the Politics of Ethnicity*, 2nd ed. (London: Zed Books, 1999).

45. Guha, *India after Gandhi*.

46. Rajni Kothari, "The Congress 'System' in India," *Asian Survey* 4, no. 12 (1964): 1161–73.

47. Thomas Blom Hansen, *The Saffron Wave: Democracy and Hindu Nationalism in Modern India* (Princeton, NJ: Princeton University Press, 1999); Jaffrelot, *The Hindu Nationalist Movement*.

48. Vaishnav, ed., *The BJP in Power*.

49. Angana Chatterji, Thomas Blom Hansen, and Christophe Jaffrelot, eds., *Majoritarian State: How Hindu Nationalism Is Changing India* (Oxford: Oxford University Press, 2019).

50. Horowitz, *Ethnic Groups in Conflict*; DeVotta, *Blowback*.

51. Paul Pierson, *Politics in Time: History, Institutions, and Social Analysis* (Princeton, NJ: Princeton University Press, 2004).

52. See, among others, Shuja Nawaz, *Crossed Swords: Pakistan, Its Army, and the Wars Within* (Oxford: Oxford University Press, 2008); Cohen, *The Idea of Pakistan*; Mary P. Callahan, *Making Enemies: War and State Building in Burma* (Ithaca: Cornell University Press, 2003); Yoshihiro Nakanishi, *Strong Soldiers, Failed Revolution: The State and Military in Burma, 1962–1988* (Singapore: NUS Press, 2013).

53. Callahan, *Making Enemies*.

54. For a distinctly sympathetic take on Ne Win's threat perceptions, see Robert Taylor, *General Ne Win: A Political Biography* (Singapore: ISEAS-Yusof Ishak Institute, 2015).

For a distinctly less sympathetic assessment, closer to my own, see Bertil Lintner, *Burma in Revolt: Opium and Insurgency since 1948*, 2nd ed. (Chiang Mai, Thailand: Silkworm Books, 1999).

55. Thant Myint-U, *The Hidden History of Burma: Race, Capitalism, and the Crisis of Democracy in the 21st Century* (New York: W. W. Norton, 2019).

56. Scott Straus, *Making and Unmaking Nations: War, Leadership, and Genocide in Modern Africa* (Ithaca: Cornell University Press, 2015); Vincent Boudreau, *Resisting Dictatorship: Repression and Protest in Southeast Asia* (Cambridge: Cambridge University Press, 2004).

CHAPTER 4. INDIA

1. The closest existing study to this is Bidisha Biswas, *Managing Conflicts in India: Policies of Coercion and Accommodation* (Lanham, MD: Lexington Books, 2015), which offers a comparative overview of the counterinsurgency operations in Kashmir, Punjab, and Naxalite areas. Rajesh Rajagopalan, *Fighting Like a Guerrilla: The Indian Army and Counterinsurgency* (New Delhi: Routledge, 2007), examines COIN doctrine in India. Both are excellent works, but focus primarily on counterinsurgency specifically, and in particular conflicts/periods. Bethany Ann Lacina, *Rival Claims: Ethnic Violence and Territorial Autonomy under Indian Federalism* (Ann Arbor: University of Michigan Press, 2017), offers a detailed study of how the formation of subnational states can relate to political violence in India.

2. Paul R. Brass, *Language, Religion and Politics in North India* (Cambridge: Cambridge University Press, 1974); Lawrence Saez, Giovanni Capoccia, and Eline de Rooij, "Where State Responses Fail: Religious Extremism and Separatism in India (1952–2002)," *Journal of Politics*, 74, no. 4 (2012): 1010–22; Steven I. Wilkinson, "Which Group Identities Lead to Most Violence? Evidence from India," in *Order, Conflict, and Violence*, ed. Stathis Kalyvas, Ian Shapiro, and Tarek Masoud (New York: Cambridge University Press, 2008), 271–300; Pradeep K. Chhibber, *Ideology and Identity: The Changing Party Systems of India*, Reprint ed. (New York: Oxford University Press, 2018).

3. For an excellent recent assessment of how ideology matters in Indian politics, see Chhibber and Verma, *Ideology and Identity*.

4. Chhibber and Verma, *Ideology and Identity*, 10.

5. Maya Jessica Tudor, *The Promise of Power: The Origins of Democracy in India and Autocracy in Pakistan* (Cambridge: Cambridge University Press, 2013).

6. Sumit Sarkar, *Modern India, 1885–1947* (Delhi: Macmillan India, 2002), 124.

7. John R. McLane, *Indian Nationalism and the Early Congress* (Princeton, NJ: Princeton University Press, 1977), 5.

8. Stuart Corbridge and John Harriss, *Reinventing India: Liberalization, Hindu Nationalism, and Popular Democracy* (Cambridge: Polity, 2000), 13.

9. McLane, *Indian Nationalism*, 15.

10. William Gould, *Religion and Conflict in Modern South Asia* (New York: Cambridge University Press, 2012), 40.

11. Gould, *Religion and Conflict in Modern South Asia*, 39.

12. Thomas Blom Hansen, *The Saffron Wave: Democracy and Hindu Nationalism in Modern India* (Princeton, NJ: Princeton University Press, 1999), 76.

13. Christophe Jaffrelot, *Religion, Caste, and Politics in India* (New York: Columbia University Press, 2011), 39.

14. Hansen, *The Saffron Wave*, 76.

15. Sudipta Kaviraj, "Nationalism," in *The Oxford Companion to Politics in India*, ed. Niraja Gopal Jayal and Pratap Bhanu Mehta (New Delhi: Oxford University Press, 2011),

325; Niraja Gopal Jayal, *Citizenship and Its Discontents* (Cambridge, MA: Harvard University Press, 2013), 132.

16. Jayal, *Citizenship and Its Discontents*, 207.

17. Hansen, *The Saffron Wave*, 44–45.

18. Alfred Stepan, Juan Linz, and Yogendra Yadav, *Crafting State-Nations: India and Other Multinational Democracies* (Baltimore: Johns Hopkins University Press, 2011).

19. Stepan, Linz and Yadav, *Crafting State-Nations*, 53.

20. Sudipta Kaviraj, *The Imaginary Institution of India: Politics and Ideas* (New York: Columbia University Press, 2010), 157.

21. Kaviraj, *The Imaginary Institution of India*, 156; Jayal, *Citizenship and Its Discontents*, 211.

22. Gould, *Religion and Conflict in Modern South Asia*, 145.

23. Sarkar, *Modern India*, 264.

24. Stepan, Linz and Yadav, *Crafting State-Nations*, 54–55.

25. Alyssa Ayres, *Speaking like a State: Language and Nationalism in Pakistan* (Cambridge: Cambridge University Press, 2009).

26. Kaviraj, "Nationalism," 326.

27. Jaffrelot, *Religion, Caste, and Politics in India*; Christophe Jaffrelot, "The Roots and Varieties of Political Conservatism in India," *Studies in Indian Politics* 5, no. 2 (December 1, 2017): 205–17.

28. Gyanendra Pandey and Yunas Samad, *Fault Lines of Nationhood* (New Delhi: Roli Books, 2007), 31.

29. Kaviraj, "Nationalism," 327.

30. Gould, *Religion and Conflict in Modern South Asia*, 131.

31. Madhav Khosla, *India's Founding Moment: The Constitution of a Most Surprising Democracy* (Cambridge, MA: Harvard University Press, 2020), 122.

32. Hansen, *The Saffron Wave*, 45–46.

33. Partha Chatterjee, *Nationalist Thought and the Colonial World: A Derivative Discourse?* (London: Zed Books, 1986), 132.

34. Jaffrelot, *Religion, Caste, and Politics in India*, 39.

35. Christophe Jaffrelot, *The Hindu Nationalist Movement in India* (New York: Columbia University Press, 1996), 83. See also Jayal, *Citizenship and Its Discontents*, 208; Gould, *Religion and Conflict in Modern South Asia*, 103–4.

36. Khosla, *India's Founding Moment*, 121.

37. William Gould, *Hindu Nationalism and the Language of Politics in Late Colonial India* (Cambridge: Cambridge University Press, 2004), 7.

38. Jaffrelot, *The Hindu Nationalist Movement*, 83.

39. Sarkar, *Modern India*, 234; Gould, *Religion and Conflict in Modern South Asia*, 179.

40. Sarkar, *Modern India*, 356.

41. Sarkar, *Modern India*, 351.

42. Sarkar, *Modern India*, 63; Faisal Devji, *Muslim Zion: Pakistan as a Political Idea* (Cambridge, MA: Harvard University Press, 2013), 66.

43. Sarkar, *Modern India*, 249.

44. Kaviraj, *The Imaginary Institution of India*, 115.

45. D. A. Lowe, "Introduction: The Climactic Years 1917–47," in *Congress and the Raj: Facets of the Indian Struggle, 1917–47* (London: Heinemann, 1977), 19.

46. Sarkar, *Modern India*, 265.

47. Chatterjee, *Nationalist Thought and the Colonial World*.

48. Sarkar, *Modern India*, 338.

49. On the evolution of this bargain after independence, see Vivek Chibber, *Locked in Place: State-Building and Late Industrialization in India* (Princeton, NJ: Princeton

University Press, 2003); Adnan Naseemullah, *Development after Statism* (Cambridge: Cambridge University Press, 2016).

50. Jayal, *Citizenship and Its Discontents*, 209.

51. Chatterjee, *Nationalist Thought and the Colonial World*, 132.

52. Chatterjee, *Nationalist Thought and the Colonial World*, 141.

53. Corbridge and Harriss, *Reinventing India*, 18.

54. Sarkar, *Modern India*, 436.

55. Ramachandra Guha, *India after Gandhi: The History of the World's Largest Democracy*, 1st ed. (New York: Ecco, 2007), 34.

56. Jaffrelot, *The Hindu Nationalist Movement*, 11.

57. Jaffrelot, *The Hindu Nationalist Movement*, 19–21.

58. Jaffrelot, *The Hindu Nationalist Movement*, 26.

59. Gould, *Religion and Conflict in Modern South Asia*, 103.

60. Khosla, *India's Founding Moment*, 126.

61. Khosla, *India's Founding Moment*, 126.

62. Khosla, *India's Founding Moment*, 127.

63. Jaffrelot, *The Hindu Nationalist Movement*, 44. The Hindu nationalist movement has viewed Buddhists, Sikhs, and Jains as authentically indigenous religions, though the relationship between the movement and these communities has often been tense.

64. Jaffrelot, *The Hindu Nationalist Movement*, 57.

65. Jaffrelot, *Religion, Caste, and Politics in India*, 38.

66. Hansen, *The Saffron Wave*, 99.

67. For a fascinating account of other ideological debates in the immediate postcolonial moment, see Chhibber and Verma, *Ideology and Identity*, chapter 3.

68. Barbara F. Walter, *Reputation and Civil War: Why Separatist Conflicts Are so Violent* (Cambridge: Cambridge University Press, 2009).

69. See Jawaharlal Nehru, *The Discovery of India* (New Delhi: Penguin, 2004).

70. Khosla, *India's Founding Moment*, 138, 140.

71. Pran Nath Chopra, *The Collected Works of Sardar Vallabhbhai Patel* (Delhi: Konark Publishers, 1990), 12:121.

72. Durga Das, *Sardar Patel's Correspondence, 1945–50* (Ahmedabad: Navajivan House, 1971), 8:220–21.

73. Ashutosh Varshney, "Ethnic Conflict and Civil Society: India and Beyond," *World Politics* 53, no. 3 (April 2001): 362–98; Ashutosh Varshney, "Is India Becoming More Democratic?" *Journal of Asian Studies* 59, no. 1 (2000): 3–25.

74. Chopra, *The Collected Works of Sardar Vallabhbhai Patel*, 15:154.

75. Jawaharlal Nehru and G. Parthasarathi, *Letters to Chief Ministers, 1947–1964* (Delhi: Oxford University Press, 1985), 1:25. See also, from 1 November 1957: "We in India have the ghost of Pakistan coming in the way of our normal activities. Behind that ghost, there lies the history not only of the past ten years of freedom, but also of the years that preceded it, with all the communal bitterness and hatred which resulted in the partition of India," Nehru, *Letters to Chief Ministers*, 4:590.

76. Das, *Sardar Patel's Correspondence*, 9:116, 118.

77. Das, *Sardar Patel's Correspondence*, 9:37.

78. Nehru, *Letters to Chief Ministers*, 1:21.

79. Granville Austin, *The Indian Constitution: Cornerstone of a Nation*, 2 ed. (Oxford: Oxford University Press, 1999), 155.

80. Das, *Sardar Patel's Correspondence*, 6:354.

81. Quoted in *Hindustan Times* article in Chopra, *The Collected Works of Sardar Vallabhbhai Patel*, 14:82.

82. Nehru, *Letters to Chief Ministers*, 1:244.

83. Nehru, *Letters to Chief Ministers*, 1:245.

84. Nehru, *Letters to Chief Ministers*, 4:102.

85. Nehru, *Letters to Chief Ministers*, 4:103.

86. See also 27 June 1961 letter in Nehru, *Letters to Chief Ministers*, 5:450–51.

87. See also Chopra, *The Collected Works of Sardar Vallabhbhai Patel*, 12:231.

88. Summary of Patel, March 1949, in *Hindustan Times* article found in Chopra, *The Collected Works of Sardar Vallabhbhai Patel*, 14:110.

89. Das, *Sardar Patel's Correspondence*, 6:24.

90. Chopra, *The Collected Works of Sardar Vallabhbhai Patel*, 13:69–270.

91. Das, *Sardar Patel's Correspondence*, 1:250.

92. For another example of Nehru linking Kashmir to communal cleavages, see 5 January 1948: "In view of the dangerous implications of the situation on our frontiers, it is of particular importance that there should be peace and order everywhere in India and that there should in particular be no communal trouble . . . communal trouble in India reacts unfavourably on the Kashmir situation as well as on the all-India situation. We cannot and must not do what Pakistan does in its territory," Nehru, *Letters to Chief Ministers*, 1:45.

93. Das, *Sardar Patel's Correspondence*, 7:671.

94. Nehru, *Letters to Chief Ministers*, 3:231; emphasis added.

95. Nehru, *Letters to Chief Ministers*, 2:464; 1 August 1951.

96. Brass, *Language, Religion and Politics*.

97. Nehru, *Letters to Chief Ministers*, 1:294; 15 February 1949.

98. Nehru, *Letters to Chief Ministers*, 2:168; 18 August 1950.

99. Nehru, *Letters to Chief Ministers*, 5:243; 18 May 1959.

100. Nehru, *Letters to Chief Ministers*, 4:1 November 1957, 590.

101. Guha, *India after Gandhi*, 272.

102. Nehru, *Letters to Chief Ministers*, 2:414, 2 June 1951.

103. Nehru, *Letters to Chief Ministers*, 3:154.

104. "These areas, so full of promise and with such a fine and often sensitive and intelligent population, were hardly remembered by New Delhi. In a vague way no doubt they existed as outlying tract which had to be kept going. But there was no intimate appreciation of their existence, their difficulties and their problems," Nehru, *Letters to Chief Ministers*, 3:152.

105. Compare to the expectations outlined in Walter, *Reputation and Civil War*.

106. Brass, *Language, Religion and Politics*.

107. Das, *Sardar Patel's Correspondence*, 9:149.

108. Austin, *The Indian Constitution*, 240.

109. Austin, *The Indian Constitution*, 307.

110. Nehru, *Letters to Chief Ministers*, 1:143; 1 July 1948.

111. Austin, *The Indian Constitution*, 309.

112. Nehru, *Letters to Chief Ministers*, 4:625.

113. On the evolution of communism in India, see Bidyut Chakrabarty, *Communism in India: Events, Processes and Ideologies*, 1st ed. (Oxford: Oxford University Press, 2014).

114. Chopra, *The Collected Works of Sardar Vallabhbhai Patel*, 13:216.

115. In *Hindustan Times* report of speech in Kerala, 15 May 1950, in Chopra, *The Collected Works of Sardar Vallabhbhai Patel*, 15:148.

116. Nehru, *Letters to Chief Ministers*, 1:143.

117. Nehru, *Letters to Chief Ministers*, 1:350.

118. Nehru, *Letters to Chief Ministers*, 1:476–77.

119. Nehru, *Letters to Chief Ministers*, 2:392.

120. Jaffrelot, *The Hindu Nationalist Movement*.

121. David E. Ludden, *Making India Hindu: Religion, Community, and the Politics of Democracy in India*, 2nd ed. (Delhi: Oxford University Press, 2005).

122. Hansen, *The Saffron Wave*.

123. Milan Vaishnav, ed., *The BJP in Power: Indian Democracy and Religious Nationalism* (Washington, DC: Carnegie Endowment for International Peace, 2019).

124. Ashutosh Varshney, "Contested Meanings: India's National Identity, Hindu Nationalism, and the Politics of Anxiety," *Daedalus* 122, no. 3 (June 22, 1993), 231.

125. Tariq Thachil, *Elite Parties, Poor Voters: How Social Services Win Votes in India*, Reprint ed. (Cambridge: Cambridge University Press, 2016).

126. Paul Staniland, "Between a Rock and a Hard Place Insurgent Fratricide, Ethnic Defection, and the Rise of Pro-State Paramilitaries," *Journal of Conflict Resolution* 56, no. 1 (February 2012): 16–40.

127. Mark Tully and Satish Jacob, *Amritsar: Mrs Gandhi's Last Battle* (London: J. Cape, 1985); Paul Brass, "The Punjab Crisis and the Unity of India," in *India's Democracy: An Analysis of Changing State-Society Relations*, ed. Atul Kohli (Princeton, NJ: Princeton University Press, 1988), 169–213.

128. Walter, *Reputation and Civil War*.

129. B. G. Verghese, *India's Northeast Resurgent: Ethnicity, Insurgency, Governance, Development* (New Delhi: Konark, 1996).

130. On the RGN, see below.

131. For background on these groups, see Paul Staniland, *Networks of Rebellion: Explaining Insurgent Cohesion and Collapse* (Ithaca: Cornell University Press, 2014).

132. Mark Tully and Satish Jacob, *Amritsar: Mrs Gandhi's Last Battle* (London: J. Cape, 1985); Paul Brass, "The Punjab Crisis and the Unity of India," in *India's Democracy: An Analysis of Changing State-Society Relations*, ed. Atul Kohli (Princeton, NJ: Princeton University Press, 1988), 169–213.

133. Staniland, "Between a Rock and a Hard Place"; C. Christine Fair, "Lessons from India's Experience in the Punjab, 1978–1993," in *India and Counterinsurgency: Lessons Learned*, ed. Sumit Ganguly and David P Fidler (London: Routledge, 2009), chapter 8.

134. The efforts to reach out to the Hizb collapsed in the face of a spoiler campaign by Pakistani militants, Pakistani pressure, and the early publicization of the talks.

135. For recent scholarly studies, see Alpa Shah, *In the Shadows of the State: Indigenous Politics, Environmentalism, and Insurgency in Jharkhand, India* (Durham, NC: Duke University Press Books, 2010); Shivaji Mukherjee, "Why Are the Longest Insurgencies Low Violence? Politician Motivations, Sons of the Soil, and Civil War Duration," *Civil Wars* 16, no. 2 (April 3, 2014): 172–207, https://doi.org/10.1080/13698249.2014.927702; Shivaji Mukherjee, "Colonial Origins of Maoist Insurgency in India: Historical Institutions and Civil War," *Journal of Conflict Resolution* 62, no. 10 (November 1, 2018): 2232–74, https://doi.org/10.1177/0022002717727818; Aditya Dasgupta, Kishore Gawande, and Devesh Kapur, "(When) Do Antipoverty Programs Reduce Violence? India's Rural Employment Guarantee and Maoist Conflict," *International Organization* 71, no. 3 (2017): 605–32, https://doi.org/10.1017/S0020818317000236; Alpa Shah and Dhruv Jain, "Naxalbari at Its Golden Jubilee: Fifty Recent Books on the Maoist Movement in India," *Modern Asian Studies* 51, no. 4 (July 2017): 1165–1219, https://doi.org/10.1017/S0026749X16000792; Kanchan Chandra and Omar García-Ponce, "Why Ethnic Subaltern-Led Parties Crowd Out Armed Organizations: Explaining Maoist Violence in India," *World Politics* 71, no. 2 (April 2019): 367–416, https://doi.org/10.1017/S004388711800028X. Accessible accounts can be found in Nandini Sundar, *The Burning Forest: India's War in Bastar* (New Delhi: Juggernaut Books, 2016); Alpa Shah, *Nightmarch: Among India's Revolutionary Guerrillas*, 1st ed. (Chicago: University of Chicago Press, 2019).

136. "Naxalism Biggest Threat to Internal Security: Manmohan," *The Hindu*, May 24, 2010, https://www.thehindu.com/news/national/Naxalism-biggest-threat-to-internal-secu rity-Manmohan/article16302952.ece.

137. On the former, see Atul Kohli, *Democracy and Discontent: India's Growing Crisis of Governability* (Cambridge: Cambridge University Press, 1990); on the latter, Sundar, *The Burning Forest*.

138. There is a rich broader literature on counterinsurgent militias and side switching. See Corinna Jentzsch, Stathis N. Kalyvas, and Livia Isabella Schubiger, "Militias in Civil Wars," *Journal of Conflict Resolution* 59, no. 5 (August 1, 2015): 755–69, https://doi.org/10.1177/0022002715576753; Kristine Eck, "Repression by Proxy: How Military Purges and Insurgency Impact the Delegation of Coercion," *Journal of Conflict Resolution* 59, no. 5 (August 1, 2015): 924–46, https://doi.org/10.1177/0022002715576746; Paul Staniland, "Militias, Ideology, and the State," *Journal of Conflict Resolution* 59, no. 5 (August 1, 2015): 770–93, https://doi.org/10.1177/0022002715576749; Sabine C. Carey, Michael P. Colaresi, and Neil J. Mitchell, "Governments, Informal Links to Militias, and Accountability," *Journal of Conflict Resolution* 59, no. 5 (August 1, 2015): 850–76, https://doi.org/10.1177/0022002715576747; Sabine C. Carey, Neil J. Mitchell, and Will Lowe, "States, the Security Sector, and the Monopoly of Violence: A New Database on pro-Government Militias," *Journal of Peace Research* 50, no. 2 (March 1, 2013): 249–58, https://doi.org/10.1177/0022343312464881; Costantino Pischedda, "Wars within Wars: Why Windows of Opportunity and Vulnerability Cause Inter-Rebel Fighting in Internal Conflicts," *International Security* 43, no. 1 (August 1, 2018): 138–76, https://doi.org/10.1162/isec_a_00322; Fotini Christia, *Alliance Formation in Civil Wars* (Cambridge: Cambridge University Press, 2012).

139. On reasons why militias are often ambiguous and opaque, see Jentzsch et al., "Militias in Civil Wars."

140. C. Christine Fair, "Lessons from India's Experience in the Punjab, 1978–1993," in *India and Counterinsurgency: Lessons Learned*, ed. Sumit Ganguly and David P Fidler (London: Routledge, 2009), chapter 8.

141. Staniland, "Between a Rock and a Hard Place."

142. S. C. Dev, *Nagaland, the Untold Story* (Calcutta: Gouri Dev, 1988); M. Horam, *Naga Insurgency: The Last Thirty Years* (New Delhi: Cosmo Publications, 1988).

143. For an overview of this history, see Alex Waterman, "Counterinsurgents' Use of Force and 'Armed Orders' in Naga Northeast India," *Asian Security* 17, no. 1 (January 2021): 119–37, https://doi.org/10.1080/14799855.2020.1724099.

144. The discussion here is based on Sundar, *The Burning Forest*.

145. Paul R Brass, *Theft of an Idol: Text and Context in the Representation of Collective Violence* (Princeton, NJ: Princeton University Press, 1997).

146. On the origins of "militarized elections" (i.e. Paul Staniland, "Armed Groups and Militarized Elections," *International Studies Quarterly* 59, no. 4 (December 1, 2015): 694–705, https://doi.org/10.1111/isqu.12195; see Kohli, *Democracy and Discontent*.

147. Thomas Blom Hansen, *Wages of Violence: Naming and Identity in Postcolonial Bombay*. (Princeton, NJ: Princeton University Press, 2001) explores the Shiv Sena's rise.

148. Jaffrelot, *The Hindu Nationalist Movement*; Hansen, *The Saffron Wave*.

149. This is a feature of India's Constitution, which gives law and order responsibility to states unless the central government needs to step in due to the state's inability to maintain order.

150. Ashutosh Varshney, "India Defies the Odds: Why Democracy Survives," *Journal of Democracy* 9, no. 3 (July 1, 1998): 36–50.

151. In recent years, more questions have emerged about the nature of democracy in India. See Soutik Biswas, "'Electoral Autocracy': The Downgrading of India's Democracy," BBC, March 16, 2021, https://www.bbc.com/news/world-asia-india-56393944.

152. Paul Staniland, "Violence and Democracy," *Comparative Politics* 47, no. 1 (2014): 99–118.

153. Recent scholarly analyses of state–armed group interactions in this context include Shalaka Thakur and Rajesh Venugopal, "Parallel Governance and Political Order in Contested Territory: Evidence from the Indo-Naga Ceasefire," *Asian Security* 15, no. 3 (September 2, 2019): 285–303, https://doi.org/10.1080/14799855.2018.1455 185; and Waterman, "Counterinsurgents' Use of Force." Both productively engage with my earlier assessments of the Naga conflict in Paul Staniland, "States, Insurgents, and Wartime Political Orders," *Perspectives on Politics* 10, no. 2 (2012): 243–64, https://doi.org/10.1017/S1537592712000655; Paul Staniland, "Armed Politics and the Study of Intra-state Conflict," *Journal of Peace Research* 54, no. 4 (July 1, 2017): 459–67, https://doi.org/10.1177/0022343317698848. See also Charles Chasie, *The Naga Imbroglio : A Personal Perspective* (Standard Printers & Publishers, 1999); Sanjoy Hazarika, *Strangers of the Mist: Tales of War and Peace from India's Northeast* (New Delhi: Viking, Penguin Books India, 1994); Sanjib Baruah, "Confronting Constructionism: Ending India's Naga War," *Journal of Peace Research* 40, no. 3 (May 1, 2003): 321–38, https://doi.org/10.1177/00223433030 40003005; Verghese, *India's Northeast Resurgent*; S. C. Dev, *Nagaland, the Untold Story* (Calcutta: Gouri Dev, 1988); Subir Bhaumik, *Troubled Periphery: Crisis of India's North East* (Los Angeles: SAGE, 2009) for overviews.

154. On related dynamics around splits and negotiations, see Kathleen Gallagher Cunningham, *Inside the Politics of Self-Determination* (Oxford: Oxford University Press, 2014); Ethan Bueno de Mesquita, "Conciliation, Counterterrorism, and Patterns of Terrorist Violence." *International Organization* 59, no. 1 (winter 2005): 145–76.

155. Waterman, "Counterinsurgents' Use of Force."

156. Wendy Pearlman, "Spoiling Inside and Out: Internal Political Contestation and the Middle East Peace Process," *International Security* 33, no. 3 (winter /2009 2008): 79–109; Kathleen Gallagher Cunningham, *Inside the Politics of Self-Determination* (Oxford: Oxford University Press, 2014); and Peter Krause, *Rebel Power: Why National Movements Compete, Fight, and Win*, 1 ed. (Ithaca: Cornell University Press, 2017). In the Naga case, see Waterman, "Counterinsurgents' Use of Force," 12–13.

157. Nehru, *Letters to Chief Ministers*, 2:414.

158. Nehru, *Letters to Chief Ministers*, 3:154.

159. Horam, *Naga Insurgency*, 81.

160. Nehru, *Letters to Chief Ministers*, 4:363.

161. Nehru, *Letters to Chief Ministers*, 4:557.

162. Nehru, *Letters to Chief Ministers*, 4:558.

163. Waterman, "Counterinsurgents' Use of Force," 10. See also Rajesh Rajagopalan, "'Restoring Normalcy': The Evolution of the Indian Army's Counterinsurgency Doctrine," *Small Wars and Insurgencies* 11, no. 1 (2000): 46–48.

164. Nari Rustomji, *Imperilled Frontiers: India's North-Eastern Borderlands* (Delhi: Oxford, 1983), 31.

165. Nehru, *Letters to Chief Ministers*, 4:558–59.

166. For instance, in July 1960 he wrote that "broadly speaking, this agreement means establishment of a new State in the Naga country, to be called Nagaland, with the normal rights and obligations of a State. But it is quite obvious that so long as the law and order situation is not quite normal there, special arrangements will have to be made to deal with it. The Governor, therefore will be responsible for law and order . . . the hostile hard core are not likely to accept this agreement, even though the great majority of the Naga people might approve of it. And so we may still have to continue to deal with the activities of these hostile groups . . . the tide has turned in Nagaland and we move now towards more peaceful conditions and normality," *Letters to Chief Ministers*, 5:399–400.

167. Nehru, *Letters to Chief Ministers*, 5:400.

168. Nehru, *Letters to Chief Ministers*, 5:523.

169. Walter, *Reputation and Civil War*.

170. Bhaumik, *Troubled Periphery*, 18.

171. Y. D. Gundevia, *War and Peace in Nagaland* (DehraDun: Palit & Palit, 1975), 72.

172. Gundevia, *War and Peace in Nagaland*, 74.

173. Gundevia, *War and Peace in Nagaland*, 77; Marcus Franke, *War and Nationalism in South Asia: The Indian State and the Nagas* (London: Routledge, 2009), 109.

174. Franke, *War and Nationalism in South Asia*, 109.

175. Franke, *War and Nationalism in South Asia*, 115.

176. D. K. Palit, *Sentinels of the North-East: The Assam Rifles* (New Delhi: Palit & Palit, 1984), 299–304.

177. Horam, *Naga Insurgency*, 144.

178. Horam, *Naga Insurgency*, 145.

179. Horam, *Naga Insurgency*, 146.

180. Horam, *Naga Insurgency*, 147.

181. Gundevia, *War and Peace in Nagaland*, 165; Franke, *War and Nationalism in South Asia*, 114.

182. Horam, *Naga Insurgency*, 140–42.

183. Horam, *Naga Insurgency*, 143.

184. For background, see Subir Bhaumik chapter in Samir Kumar Das, ed. *Peace Processes and Peace Accords* (2005), 2:217; Dev, *Nagaland*, 82.

185. Subir Bhaumik chapter in Samir Kumar Das, ed., *Peace Processes and Peace Accords*, 2:217.

186. Horam, *Naga Insurgency*, 143.

187. Horam, *Naga Insurgency*, 147,

188. Horam, *Naga Insurgency*, 146.

189. Dev, *Nagaland*, 82.

190. There were also several very small splinter groups that came over to India. See Dev, *Nagaland*, 56–79.

191. B. K. Nehru, *Nice Guys Finish Second* (New Delhi: Viking, 1997), 522.

192. Nehru, *Nice Guys Finish Second*, offers the government's perspective on this shift.

193. Nehru, *Nice Guys Finish Second*, 503–4.

194. Nehru, *Nice Guys Finish Second*, 505.

195. Verghese, *India's Northeast Resurgent*, 94. For corroboration, see Gundevia, *War and Peace in Nagaland*, 207.

196. K. V. Krishna Rao, *In the Service of the Nation: Reminiscences* (New Delhi: Viking, 2001), 279–80.

197. Gundevia, *War and Peace in Nagaland*, 206.

198. Dev, *Nagaland*, 98–99.

199. Franke, *War and Nationalism in South Asia*, 116.

200. Horam, *Naga Insurgency*, 177.

201. Horam, *Naga Insurgency*, 190.

202. Dev, *Nagaland*, 139.

203. MHA Annual Report 77–78, 13.

204. Waterman, "Counterinsurgents' Use of Force," 14.

205. Horam, *Naga Insurgency*, 151.

206. Horam, *Naga Insurgency*, 151.

207. Dev, *Nagaland*, 83.

208. Nehru, *Nice Guys Finish Second*, 523.

209. *Ministry of Home Affairs Annual Report* (Government of India, 1986–87), 7.

210. Udayon Misra, *The Periphery Strikes Back: Challenges to the Nation-State in Assam and Nagaland* (Shimla: Indian Institute of Advanced Study, 2000), 53.

211. Rita Manchanda and Tapan Bose, "Expanding the Middle Space in the Naga Peace Process," *Economic and Political Weekly* 46, no. 53 (2011): 52.

212. Bhaumik, *Troubled Periphery*, 102.

213. Ved Marwah, *India in Turmoil : Jammu & Kashmir, the Northeast and Left Extremism* (New Delhi: Rupa & Co., 2009), 193.

214. Baruah, *Confronting Constructionism*, 335.

215. Åshild Kolås, "Naga Militancy and Violent Politics in the Shadow of Ceasefire," *Journal of Peace Research* 48, no. 6 (November 1, 2011): 781–92.

216. Bhaumik, *Troubled Periphery*, 207–8.

217. Kolås, "Naga Militancy," 791.

218. Alex Waterman, "Counterinsurgents' Use of Force and 'Armed Orders' in Naga Northeast India," 5.

219. Kolby Hanson, "Good Times and Bad Apples: Rebel Recruitment in Crackdown and Truce," *American Journal of Political Science*, accessed October 5, 2020, https://doi.org/10.1111/ajps.12555, argues that the cease-fires have decreased the individual "quality" of recruits, since the lower costs and risks, as well as the increased importance of material rewards, have shifted the nature of participants away from ideological commitments.

220. Thakur and Venugopal, "Parallel Governance and Political Order," 9.

221. Thakur and Venugopal, "Parallel Governance and Political Order," 10.

222. Sangeeta Barooah Pisharoty, "NSCN (I-M) Blames Interlocuturo—the Nagaland Governor—for Peace Accord Delays," *The Wire*, August 2, 2020, https://thewire.in/politics/nagaland-rn-ravi-framework-agreement-delay.

223. Sadiq Naqvi, "Naga Insurgent Group NSCN(K) Splits Down the Middle, Konyak Faction Considering Talks with the Centre," *Hindustan Times*, September 30, 2018, https://www.hindustantimes.com/india-news/naga-insurgent-group-nscn-k-splits-down-the-middle-konyak-faction-considering-talks-with-centre/story-n9F1UQcbCaNuLU6Vsngy2M.html.

224. See Waterman, "Counterinsurgents' Use of Force," on these post-2015 dynamics.

225. Compare Sunil Khilnani, *The Idea of India* (New York: Farrar Straus Giroux, 1998), to the overview offered in Milan Vaishnav, ed., *The BJP in Power: Indian Democracy and Religious Nationalism* (Washington, DC: Carnegie Endowment for International Peace, 2019); and Angana Chatterji, Thomas Blom Hansen, and Christophe Jaffrelot, eds., *Majoritarian State: How Hindu Nationalism Is Changing India* (Delhi: HarperCollins India, 2019).

226. "'Control of State Power by Hindus Absolutely Essential': BJP MP Tejasvi Surya Wades into Controversy Again," *Indian Express*, August 5, 2020, https://indianexpress.com/article/cities/bangalore/tejasvi-surya-ayodhya-ram-mandir-bengaluru-hindus6541125/.

227. Kanchan Chandra, "Ethnic Parties and Democratic Stability," *Perspectives on Politics* 3, no. 2 (June 2005): 235–52.

CHAPTER 5. PAKISTAN

1. Haroon K. Ullah, *Vying for Allah's Vote: Understanding Islamic Parties, Political Violence, and Extremism in Pakistan* (Washington, DC: Georgetown University Press, 2013), 9.

2. Paul Staniland, Asfandyar Mir, and Sameer Lalwani, "Politics and Threat Perception: Explaining Pakistani Military Strategy on the North West Frontier," *Security Studies* 27, no. 4 (October 2, 2018): 535–74.

3. John R. McLane, *Indian Nationalism and the Early Congress* (Princeton, NJ: Princeton University Press, 1977), 362.

4. McLane, *Indian Nationalism*, 363.

5. McLane, *Indian Nationalism*, 364.

6. Farzana Shaikh, *Community and Consensus in Islam: Muslim Representation in Colonial India, 1860–1947* (Cambridge: Cambridge University Press, 1989), 135.

7. Shaikh, *Community and Consensus*, 136.

8. Shaikh, *Community and Consensus*.

9. William Gould, *Religion and Conflict in Modern South Asia* (New York: Cambridge University Press, 2012), 25.

10. Christophe Jaffrelot, *The Pakistan Paradox: Instability and Resilience* (New York: Oxford University Press, 2015), 49.

11. Jaffrelot, *The Pakistan Paradox*, 66.

12. Shaikh, *Community and Consensus*, 161.

13. Shaikh, *Community and Consensus*, 161.

14. Shaikh, *Community and Consensus*, 174.

15. Shaikh, *Community and Consensus*, 184; Jaffrelot, *The Pakistan Paradox*, 54.

16. Jaffrelot, *The Pakistan Paradox*, 67; Shaikh, *Community and Consensus*, 187.

17. Jaffrelot, *The Pakistan Paradox*, 67.

18. Ayesha Jalal, "Exploding Communalism: the Politics of Muslim Identity in South Asia," in *Nationalism, Democracy and Development: State and Politics in India*, ed. Sugata Bose and Ayesha Jalal (Delhi: Oxford University Press, 1997), 90.

19. Farzana Shaikh, *Making Sense of Pakistan* (New York: Columbia University Press, 2009), 19.

20. Shaikh, *Making Sense of Pakistan*, 25.

21. David Gilmartin, *Empire and Islam: Punjab and the Making of Pakistan* (Berkeley: University of California Press, 1988), 96.

22. Jaffrelot, *The Pakistan Paradox*, 65.

23. Shaikh, *Community and Consensus*, 197.

24. David Gilmartin, "The Historiography of India's Partition: Between Civilization and Modernity," *Journal of Asian Studies* 74, no. 1 (February 2015): 32.

25. Shaikh, *Community and Consensus*, 229.

26. Shaikh, *Making Sense of Pakistan*, 2.

27. Jalal, "Exploding Communalism," 92.

28. Faisal Devji, *Muslim Zion: Pakistan as a Political Idea* (Cambridge, MA: Harvard University Press, 2013), 89.

29. Jaffrelot, *The Pakistan Paradox*, 69.

30. Niraja Gopal Jayal, *Citizenship and Its Discontents* (Cambridge, MA: Harvard University Press, 2013), 223.

31. Gilmartin, *Empire and Islam*, 109.

32. Gilmartin, *Empire and Islam*, 112.

33. Gilmartin, *Empire and Islam*, 114.

34. Gilmartin, *Empire and Islam*, 114.

35. Shaikh, *Making Sense of Pakistan*, 41.

36. See Maya Tudor, *The Promise of Power: The Origins of Democracy in India and Autocracy in Pakistan* (Cambridge: Cambridge University Press, 2010), on the tensions, including serious redistributive disagreements, that accompanied the efforts to bring Bengal into the League.

37. Alyssa Ayres, *Speaking like a State: Language and Nationalism in Pakistan* (Cambridge: Cambridge University Press, 2009), 27.

38. Stephen P. Cohen, *The Idea of Pakistan* (Washington, DC: Brookings Institution Press, 2004), 161; Aqil Shah, *The Army and Democracy: Military Politics in Pakistan* (Cambridge, MA: Harvard University Press, 2014), 37.

39. Gyanendra Pandey and Yunas Samad, *Fault Lines of Nationhood* (New Delhi: Roli Books, 2008), 80.

40. Pandey and Samad, *Fault Lines of Nationhood*, 83.

41. Shaikh, *Making Sense of Pakistan*, 42.

42. Shaikh, *Making Sense of Pakistan*, 38. Jalal goes further in suggesting that he would have been open to a federal/confederal arrangement even after the Lahore Resolution, until 1946 (Jalal, "Exploding Communalism," 93).

43. Sumit Sarkar, *Modern India, 1885–1947* (Delhi: Macmillan India, 2002), 379.

44. Devji, Muslim Zion; Jaffrelot, The Pakistan Paradox; Venkat Dhulipala, *Creating a New Medina: State Power, Islam, and the Quest for Pakistan in Late Colonial North India* (Cambridge: Cambridge University Press, 2015).

45. Shaikh, *Making Sense of Pakistan*, 400.

46. Joya Chatterji, *Bengal Divided: Hindu Communalism and Partition, 1932–1947* (Cambridge: Cambridge University Press, 2002), 221–22.

47. Shah, *The Army and Democracy*, 56.

48. Madhav Khosla, *India's Founding Moment: The Constitution of a Most Surprising Democracy* (Cambridge, MA: Harvard University Press, 2020), 114.

49. Cohen, *The Idea of Pakistan*, 72.

50. Ayres, *Speaking like a State*, 128.

51. Tudor, *The Promise of Power*.

52. Allen McGrath, *The Destruction of Pakistan's Democracy* (Karachi: Oxford University Press, 1996), 64.

53. McGrath, *The Destruction of Pakistan's Democracy*, 67.

54. Shaikh, *Making Sense of Pakistan*, 2.

55. McGrath, *The Destruction of Pakistan's Democracy*, 71.

56. McGrath, *The Destruction of Pakistan's Democracy*, 73.

57. Farahnaz Ispahani, *Purifying the Land of the Pure: Pakistan's Religious Minorities* (Noida: HarperCollins India, 2016), 37.

58. Shaikh, *Making Sense of Pakistan*, 84.

59. McGrath, *The Destruction of Pakistan's Democracy*, 93.

60. Ispahani, *Purifying the Land of the Pure*, 48.

61. Ullah, *Vying for Allah's Vote*, 22.

62. Johann Chacko, "Religious Parties: The Politics of Denominational Diversity in an Islamic Republic," in *Pakistan's Political Parties: Surviving between Dictatorship and Democracy*, ed. Mariam Mufti, Sahar Shafqat, and Niloufer Siddiqui (Washington, DC: Georgetown University Press, 2020), 116.

63. Chacko, "Religious Parties," 109.

64. Ayres, *Speaking like a State*, 13.

65. Ayres, *Speaking like a State*, 28.

66. Shah, *The Army and Democracy*, 34.

67. Cohen, *The Idea of Pakistan*, 54.

68. Jaffrelot, *The Pakistan Paradox*, 98.

69. Jaffrelot, *The Pakistan Paradox*, 202.

70. Ayres, *Speaking like a State*, 42.

71. Jaffrelot, *The Pakistan Paradox*, 99.

72. Ayres, *Speaking like a State*, 43.

73. Shah, *The Army and Democracy*, 60.

74. Jaffrelot, *The Pakistan Paradox*, 101.

75. Ayres, *Speaking like a State*, 46.

76. Shah, *The Army and Democracy*, 14.

77. McGrath, *The Destruction of Pakistan's Democracy*, 119.

78. Ispahani, *Purifying the Land of the Pure*, 55–56.

79. Shah, *The Army and Democracy*, 55.

80. Ramachandra Guha, *India after Gandhi: The History of the World's Largest Democracy*, 1st ed. (New York: Ecco, 2007), 743.

81. Shah, *The Army and Democracy*, 75.

82. Shah, *The Army and Democracy*, 75.

83. McGrath, *The Destruction of Pakistan's Democracy*, 53.

84. Ishtiaq Ahmed, *The Pakistan Garrison State: Origins, Evolution, Consequences* (Karachi: Oxford University Press, 2013), 107.

85. Ullah, *Vying for Allah's Vote*, 61.

86. Shah, *The Army and Democracy*, 76.

87. Shah, *The Army and Democracy*, 79.

88. Ayesha Jalal, *The State of Martial Rule: The Origins of Pakistan's Political Economy of Defence* (Cambridge: Cambridge University Press, 1990).

89. Philip Jones, "Pakistan People's Party: From Populism to Patronage," in *Pakistan's Political Parties: Surviving between Dictatorship and Democracy*, ed. Mariam Mufti, Sahar Shafqat, and Niloufer Siddiqui (Washington, DC: Georgetown University Press, 2020), 43.

90. Jalal, *The State of Martial Rule*; Shah, *The Army and Democracy*.

91. C. Christine Fair, *Fighting to the End: The Pakistan Army's Way of War* (New York: Oxford University Press, 2014), 73.

92. Shah, *The Army and Democracy*, 88, 93.

93. Samuel P. Huntington, *Political Order in Changing Societies* (New Haven: Yale University Press, 1968).

94. Jaffrelot, *The Pakistan Paradox*, 321.

95. Mohammad Ayub Khan and Craig Baxter, *Diaries of Field Marshal Mohammad Ayub Khan, 1966–1972* (Karachi: Oxford University Press, 2007), 18 Feb 1967, 63.

96. Khan and Baxter, 25 May 1967, 100–101.

97. Khan and Baxter, 12 Aug 1967, 132.

98. Khan and Baxter, 23 August 1967, 138.

99. Khan and Baxter, 7 Sept 1967, 145.

100. Jaffrelot, *The Pakistan Paradox*, 120.

101. Richard Sisson and Leo E. Rose, *War and Secession: Pakistan, India, and the Creation of Bangladesh* (Berkeley: University of California Press, 1990); and Srinath Raghavan, *1971: A Global History of the Creation of Bangladesh* (Cambridge, MA: Harvard University Press, 2013), provide detailed background to the crisis.

102. On Bhutto's abandonment of the socialist Left in 1970s, see Ayesha Siddiqa, "The Kingmaker: Pakistan's Military and Political Parties," in *Pakistan's Political Parties: Surviving between Dictatorship and Democracy*, ed. Mariam Mufti, Sahar Shafqat, and Niloufer Siddiqui (Washington, DC: Georgetown University Press, 2020), 220.

103. Background on Bhutto can be found in Stanley A. Wolpert, *Zulfi Bhutto of Pakistan: His Life and Times* (New York: Oxford University Press, 1993); Philip Jones, *The Pakistan People's Party: Rise to Power* (New York: Oxford University Press, 2003); Owen Bennett-Jones, *The Bhutto Dynasty: The Struggle for Power in Pakistan* (New Haven: Yale University Press, 2020).

104. Hasan-Askari Rizvi, *The Military and Politics in Pakistan 1947–1997* (Lahore: Sang-e-Meel Publications, 2000), 170.

105. Ullah, *Vying for Allah's Vote*, 23.

106. Ullah, *Vying for Allah's Vote*, 24; Rizvi, *The Military and Politics*, 170.

107. Vali R. Nasr, "International Politics, Domestic Imperatives, and Identity Mobilization: Sectarianism in Pakistan, 1979–1998," *Comparative Politics* 32, no. 2 (2000): 175.

108. For a long list of specifics, see Rizvi, *The Military and Politics*, 170–73. Fair, *Fighting to the End*; and Shah, *The Army and Democracy*, devote extensive attention to Zia's period of rule.

109. Jones, "Pakistan People's Party," 52.

110. Ayres, *Speaking like a State*, 35.

111. Ayres, *Speaking like a State*, 40.

112. Cohen, *The Idea of Pakistan*, 84.

113. Nasr, "International Politics, Domestic Imperatives, and Identity Mobilization"; Mariam Abou Zahab and Olivier Roy, *Islamist Networks: The Afghan-Pakistan Connection* (New York: Columbia University Press, 2004).

114. Rizvi, *The Military and Politics*, 245.

115. Saeed Shafqat, "The Formation, Development, and Decay of the Pakistan Muslim League-Nawaz," in *Pakistan's Political Parties: Surviving between Dictatorship and Democracy*, ed. Mariam Mufti, Sahar Shafqat, and Niloufer Siddiqui (Washington, DC: Georgetown University Press, 2020), 27.

116. Nasr, "International Politics, Domestic Imperatives, and Identity Mobilization," 177.

117. Ullah, *Vying for Allah's Vote*, 23.

118. See Cohen, *The Idea of Pakistan*; Jaffrelot, *Pakistan Paradox*; and Mariam Mufti, Sahar Shafqat, and Niloufer Siddiqui, eds., *Pakistan's Political Parties: Surviving between Dictatorship and Democracy* (Washington, DC: Georgetown University Press, 2020), for general discussions of the differences among these parties.

119. Ullah, *Vying for Allah's Vote*, 25.

120. Ullah, *Vying for Allah's Vote*, 6.

121. Ullah, *Vying for Allah's Vote*.

122. Tabinda Khan, "Pakistan Tehreek-e-Insaf: From a Movement to a Catch-All Party," in *Pakistan's Political Parties: Surviving between Dictatorship and Democracy,* ed. Mariam Mufti, Sahar Shafqat, and Niloufer Siddiqui (Washington, DC: Georgetown University Press, 2020), 70.

123. Jones, "Pakistan People's Party," 41.

124. Chacko, "Religious Parties," 109, 116.

125. Chacko, "Religious Parties," 118.

126. Two important components of military power in Pakistan are its control over economic resources and its network of retired personnel in state institutions. Ayesha Siddiqa, *Military Inc.: Inside Pakistan's Military Economy* (London: Pluto, 2007); Paul Staniland, Adnan Naseemullah, and Ahsan Butt, "Pakistan's Military Elite," *Journal of Strategic Studies* 43, no. 1 (January 2, 2020): 74–103.

127. Shuja Nawaz, *The Battle for Pakistan: The Bitter US Friendship and a Tough Neighbourhood* (New York: Vintage Books, 2019), 43.

128. Nawaz, *The Battle for Pakistan*, 297.

129. Rizvi, *The Military and Politics*, 245.

130. Rizvi, *The Military and Politics*, 247.

131. Jaffrelot, *The Pakistan Paradox*.

132. Siddiqa, "The Kingmaker," 231.

133. Nasr, "International Politics, Domestic Imperatives, and Identity Mobilization," 180.

134. Nawaz, *The Battle for Pakistan*.

135. Nawaz, *The Battle for Pakistan*.

136. https://www.crisisgroup.org/asia/south-asia/pakistan/b150-shaping-new-peace-pakistans-tribal-areas.

137. There was some limited armed leftist mobilization in East Pakistan in the late 1940s, and some leftist radicals joined Baloch insurgents in the 1960s. But there is no equivalent to the Naxalites in India, JVP in Sri Lanka, or CPB in Burma/Myanmar.

138. Nawaz, *The Battle for Pakistan*, 291.

139. A valuable history of armed politics can be found in Laurent Gayer, *Karachi: Ordered Disorder and the Struggle for the City* (Oxford: Oxford University Press, 2014).

140. Jaffrelot, *The Pakistan Paradox*.

141. Staniland et al., "Politics and Threat Perception."

142. Compare to the account of Indian linguistic policies in Alfred Stepan, Juan Linz, and Yogendra Yadav, *Crafting State-Nations: India and Other Multinational Democracies* (Baltimore: Johns Hopkins University Press, 2011).

143. Fair, *Fighting to the End*, 144.

144. For a detailed background of the rise of the conflict, see Raghavan, *1971*.

145. Sisson and Rose, *War and Secession*.

146. December 11, 1970, "Operation Blitz" document by Lt. Gen Sahibzada Yaqub Khan, quoted in Shuja Nawaz, *Crossed Swords: Pakistan, Its Army, and the Wars Within* (Oxford: Oxford University Press, 2008), 265–66.

147. Nawaz, *Crossed Swords*, 267–69.

148. Gary J. Bass, *The Blood Telegram: Nixon, Kissinger, and a Forgotten Genocide*, Illustrated ed. (New York: Vintage, 2014).

149. Nawaz argues that the army "badly missed the political dimension of the conflict." Nawaz, *The Battle for Pakistan*.

150. Salil Tripathi, *The Colonel Who Would Not Repent: The Bangladesh War and Its Unquiet Legacy* (New Haven: Yale University Press, 2016), offers a harrowing account of this violence, as well as that by the Mukti Bahini against suspected collaborators.

151. Nawaz, *Crossed Swords*, 283.

152. Sisson and Rose, *War and Secession*; Srinath Raghavan, *1971*. Ahsan I. Butt, *Secession and Security: Explaining State Strategy against Separatists* (Ithaca: Cornell University Press, 2017) further argues that Indian backing exacerbated this perception. The main dissenting voice is Sarmila Bose, *Dead Reckoning: Memories of the 1971 Bangladesh War*, 1st ed. (London: Hurst, 2011), which aims to vindicate the Pakistan Army from the main charges against it. The critical reception to Bose's book, however, has been rather devastating.

153. Nawaz, *Crossed Swords*, 282.

154. For some historical background, see Selig S. Harrison, *In Afghanistan's Shadow: Baluch Nationalism and Soviet Temptations*, 1st ed. (New York: Carnegie Endowment for International Peace, 1981); Frederic Grare, "Balochistan: The State Versus the Nation," Carnegie Endowment for International Peace, accessed October 21, 2020, https://carnegieendowment.org/2013/04/11/balochistan-state-versus-nation-pub-51488.

155. International Crisis Group, "Pakistan: The Forgotten Conflict in Balochistan," October 2007, http://www.crisisgroup.org/en/regions/asia/south-asia/pakistan/B069-pakistan-the-forgotten-conflict-in-balochistan.aspx; "Balochistan: Neglected Still," *Human Rights Commission of Pakistan* (Lahore, 2019).

156. Grare, "Balochistan."

157. Human Rights Watch, "Pakistan: Upsurge in Killings in Balochistan," Human Rights Watch, July 13, 2011, https://www.hrw.org/news/2011/07/13/pakistan-upsurge-killings-balochistan.

158. International Crisis Group, "Pakistan."

159. Shah Meer Baloch, "Balochistan and the Killing of Akbar Bugti: 10 Years Later," August 26, 2016, https://thediplomat.com/2016/08/balochistan-and-the-killing-of-akbar-bugti-10-years-later/.

160. Ullah, *Vying for Allah's Vote*.

161. Ronald R. Krebs and Patrick Thaddeus Jackson, "Twisting Tongues and Twisting Arms: The Power of Political Rhetoric," *European Journal of International Relations*, July 25, 2016, https://doi.org/10.1177/1354066107074284.

162. For some background, see Zahid Hussain, *Frontline Pakistan: The Struggle with Militant Islam* (New York: Columbia University Press, 2007).

163. Nawaz, *The Battle for Pakistan*, 291.

164. Nawaz, *The Battle for Pakistan*, 77.

165. Nawaz, *The Battle for Pakistan*, 190.

166. Nawaz, *The Battle for Pakistan*, 274–75.

167. Fair, *Fighting to the End*, 250, 256.

168. Jaffrelot, *Pakistan Paradox*, 608.

169. Gayer, *Karachi*.

170. Siddiqa, "The Kingmaker," 224.

171. Paul Staniland, "Armed Groups and Militarized Elections," *International Studies Quarterly* 59, no. 4 (December 1, 2015): 694–705, https://doi.org/10.1111/isqu.12195.

172. Siddiqa, "The Kingmaker," 225.

173. Siddiqa, "The Kingmaker," 225, 226.

174. Siddiqa, "The Kingmaker," 226.

175. Syed Raza Hassan, "Fearful for Decades, Pakistan's Main Parties Now Openly Campaign in Karachi," Reuters, July 19, 2018, https://www.reuters.com/article/us-pakistan-election-karachi/fearful-for-decades-pakistans-main-parties-now-openly-campaign-in-karachi-idUSKBN1K9162.

176. Gayer, *Karachi*.

177. Alisha Holland, *Forbearance as Redistribution: The Politics of Informal Welfare in Latin America* (Cambridge: Cambridge University Press, 2017).

178. Staniland et al., "Politics of Threat Perception." There have of course been further developments since 2015 that are not covered here.

179. From 2002 to 2013, we estimate that there were twenty-two armed groups in the Northwest with a size of two hundred or more foot soldiers. We restricted our analysis to twenty of them. There is very limited information the Noor Islam Group and Asmatullah Shaheen Group, especially its interaction with the Pakistani state.

180. This is a conservative estimate. The Pakistan Army does not release information on its military campaigns. We have tried to use secondary sources to triangulate information on military operations. See the section on "Applying the Framework" below for details on data collection methodology.

181. KP has had 30 percent of violence in Pakistan compared to 26 percent of its violence in FATA from 2007 to 2014, according to data compiled by the Pakistan Institute of Peace Studies (PIPS). See the PIPS Database at https://www.pakpips.com/about-pips-database.

182. Ayres, *Speaking Like a State*.

183. Ayres, *Speaking Like a State*, 34.

184. On recent army chiefs and their use of religion, see Jaffrelot, *Pakistan Paradox*, 528–35.

185. Kalbe Ali, "Islam Should Serve as Unifying Force: Kayani," *Dawn*, April 21, 2013.

186. Shaikh, *Making Sense of Pakistan*.

187. Jaffrelot's *The Pakistan Paradox* is structured around this tension between forms of Pakistani nationalism.

188. Ahmed Rashid, *Descent into Chaos: The US and the Failure of Nation Building in Pakistan, Afghanistan, and Central Asia* (New York: Penguin, 2008), 265–67.

189. On local embeddedness, see Paul Staniland, *Networks of Rebellion: Explaining Insurgent Cohesion and Collapse* (Ithaca: Cornell University Press, 2014).

190. For full details of coding and case selection, see Staniland et al., "Politics and Threat Perception."

191. Jaffrelot, *Pakistan Paradox*, 535.

192. The question of who knew what about Bin Laden remains open. Two important accounts on the topic are Carlotta Gall, *The Wrong Enemy: America in Afghanistan, 2001–2014* (London: Houghton Mifflin Harcourt, 2014); and Adrian Levy and Cathy Scott-Clark, *The Exile: The Stunning Inside Story of Osama bin Laden and Al Qaeda in Flight* (New York: Bloomsbury, 2017). Gall argues that the Pakistani military facilitated Bin Laden's stay whereas Levy and Scott-Clark find evidence of the role of select Pakistani military/intelligence leaders in facilitating Bin Laden.

193. Nawaz, *The Battle for Pakistan*, 293.

194. Gary King, Robert O. Keohane, and Sidney Verba, *Scientific Inference in Qualitative Research* (Princeton, NJ: Princeton University Press, 1994).

195. Alexander L. George and Andrew Bennett, *Case Studies and Theory Development in the Social Sciences* (Cambridge, MA: MIT Press, 2005).

196. The Haqqanis have pledged allegiance to the Afghan Taliban, but predate the Taliban's origins and have a relatively loose tactical relationship with the Quetta Shura. Anand Gopal, Mansoor Khan Mahsud, and Brian Fishman, "The Taliban in North Waziristan," in *Negotiating the Borders Between Terror, Politics, and Religion*, ed. Peter Bergen and Katherine Tiedemann (New York: Oxford University Press, 2013), 137–39.

197. Mark Mazzetti, *The Way of the Knife: The CIA, a Secret Army, and a War at the Ends of the Earth* (New York: Penguin Books, 2014).

198. Azaz Syed, *The Secrets of Pakistan's War on Al-Qaeda* (Islamabad: Al-Abbas International, 2014), 62.

199. Ismail Khan, "Forces, Militants Heading for Truce," *Dawn*, June 23, 2006.

200. Gopal, Mahsud, and Fishman, "Taliban in North Waziristan," 143.

201. Vahid Brown and Don Rassler, *Fountainhead of Jihad: The Haqqani Nexus, 1973–2012* (New York: Oxford University Press, 2013), 122.

202. Jaffrelot, *Pakistan Paradox*, 539.

203. Aslam Khan, "Taliban Warn of Long Guerrilla War," *The News*, October 1, 2001.

204. Brown and Rassler, *Fountainhead of Jihad*.

205. Brown and Rassler, *Fountainhead of Jihad*, 152.

206. Brown and Rassler, *Fountainhead of Jihad*, 130.

207. Brown and Rassler, *Fountainhead of Jihad*, 125.

208. Gopal, Mahsud, and Fishman, "Taliban in North Waziristan," 130.

209. Brown and Rassler, *Fountainhead of Jihad*, 152.

210. Gall, *Wrong Enemy*, 260.

211. Brown and Rassler, *Fountainhead of Jihad*, 165; David Rohde, "You have Atomic Bombs, But We Have Suicide Bombers," *New York Times*, October 19, 2009.

212. Matthew Aid, *Intel Wars: The Secret History of the Fight Against Terror* (New York: Bloomsbury, 2012), 108.

213. Gopal, Mahsud, and Fishman, "The Taliban in North Waziristan," 146.

214. Brown and Rassler, *Fountainhead of Jihad,* 141.

215. Brown and Rassler, *Fountainhead of Jihad,* 141.

216. Mansoor Khan Mahsud, "The Taliban in South Waziristan" In *Negotiating the Borders Between Terror, Politics, and Religion*, edited volume by Peter Bergen and Katherine Tiedemann (New York: Oxford University Press, 2013), 190.

217. Bureau Report, "Mehsud Described As Soldier of Peace," *Dawn*, August 7, 2005.

218. Seth Jones and C. Christine Fair, *Counterinsurgency in Pakistan* (Santa Monica, CA: RAND Corporation, 2010), 57.

219. Jaffrelot, *The Pakistan Paradox*, 573.

220. Amir Mir, "Of Pakistani Jehadi Groups and Their Al-Qaeda and Intelligence Links," *The News*, March 24, 2009.

221. Ahmad Zaidan, "Baitullah Mehsud Interview," *Al-Jazeera*, January 21–22, 2008.

222. Jason Burke, *The 9/11 Wars* (London: Penguin, 2011), 374.

223. Burke, *The 9/11 Wars*, 390.

224. Jaffrelot, *Pakistan Paradox*, 595.

225. Mahsud, "Taliban in South Waziristan," 190–91.

226. Hamid Mir, "Army Official Calls Baitullah Mehsud, Fazlullah 'Patriots,'" *The News*, December 1, 2008.

227. On arguments about peace deals and fragmentation, see Andrew Kydd and Barbara Walter, "Sabotaging the Peace: The Politics of Extremist Violence," *International Organization* 56, no. 2 (2002): 263–96. See also Kathleen Gallagher Cunningham, *Inside the Politics of Self-Determination* (New York: Oxford University Press, 2014).

228. Jaffrelot, *Pakistan Paradox*, 572; Jones and Fair, *Counterinsurgency in Pakistan*, 72.

229. Jaffrelot, *Pakistan Paradox*, 596.

230. Mahsud, "Taliban in South Waziristan," 191.

231. Jaffrelot, *Pakistan Paradox*, 601.

232. Jaffrelot, *Pakistan Paradox*, 601.

233. Jaffrelot, *Pakistan Paradox*, 601, 603.

234. Jaffrelot, *Pakistan Paradox*, 600.

235. See Stephen Tankel, "Beyond the Double Game: Lessons from Pakistan's Approach to Islamist Militancy," *Journal of Strategic Studies* 41, no. 4 (June 7, 2018): 545–75, https://doi.org/10.1080/01402390.2016.1174114. Tankel refers to them as "frenemies."

236. Fair, *Fighting to the End*, 252.

237. Zia-ur Rehman, "The Significance of Maulvi Nazir's Death in Pakistan," *CTC Sentinel* 6, no. 2 (February 2013): 18.

238. Rehman, "Maulvi Nazir's Death."

239. Jaffrelot, *Pakistan Paradox*, 572.

240. Mahsud, "Taliban in South Waziristan," 185.

241. Rehman "Maulvi Nazir's Death."

242. Jaffrelot, *Pakistan Paradox*, 572.

243. Jones and Fair, *Counterinsurgency in Pakistan*, 58.

244. Confirmed by Maulvi Nazir in an interview to journalist Syed Saleem Shahzad. See Syed Saleem Shahzad, "Taliban and Al-Qaeda: Friends in Arms," *Asia Times Online*, May 5, 2011.

245. Zia-ur Rehman, "Realignment in Waziristan" *Friday Times*, June 6, 2014.

246. Jones and Fair, *Counterinsurgency in Pakistan*, 73.

247. Gopal, Mahsud, and Fishman, "Taliban in North Waziristan," 140.

248. Gopal, Mahsud, and Fishman, "Taliban in North Waziristan," 147.

249. Jaffrelot, *Pakistan Paradox*, 574.

250. Gopal, Mahsud, and Fishman, "Taliban in North Waziristan," 148; Mahsud, "Taliban in South Waziristan," 169.

251. Gopal, Mahsud, and Fishman, "Taliban in North Waziristan," 148; Fair, *Fighting to the End*, 246.

252. Gopal, Mahsud, and Fishman, "Taliban in North Waziristan," 152.

253. There has been no confirmation of his death, but rumors were first reported in December 2014.

254. Aamir Iqbal, "Militant Commander Declares War on Pakistan," *Newsweek*, June 20, 2014.

255. Walter C. Ladwig III, *The Forgotten Front: Patron-Client Relationships in Counter Insurgency* (Cambridge: Cambridge University Press, 2017). Ladwig finds greater success for international pressures than we have found in Pakistan.

256. Chacko, "Religious Parties," 113.

CHAPTER 6. BURMA/MYANMAR

1. Martin J. Smith, *Burma: Insurgency and the Politics of Ethnicity*, 2nd ed. (London: Zed Books, 1999), 48.

2. Kerstin Duell, "Non-Traditional Security Threats, International Concerns, and the Exiled Opposition," in *Internal Conflicts in Myanmar: Transnational Consequences 2011*, ed. V. R. Raghavan (Chennai: 2011), 47.

3. Albert D. Moscotti, *British Policy and the Nationalist Movement in Burma, 1917–1937* (Honolulu: University Press of Hawaii, 1974), 23.

4. Hugh Tinker, *The Union of Burma: A Study of the First Years of Independence.*, 4th ed. (London: Oxford University Press and Royal Institute of International Affairs, 1967), 2.

5. "The nationalist movement was by this time no longer confined to a few politically conscious Burmese but was evident at the village level"; Moscotti, *British Policy*, 33. See also John F. Cady, *A History of Modern Burma* (Ithaca: NCROL, 1958), 233.

6. Cady, *A History of Modern Burma*, 255.

7. Cady, *A History of Modern Burma*, 221.

8. Michael W. Charney, *A History of Modern Burma* (Cambridge: Cambridge University Press, 2009), 13–15.

9. Charney, *A History of Modern Burma*, 18.

10. Cady, *A History of Modern Burma*, 231.

11. Mary Callahan, *Making Enemies: War and State Building in Burma* (Ithaca: Cornell University Press, 2003), 36.

12. Moscotti, *British Policy*, 183.

13. Moscotti, *British Policy*, 182.

14. Charney, *A History of Modern Burma*, 30.

15. Charney, *A History of Modern Burma*, 36–37.

16. Cady, *A History of Modern Burma*, 228. As Moscotti agrees, "The British policy toward minorities in Burma was continually suspect by Burmese nationalists who viewed special measures for minorities as part of a plan of 'divide and rule'"; Moscotti, *British Policy*, 122.

17. Cady, *A History of Modern Burma*, 229.

18. Smith, *Burma*, 49.

19. Charney, *A History of Modern Burma*, 42–43.

20. Callahan, *Making Enemies*, 35.

21. Callahan, *Making Enemies*, 36.

22. Moscotti, *British Policy*, 56.

23. Cady, *A History of Modern Burma*, 322.

24. Cady, *A History of Modern Burma*, 383.

25. Yoshihiro Nakanishi, *Strong Soldiers, Failed Revolution: The State and Military in Burma, 1962–1988* (Singapore: NUS Press, 2013), 38–39.

26. Cady, *A History of Modern Burma*, 378.

27. Tinker, *The Union of Burma*, 7.

28. Tinker, *The Union of Burma*, 7.

29. Smith, *Burma*, 56.

30. Nakanishi, *Strong Soldiers, Failed Revolution*, 39.

31. Tinker, *The Union of Burma*, 6.

32. Tinker, *The Union of Burma*, 6.

33. Charney, *A History of Modern Burma*, 71.

34. Cady, *A History of Modern Burma*, 416.

35. Cady, *A History of Modern Burma*, 416.

36. Smith, *Burma*, 54.

37. Cady, *A History of Modern Burma*, 427–28.

38. Smith, *Burma*, 60.

39. Smith, *Burma*, 61.

40. Charney, *A History of Modern Burma*, 55.

41. Smith, *Burma*, 64.

42. Smith, *Burma*, 62.

43. Tinker, *The Union of Burma*, 9.

44. Charney, *A History of Modern Burma*, 55.

45. Charney, *A History of Modern Burma*, 57.

46. Charney, *A History of Modern Burma*, 62.

47. Cady, *A History of Modern Burma*, 428.

48. Cady, *A History of Modern Burma*, 478.

49. Cady, *A History of Modern Burma*, 478.

50. Cady, *A History of Modern Burma*, 519.

51. Smith, *Burma*, 67.

52. Smith, *Burma*, 66.

53. Smith, *Burma*, 67.

54. Smith, *Burma*, 68.

55. Smith, *Burma*, 68.

56. Cady, *A History of Modern Burma*, 535.

57. Cady, *A History of Modern Burma*, 535.

58. Smith, *Burma*, 69.

59. Tinker, *The Union of Burma*, 17.

60. For a discussion of Aung San and the AFPFL's position toward ethnic minorities, see Matthew J. Walton, "Ethnicity, Conflict, and History in Burma: The Myths of Panglong," *Asian Survey* 48, no. 6 (2008): 889–910, https://doi.org/10.1525/as.2008.48.6.889.

61. Charney, *A History of Modern Burma*, 73.

62. Smith, *Burma*, 68.

63. Tinker, *The Union of Burma*, 32.

64. Bertil Lintner, *The Rise and Fall of the Communist Party of Burma (CPB)* (Ithaca: Southeast Asia Program Publication, 1990), 11.

65. Lintner, *The Rise and Fall of the Communist Party of Burma*, 14.

66. Charney, *A History of Modern Burma*, 65–66.

67. Cady, *A History of Modern Burma*, 558.

68. Charney, *A History of Modern Burma*, 66.

69. Smith, *Burma*, 80.

70. Charney, *A History of Modern Burma*, 67.

71. Callahan, *Making Enemies*, 3.

72. Charney, *A History of Modern Burma*, 72.

73. Callahan, *Making Enemies*, 3.

74. Callahan, *Making Enemies*, 111.

75. Callahan, *Making Enemies*, 127.

76. Callahan, *Making Enemies*, 129.

77. Callahan, *Making Enemies*, 135.

78. Callahan, *Making Enemies*, 137, 140.

79. Callahan, *Making Enemies*, 141–42; 145–46.

80. Callahan, *Making Enemies*, 137–38.

81. Smith, *Burma*, 199.

82. Smith, *Burma*, 199.

83. Matthew J. Walton, "The 'Wages of Burman-ness:' Ethnicity and Burman Privilege in Contemporary Myanmar," *Journal of Contemporary Asia* 43, no. 1 (February 1, 2013): 9.

84. Callahan, *Making Enemies*, 145.

85. Local private armies persisted deep into the 1950s, despite some attempts from Rangoon to try to incorporate them; Callahan, *Making Enemies*, 143. For more on collusion involving Tatmadaw commanders and local armed groups see Callahan, *Making Enemies*, 147.

86. Vincent Boudreau, *Resisting Dictatorship: Repression and Protest in Southeast Asia* (New York: Cambridge University Press, 2004), 46.

87. Callahan, *Making Enemies*, 127.

88. Boudreau, *Resisting Dictatorship*, 47.

89. Bertil Lintner, *Burma in Revolt: Opium and Insurgency since 1948*, 2 ed. (Chiang Mai, Thailand: Silkworm Books, 1999), 167.

90. Lintner, *Burma in Revolt*, 168.

91. Lintner, *The Rise and Fall of the Communist Party of Burma*, 18.

92. Smith, *Burma*, 163.

93. Nakanishi, *Strong Soldiers, Failed Revolution*, 85.

94. Smith, *Burma*, 167.

95. Lintner, *Burma in Revolt*, 169.

96. Callahan, *Making Enemies*, 149, 185.

97. Smith, *Burma*, 169.

98. Smith, *Burma*, 168.

99. Smith, *Burma*, 168.

100. Smith, *Burma*, 175.

101. Mary P. Callahan, "The Sinking Schooner: Murder and the State in Independent Burma, 1948–1958," in *Gangsters, Democracy, and the State in Southeast Asia* (Ithaca: Cornell University Press, 1998), 17–38.

102. Smith, *Burma*, 177.

103. Lintner, *Burma in Revolt*, 157.

104. Lintner, *Burma in Revolt*, 173.

105. Lintner, *Burma in Revolt*, 180.

106. Lintner, *Burma in Revolt*, 178.

107. Smith, *Burma*, 174.

108. Callahan, *Making Enemies*, 204.

109. Callahan, *Making Enemies*, 186.

110. Smith, *Burma*, 177.

111. Callahan, *Making Enemies*, 189.

112. Callahan, *Making Enemies*, 190.

113. Lintner, *Burma in Revolt*, 179.

114. Lintner, *Burma in Revolt*, 178.

115. Smith, *Burma*, 182–83.

116. Smith, *Burma*, 186.

117. Smith, *Burma*, 191; Lintner, *Burma in Revolt*, 197.

118. Lintner, *Burma in Revolt*, 201.

119. Lee Jones, "Explaining Myanmar's Regime Transition: The Periphery Is Central," *Democratization* 21, no. 5 (July 29, 2014): 787.

120. Smith, *Burma*, 191.

121. Smith, *Burma*, 192.

122. Smith, *Burma*, 195.

123. Lintner, *Burma in Revolt*, 203.

124. Lintner, *Burma in Revolt*, 210.

125. Smith, *Burma*, 196.

126. Smith, *Burma*, 196.

127. Smith, *Burma*, 198.

128. Smith, *Burma*, 198.

129. Ashley South, *Ethnic Politics in Burma: States of Conflict*, Reprint ed. (Abingdon, UK: Routledge, 2008), 27.

130. Nakanishi, *Strong Soldiers, Failed Revolution*, 101.

131. Nakanishi, *Strong Soldiers, Failed Revolution*, 219.

132. Walton, "The 'Wages of Burman-Ness,'" 13.

133. For background, see Robert Taylor, *General Ne Win: A Political Biography* (Singapore: ISEAS-Yusof Ishak Institute, 2015); David Steinberg, *Burma/Myanmar: What Everyone Needs to Know*, 2nd ed. (New York: Oxford University Press, 2013).

134. John Buchanan, *Militias in Myanmar* (New York: The Asia Foundation, 2016), 9, notes that there was another set of murky counterinsurgent militias, the Ta Ka Sa Pha, but that little is known about them.

135. Buchanan, *Militias in Myanmar*, 11.

136. Buchanan, *Militias in Myanmar*, 11.

137. For a detailed account of this incident, see Bertil Lintner, *Outrage: Burma's Struggle for Democracy* (Bangkok: White Lotus, 1990).

138. Lintner, *The Rise and Fall of the Communist Party of Burma*, 41–46.

139. Lintner, *The Rise and Fall of the Communist Party of Burma*, 49–52.

140. Lintner, *The Rise and Fall of the Communist Party of Burma*, 53.

141. Thant Myint-U, *The Hidden History of Burma: Race, Capitalism, and the Crisis of Democracy in the 21st Century* (New York: W. W. Norton, 2019), 49–50.

142. Myint-U, *The Hidden History of Burma*, 49.

143. Myint-U, *The Hidden History of Burma*, 50.

144. Tom Kramer, *The United Wa State Party: Narco-Army or Ethnic Nationalist Party* (Washington, DC: East-West Center Washington, 2007), 2, 28–29, 29.

145. Jones, "Explaining Myanmar's Regime Transition," 788.

146. Buchanan, *Militias in Myanmar*, 14.

147. David Brenner, *Rebel Politics: A Political Sociology of Armed Struggle in Myanmar's Borderlands* (Ithaca: Southeast Asia Program Publication, 2019), 42.

148. Mary P. Callahan, *Political Authority in Burma's Ethnic Minority States: Devolution, Occupation, and Coexistence* (Washington, DC: East-West Center, 2007); Zaw Oo and Win Min, *Assessing Burma's Ceasefire Accords* (Washington, DC: East-West Center Washington, 2007).

149. Brenner, *Rebel Politics*, 45.

150. Brenner, *Rebel Politics*, 48–51.

151. Jones, "Explaining Myanmar's Regime Transition," 792.

152. Kevin Woods, "Ceasefire Capitalism: Military—Private Partnerships, Resource Concessions and Military—State Building in the Burma—China Borderlands," *Journal of Peasant Studies* 38, no. 4 (October 1, 2011): 747–70, https://doi.org/10.1080/03066150.2011.607699, 749.

153. Jones, "Explaining Myanmar's Regime Transition," 791.

154. Myint-U, *The Hidden History of Burma*, 168–71.

155. Brenner, *Rebel Politics*, 98.

156. Buchanan, *Militias in Myanmar*, 15, 18–20; 24–26.

157. Buchanan, *Militias in Myanmar*, 22.

158. Buchanan, *Militias in Myanmar*, 15; 26–27; Brenner, 51–52.

159. Brenner, *Rebel Politics*, 52.

160. Myint-U, *The Hidden History of Burma*, 112–13.

161. https://www.irrawaddy.com/news/burma/dkba-unveils-overture-united-karen-armed-forces.html.

162. Myint-U, *The Hidden History of Burma*, 165.

163. Walton, "The 'Wages of Burman-ness,'" 1–27.

164. Myint-U, *The Hidden History of Burma*, 179.

165. Myint-U, *The Hidden History of Burma*, 207.

166. Myint-U, *The Hidden History of Burma*, 36–37.

167. Myint-U, *The Hidden History of Burma*, 107.

168. Myint-U, *The Hidden History of Burma*, 108–9. See also Nick Cheesman, "How in Myanmar 'National Races' Came to Surpass Citizenship and Exclude Rohingya," *Journal of Contemporary Asia* 47, no. 3 (May 27, 2017): 461–83, https://doi.org/10.1080/0047233 6.2017.1297476.

169. For a discussion of how elite strategies of mobilization amid constrained democratization led to a situation in which "a moral panic effectively created a crisis where none existed," see Gerry van Klinken and Su Mon Thazin Aung, "The Contentious Politics of Anti-Muslim Scapegoating in Myanmar," *Journal of Contemporary Asia* 47, no. 3 (May 27, 2017): 353–75, https://doi.org/10.1080/00472336.2017.1293133.

170. Myint-U, *The Hidden History of Burma*, 237.

171. Myint-U, *The Hidden History of Burma*, 242.

CHAPTER 7. SRI LANKA

1. James Manor, *The Expedient Utopian: Bandaranaike and Ceylon* (Cambridge: Cambridge University Press, 2009); K. M. De Silva, *A History of Sri Lanka*, Rev. ed. (New Delhi: Penguin Books, 2005).

2. Neil DeVotta, *Blowback: Linguistic Nationalism, Institutional Decay, and Ethnic Conflict in Sri Lanka* (Stanford, CA: Stanford University Press, 2004), 21.

3. De Silva, *A History of Sri Lanka*, 457.

4. DeVotta, *Blowback*, 29–30.

5. DeVotta, *Blowback*, 30.

6. DeVotta, *Blowback*, 30.

7. DeVotta, *Blowback*, 32. K. N. O. Dharmadasa, *Language, Religion, and Ethnic Assertiveness: The Growth of Sinhalese Nationalism in Sri Lanka* (Ann Arbor: University of Michigan Press, 1992),143, agrees.

8. Steven Kemper, *The Presence of the Past: Chronicles, Politics, and Culture in Sinhala Life* (Ithaca: NCROL, 1992).

9. Dharmadasa, *Language, Religion, and Ethnic Assertiveness*, 125.

10. Dharmadasa, *Language, Religion, and Ethnic Assertiveness*, 143.

11. De Silva, *A History of Sri Lanka*, 468–69.

12. De Silva, *A History of Sri Lanka*, 474.

13. De Silva, *A History of Sri Lanka*, 475.

14. Nira Wickramasinghe, *Sri Lanka in the Modern Age: A History*, Updated 2nd ed. (New York: Oxford University Press, 2014), 127.

15. Robert N. Kearney, *Communalism and Language in the Politics of Ceylon*, vol. 2 (Durham, NC: Duke University Press, 1967), 48.

16. Jane Russell, *Communal Politics under the Donoughmore Constitution, 1931–1947*, 1st ed. (Dehiwala, Sri Lanka: Tisara Prakasakayo, 1982), 47.

17. Wickramasinghe, *Sri Lanka in the Modern Age*, 157.

18. Dharmadasa, *Language, Religion, and Ethnic Assertiveness*, 225.

19. Wickramasinghe, *Sri Lanka in the Modern Age*, 55.

20. Kearney, *Communalism and Language in the Politics of Ceylon*, 28.

21. Dharmadasa, *Language, Religion, and Ethnic Assertiveness*, 223.

22. Dharmadasa, *Language, Religion, and Ethnic Assertiveness*, 216.

23. Dharmadasa, *Language, Religion, and Ethnic Assertiveness*, 227.

24. Russell, *Communal Politics*, 224.

25. DeVotta, *Blowback*, 37.

26. Stanley Jeyaraja Tambiah, *Buddhism Betrayed? Religion, Politics, and Violence in Sri Lanka* (Chicago: University of Chicago Press, 1992), 11.

27. Wickramasinghe, *Sri Lanka in the Modern Age*, 150; De Silva, *A History of Sri Lanka*, 522.

28. De Silva, *A History of Sri Lanka*, 538.

29. Russell, *Communal Politics*, 182.

30. De Silva, *A History of Sri Lanka*, 478.

31. DeVotta, *Blowback*, 37.

32. Dharmadasa, *Language, Religion, and Ethnic Assertiveness*, 257.

33. Russell, *Communal Politics*, 146.

34. Dharmadasa, *Language, Religion, and Ethnic Assertiveness*, 256.

35. Russell, *Communal Politics*, 224, Dharmadasa, *Language, Religion, and Ethnic Assertiveness*, 258; Manor, *The Expedient Utopian*, 138.

36. Dharmadasa, *Language, Religion, and Ethnic Assertiveness*, 258; Tambiah, *Buddhism Betrayed*, 13, concurs.

37. Russell, *Communal Politics*, 224; Kearney, *Communalism and Language in the Politics of Ceylon*, 35.

38. De Silva, *A History of Sri Lanka*, 549.

39. Manor, *The Expedient Utopian*, 4.

40. Manor, *The Expedient Utopian*, 127.

41. Manor, *The Expedient Utopian*, 129.

42. Kearney, *Communalism and Language in the Politics of Ceylon*, 35.

43. De Silva, *A History of Sri Lanka*, 538.

44. Dharmadasa, *Language, Religion, and Ethnic Assertiveness*, 257.

45. Tambiah, *Buddhism Betrayed*, 12.

46. Russell, *Communal Politics*, 267.

47. Russell, *Communal Politics*, 261.

48. Dharmadasa, *Language, Religion, and Ethnic Assertiveness*, 219.

49. Kearney, *Communalism and Language in the Politics of Ceylon*, 26–27.

50. Manor, *The Expedient Utopian*, 140.

51. Manor, *The Expedient Utopian*, 123.

52. De Silva, *A History of Sri Lanka*, 551.

53. Russell, *Communal Politics*, 305.

54. Dharmadasa, *Language, Religion, and Ethnic Assertiveness*, 1939, 240.

55. DeVotta, *Blowback*, 48–49.

56. DeVotta, *Blowback*, 44.

57. DeVotta, *Blowback*, 44.

58. Dharmadasa, *Language, Religion, and Ethnic Assertiveness*, 298.

59. De Silva, *A History of Sri Lanka*, 601.

60. Dharmadasa, *Language, Religion, and Ethnic Assertiveness*, 299.

61. Dharmadasa, *Language, Religion, and Ethnic Assertiveness*, 245.

62. Russell, *Communal Politics*, 303; Manor, *The Expedient Utopian*, 158.

63. De Silva, A *History of Sri Lanka*, 554–55.

64. De Silva, *A History of Sri Lanka*, 555.

65. Manor, *The Expedient Utopian,* 169.

66. Manor, *The Expedient Utopian,* 168.

67. Manor, *The Expedient Utopian,* 168.

68. Manor, *The Expedient Utopian,* 177.

69. Manor, *The Expedient Utopian,* 180.

70. De Silva, *A History of Sri Lanka*, 607.

71. De Silva *A History of Sri Lanka*, 603.

72. De Silva, *A History of Sri Lanka*, 609.

73. De Silva, *A History of Sri Lanka*, 609.

74. De Silva, *A History of Sri Lanka*, 569.

75. Manor, *The Expedient Utopian,* 219.

76. DeVotta, *Blowback*, 52.

77. De Silva, *A History of Sri Lanka*, 609.

78. Wickramasinghe, *Sri Lanka in the Modern Age,* 192.

79. De Silva, *A History of Sri Lanka*, 609.

80. De Silva, *A History of Sri Lanka*, 605.

81. De Silva, *A History of Sri Lanka*, 608.

82. De Silva, *A History of Sri Lanka*, 610.

83. Manor, *The Expedient Utopian,* 212–13.

84. Manor, *The Expedient Utopian,* 228.

85. DeVotta, *Blowback*, 52.

86. De Silva, *A History of Sri Lanka*, 614.

87. De Silva, *A History of Sri Lanka*, 626.

88. Donald L Horowitz, *Ethnic Groups in Conflict* (Berkeley: University of California Press, 1985).

89. De Silva, *A History of Sri Lanka*, 633.

90. De Silva, *A History of Sri Lanka*, 650.

91. De Silva, *A History of Sri Lanka*, 649.

92. Horowitz, *Ethnic Groups in Conflict*.

93. A. Jeyaratnam Wilson, *Sri Lankan Tamil Nationalism: Its Origins and Development in the Nineteenth and Twentieth Centuries* (New Delhi: Penguin, 2001), 99.

94. Wilson, *Sri Lankan Tamil Nationalism*, 99.

95. DeVotta, *Blowback*, 163.

96. Neil DeVotta, *Sinhalese Buddhist Nationalist Ideology: Implications for Politics and Conflict Resolution in Sri Lanka* (Washington, DC: East-West Center Washington, 2007), 3.

97. DeVotta, *Sinhalese Buddhist Nationalist Ideology*.

98. A grim assessment of the interlocking calculations and miscalculations of the final days of the war can be found in Gordon Weiss, *The Cage: The Fight for Sri Lanka and the Last Days of the Tamil Tigers* (London: Bodley Head, 2011). For a discussion of the potential for civilian agency under the LTTE, see Nimmi Gowrinathan and Zachariah Mampilly, "Resistance and Repression under the Rule of Rebels: Women, Clergy, and Civilian Agency in LTTE Governed Sri Lanka," *Comparative Politics* 52, no. 1 (October 1, 2019): 1–20.

99. On the JVP as an example of a broader category of leftist revolts in democracies, see Staniland, "Leftist Insurgency in Democracies."

100. A. C. Alles, *Insurgency, 1971: An Account of the April Insurrection in Sri Lanka* (n.p., 1976), provides an extensive overview of the first revolt. On the insurgents themselves,

see Robert N. Kearney, "A Note on the Fate of the 1971 Insurgents in Sri Lanka," *Journal of Asian Studies* 36, no. 3 (1977): 515–19; Gananath Obeyesekere, "Some Comments on the Social Backgrounds of the April 1971 Insurgency in Sri Lanka (Ceylon)," *Journal of Asian Studies* 33, no. 3 (1974): 367–84.

101. See Paul Staniland, "Leftist Insurgency in Democracies," *Comparative Political Studies*, July 8, 2020, https://doi.org/10.1177/0010414020938096.

102. Studies of this period and the 1987–1990 uprising itself include Rohan Gunaratna, *Sri Lanka, a Lost Revolution? The Inside Story of the JVP* (Kandy, Sri Lanka: Institute of Fundamental Studies, 1990); Mick Moore, "Thoroughly Modern Revolutionaries: The JVP in Sri Lanka," *Modern Asian Studies* 27, no. 3 (1993): 593–642; Jagath P. Senaratne, *Political Violence in Sri Lanka, 1977–1990: Riots, Insurrections, Counter-Insurgencies, Foreign Intervention*, vol. 4, Sri Lanka Studies (Amsterdam: VU University Press, 1997).

103. C. A. Chandraprema, *Sri Lanka, the Years of Terror: The J.V.P. Insurrection, 1987–1989*, 1st ed. (Colombo: Lake House Bookshop, 1991).

104. For anyone looking for an exceptionally depressing but very good novel about civil war, Michael Ondaatje, *Anil's Ghost*, Reprint ed. (New York: Vintage, 2001), is set in late 1980s Sri Lanka during the grim overlap of the JVP and LTTE wars.

105. Rajesh Venugopal, "Sectarian Socialism: The Politics of Sri Lanka's Janatha Vimukthi Peramuna (JVP)," *Modern Asian Studies* 44, no. 3 (2010): 567–602.

106. Paul Staniland, *Networks of Rebellion: Explaining Insurgent Cohesion and Collapse*, 1st ed. (Ithaca: Cornell University Press, 2014).

107. M. R Narayan Swamy, *Tigers of Lanka, from Boys to Guerrillas*, 7th ed. (Colombo: Vijitha Yapa Publications, 2006).

108. See Wilson, *Sri Lankan Tamil Nationalism*.

109. DeVotta, *Blowback*; Horowitz, *Ethnic Groups in Conflict*; Manor, *The Expedient Utopian*.

110. DeVotta, *Blowback*, 167.

111. DeVotta, *Blowback*, 169–70.

112. For details, see Staniland, *Networks of Rebellion*.

113. Gunaratna, *The Lost Rebellion*; Swamy, *Tigers of Lanka*.

114. Staniland, *Networks of Rebellion*.

115. De Silva, *A History of Sri Lanka*, 698–705.

116. DeVotta, *Blowback*, 173.

117. Swamy, *Tigers of Lanka*, 299–300; 303–4.

118. M. R. Narayan Swamy, *Inside an Elusive Mind, Prabhakaran: The First Profile of the World's Most Ruthless Guerrilla Leader* (Delhi: Konark Publishers, 2003), 80–85.

119. DeVotta, *Blowback*, 174.

120. Swamy, *Inside an Elusive Mind*, 218–19.

121. DeVotta, *Sinhalese Buddhist Nationalist Ideology*, 38.

122. Swamy, *Inside an Elusive Mind*, 251–53.

123. "High Hopes for a Sri Lanka Ceasefire," CNN, December 24, 2001, https://www.cnn.com/2001/WORLD/asiapcf/south/12/24/slanka.ceasefire/index.html.

124. For analyses of the failed process, see Amita Shastri, "Ending Ethnic Civil War: The Peace Process in Sri Lanka," *Commonwealth & Comparative Politics* 47, no. 1 (February 1, 2009): 76–99, https://doi.org/10.1080/14662040802659025; and Jonathan Goodhand and Oliver Walton, "The Limits of Liberal Peacebuilding? International Engagement in the Sri Lankan Peace Process," *Journal of Intervention and Statebuilding* 3, no. 3 (November 1, 2009): 303–23, https://doi.org/10.1080/17502970903086693.

125. See Human Rights Watch 2007, https://www.hrw.org/report/2007/01/23/complicit-crime/state-collusion-abductions-and-child-recruitment-karuna-group.

126. Most of these groups functionally ended as armed actors from 2009.

127. Paul Staniland, "Between a Rock and a Hard Place Insurgent Fratricide, Ethnic Defection, and the Rise of Pro-State Paramilitaries," *Journal of Conflict Resolution* 56, no. 1 (February 2012): 16–40, https://doi.org/10.1177/0022002711429681.

128. Sameer P. Lalwani, "Size Still Matters: Explaining Sri Lanka's Counterinsurgency Victory over the Tamil Tigers," *Small Wars & Insurgencies* 28, no. 1 (January 2, 2017): 119–65, https://doi.org/10.1080/09592318.2016.1263470.

129. Weiss, *The Cage*; Rohini Mohan, *The Seasons of Trouble: Life Amid the Ruins of Sri Lanka's Civil War* (Brooklyn, NY: Verso, 2014) explore the last days of the war.

130. DeVotta, *Sinhalese Buddhist Nationalist Ideology*, 29.

131. For a critique, see Stuart J. Kaufman, "Symbolic Politics or Rational Choice? Testing Theories of Extreme Ethnic Violence," *International Security* 30, no. 4 (2006): 45–86.

132. Kanchan Chandra, "Ethnic Parties and Democratic Stability," *Perspectives on Politics* 3, no. 2 (June 2005): 235–52, https://doi.org/10.1017/S1537592705050188; Alfred Stepan, Juan Linz, and Yogendra Yadav, *Crafting State-Nations: India and Other Multinational Democracies* (Baltimore: Johns Hopkins University Press, 2011).

133. DeVotta, *Sinhalese Buddhist Nationalist Ideology*, ix.

134. Kate Cronin-Furman, "Human Rights Half Measures: Avoiding Accountability in Postwar Sri Lanka," *World Politics* (2020), https://doi.org/10.1017/S0043887119000182.

CONCLUSION

1. See, among others, Daniel L. Byman and Kenneth M. Pollack, "Let Us Now Praise Great Men: Bringing the Statesman Back In," *International Security* 25, no. 4 (2001): 107–46; Elizabeth N. Saunders, "Transformative Choices: Leaders and the Origins of Intervention Strategy," *International Security* 34, no. 2 (October 1, 2009): 119–61, https://doi.org/10.1162/isec.2009.34.2.119; Giacomo Chiozza and H. E. Goemans, *Leaders and International Conflict* (Cambridge: Cambridge University Press, 2011); Michael C. Horowitz, Allan C. Stam, and Cali M. Ellis, *Why Leaders Fight* (New York: Cambridge University Press, 2015).

2. Kathleen Gallagher Cunningham, Reyko Huang, and Katherine M. Sawyer, "Voting for Militants: Rebel Elections in Civil War," *Journal of Conflict Resolution*, July 9, 2020, https://doi.org/10.1177/0022002720937750; Jenna Jordan, *Leadership Decapitation: Strategic Targeting of Terrorist Organizations*, 1st ed. (Stanford, CA: Stanford University Press, 2019); Asfandyar Mir, "What Explains Counterterrorism Effectiveness? Evidence from the U.S. Drone War in Pakistan," *International Security* 43, no. 2 (November 1, 2018): 45–83, https://doi.org/10.1162/isec_a_00331.

3. Kristin M. Bakke, Kathleen Gallagher Cunningham, and Lee J. M. Seymour, "A Plague of Initials: Fragmentation, Cohesion, and Infighting in Civil Wars," *Perspectives on Politics* 10, no. 2 (2012): 265–83, https://doi.org/10.1017/S1537592712000667; Kathleen Gallagher Cunningham, Kristin M. Bakke, and Lee J. M. Seymour, "Shirts Today, Skins Tomorrow Dual Contests and the Effects of Fragmentation in Self-Determination Disputes," *Journal of Conflict Resolution* 56, no. 1 (February 1, 2012): 67–93, https://doi.org/10.1177/0022002711429697; Peter Krause, *Rebel Power: Why National Movements Compete, Fight, and Win*, 1st ed. (Ithaca: Cornell University Press, 2017); Costantino Pischedda, "Wars within Wars: Why Windows of Opportunity and Vulnerability Cause Inter-Rebel Fighting in Internal Conflicts," *International Security* 43, no. 1 (August 1, 2018): 138–76, https://doi.org/10.1162/isec_a_00322; Wendy Pearlman, *Violence, Nonviolence, and the Palestinian National Movement*, 1st ed. (Cambridge: Cambridge University Press, 2011); Paul Staniland, "Between a Rock and a Hard Place Insurgent Fratricide,

Ethnic Defection, and the Rise of Pro-State Paramilitaries," *Journal of Conflict Resolution* 56, no. 1 (February 2012): 16–40, https://doi.org/10.1177/0022002711429681.

4. David Brenner, *Rebel Politics: A Political Sociology of Armed Struggle in Myanmar's Borderlands* (Ithaca: Southeast Asia Program Publication, 2019).

5. Zachariah Cherian Mampilly, *Rebel Rulers: Insurgent Governance and Civilian Life During War* (Ithaca: Cornell University Press, 2011); Ana Arjona, *Rebelocracy: Social Order in the Colombian Civil War by Ana Arjona* (Cambridge: Cambridge University Press, 2016).

6. See, for instance, Graeme Blair, "Survey Topics for Sensitive Topics," *APSA Comparative Politics Newsletter* 2015 (24:1), 12–16.

7. Charles Tilly, *From Mobilization to Revolution* (Reading, MA: Addison-Wesley, 1978). This is the approach that Lars-Erik Cederman, Andreas Wimmer, and Brian Min, "Why Do Ethnic Groups Rebel? New Data and Analysis," *World Politics* 62, no. 1 (2010): 87–119, very impressively deploy for studying ethnic power relations. Theda Skocpol, *States and Social Revolutions: A Comparative Analysis of France, Russia, and China* (Cambridge: Cambridge University Press, 1979).

8. An excellent recent work on this question is Sheena Chestnut Greitens, *Dictators and Their Secret Police: Coercive Institutions And State Violence* (Cambridge: Cambridge University Press, 2016).

9. William Reno, *Warlord Politics and African States* (Boulder, CO: Lynne Rienner Publishers, 1998); Philip Roessler, *Ethnic Politics and State Power in Africa: The Logic of the Coup-Civil War Trap* (Cambridge: Cambridge University Press, 2016).

10. On this type of work, see Alexander L. George and Andrew Bennett, *Case Studies and Theory Development in the Social Sciences* (Cambridge, MA: MIT Press, 2005); Henry E. Brady and David Collier, eds., *Rethinking Social Inquiry: Diverse Tools, Shared Standards* (Lanham, MD: Rowman & Littlefield, 2004); Gary Goertz and James Mahoney, "Concepts and Measurement: Ontology and Epistemology," *Social Science Information* 51, no. 2 (2012): 205–16, https://doi.org/10.1177/0539018412437108.

11. This builds on a rich literature on ideas, nationalism, and political violence. Recent work includes Scott Straus, *Making and Unmaking Nations: War, Leadership, and Genocide in Modern Africa* (Ithaca: Cornell University Press, 2015); Vincent Boudreau, *Resisting Dictatorship: Repression and Protest in Southeast Asia* (Cambridge: Cambridge University Press, 2004); Francisco Gutiérrez Sanín and Elisabeth Jean Wood, "Ideology in Civil War: Instrumental Adoption and Beyond," *Journal of Peace Research* 51, no. 2 (March 1, 2014): 213–26, https://doi.org/10.1177/0022343313514073; Jonathan Leader Maynard, "Ideology and Armed Conflict," *Journal of Peace Research* 56, no. 5 (September 1, 2019): 635–49, https://doi.org/10.1177/0022343319826629; Amelia Hoover Green, *The Commander's Dilemma: Violence and Restraint in Wartime* (Ithaca: Cornell University Press, 2018); Laia Balcells, *Rivalry and Revenge: The Politics of Violence during Civil War* (Cambridge: Cambridge University Press, 2017); Deborah J. Yashar, *Contesting Citizenship in Latin America: The Rise of Indigenous Movements and the Postliberal Challenge* (Cambridge: Cambridge University Press, 2005); Stephen E. Hanson, *Post-Imperial Democracies: Ideology and Party Formation in Third Republic France, Weimar Germany, and Post-Soviet Russia*, 1st ed. (Cambridge: Cambridge University Press, 2010).

12. James D. Fearon and David D. Laitin, "Violence and the Social Construction of Ethnic Identity," *International Organization* 54, no. 4 (2000): 845–77, https://doi.org/10.1162/002081800551398.

13. Reno, *Warlord Politics*; Roessler, *Ethnic Politics and State Power*; Robert I. Rotberg, ed., *When States Fail: Causes and Consequences* (Princeton, NJ: Princeton University Press, 2004); Paul Collier and Anke Hoeffler, "Greed and Grievance in Civil War," *Oxford Economic Papers* 56, no. 4 (October 2004): 563–95.

14. Barbara F. Walter, "The New New Civil Wars," *Annual Review of Political Science* 20, no. 1 (2017): 469–86, https://doi.org/10.1146/annurev-polisci-060415-093921.

15. John Mueller, "The Banality of 'Ethnic War,'" *International Security* 25, no. 1 (summer 2000): 42–70.

16. See footnote 12 above.

17. Barbara F. Walter, *Committing to Peace: The Successful Settlement of Civil Wars* (Princeton, NJ: Princeton University Press, 2002); Virginia Page Fortna, *Does Peacekeeping Work? Shaping Belligerents' Choices After Civil War* (Princeton, NJ: Princeton University Press, 2008); Michael W. Doyle and Nicholas Sambanis, *Making War and Building Peace* (Princeton, NJ: Princeton University Press, 2006); Lise Morjé Howard, *Power in Peacekeeping* (Cambridge: Cambridge University Press, 2019), https://doi.org/10.1017/9781108557689.

18. Lise Morjé Howard and Alexandra Stark, "How Civil Wars End: The International System, Norms, and the Role of External Actors," *International Security* 42, no. 3 (January 1, 2018): 127–71, https://doi.org/10.1162/ISEC_a_00305; Walter, "The New New Civil Wars"; Thérése Pettersson and Kristine Eck, "Organized Violence, 1989–2017," *Journal of Peace Research* 55, no. 4 (July 1, 2018): 535–47, https://doi.org/10.1177/0022 343318784101.

19. For my assessment of this process over the last two decades in South Asia, see Paul Staniland, "Political Violence in South Asia: The Triumph of the State?" Carnegie Endowment for International Peacehttps://carnegieendowment.org/2020/09/03/political-violence-in-south-asia-triumph-of-state-pub-82641.

20. Séverine Autesserre, *Peaceland: Conflict Resolution and the Everyday Politics of International Intervention* (Cambridge: Cambridge University Press, 2014).

21. Barry R. Posen, "The Security Dilemma and Ethnic Conflict," *Survival: Global Politics and Strategy* 35, no. 1 (1993): 27–47, https://doi.org/10.1080/00396339308442672; Walter, *Committing to Peace.*

22. For arguments on the important role of the international community in conflict resolution, see Walter, *Committing to Peace;* Aila M. Matanock, *Electing Peace: From Civil Conflict to Political Participation* (New York: Cambridge University Press, 2017).

23. Aila M. Matanock and Paul Staniland, "How and Why Armed Groups Participate in Elections," *Perspectives on Politics* 16, no. 3 (September 2018): 710–27, https://doi.org/10.1017/S1537592718001019.

24. Straus, *Making and Unmaking Nations.*

25. H. Zeynep Bulutgil, "Prewar Domestic Conditions and Civilians in War," *Journal of Global Security Studies*, accessed October 28, 2019, https://doi.org/10.1093/jogss/ogz039.

26. Paul Pierson, *Politics in Time: History, Institutions, and Social Analysis* (Princeton, NJ: Princeton University Press, 2004).

27. Lee Ann Fujii, "The Puzzle of Extra-Lethal Violence," *Perspectives on Politics* 11, no. 02 (2013): 410–26, https://doi.org/10.1017/S1537592713001060.

28. This is similar to Valentino's approach to strategic violence—ideology can create preferences and threat perceptions, which then lay the basis for "rational" cost-benefit calculations. Benjamin A. Valentino, *Final Solutions: Mass Killing and Genocide in the Twentieth Century* (Ithaca: Cornell University Press, 2004).

29. Geoffrey B. Robinson, *The Killing Season: A History of the Indonesian Massacres, 1965–66* (Princeton, NJ: Princeton University Press, 2018).

30. Ali Riaz, *Bangladesh: A Political History since Independence*, Sew edition (London: I. B. Tauris, 2016); Salil Tripathi, *The Colonel Who Would Not Repent: The Bangladesh War and Its Unquiet Legacy* (New Haven: Yale University Press, 2016).

31. For an excellent overview of the electoral violence literature, see Sarah Birch, Ursula Daxecker, and Kristine Höglund, "Electoral Violence: An Introduction," *Journal of Peace Research* 57, no. 1 (January 1, 2020): 3–14, https://doi.org/10.1177/0022343319889657.

32. Matanock and Staniland, "How and Why Armed Groups Participate in Elections."

33. Valentino, *Final Solutions.*

34. Christian Davenport, "State Repression and Political Order," *Annual Review of Political Science* 10, no. 1 (2007): 1–23, https://doi.org/10.1146/annurev.polisci.10.101405.143216; Christian Davenport et al., "The Consequences of Contention: Understanding the After-effects of Political Conflict and Violence," *Annual Review of Political Science* 22, no. 1 (2019): 361–77, https://doi.org/10.1146/annurev-polisci-050317-064057.

35. Davenport, "State Repression and Political Order"; Paul Staniland, "Violence and Democracy," *Comparative Politics* 47, no. 1 (2014): 99–118; Thad Dunning, "Fighting and Voting: Violent Conflict and Electoral Politics," *Journal of Conflict Resolution* 55, no. 3 (June 1, 2011): 327–39, https://doi.org/10.1177/0022002711400861; Catherine Boone, "Politically Allocated Land Rights and the Geography of Electoral Violence: The Case of Kenya in the 1990s," *Comparative Political Studies* 44, no. 10 (October 1, 2011): 1311–42, https://doi.org/10.1177/0010414011407465; Enrique Desmond Arias and Daniel M. Goldstein, eds., *Violent Democracies in Latin America* (Durham, NC: Duke University Press Books, 2010).

36. Nicholas Barnes, "Criminal Politics: An Integrated Approach to the Study of Organized Crime, Politics, and Violence," *Perspectives on Politics* 15, no. 4 (December 2017): 967–87, https://doi.org/10.1017/S1537592717002110; Benjamin Lessing, *Making Peace in Drug Wars: Crackdowns and Cartels in Latin America* (New York: Cambridge University Press, 2017); Christine Cheng, *Extralegal Groups in Post-Conflict Liberia: How Trade Makes the State* (Oxford: Oxford University Press, 2018).

37. Max Weber, *Weber: Political Writings* (Cambridge: Cambridge University Press, 1994).

38. Such as James D. Fearon and David D. Laitin, "Neotrusteeship and the Problem of Weak States," *International Security* 28, no. 4 (spring 2004): 5–43.

39. They also vary in the level of violence they use against such dissidents. Greitens, *Dictators and their Secret Police.*

40. This basic dynamic can exist in a wide range of contexts—examples can be found in Javier Auyero and Katherine Sobering, *The Ambivalent State: Police-Criminal Collusion at the Urban Margins* (Oxford: Oxford University Press, 2019); Marie-Eve Reny, *Authoritarian Containment: Public Security Bureaus and Protestant House Churches in Urban China* (Oxford: Oxford University Press, 2018); Vincent Boudreau, *Resisting Dictatorship: Repression and Protest in Southeast Asia* (Cambridge: Cambridge University Press, 2004); Philip G. Roessler, "Donor-Induced Democratization and the Privatization of State Violence in Kenya and Rwanda," *Comparative Politics* 37, no. 2 (January 1, 2005): 207–27, https://doi.org/10.2307/20072883; Christian Davenport, Sarah A. Soule, and David A. Armstrong, "Protesting While Black? The Differential Policing of American Activism, 1960 to 1990," *American Sociological Review* 76, no. 1 (February 1, 2011): 152–78, https://doi.org/10.1177/0003122410395370; Joe Soss and Vesla Weaver, "Police Are Our Government: Politics, Political Science, and the Policing of Race–Class Subjugated Communities," *Annual Review of Political Science* 20, no. 1 (2017): 565–91, https://doi.org/10.1146/annurev-polisci-060415-093825.

41. On transnational groups, see Daniel Byman and Sarah E. Kreps, "Agents of Destruction? Applying Principal-Agent Analysis to State-Sponsored Terrorism," *International Studies Perspectives* 11, no. 1 (2010): 1–18, https://doi.org/10.1111/j.1528-3585.2009.00389.x; and Idean Salehyan, *Rebels without Borders: Transnational Insurgencies in World Politics* (Ithaca: Cornell University Press, 2009).

42. Christopher R. Day and William S. Reno, "In Harm's Way: African Counter-Insurgency and Patronage Politics," *Civil Wars* 16, no. 2 (April 3, 2014): 105–26, https://doi.org/10.1080/13698249.2014.927699.

43. Marielle Debos, *Living by the Gun in Chad: Combatants, Impunity, and State Formation* (London: Zed Books, 2016).

44. Matthew Adam Kocher, "State Capacity as a Conceptual Variable," *Yale Journal of International Affairs* 5, no. 2 (spring/summer 2010): 137–45, outlines some of the challenges in grappling with this concept.

45. On the general importance of state strength in shaping opportunities for revolt, see James D. Fearon and David D. Laitin, "Ethnicity, Insurgency, and Civil War," *American Political Science Review* 97, no. 1 (February 2003): 75–90.

46. For a critique in the IR literature, see Paul Poast, "Dyads Are Dead, Long Live Dyads! The Limits of Dyadic Designs in International Relations Research," *International Studies Quarterly* 60, no. 2 (June 1, 2016): 369–74, https://doi.org/10.1093/isq/sqw004; on civil wars, see Nicholas Sambanis and Jonah Schulhofer-Wohl, "Sovereignty Rupture as a Central Concept in Quantitative Measures of Civil War," *Journal of Conflict Resolution* 63, no. 6 (July 1, 2019): 1542–78, https://doi.org/10.1177/0022002719842657.

47. Recent work using a network approach includes Cassy Dorff, Max Gallop, and Shahryar Minhas, "Networks of Violence: Predicting Conflict in Nigeria," *Journal of Politics*, February 5, 2020, https://doi.org/10.1086/706459.

48. See also Davenport, "Consequences of Contention."

49. Paul Staniland, "Armed Politics and the Study of Intrastate Conflict," *Journal of Peace Research*, June 5, 2017, 0022343317698848, https://doi.org/10.1177/0022343317698848.

50. For an excellent literature on civil war termination, see Walter, *Committing to Peace*; Doyle and Sambanis, *Making War and Building Peace*; Monica Duffy Toft, *Securing the Peace: The Durable Settlement of Civil Wars* (Princeton, NJ: Princeton University Press, 2010); Matanock, *Electing Peace*; Joakim Kreutz, "How and When Armed Conflicts End: Introducing the UCDP Conflict Termination Dataset," *Journal of Peace Research* 47, no. 2 (March 1, 2010): 243–50; Howard and Stark, "How Civil Wars End"; Sarah Zukerman Daly, *Organized Violence after Civil War: The Geography of Recruitment in Latin America* (Cambridge: Cambridge University Press, 2017).

51. Brenner, *Rebel Politics*.

52. Toft, *Securing the Peace*; Edward Luttwak, "Give War a Chance," *Foreign Affairs* 78, no. 4 (July/August 1999): 36–44.

53. Autesserre, *Peaceland*.

54. Rachel Kleinfeld and Elena Barham, "Complicit States and the Governing Strategy of Privilege Violence: When Weakness Is Not the Problem," *Annual Review of Political Science* 21, no. 1 (2018): 215–38.

55. Christine Cheng, Jonathan Goodhand, and Patrick Meehan, *Synthesis Paper: Securing and Sustaining Elite Bargains that Reduce Violent Conflict* (London: UK Stabilisation Unit, Her Majesty's Government, 2018).

56. Howard and Stark, "How Civil Wars End."

57. Asfandyar Mir, "What Explains Counterterrorism Effectiveness? Evidence from the U.S. Drone War in Pakistan," *International Security* 43, no. 2 (November 1, 2018): 45–83; Eli Berman et al., *Small Wars, Big Data: The Information Revolution in Modern Conflict* (Princeton, NJ: Princeton University Press, 2018).

58. Autesserre, *Peaceland*, offers a deep critique of the easy applicability of conflict resolution templates across contexts.

59. See James D. Fearon, "Why Do Some Civil Wars Last so Much Longer than Others?" *Journal of Peace Research* 41, no. 3 (May 2004): 275–301; Barbara F. Walter, *Reputation and Civil War: Why Separatist Conflicts Are so Violent* (Cambridge: Cambridge University Press, 2009); and Robert Powell, "War as a Commitment Problem," *International Organization* 60, no. 1 (2006): 169–203, on the intricacies of bargaining and conflict.

60. Austin Carson, *Secret Wars: Covert Conflict in International Politics* (Princeton, NJ: Princeton University Press, 2018), identifies a double-edged aspect to transparency in some international crisis contexts.

61. For a broader study of civil war outcomes, see Kreutz, "How and When Armed Conflicts End."

62. Paul Staniland, Asfandyar Mir, and Sameer Lalwani, "Politics and Threat Perception: Explaining Pakistani Military Strategy on the North West Frontier," *Security Studies* 27, no. 4 (October 2, 2018): 535–74, https://doi.org/10.1080/09636412.2018.1483160.

63. Geoffrey B. Robinson, *The Killing Season: A History of the Indonesian Massacres, 1965–66* (Princeton, NJ: Princeton University Press, 2018).

64. Thant Myint-U, *The Hidden History of Burma: Race, Capitalism, and the Crisis of Democracy in the 21st Century* (New York: W. W. Norton, 2019).

Index

Pages numbers followed by *f* or *t* indicate figures or tables.